Feminist Counselling

Theory, Issues, and Practice

Feminist Counselling

Theory, Issues, and Practice

Edited by Lynda R. Ross

Feminist Counselling
Edited by Lynda R. Ross

Published by
Women's Press, an imprint of Canadian Scholars' Press Inc.
180 Bloor Street West, Suite 801
Toronto, Ontario
M5S 2V6

www.womenspress.ca

Canadian Scholars' Press Inc. gratefully acknowledges financial support for our publishing activities from the Government of Canada through the Book Publishing Industry Development Program (BPIDP).

Library and Archives Canada Cataloguing in Publication

Feminist counselling : theory, issues, and practices / edited by Lynda R. Ross.

1. Women-Counselling of. 2. Women-Psychology. 3. Counselling.
4. Feminist psychology. I. Ross, Lynda Rachelle, 1950-

HQ1206.F4442 2010   361'.06082   C2010-901328-X

ISBN: 978-0-88961-471-0

Cover design by Colleen Wormald.
Interior design by Aldo Fierro.
Cover photo: copyright © STILLFX/Shutterstock.com

10 11 12 13 14   1 2 3 4 5

Printed and bound in Canada by Marquis Book Printing, Inc.

Canad??

Contents

Negotiating Social Complexities in Counselling Practice by Lynda R. Ross and Marie Lovrod

WHAT IS FEMINIST THERAPY?

No movement occurs in isolation. The growth and development of feminist therapy, as an integral expression of needs and goals defined through therapeutic and social justice movements in the twentieth and twenty-first centuries, is no exception. Although not a single, clearly definable entity, feminist therapy in Canada has emerged from among what are often cited as the "waves" of feminisms, fused as these are with community-centered efforts for social equity and within academic research in the field. Guided by a multiplicity of feminist theories, theorists, and contexts, feminist therapy is a constantly evolving yet interrelated set of methodologies for effecting personal and social change. Among its core principles are a commitment to valuing women's experiences, a recognition that informed consent is an inherent right, and an acknowledgement that "much of the distress that brings people to therapy is socio-culturally based" (Hill & Ballou, 1998, p. 2). Feminist therapy is characterized by an explicit ownership of power differentials in therapeutic contexts, a constant effort to maintain current analyses of social power imbalances, and the capacity to imagine social transformation as a potential horizon for individual and interpersonal healing.

Feminist therapy operates within diverse political, social, and cultural contexts, ever shaped and reshaped by new knowledges and emergent "publics" and

1

"counter publics" (Cvetkovich, 2003). Simultaneously, it is conditioned by an overarching goal of promoting and understanding women's own and relational wellness. "At its most basic level, feminist therapy represents a conceptual framework for organizing assumptions about counselling and psychotherapy" (Enns, 2004, p. 7). Because deeply informed conceptual frameworks are crucial to constructive client outcomes, this collection seeks to foster ever more inclusive articulations of the shared project of facilitating more livable lives for women. At the same time, because processes of professional credentialing must inevitably strive to keep up with the lived realities of clients and practitioners, this volume emphasizes the persistent need to revise lexicons, training models, and practices as new insights surface. The importance of continuing to own and learn from "missteps" (Hill & Rothblum, 1998) is a vital part of this process, for the profession, practitioners, and participants alike.

The articles in this collection address a range of pressing contemporary issues and speak theoretically and, in some instances, practically to topics that are relevant to women's lives and to situated feminist counselling practice. Like the clients who enter into counselling relationships, the authors whose work is gathered here come from diverse backgrounds, bring different experiences to their writing, and speak in a variety of voices. The chapters address a selection of topics relevant to understanding contemporary women's experiences in Canada, including cultural diversity, motherhood, violence perpetrated against and by women, the persistent effects of colonization, the ways in which language choices replicate or reposition dominance relationships with and among Aboriginal and Metis women, and the effects of socially produced mental health concerns on Indigenous and settler realities. Authors take on questions of embodiment projects, ethics, crisis counselling, storytelling, and mandated therapy, as well as gender and sexual diversity. Some of the writers gathered here offer guidance for approaching feminist counselling practice in situated contexts. Others outline questions and debates informing feminist theoretical perspectives on socially mired experiences. The range of topics addressed is broad, but inevitably not inclusive. There are, however, common threads that weave through the chapters. Regardless of the issues addressed or the approaches discussed, underlying each of the essays in this collection is an acknowledgement of the absolute need to understand and respect diversity. Readers are invited to gather insights generated within and across these essays in pursuit of an intersectional analysis (Crenshaw, 1991) of what it means to identify with the socially constructed category of "woman" in contemporary Canada. The juxtaposition of experiences in this spectrum provides an opportunity to imagine feminist consciousness and therapeutic practice in ways that remain accountable to the widest possible constituencies of women and allies invested in the mutual processes of personal healing and social justice.

Central to any organizational framework or collection of frameworks in the field is the recognition that feminist therapy occupies a critical set of potentially creative contradictions. It seeks to engage individual therapists, clients, and members of therapeutic groups at the site of lived experience, while maintaining awareness that situated interpretations of personal events are politically produced under conditions that Weedon (1996) has termed "agency without sovereignty" (p. 41). As her work suggests, scattered but hegemonic structural social forces (Grewal & Kaplan, 1994) inevitably impact potentials for personal, interpersonal, and collective actualization, even as each therapist and client practices agency at the level of consciousness, and affect choices made within and beyond the shared therapeutic setting. These choices, in turn, shape the lived possibilities enabled or disabled by the social surround, often engaging points of potentially challenging *and* productive tension for the client and therapist.

"Non-authoritarian, open-ended and process-oriented" (Flax, 1990, p. 3), feminist therapy must be understood to operate at the material and conceptual nexus of feminisms' central paradox. As articulated by Vance (2001), feminisms must challenge the contents and effects of the socially constructed category— "woman"—even as they engage with lived experiences of that category in processes of healing. As such, feminist therapists are asked to look at "womanhood" from two perspectives, attending to both the constraints it imposes and the rewards it provides for compliance. Notions of "femininity" and "masculinity" inevitably become more fluid, assuming less fixed associations with particular embodiments or sexualities, as diverse intersectional perspectives continue to unpack gender roles and the ways they overlap with other socially constructed identities. When the implications of de Beauvoir's (1952) insight that "one is not born but becomes a woman" (p. 249) is fully assimilated, gender performances increasingly can be understood as contested political processes of power positioning and meaning-making. Empowerment itself may be redefined when the goals of personal, intersubjective, and social well-being reconfigure the directions people choose in constructing their lives. Finally, because feminist therapeutic practice evolves in the context of emergent forms of critical feminist consciousness, the conditions negotiated by practitioners and participants are simultaneously various, incongruous, interconnected, and changing.

FEMINIST COUNSELLING IN THE CONTEXT OF FEMINISMS' WAVES

Historicizing this persistent multi-dimensional paradox in relation to the often-circulated model of "waves" of feminisms shows us how feminist therapy participates in the wider politics of "diffractive" feminist visioning (Haraway, 1992). The wave model implies a progression of cumulative political energy

3

and imagines stages of feminist consciousness emerging at the shoreline of sometimes conflicted but always mutually influential political actions. While Western feminists have tended to envision each wave temporally and in succession, with occasional debates about how to categorize particular episodes or projects, feminist waves, like aqueous ones, include a circulatory motion when political energy interfaces with transformative goals and social response. Thus, no single wave is ever really over because as each political project is absorbed into the shoreline of the social environment, modifying its configurations, the wave curls reflexively back on itself and gathers the energy collecting in the wake of its effects in order to approach and attempt to reshape the edges of possibility again. Neither are the waves necessarily simply successive. Depending upon the contested conditions in question, approaches associated with any of the waves might be more or less effective. Needless to say, some shorelines are more malleable than others. The wave model offers a helpful paradigm for examining the direction and impact of feminist therapeutic engagements with social activisms and concurrent feminist academic endeavours. The following descriptive outline provides a brief overview of feminist therapy as part of a collection of intersecting movements, all of which have emerged under situated political conditions to promote greater actualization among women and their allies.

The First Wave

As commonly represented among feminist theorists, the first wave is often seen to bear some affinity to liberal feminisms, having sought to make social institutions more inclusive through focussed political efforts such as demands for access to education, the vote, citizenship, or human rights, and for revisions to research and academic paradigms in order to correct previous misunderstandings of "woman." Naming and replacing women's absence in research endeavours is part of the liberal feminist legacy. In 1971, for example, Weisstein wrote in her memorable article entitled "Psychology Constructs the Female, or the Fantasy Life of the Male Psychologist (with some attention to the fantasies of his friends the male biologists and the male anthropologists)": "Psychology has nothing to say about what women are really like, what they need and what they want, essentially because psychology does not know" (p. 63). Weisstein's analysis challenged existing androcentric views, which assumed that males define normative behaviour. She decried practices of leaving women out of the research process and absent from theory, and resisted distorting, trivializing, and dismissive constructions of women's experiences (Paludi, 1998). Gender was beginning to be understood not as an essential, inherent characteristic based on biological sex, but as a social product of political difference (West & Zimmerman, 1992). Feminist theorists

4

removed notions of gender from the personal and situated them in the social realm (Beall, 1993; Bohan, 1993; West & Zimmerman). This represented a critical initiative in promoting awareness not only of the impact of socialization practices on defining "woman," but of how gender constructions serve to enhance power imbalances between "two" defined sexes, thereby affecting women's positions in all societies.

From theoretical debates to activist frontlines, first wave initiatives promote avenues of influence and inclusion among existing practices and institutions. Gaining access to property ownership or challenging male dominance in the professions might be understood as first wave feminist strategies, emerging in the shadow of the modern nation-state and its legitimating projects. Today, first wave feminisms are continually recontextualized by the use of similar strategies in related struggles. For example, the United Nations Declaration on the Rights of Indigenous Peoples in 2007, with its explicit gender-equity guarantees to all community members (in Article 44), offers a challenge to the sexism of Canada's divisive Indian Act, in each of its iterations. The declaration's important contemporary teaching about institutional change and gender-inclusive respect, as derived from Aboriginal cultural and diplomatic practices, illuminates opportunities to reconsider some of feminisms' past affiliations with colonialist institutions and to affirm the aspirations of Indigenous peoples to survive them. Similarly, the contemporary project of establishing gender diversity as prohibited grounds of discrimination in human rights instruments in Canada can be understood as a potentially expansive solidarity project, drawing on but not necessarily confined to the lessons or frameworks that initially informed first wave feminisms in the West.

Horney (1926/1974) prefigured a growing awareness that internalized experiences of "difference" are socially produced and laid some of the groundwork for appreciating complex experiences of gender identity. Early in the twentieth century, she argued against social subordinations based on gender, and their deleterious effects, as attributed to embodiments. A psychoanalyst and member of Freud's circle, Horney questioned the idea, then current, that women look on their bodies and experiences as inferior and argued that socialized masculine self-worship is the only basis for the assumption that females are all naturally discontented with the biological sex they are assigned (Lips, 1994). Her work contributed to the recognition that interpretations of embodiments are produced through social institutions with vested interests in power relations. Horney was one of the first psychoanalysts to draw attention to the possibility that culture and inner forces interact to inform gender identity and personality development. She proposed that the rejection of the feminine *role* was partially, and understandably, a response to a society that views women as inadequate and inferior (Horney). Today, as gender identities become more fluid, the recognition that subjective inferiority does not always match received gender scripts enables more compassionate responses to experiences of gender dysphoria.

Feminist activists, scholars, and researchers who deploy first wave strategies share many perspectives, including their recognition of the social construction of gender and of the effects of hegemonic power on women's positions in society, an acknowledgement of "the personal as political," a valuing of women's experiences and their diversity, and a concern for the global as well as the local status of women (Chrisler, Golden, & Rozee, 2003). First wave feminists have worked to provide women with new understandings about gender and power relations, a valued place in the social order, and a public voice. As women worked together in establishing more resistant feminist publics and counter-publics, the practices of women's commitments to learning from one another began to precipitate the second wave. Contratto and Rossier (2005) remind us how feminist therapy and the theory surrounding it emerged out of the ferment of the women's movement in the 1960s and 1970s. It was a time when women's consciousness-raising groups began to make public aspects of their lives that were previously private and unlabelled. Not only did women begin to realize and acknowledge similarities in their experiences, but what came to the forefront in the early years was how women's socialization and the "real life" situations surrounding them created problems and potential for social change that traditional psychology and therapy ignored (Contratto & Rossier). By rejecting the limitations of received identities for women, first wave feminisms began to amplify the possibilities of what being a woman might mean. While recognizing the power of shared experiences, Contratto and Rossier suggest that as a result of ongoing efforts to include wider ranges of possibilities for actualization drawn from women's perspectives, feminist therapists "don't have a straightforward how-to book" (p. 9). Nonetheless, a number of common themes emerged from earlier feminist therapy theorists, who worked to affirm women's competence in negotiating the restrictive environments they inherited.

The Second Wave

Where the first wave seeks to bring transformative change to existing social institutions and academic endeavours, the second is a product of women consulting their own and one another's experiences. This approach has generated multiple alternative practices and projects, and informed the emergence of domestic violence shelters, sexual assault centres, culturally appropriate healing methods, queer pride, feminist media, and locally bound but often transnationally affiliated NGOs, among others. As well, the second wave introduced exciting feminist epistemological approaches to knowledge transformation. Understanding the effects of bias and misguided notions of objectivity in the research process has been a major force in helping to deconstruct "truths" of the past and in informing new knowledge and understandings. Feminist scholars highlighted the need to incorporate subjectivity into the research process (e.g., Lather, 1991; Reinharz, 1992) and for models to explain human behaviour by looking at the world in ways far more complex than those offered by traditional empiricism (Morrow, 2000; White, Russo, & Tavris, 2001). Pioneering theorists, like Allen and Baber (1992), Crawford and Marecek (1989), and Lather, developed new epistemological paradigms to drive social enquiry, challenging the moral and political assumptions underlying contemporary knowledge bases. Feminist disillusionment with existing modes of enquiry—male and scientific—emerged from a conscious understanding that women were absent both as producers and products of knowledge (e.g., Fox-Keller, 2001). The feminist critique of positivism and scientific enquiry was rooted in an awareness that social inquiry could never be context free and "neutral," and that empirical observations are saturated with personal, social, cultural, political, and gendered influences.

The second wave saw new frameworks emerging for social inquiry, challenging at fundamental levels the dominant and dominating male perspectives. Revisions to traditional empiricism, aimed at "countering erasure" (Wylie, 2001, p. 30) of women from history, politics, and academic discourse helped to focus research on questions of relevance to women (Fedigan, 2001; Wylie). Further, standpoint theory began to open up new ways to value and acknowledge women's unique social positions, experiences, and views of the world, privileging their activities and understandings as a starting point for the development of less distorted knowledge claims (Flax, 1983; Hartsock, 1987; Smith, 1987). Feminist postmodernists took a further step in the production of context-sensitive knowledge, moving radically away from endorsing positivism and remaining skeptical of universalizing meta-narratives and claims of absolute truths. Using deconstructive narrative techniques, feminist postmodernists helped to further focus attention on gender and gender relations and on altering the balance of power between men and women (Fraser & Nicholson, 1990; Halberstam, 1998a; Lather, 1991).

These second wave epistemological approaches expanded feminist agendas on political, social, and academic fronts. They revised both the kinds of questions that could be generated for research as well as the ways in which research could be conducted. They encouraged feminist counsellors to privilege women's interests, needs, and the contexts in which they lived, as well as to incorporate broad gender analyses into all of our work. This opening up of research practice profoundly influenced the shared knowledge of women's psychological needs and consequently changed various strategies used in applied practice. Recently, theorists like Brown (2006) have suggested that feminist therapy is one of the few approaches to practice that both owns and names the interpersonal politics shaping realities that affect all of us. Feminist therapists continue to focus on the politics of the personal and relational experiences of power and powerlessness. "Self-in-relation" theorists have drawn on women's experiences to posit models of moral reasoning and knowledge development that derive from relational attachments and imperatives seen to characterize women's socialization (e.g., Belenky, Clinchy, Goldberger, & Tarule, 1986; Gilligan, 1982). The implication that differential gender training distributes problem-solving skills in ways that undermine personal and social actualization for all permeates these texts, as their authors work to revalue qualities attributed to women.

In the 1970s and 1980s, academic and counselling professions were both dominated by white males. Rooted in evolutionary and radical psychiatry movements, consciousness-raising groups, and civil rights initiatives, early feminist therapy was committed to listening to women as the experts in their own lives, to engaging in political struggles that would change women's realities, and to challenging dehumanizing diagnostic labels applied to women's experiences by the dominant mainstream psychiatric profession. The notion that women's perspectives inevitably expand on androcentric world views was implicit in the recognition that much had been "left out" by knowledge-building practices that excluded women. Sarachild (1975), an early proponent of consciousness-raising, remarks that the "objectivity" of the scientific method had been skewed by gender bias:

> The decision to emphasize our own feelings and experiences as women and to test all generalizations and reading we did by our own experience was actually the scientific method of research. We were in effect repeating the 17th century challenge of science to scholasticism ... and put all theories to the testing of living practice and action (p. 145).

Critical attention to subjectivity was increasingly understood by second wave feminists to be central to any credible knowledge claims about women.

In early writings on feminist counselling theory and practice, gender socialization was seen as a primary stressor and focus, while less attention was paid to women's physiological orientations or experiences, or to lived sociocultural specificities (Contratto & Rossier, 2005). In *This Sex Which Is Not One*, French feminist Irigaray (1985) made a powerful intervention in dominant discourses of the period by emphasizing female embodiment as a ground of political knowledge. Irigaray was trained as a psychoanalyst, but sought to show how theories based in male physiogamy were insufficient to understanding women's consciousness or potentials for actualization. Constructed on a theory based on the female body as a site for radical reinterpretation, her work eloquently demonstrates that beginning with a focus on women's bodies reveals the inherent political implications that shape gendered subjectivity. Irigaray's lived navigation of the contradictions she examined included being dismissed for her insubordination to a psychoanalytic tradition in which she nevertheless remains an important player, having launched a very successful and influential career celebrating "woman's difference." Feminist health projects in North America, which sought to destabilize discourses that constructed women as "imperfect men" for medical treatment purposes, also placed women at the centre of naming their own physical needs and desired approaches to them. Reproductive rights activisms and childbirth reform movements both draw on this reappraisal of women's expertise about their own embodied experiences and needs, and remain relevant to women's aspirations.

Hare-Mustin and Marecek (1990) clarified the ways that bias could enter into discussions of difference by delineating "alpha" and "beta" biases: the former operating to exaggerate interpretations of difference, and the latter to obscure them. Their interventions helped to bring much-needed nuance to the "equality versus difference" debates surrounding strategies for women's empowerment by demonstrating the political consequences of extreme arguments in either direction. Today, as transgender embodiment and performance projects emerge into public consciousness, Butler's (2004) analysis of the political implications of "undoing gender," Halberstam's (1998b) attentions to "female masculinity," and Noble's (2003) work on "masculinities without men" all interrogate any overdetermined attribution of femininities or masculinities to particular embodiments.

Each of the waves, then, continue to evolve and generate creative tensions that inform contemporary feminist therapy and social activism. Such contradictions do not disable effective agency in the world, but can rather enable it in ways that create more space for diversities. For example, as indicated, Hartsock's (2004) profound insight that women's standpoints illuminate dominant structures remains foundational to second wave principles placing women at the centre of the feminist therapeutic project. Spivak's (1998) resonant and complex question for the title of her groundbreaking essay "Can the Subaltern Speak?" extends this analysis by defining the need for a social apparatus capable of attending to subaltern standpoints and the light they shed on "ruling relations" (Smith, 1974). Feminist therapy, because of its deeply interpersonal interface with clients and political engagement with the social surround, attempts to bridge the constructive tension mobilized by the deep and ultimately related insights of these influential theorists into the political operations of difference. As Lorde (1984) argued, rightly understood difference "is a fund of necessary polarities between which our creativity can spark like a dialectic" (p. 111), when the needs of those most affected are made central to social change projects.

The Third Wave

The second wave consolidated a sense that women might begin to envision possibilities for informed collective action around shared experiences, based on knowledge gained through challenges offered by social constructionist perspectives, standpoint epistemologies, and postmodernist deconstructive techniques (e.g., Beall, 1993; Bohan, 1993; Burr, 2003; West & Zimmerman, 1992). A social constructionist perspective resists any universal construction of "woman" and "insists that we take a critical stance toward our taken-for-granted ways of understanding the world, including ourselves" (Burr, pp. 2–3). Third wave feminisms built on this insight and at the same time recognized that new strategies for collective political action would require deeper work on questions of how socially constructed differences operate among women. Mohanty's (2003) notion of "strategic essentialism" grows out of the sobering recognition that women themselves are often mutually implicated in inequitable power structures. Women's complexly situated relations with one another in power systems that benefit some at the expense of others reveal the importance of developing solidarity projects, while remaining critically mindful of diversely positioned lives and constructed choices. In light of these challenges, Cockburn (1998) calls for "the difficult reality of unavoidable, unending, careful, respectful struggle" (p. 216) in creating constructive third wave social change. In writing about globally focussed women's movements, Antrobus (2004) stresses how the objectives of one group of women might contradict those of another.

Increasingly, there is recognition that each of the feminist waves engages a set of structural features that characterize the prevailing order, at sites ranging from the intimate to the international. For example, discussions of human rights have, until very recently, failed to acknowledge the unique concerns of women. Bunch (1990) noted that "despite a clear record of deaths and demonstrable abuse, women's rights are not commonly classified as human rights" (p. 486). The eradication of violence against women has always been a central focus among feminist activists, academics, and counsellors, whose efforts have informed worldwide awareness that the most effective strategies for eliminating violence against women continue to be centred in the promotion of gender equality and women's empowerment (UN, 2006). The feminization of poverty, cultural prescriptions for women's roles, the limited value placed on women's lives, and inequitable power relations are now commonly accepted as fundamental to the violence perpetrated against women. Today's feminist therapies can be understood to draw on and reflect upon past strategies newly applied—receiving, influencing, participating in, and challenging them—depending on the needs each therapeutic encounter gathers and represents.

Bringing a multifocal pluralist set of lenses to shared projects has profound implications for feminist therapists, clients, and facilitated self-help groups. For example, sexual assault crisis counsellors have long demanded changes to political, legal, and religious structures and the assumptions that inform them, so that people targeted in acts of sexual violence can resist re-traumatization by dominating interpretive frameworks. Advocacy, then, may become part of a social healing process for the therapist, the client, and/or other allies. Yet, as the difficult case of Canadian transwoman Kimberly Nixon (Shelley, 2008) demonstrates, this is an ongoing struggle within feminism as well as beyond it, characterized by emergent questions that reshape political environments. Today, sexual assault survivors may choose, in therapy or on their own, whether or not, or perhaps when and how, they might wish to engage a struggle for recognition of the power politics informing their own case. Kimberly Nixon's experiences of having transitioned from a male body were deemed by the Supreme Court of Canada as sufficient grounds for excluding her from a volunteer position in a sexual assault crisis centre in Vancouver. The argument that clients may have felt threatened by her presence, even if her services were exclusively offered to other transwomen surviving sexual assault, reveals an important critical site of theoretical and practical problem solving. Finding ways to imagine constructive approaches to such impasses will inevitably impact the feminist therapeutic project.

Contradictions and flows within wave theory, then, are potentially simultaneous and cumulative, opening wide ranges of potential interventions to feminist therapists and clients as social actors responding to situated historical and geopolitical forces and events. From a feminist therapeutic standpoint, the intergenerational effects of traumatic experiences are perhaps binding all the waves together. Erickson (1995) has argued that trauma can be acute and/or insidious, sharply felt, or gnawing and persistent; she has further demonstrated trauma's individual and collective dimensions. *The Unsayable: The Hidden Language of Trauma*, Rogers's (2007) sensitive work with unconscious grammars of unresolved pain from the past, reveals how buried traumatic experiences can penetrate the lives of subsequent generations and re-emerge as verbal cues and uncanny re-enactments of truths that exceed received frames of reference in the present. Similarly, Tuhiwai Smith (1999) affirms Indigenous efforts to heal from the effects of colonial histories that impinge upon the contemporary moment. She argues that, "[t]o hold alternative histories is to hold alternative knowledges.... This in turn requires an approach that enables us to engage with, understand and then act upon history" (p. 34). Situated at the heart of such hermeneutic struggles, feminist therapists collaborate with clients, theorists, and activists in attempts to heal the social by responding to the needs presented by clients. As a result, feminist therapies, and the narratives they develop and engage, participate in revising collective as well as personal histories and futures.

FEMINIST COUNSELLING AND THERAPIES

No volume of Canadian essays on feminist counselling would be complete without an acknowledgement of the contributions of Canadian feminist therapists and theorists in creating a more hospitable environment for women's healing. While it is true that academic training and professional counselling practices were initially dominated by white men in the West, by 1986 the *Canadian Journal of Community Mental Health* had published a special issue on women and mental health, outlining feminist approaches to therapy from the point of view of Canadian writers in the field. In 1990, the University of Manitoba Press published *Living the Changes*, edited by Joan Turner, in an effort to initiate more inclusive approaches to the diversity of experiences clients and therapists bring to feminist counselling. Status of Women Canada has worked diligently over the course of the past decade to promote gender-based analysis of social policy, and it can be argued that the Canadian environment has consistently emphasized community-centred mental health initiatives in building feminist therapy as a profession.

Today, as is evident in this collection, contemporary feminist theorists continue to provide rich critical analyses of historical and contemporary society. Adding to the earlier focus on gender, today's feminist counselling theorists highlight the profound necessity of understanding women in their diverse contexts, including race, ethnicity, class, sexual orientation, disability, and age (Porter, 2005). Contemporary feminist counsellors no longer look at women's lives in relation to a single index of power relations, but explore women's realities as they are defined by the interactions of multiple contexts, over time. Although contemporary feminist theorists have approached feminist counselling practice from wide-ranging perspectives, placing emphasis on different aspects of the therapeutic encounter, a number of common themes informing the works of contemporary theorists, such as Ellyn Kaschak, Laura Brown, Mary Ballou, Pam Remer and Judith Worrell, and Bonnie Burstow, can be found (Porter). Drawing from each of the "waves," all share recognition of the need for a continued deconstruction of patriarchy. They each focus, to some extent, on multiple contexts in order to understand women's lived realities. There is a common recognition that feminist therapy theory must involve the reconstruction of therapeutic goals, values, and frameworks, as well as an acknowledgement that there is no single reality, no one "right" feminist theory or epistemological position about women. All of these writers are influenced by critical perspectives emerging from the radical edges of existentialism, social constructionism, and post-structural theories, with their inherent critiques of empiricism and concomitant engagements with the intersubjective contexts of self-formation in power systems. According to Porter, "'Location, location, location,' are central features of contemporary feminist theory development. The location of the feminist theorist, the location of the feminist therapist, and the location of the client must all be brought to the endeavor of feminist theorists and therapists understanding the contexts of women's lives and working toward the well being and healing of women" (p. 144). The socio-political locations of women's individual and collective vulnerabilities and capacities for empowerment are significant to the present volume as well. The articles in this volume are organized in thematic sections that affirm women's contextual experiences, the nexus of personal and political structures, and feminist therapy as feminist praxis.

CONCLUSION

The authors and articles in this collection highlight and bring together critical issues central to the study and practice of feminist counselling in Canada. Given the feminist orientations of all of the authors, a number of common themes related to understanding women's lived realities permeate their discussions. These themes both reflect and enhance a broader feminist therapy literature and reinforce the need for continued vigilance in working towards understanding women in varied contexts, acknowledging women as the experts in defining their own lived realities, and promoting counselling strategies to assist individual women in negotiating changes in their lives.

The increasing demand for feminist counselling provides an important barometer of gendered processes of social alienation and emergent consciousness about barriers to actualization, as embedded in evolving power structures and rooted in practices of dominance. This collection arises out of a series of conversations among practitioners, counsellor teachers, and advanced students from across Canada many who met, initially, through Athabasca University's Counselling Women Program. The existence and success of this program in itself speaks to the need for specific training in feminist counselling practices and the ongoing development of appropriate pedagogies and processes of professional credentialing that reflect this growing field of expertise. Our continued political commitments to centring the perspectives of those most affected in socially situated healing practices formed a key organizing principle in our initial conversations. Building on a growing demand for sensitivity to the specificities of the Canadian context, a core group of counsellors and teachers began to identify issues for a text that could be regularly updated to reflect insights emerging from the experiences and perspectives that bring counsellors and clients to the projects of feminist therapy, theory, and research. How might emergent voices continually inform and shape feminist counselling practices and debates with greatest currency, effectiveness, and impact? How might diagnostic categories contribute to the creation of social alienation and mental illnesses? Lively discussions around these and related questions had a snowball effect in drawing together a group of authors invested in the vision of a feminist counselling textbook that, in each new edition, would remain responsive to intersecting publics for the insights generated by feminist therapeutic approaches to the politics of personal and relational challenges and changes. Imagined as a work in progress, this text invites ongoing collaborations in extending the explanatory power of feminist theory and the effectiveness of feminist counselling practices for personal empowerment and social transformation.

REFERENCES

Allen, K., & Baber, K. (1992). Ethical and epistemological tensions in applying postmodern perspective to feminist research. *Psychology of Women Quarterly, 16,* 1—15.

Antrobus, P. (2004). *The global women's movement: Origins, issues and strategies.* London & New York: Zed Books.

Beall, A. (1993). A social constructionist view of gender. In A. Beall & R. Sternberg (Eds.), *The psychology of gender* (pp. 127–147). New York: Guilford Press.

Belenky, M., Clinchy, B., Goldberger, N., & Tarule, J. (1986). *Women's ways of knowing: The development of self, voice and mind.* New York: Basic Books Inc.

Bohan, J. (1993). Regarding gender: Essentialism, constructionism, and feminist psychology. *Psychology of Women Quarterly, 17,* 5–21.

Brown, L. (2006). Still subversive after all these years: The relevance of feminist therapy in the age of evidence based practice. *Psychology of Women Quarterly, 30,* 15–24.

Bunch, C. (1990). Women's rights as human rights: Towards a re-vision of human rights. *Human Rights Quarterly, 12,* 486–498.

Burr, V. (2003). *Social constructionism, 2nd Edition.* New York: Routledge.

Butler, J. (2004). *Undoing gender.* New York: Routledge.

Canadian Periodical for Community Studies, Inc. (1986) *Canadian Journal of Community Mental Health, Special Issue: Women and Mental Health,* 5(Fall).

Chrisler, J., Golden, C., & Rozee, P. (2004). Introduction. In J. Chrisler, C. Golden, & P. Rozee (Eds.), *Lectures on the psychology of women* (pp. xi–xvii). Boston: McGraw Hill.

Contratto, S., & Rossier, J. (2005). Early trends in feminist therapy theory and practice. *Women & Therapy*, 28(2), 7–26.

Cockburn, C. (1998). *The space between us: Negotiating gender and national identities in conflict*. London: Zed Books.

Crawford, M., & Marecek, J. (1989). Feminist theory, feminist psychology: A bibliography of epistemology, critical analysis, and applications. *Psychology of Women Quarterly*, 13, 477–491.

Crenshaw, K. (1991). Mapping the margins: Intersectionality, identity politics, and violence against women of color. *Stanford Law Review*, 43(6), 1241–1299.

Cvetkovich, A. (2003). *An archive of feelings: Trauma, sexuality and lesbian public cultures*. Durham, NC: Duke University Press.

de Beauvoir, S. (1952) *The second sex: Woman as other*. New York: Bantham Books.

Enns, C. (2004). *Feminist theories and feminist psychotherapies: Origins, themes, and diversity (2nd edition)*. New York: The Haworth Press.

Erickson, K. (1995). Notes on trauma and community. In C. Caruth (Ed.), *Trauma: Explorations in memory* (pp. 183–199). Baltimore: Johns Hopkins University Press.

Fedigan, L. (2001). The paradox of feminist primatology: The goddess's discipline? In A. Craeger, E. Lunbeck, & L. Schiebinger (Eds.), *Feminism in twentieth-century science, technology, and medicine* (pp. 46–72). Chicago: The University of Chicago Press.

Flax, J. (1983/2003). Political philosophy and the patriarchal unconscious: A psychoanalytic perspective on epistemology and metaphysics. In S. Harding & M. Hintikka (Eds.), *Discovering reality* (pp. 245–282). Dordrecht: Reidel.

Flax, J. (1990). *Thinking fragments: Psychoanalysis, feminism and the postmodern in the contemporary west*. Berkeley: University of California Press.

Fox-Keller, E. (2001). Making a difference: Feminist movement and feminist critiques of science. In A. Creager, E. Lunbeck, & L. Schiebinger (Eds.), *Feminism in twentieth-century science, technology, and medicine* (pp. 98–109). Chicago: The University of Chicago Press.

Fraser, N. & Nicholson, L. (1990). Social criticism without philosophy: An encounter between feminism and postmodernism. In L. Nicholson (Ed.), *Feminism/ postmodernism* (pp. 19–38). N.Y.: Routledge.

Gilligan, C. (1982). *In a different voice: Psychological theory and women's development*. Cambridge: Harvard University Press.

Grewal, I. & Kaplan, C. (1994). *Scattered hegemonies: Postmodernity and transnational feminist practices*. Minneapolis: University of Minnesota Press.

Halberstam, J. (1998a). Automating gender: Postmodern feminism in the age of the intelligent machine. In P. Hopkins (Ed.), *Sex/machine: Readings in culture, gender, and technology* (pp. 468–483). Bloomington: Indiana University Press.

Halberstam, J. (1998b). *Female masculinity*. Durham, NC: Duke University Press.

Haraway, D. (1992). The promises of monsters: A regenerative politics for inappropriate/d others. In L. Grossberg, C. Nelson, & P. Treichler (Eds.), *Cultural Studies* (pp. 295–337). New York: Routledge.

Hare-Mustin, R., & Marecek, J. (1990). *On making a difference: Psychology and the construction of gender.* New Haven, CT: Yale University Press.

Hartsock, N. (1987). The feminist standpoint: Developing the ground for a specifically feminist historical materialism. In S. Harding (Ed.), *Feminism and methodology: Social science issues* (pp. 157–180). Indiana: University Press.

Hartsock, N. (2004). *The feminist standpoint theory reader: Intellectual and political controversies.* New York: Routledge.

Hill, M., & Ballou, M. (1998). Making therapy feminist: A practice survey. In M. Hill (Ed.), *Feminist therapy as a political act* (pp. 1–16). Binghampton, NY: Haworth Press.

Hill, M., & Rothblum, E. (1998). *Learning from our mistakes: Difficulties and failures in feminist therapy.* New York: Haworth Press.

Horney, K. (1926/1974). The flight from womanhood: The masculinity-complex in women as viewed by men and women. In J. Strouse (Ed.), *Women and analysis: dialogues on psychoanalytic views of femininity* (pp. 171–186). New York: Viking.

Irigaray, L. (1985). *This sex which is not one* (Trans. C. Porter & C. Burke). Ithaca: Cornell University Press.

Lather, P. (1991). *Getting smart: Feminist research and pedagogy with/in the postmodern.* New York: Routledge.

Lips, H. (1994). *Sex & gender (2nd Edition).* London: Mayfield.

Lorde, A. (1984) *Sister outsider: Essays and speeches.* Berkeley, CA: The Crossing Press.

Mohanty, C. (2004). *Feminism without borders: Decolonizing theory, practicing solidarity.* Durham, NC: Duke University Press.

Morrow, S. (2000). Feminist reconstructions of psychology. In S. Morrow, M. Biaggio, & M. Herson (Eds.), *Issues in the psychology of women* (pp.15–31). New York: Plenum Publishers.

Noble, J.B. (2003). *Masculinities without men? Female masculinity in twentieth-century fictions.* Vancouver: UBC Press.

Paludi, M. (1998). *The psychology of women.* Upper Saddle River, NJ: Prentice Hall.

Porter, N. (2005). Location, location, location: Contributions of contemporary feminist theorists to therapy theory and practice. *Women & Therapy, 28*(3/4), 143–160.

Reinharz, S. (1992). *Feminist methods in social research.* Oxford: Oxford University Press.

Rogers, A. (2007). *The unsayable: The hidden language of trauma.* New York: Ballantine Books.

Sarachild, K. (1975). Consciousness-raising: A radical weapon. In Redstockings (Ed.), *Feminist revolution* (131–137). New York: Random House.

Shelley, C. (2008). *Transpeople: Repudiation, trauma, healing.* Toronto: University of Toronto Press.

Smith, D. (1974). Women's perspective as a radical critique of sociology. *Sociological Inquiry, 44*(1), 7–13.

Smith, D. (1987). *The everyday world as problematic: A feminist sociology.* Toronto: University of Toronto Press.

Spivak, G. (1988). Can the subaltern speak? In C. Nelson & L. Grossberg (Eds.), *Marxism and the interpretation of culture* (pp. 271–313). Urbana: University of Illinois Press.

Turner, J. (1990). *Living the changes.* Winnipeg: University of Manitoba Press.

Tuhiwai Smith, L. (1999). *Decolonizing methodologies: Research and Indigenous peoples.* New York: Zed Books.

Vance, C. (2001). Social construction theory: Problems in the history of sexuality. In K. Plummer (Ed.), *Sexualities: Critical assessments* (pp. 356–371). London: Routledge.

Weedon, C. (1996). *Feminist practice and poststructuralist theory.* United Kingdom: Blackwell Publishing.

White, J., Russo, N., & Tavris, C. (2001). Feminism and the decade of behavior. *Psychology of Women Quarterly, 25,* 267–279.

Weisstein, N. (1971/1992). Psychology constructs the female, or the fantasy life of the male psychologist (with some attention to the fantasies of his friends the male biologists and the male anthropologists). In J. Bohan (Ed.), *Seldom seen, rarely heard: Women's place in psychology* (pp. 61–78). Boulder: Westview Press.

West, C. & Zimmerman, D. (1992). Doing gender. In J. Bohan (Ed.), *Seldom seen, rarely heard: Women's place in psychology* (pp. 379–403). Boulder: Westview Press.

Wylie, A. (2001). Doing social science as a feminist: The engendering of archaeology. In A. Craeger, E. Lunbeck, & L. Schiebinger (Eds.), *Feminism in twentieth-century science, technology, and medicine* (pp. 23–45). Chicago: The University of Chicago Press.

Women in Context: Feminist Theory's Contribution to Understanding Women's Lived Realities

U nderlying the feminist agenda as it applies to counselling theory and practice is "the capacity to think critically about the politics of power in personal life as filtered through the lenses of gender and other facets of social location" (Brown, 2006, p. 22). By extension, theory guiding feminist therapy places demands on counsellors to have a deep understanding of the specific problems women bring to counselling, and also to be aware of how issues often extend well beyond women's presenting problems or therapeutic counselling rooms (Twist, 2005). As such, feminist counsellors are aware of the need for systemic change in response to power differentials and the inequities that permeate many women's lives. Feminist counsellors also work hard to understand their own contextualized and socially constructed understandings of the varied worlds in which women live their lives. The theoretical focus of the first grouping of papers in this collection addresses a variety of topics that affect women's individual and collective identities. The authors interrogate theory with the ultimate goals of asking feminist counsellors to reflect on the impact that theories have, not only on informing our understanding about women's places in diverse societies, but on shaping the private and public realities that profoundly affect women's lived experiences.

The first chapter in this section, *Women on the Margins: Honouring Multiple and Intersecting Cultural Identities*, explores feminist and multicultural theories and the implications of these theories for counselling women who identify with multiple non-dominant statuses. Sandra Collins discusses the absence of gender in the multicultural literatures, and conversely, the lack of attention that is paid to ethnicity in the feminist literatures. She suggests ways in which these omissions marginalize groups who reside outside as well as inside of these established "silos." The author searches for common ground between the two approaches in an effort to promote an integration of these theories, one with the other. In doing so, she addresses the need to bring feminisms and multiculturalism closer together so that, in combination, they can more fully be used to meaningfully inform mainstream counselling practice. Collins introduces principles for understanding women on the margins from a variety of perspectives. She asks that we look at women's multiple identities as interconnected and interdependent. As such, we are asked to reflect on the consequences of these multiple identities as they contribute to conflict and dissonance, layers of oppression, and the tensions that many women will confront. Collins uses the metaphor of a kaleidoscope to illustrate the dynamic and fluid intersection of the multiple elements affecting individual women's well-being and proposes a model to integrate feminist and multicultural theories that can be used to inform our understanding about women's individual and collective identities.

The next chapter, *Mom's the Word: Attachment Theory's Role in Defining the "Good Mother,"* departs from multiple non-dominant statuses but continues with the discussion of the need to change core values and assumptions imposed by both society and psychological theory. Lynda Ross explores how theory has contributed to our constructed notions of motherhood and outlines one popular psychological theory—that of attachment (Bowlby 1969, 1973, 1980)—formulated to explain mother-infant bonding. She discusses how Bowlby, like many other theorists in the mid-twentieth century, assumed that women mother instinctively and are biologically suited and best able to perform tasks surrounding child rearing. Although revised to reflect more contemporary views of parenting, the theory as originally formulated continues to influence the now almost-commonplace view that the "good mother" remains as the most critical factor in ensuring healthy child development. The chapter explores the impact attachment theory has had on pathologizing the outcomes of mothering and on the mental health of women who are socially and culturally tied to a role that many do not and cannot "naturally" fulfill.

Like the discussion about motherhood, *Male Violence against Women and Girls: What Feminist Counsellors Need to Know to Begin Their Work with Women* asks readers to explore a topic affecting the lives of many women. Charlene Senn provides detailed Canadian statistics as a framework for understanding both the scope and damaging impact of violence on women's lives. Focussing on child sexual abuse, abuse of women by intimate partners, and sexual assault, the author argues that a feminist framework is necessary in order to provide women with the best possible type of support. She also highlights how, in spite of the startling prevalence rates associated with male violence against women, we must acknowledge as feminists that most women who experience male violence are temporary victims who ultimately "resist, survive, and thrive." Senn outlines the unique contributions and critical features of a feminist approach to counselling women and girls who are the survivors of male violence. She discusses the importance of naming and labelling as an issue fundamental to the feminist political struggle to end violence against women and to beginning the work of healing. Through a feminist lens, she looks at how feminisms have begun to shape the way we understand male violence against women.

In the final chapter of this section, *Hitting Like a Girl: An Integrated and Contextualized Approach to Confronting the Feminist Dilemma of Women's Use of Violence*, Susan Le Blanc explores a different perspective on violence and women. She discusses the long history, validation, and socially rewarded aspects of male violence. In exploring the standardized ideological framework for understanding violence, she describes it as entrenched in masculine experience. The chapter uses patriarchy and its history as the relevant framework to understanding both male and female use of violence. Drawing on existing literatures, Le Blanc looks at women's use of violence in intimate partner relationships and suggests such an exploration as a necessary approach to inform arguments that have, in the past, been used to misrepresent female violence. Consistent with a minority of authors, she suggests that the study of female violence has the potential to inform prevention of violence against women. Le Blanc presents compelling arguments for a feminist engagement in the study of violent women. Her analysis provides a framework for interrogating women's use of violence from a feminist perspective, one that can ultimately lead to transformatory change for women.

REFERENCES: SECTION I

Bowlby, J. (1969). *Attachment and loss: Vol. 1., Attachment.* New York: Basic Books.
Bowlby, J. (1973). *Attachment and loss: Vol. 2., Separation: Anxiety and anger.* New York: Basic Books.
Bowlby, J. (1980). *Attachment and loss: Vol. 3., Loss, sadness and depression.* New York: Basic Books.
Brown, L. (2006). Still subversive after all these years: The relevance of feminist therapy in the age of evidence based practice. *Psychology of Women Quarterly, 30*, 15-24.
Twist, M. (2005). A response to the Babies and Bosses Report: The effects of policies on therapy and the influence of therapists on politics. *Journal of Feminist Family Therapy, 17*(3/4), 67-77.

CHAPTER 1

Women on the Margins: Honouring Multiple and Intersecting Cultural Identities by Sandra Collins

W*riting about women on the margins has led me to reflect on the transformations over time and context of my own cultural identities and the interactions between my self-identity and my views of others and of the counselling process. I speak from both a position of privilege (as a white, middle-class, Canadian-born, well-educated woman) and from a position of dis-privilege (as a lesbian, a pagan, and a woman with invisible physical limitations). I ponder the way in which my experience of gender changed as I moved in adulthood from heterosexuality to lesbian identity and as I continue to struggle to find meaningful expression of my femaleness in male-dominated social and professional contexts. I reflect on how social class and education shape my perspectives and how my increasing awareness of my own privilege has challenged previously unexamined values and beliefs. I'm aware of my hesitancy to identify as a woman with a disability in spite of the fact that health challenges impact many of my personal and career choices. I open myself to honest reflection on the meaning of my resistance. These are the cutting edges of my own path of self-exploration and awareness. This process is also the foundation for my authentic connection to my colleagues and my clients, and for my appreciation of their unique, complex, and evolving identities. I welcome you to join me in deepening awareness and respect for self and other. Only then can we move together to transform the practice of psychology to be more fully responsive to all women—especially those women currently on the margins.*

INTRODUCTION

Canada is known internationally for its diverse cultural makeup and its inclusive policies on multiculturalism (Bowman, 2000; Kymlicka, 1997).

However, according to Statistics Canada's (2003) *Ethnic Diversity Survey*, 1.8 million Canadians (8% of the population) expressed feeling discomfort or out of place by virtue of ethnicity, skin colour, language, or other cultural factors. Canadian women are also generally perceived as benefitting from gender equality. However, women in Canada continue to have lower wages than men, are more likely to live in poverty, and are more likely to experience domestic violence (Neville, 2005). Aboriginal women, lesbian, bisexual, and transgendered women, women of colour, women with disabilities, and other women with multiple non-dominant identities are further disadvantaged.

The implicit definition of a "true Canadian" is still often white, male, heterosexual, able-bodied, Christian, young, and middle class. Much of traditional Western psychological theory and practice is similarly infused with assumptions that reflect these larger patriarchal systems and cultural norms (Evans, Kincade, Marbley, & Seem, 2005; Morrow, Hawxhurst, Montes de Vegas, Abousleman, & Castaneda, 2006; Reynolds & Constantine, 2004). Feminist and multicultural theories have emerged in response to the needs of those individuals or groups not well represented in the dominant socio-political or theoretical discourse and have challenged the professions of counselling and psychology to become more inclusive and responsive to the diversity of human experience.

In spite of common perspectives and goals, feminist and multicultural theories have developed as relatively independent streams within psychology, and few meaningful attempts have been made to integrate the two perspectives in the psychological literature (Reynolds & Constantine, 2004; Whalen et al., 2004). Some feminist and multicultural approaches have been criticized for "being myopic with regard to the intricacies of personal identity" (Williams & Barber, 2004, p. 392) because they tend to focus predominantly on only one factor: either gender or ethnicity. More recent approaches in both fields, however, adopt a more inclusive perspective. The purpose of this chapter is to explore the intersection of feminist and multicultural theories and the implications of these models for counselling women who identify with multiple non-dominant statuses based on ethnicity, ability, social class, sexual orientation, religion, and age, for example. The concept of cultural identity as complex, intersectional, and contradictory is introduced as a central component for understanding and counselling women, and as a point of connection between these models. The needed impetus to integrate the core constructs and goals of both feminism and multiculturalism into the mainstream of psychological theory and practice may be provided by an appreciation for the complexity of cultural identity of every counsellor and every client.

FEMINISM AND MULTICULTURALISM AS SEPARATE BUT PARALLEL STREAMS

Reynolds and Constantine (2004) provide a brief overview of the historical development of both feminist and multicultural psychology, highlighting the separate but parallel paths. Similar distinct movements and bodies of literature have emerged to address issues of sexual orientation, ability, and social class. Separate chapters within professional associations have also evolved, focussing predominantly on one element of cultural identity (Israel, 2003). The new Social Justice Chapter of the Canadian Counselling Association is a notable exception (see www.ccacc.ca). Both feminism and multiculturalism have been criticized for this lack of integration (Williams & Barber, 2004). Although more recent developments in each movement emphasize the intersection of these elements of cultural identity, it is important to attend to the pitfalls of maintaining a silo approach.

Gender in Multicultural Literature

The multicultural movement in psychology has had such a profound effect on the discipline that it is often referred to as the "fourth force"(Pederson, 2001). The focus has shifted beyond the individual to the contexts that shape experience, self-perception, and relationships with others (Arthur & Collins, 2005a). However, much of the multicultural literature has failed to attend to the intersection of gender and ethnicity, sexism and racism (Barret et al., 2005; Silverstein, 2006). Reference to feminist principles is most often missing (Reynolds & Constantine, 2004). Similarly, the issue of sexual orientation has been largely left out of the discourse (Lowe & Mascher, 2001; Silverstein).

This has occurred in part because both culture and multiculturalism have been narrowly defined to refer exclusively to race and ethnicity (Lowe & Mascher, 2001; Silverstein, 2006), rather than more inclusively to include gender, sexual orientation, ability, age, religion, socio-economic status, and language (Daya, 2001; Pedersen, 2001). Even where the concept of cultural is more broadly defined, it has often been narrowly applied (Gustafson, 2005). The tendency has been to define culture in terms of discrete and essentialized categories that result in a relatively stable individualized identity rather than as highly politicized ideological constructs directly related to power and privilege (Gustafson, 2005). This narrow application of the concept of culture has led to a focus on the individual rather than on the historical and social contexts leading to oppression and exploitation. The term *culture* itself is not a neutral concept; rather, it holds powerful social, historical, and political meanings (Anderson et al., 2003). These broader forces serve to create and mask misrepresentations of culture, reinforcing biases and marginalizing particular voices and experiences (Anderson et al.).

The tendency in psychology and elsewhere has been to define culture in terms of the "other" and in so doing, to set up white, male, heterosexual, able-bodied, Christian, young, and middle class as the norm.

The classic multicultural counselling competencies (Arredondo et al., 1996; Sue, Arredondo, & McDavis, 1992; Sue et al., 1982) have been criticized for the primacy given to race and ethnicity, with other dimensions of cultural identity excluded or marginalized (Coleman, 2004; Vontress & Jackson, 2004; Wienrach & Thomas, 2002). Many authors now argue that any definition of multicultural competence must include these broader dimensions of culture (Arredondo & Perez, 2006; Arthur & Collins, 2005b; Fassinger & Richie, 1997; Mollen, Ridley, & Hill, 2003). A number of writers have expanded the multicultural counselling competencies to be more inclusive of gender, sexual orientation, and other identity factors (Collins & Arthur, 2005b; Hansen, Petitone-Arreola-Rockwell, & Greene, 2000; Israel, 2003); however, there is still debate and resistance to taking a more inclusive stance (Sue, 2001; Sue & Sue, 2003). Although other specific population guidelines have been developed, such as the *Guidelines for Psychotherapy with Lesbian, Gay, and Bisexual Clients* (American Psychological Association [APA], 1998) and the *Guidelines for Psychological Practice with Older Adults* (APA, 2003), the current *Guidelines on Multicultural Education, Training, Research, Practice, and Organizational Change for Psychologists* (APA, 2002) remains almost exclusively focussed on racial and ethnic groups and does not even integrate a focus on gender or on feminist practice (Silverstein, 2006).

Further, the focus of multicultural competence still remains primarily on applied practice with individuals and groups and does not effectively integrate competencies for broader social and political analysis or systems change (Arthur & Collins, 2005a). Williams (2007) notes that the traditional multicultural approach tends to emphasize personal or interpersonal multicultural awareness and sensitivity without pushing for pluralism at the broader systems levels (social, economic, political). A number of cultural identity models have been proposed that integrate other cultural identity factors; however, these models still tend to place the emphasis on race and ethnicity (Munley, Lidderdale, Thiagarajan, & Null, 2004) and to view various dimensions of culture as fixed, non-interactive, and localized within the individual. Women of colour, lesbians of colour, and others who hold multiple, non-dominant identities do not see their experiences adequately represented in this body of literature.

The recent emergence of social justice as a central agenda in the multicultural literature provides evidence of a shift in the way in which culture is defined and applied to psychological practice. Arguing for a new model of feminist multicultural counselling, Morrow and colleagues (2006) call on the field to address the "braidings of racism; sexism; heterosexism; and other forms of privilege, power, and oppression" (p. 236) through an active commitment to challenging socio-cultural injustice (Morrow et al., 2006; Whalen et al., 2004). The recent *Handbook for Social Justice in Counselling Psychology* was developed as a result of a coalition between several sections of the American Psychological Association: Section for Lesbian, Gay, and Bisexual Awareness, Section for Ethnic and Racial Diversity, and Section for the Advancement of Women (Fouad, Gerstein, & Toporek, 2006). Attempts are also being made to expand the multicultural competencies in response to this social justice agenda (Arthur & Collins, 2005a).

Ethnicity in the Feminist Literature

Feminist practice has provided a strong voice for women in psychology over the past several decades, challenging the status quo and moving both the profession and the broader socio-political contexts towards more inclusive and equitable norms. Nonetheless, similar criticisms have been levied against certain strains of feminist theory and practice for their monocultural perspective.

The focus of some feminist writing has been predominantly on white, Western, middle-class women (Bowman et al., 2001; Evans et al., 2005; Silverstein, 2006; Williams & Barber, 2004). An essentialist position on gender has been adopted, with what are assumed to be commonalities between all women really reflecting only the world views and realities of the dominant population (who have also been doing the theorizing) (Ludvig, 2006; Valentine, 2007). These theorists and researchers have often failed to integrate other socio-cultural factors beyond gender (Williams & Barber). As a result, some authors have argued that the issues addressed by white feminists and their particular struggles have dominated the literature at the expense of those faced by women with multiple non-dominant identities (Bowman et al.; West, 2005).

Particularly in earlier writings, issues of race and ethnicity were ignored or included only sporadically (Morrow et al., 2006; Reid, 2002; Silverstein, 2006). Where a dialogue about race occurred, gender was often identified as the primary variable in defining identity (Bowman et al., 2001). Although gender-based analysis effectively highlights issues of patriarchy on policies and programs for women, for example, it also tends to prioritize this aspect of identity over others (Canadian Research Institute for the Advancement of Women: CRIAW, 2006). Women of colour and antiracist feminists did not see themselves or their realities represented in this version of "white feminism" and accused the movement of being both ethnocentric and class bound (Bowman et al.; Gustafson, 2007; Morrow et al.).

Feminists who are also women of colour argue that other dimensions of their identities are equally important (Evans et al., 2005; Morrow et al., 2006). They point out that racism is often a more critical oppressive force in their lives than sexism and advocate expanding the focus of feminism to the elimination of all forms of oppression (Bowman et al., 2001; Zerbe Enns, Sinacore, Ancis, & Phillips, 2004). Similarly, sexual orientation has not always been part of the mainstream feminist discourse (Brown, Reipe, & Coffey, 2005), although it has fared better than other dimensions of cultural identity. Women with disabilities, for example, have been historically excluded from the feminist theory, along with attention to socio-economic status or class (Bowman et al.; Brown et al.; Silverstein, 2006). Adair (2005) asserts that even those writers who attempt to explore the intersections of ethnicity, gender, sexual orientation, and other cultural identity factors often exclude women in poverty from the analysis or address them only marginally. There has also been insufficient attention paid to the impact of geographic dislocation on the unique identity experiences of refugee and immigrant women (Brown et al.).

These criticisms do not apply across the board, however, with many current feminist theorists and researchers leading the way in centralizing the perspectives of marginalized women and girls. During the 1990s, challenges to gender as a homogenous category emerged (Gustafson, 2007) as more emphasis was placed on the interactions of gender with race, ethnicity, and class (Evans et al., 2005). White feminist writers like Gustafson (2007) began to question how their own social locations have had an impact on their perspective on feminist research and teaching. The writings of Miller (1987) and the feminist theorists from the Stone Centre (Jordon, Kaplan, Miller, Stiver, & Surrey, 1991) introduced a new model of development centred in and propelled by relational connection. While their earlier work was also fairly monocultural in perspective, Jordon's (1997) edited collection embraced diversity in women's experiences and began to explore ways in which their relational model found expression across ethnicity, sexual orientation, ability, age, and socio-economic difference. The current relational–cultural theory (Jordon, Walker, & Hartling, 2004) crystallizes a growing awareness of the pervasive influence of culture on women's experiences and development. "To place culture, alongside connection, at the center of theory is to break a critical silence" (Jordon & Walker, 2004, p. 4).

Proponents of feminist critical theory argue that the complexities inherent in the intersection of multiple cultural identities must be embraced (Morrow et al., 2006). Gustafson (2005), for example, challenges the artificial boundaries between gender and ethnicity, viewing them as "deeply interconnected social, political, and ideological categories to which positive and negative meanings are attached" (p. 4). Gustafson also locates the focus of responsibility and change at the level of social, professional, and political systems. Similarly, intersectional feminist frameworks explore how cultural identities combine with broader systems of discrimination to reinforce the marginalization of particular groups

(CRIAW, 2006). Central to this perspective is the idea that gender informs ethnicity just as ethnicity is shaped by gender. Dossa (2008) and others have expanded this paradigm to explore the intersection of other "markers of difference" (p. 79), including class, ability, and age. Suyemoto and Liem (2007) provide cultural sensitivity training focussed on the complexity of intersections for marginalized women and the systems of privilege that serve to shape their world views. Those writing from a post-colonial feminist perspective assert that "the intersections of gender, class, race, age, and other social relations are … necessary axes of analyses to explicate the complex nexus of everyday meanings and realities" (Anderson et al., 2003, p. 200). These more recent feminist theories centre political and social analysis on the experiences of those most marginalized in society (CRIAW, 2006; Morris & Bunjun, 2007).

Women on the Margins

In spite of these advances in both multicultural and feminist theory, the study of girls and women of colour is still under-represented in the psychological literature generally (Reynolds & Constantine, 2004; Silverstein, 2006; Williams & Barber, 2004). The multicultural and feminist movements and bodies of literature have had a tremendous impact in challenging the monocultural foundations of traditional psychological theory. However, since the historical focus of both feminist and multicultural dialogues has predominantly been on a single domain of diversity, the experiences of many women have been marginalized in both bodies of literature (Bowman et al., 2001; Silverstein). Even where different domains of diversity are acknowledged, they have not always been considered equally important (Bowman et al; Fassinger, 2004), with the feminists stressing gender, the multiculturalists stressing ethnicity and nationality, and many others being excluded from the discussion entirely.

Maintaining the silos does not simply marginalize other groups but also marginalizes many individuals within each group, particularly women with multiple and complex cultural identity affiliations: "Conceptualizing individuals, particularly members of non-dominant populations, into monolithic and singular identity categories assumes a reductionist perspective that devalues all other dimensions of the individual" (Justin, 2005, p. 367). Further, the continued lack of dialogue and convergence of ideologies leaves responsibility for the negotiation of multiple identities with the individual (Lowe & Mascher, 2001).

The next section will explore the commonalties between the feminist and multicultural perspectives and will look at some of the challenges to a fuller integration of these movements. This will set the stage for an in-depth exploration of the complexity of culture and cultural identity and the central role that the experiences of women with multiple non-dominant identities play in forging ties between the feminist and multicultural models, bringing the importance of cultural sensitivity to the forefront of psychological practice.

SEARCHING FOR COMMON GROUND

Although there are increased calls in the literature for integrating a broader definition and application of cultural diversity into both feminist and multi-cultural models, less specific direction is provided about how such integration might occur (Williams & Barber, 2004). However, synergies do exist in some core constructs of both feminist and multicultural models.

Unlike most of traditional Western psychological theory, both feminist and multicultural models emerged through grassroots movements. Feminism was driven by expressed needs of women in the women's movement (Evans et al., 2005; West, 2005); multiculturalism emerged from the civil rights movement and in response to the lack of recognition of racial issues in mainstream psychology (Fouad, Gerstein, & Toporek, 2006). As a result, both highlight the racist and sexist assumptions that underlie much of traditional Western psychology (Morrow et al., 2006; Reynolds & Constantine, 2004). They both place emphasis on changing the status quo within theory and practice (Reynolds & Constantine).

The importance of environmental context to understanding individuals or groups is core to both approaches (Williams & Barber, 2004). Systemic oppression asserts an impact on all aspects of women's experiences and manifests in many "symptoms" of psychological unrest (Reynolds & Constantine, 2004; Whalen et al., 2004). It is, therefore, the oppressive environment that forms the locus of assessment and intervention. Without this, a high potential for misdiagnosis exists because women's responses are viewed without understanding the cultural identities and contexts that might provide insight into culturally appropriate reactions (Morrow et al., 2006).

Socio-political analysis becomes an important means of examining power dynamics and the impact of oppression at both the interpersonal and socio-cultural levels (Bowman et al., 2001; Reynolds & Constantine, 2004; Whalen et al., 2004; Williams & Barber, 2004). The interface between client experiences and identities and these systems of power also needs to be analyzed (Morrow et al., 2006). Consciousness-raising is central to both movements (Morrow et al.; Reynolds & Constantine). Part of the process of consciousness-raising is to demystify client experiences by opening understanding about the impact of systemic discrimination and oppression (Morrow et al.).

Coined by feminist theorists, the phrase "the personal is political" applies equally well to the multicultural movement, where social change is also seen as necessary for any lasting change at the individual level (Evans et al., 2005;

Reynolds & Constantine, 2004). Although the importance of work with individual clients is acknowledged, change in individuals is not sufficient (Arthur & Collins, 2005a; Williams & Barber, 2004). Social transformation is essential, and the locus of change must be broadened to include larger familial, organizational, social, and political systems (Arthur & Collins, 2005a; Gustafson, 2005; Israel, 2003; Reynolds & Constantine; Williams & Barber). The goal is to reduce inequities in power and privilege between dominant and non-dominant groups in society (Bowman et al., 2001; Williams & Barber). With the emphasis on social responsibility comes the expectation that advocacy is a core role of practitioners (Arthur & Collins, 2005a; Reynolds & Constantine).

Both feminist and multicultural writings emphasize that counsellors need to increase their awareness of the meaning of gender, ethnicity, ability, class, sexual orientation, and other cultural factors to their own identities, as people and as professionals (Collins & Arthur, 2005b, 2007; Reynolds & Constantine, 2004). This includes careful examination of both the experience of oppression and the experience of privilege (Lowe & Mascher, 2001; Williams & Barber, 2004). Counsellors and psychologists are challenged to begin with an analysis of their own attitudes, assumptions, biases, and world views, particularly as they relate to working with women of colour or lesbians or women with other multiple non-dominant identities (Bowman & King, 2003; Reynolds & Constantine). Such personal transformation must precede collective efforts at transformation of the profession.

The importance of a collaborative relationship between counsellor and client is also acknowledged in both multicultural and feminist perspectives (Collins & Arthur, 2005a; Williams & Barber, 2004). Power is openly and actively addressed in the therapeutic context to both understand and reduce the impact of inherent power differences (Morrow et al., 2006; Reynolds & Constantine, 2004). Traditional boundaries for the therapeutic relationship are re-examined in light of both cultural norms and social action agendas (Morrow et al.). The more egalitarian therapeutic relationship facilitates empowerment of women to positively influence their own lives (Reynolds & Constantine). Bowman and colleagues (2001) define empowerment as "the process by which a marginalized person becomes aware of power dynamics and develops skills to gain control over his or her life without infringing on others' rights" (p. 787). Clients are empowered to take action to change the circumstances or systems in which they experience oppression (Morrow et al.).

Why the Divergent Streams?

With the calls for integration and the obvious commonalties in both theoretical constructs and change agendas, why has little progress been made in bringing feminism and multiculturalism together or in integrating both streams more fully into mainstream counselling practice (Williams & Barber, 2004)? Although a more detailed analysis is beyond the scope of this chapter, I will briefly outline some of the challenges identified in the literature.

From a purely practical perspective, theorists and researchers are rarely completely versed in both fields (Reynolds & Constantine, 2004). There are also debates across and within each field about the interconnections between and relative importance of various forms of oppression (Valentine, 2007; Williams & Barber, 2004). This pitting of racism and race against sexism and gender perpetuates the divisions within the profession (Bowman & King, 2003). Assigning both quantitative and qualitative difference to various "isms" also prevents establishing strategic alliances among members of non-dominant populations (Lowe & Mascher, 2001). The debates are further complicated by the interplay of multiple identities and multiple oppressions (Bowman et al., 2001; Valentine, 2007; Wiegman, 2000; Williams & Barber).

In the context of a particular client's experience, the world views and values of feminism and the world views and values of multiculturalism may also conflict, which creates tensions for both the counsellor and the client (Morrow et al., 2006; Reynolds & Constantine, 2004). The feminist and the lesbian-, gay-, bisexual-, and transgendered- (LGBT) affirmative literatures challenge the sexist and heterosexist norms of both non-dominant ethnic and dominant North American cultures (Israel, 2003). Conflicts may then arise between valuing women's equality to men and respecting cultural or religious norms that impact gender role definitions (Justin, 2005; Morrow et al.). Women of colour may band together with other members of their ethnic community to fight against racism and see internal gender inequalities as less important (Bowman et al., 2001). Some perceive that to embrace the cause of gender equality is to weaken the strength of non-dominant ethnic communities in their fight for equality within the dominant culture (Evans et al., 2005). Practitioners and theorists often feel forced to choose between allegiances, not only in their personal lives but also in their professional affiliations (Bowman & King, 2003; Rivière, 2004).

Lesbian, bisexual, and transgendered women from non-dominant ethnic populations may similarly face oppression within the larger LGBT community. They may choose to suppress expression of sexual orientation in favour of ethnic identity affiliations, because their ethnic communities provide a stronger source of social support (Barret et al., 2005; Israel, 2003; Lowe & Mascher, 2001). Ironically, "individuals may seek refuge from one type of prejudice in a community that harbors intolerance for another aspect of their identity" (Israel, p. 73). There are also conflicts between feminist and disability rights activists in the area of women's reproductive health. The right to choose the termination of a pregnancy may conflict with advocating for equality for persons with disabilities when such a choice is based on fetal diagnosis of disability (Brown et al., 2005).

In each of these scenarios, there is not a clear external, values-driven path, and each individual client (and counsellor) will have to explore her own cultural affiliations and the potential losses and gains with either choice. Counsellors must decide whether to challenge beliefs and practices that are culturally appropriate but oppressive to women (Israel, 2003). At the same time, they must evaluate their feminist perspectives to ensure that they are not making assumptions based on a lack of cultural understanding or on their own culture-, class-, or ability-bound assumptions about gender and sexuality (Bowman et al., 2001; Israel).

Another significant challenge for the profession lies in the fact that white women have benefitted from their position of privilege and have contributed to the oppression of women of colour (Bowman & King, 2003; Bowman et al., 2001; Evans et al., 2005). While traditional feminist practices may help equalize power between white men and white women, they do not remove the power associated with white women's racial privilege (Bowman et al.). Mahalingam and Leu (2005) point out the complex relationship between the socio-economic advancement of white women and the social marginalization and reinforcement of more traditional gender roles among immigrant women who step in to fill the domestic void. Gustafson (2005) explores her own emergent consciousness of white privilege within the health care system and the shift of focus from simply the gendered environment to the interactions of ethnicity and gender. Bowman and colleagues (2001) describe their own experiences and frustrations as women of colour seeking to have voice within the larger psychological community. Consciousness-raising among feminist practitioners and a genuine willingness to expose and address issues of privilege are essential for rapprochement (Bowman et al.). West (2005) cautions us that "to have experienced and felt the damaging effects of exclusion and fail to be inclusive could be to merely substitute one paradigmatic caricature for another" (p. 98).

The very source of commonalty across these movements has also served the purpose of dividing their energies and pushing them apart. The success of colonization rests in its classification of individuals into separate and exclusive groups (Lowe & Mascher, 2001). The result has been both a distancing between cultural relations and a pressure to choose one identity over another. As long as white, heterosexual, Christian, able-bodied, middle-class, young males are considered descriptors of what is *normal* and *privileged* (Lowe & Mascher), then the dominant discourse serves to divide and conquer.

In the context of mainstream psychology, both the feminist and multicultural approaches continue to be treated as specialized streams that apply only to work with certain non-dominant groups (Williams & Barber, 2004). Their marginalization by mainstream psychology also serves to take the focus off the work of integrating their ideas (Williams & Barber). The energy devoted by each to championing their own cause within oppressive professional and socio-cultural environments leaves less energy for forging strategic alliances (Lowe & Mascher, 2001; Reynolds & Constantine, 2004).

The result of maintaining the silos is that women on the margins of multiple non-dominant identity affiliations are not only ill-served by psychological theory and practice but risk being pathologized when the real source of pathology is in the dominant discourse within society and within the profession of psychology (Lowe & Mascher, 2001). Attention is also misdirected onto culture at the micro level exclusively instead of challenging the dominant discourses that perpetuate injustices.

The answer may not be an *either/or* but rather a *both/and* approach (Reynolds & Constantine, 2004), where the broader definition of culture and subsequent integration of a more complex view of cultural identity is complemented by continued attention to the specific needs and challenges of particular non-dominant groups (Arthur & Collins, 2005b; Collins & Arthur, 2005b). This approach would include not only multiple cultural identity factors—ethnicity, gender, sexual orientation, nationality, socio-economic status, ability, age, and religion (Fassinger, 2004; Ludvig, 2006)—but also the complex interactions between them (Reid, 2002) and their location within systems of oppression that continue to perpetuate inequities (CRIAW, 2006; Gustafson, 2005). Rather than judging the relative severity of various forms of oppression, the shared focus would be on fully understanding the complexity and cultural contexts of each woman's experience (Mahalingam & Trotman, 2007).

RECOGNIZING AND APPRECIATING THE UNIQUENESS OF ALL WOMEN

Attempts to more fully integrate the feminist and multicultural streams are fairly recent (Morrow et al., 2006). Much of the writing in this area has been generated by and has centred on women whose lived experiences and identities do not fit neatly into any of the professional silos erected around ethnicity, gender, sexual orientation, ability, and other cultural factors (Anderson et al., 2003; Bowman & King, 2003; Brown et al., 2005; CRIAW, 2006; Israel, 2003; Lowe & Mascher, 2001; Morris & Bunjun, 2007). The purpose of this section is to introduce some principles for understanding these women on the margins, drawing on both feminist and multicultural perspectives.

The models used to conceptualize cultural identity vary in terms of their focus and their degree of integration across various identity factors (Arredondo et al., 1996; Arredondo & Glauner, 1992; Collins & Arthur, 2005b; Ho, 1995; Ivey, D'Andrea, Bradford Ivey, & Simek-Morgan, 2002; Robinson, 1999; Sue, 2001). Drawing on these various models, the following factors emerge as central to cultural identity. These factors apply to both the counsellor and the client in any counselling interaction (Collins & Arthur, 2005b).

- *Cultural factors* represent the group affiliations held by individuals, including age, gender, ethnicity, physical and mental ability, sexual orientation, religion, language, and social class. These may be visible or invisible. The focus at this level is on between-group differences.

- *Personal identity factors* include idiosyncratic experiences, genetic makeup, developmental paths, socialization, and so on. I include in this dimension factors such as education, marital status, and work experience that are unique to the particular individual. At this level, attention is focussed on within-group differences.

- *Contextual factors* refer to the historical, social, political, environmental, or economic contexts in which individuals live. These factors can have a significant impact on personal experiences, world view, and values.

- *Ideological factors* refer to the dominant discourses about power and privilege within society that lead to widespread social or institutionalized oppression based on one or more cultural identity factor. The various "isms" that impact women's views of themselves are included here. Some include these elements under contextual factors (Arredondo & Glauner, 1992); however, this tends to weaken the import they have on women's lives.

- *Universal factors* include those elements of experience that are common to all women and, to some degree, set human beings apart from other forms of life, including self-awareness, ability to use symbols, and psychological or biological similarities. At this level, we are reminded that "all individuals are, in some respects, like all other individuals" (Sue, 2001, p. 793).

Figure 1.1

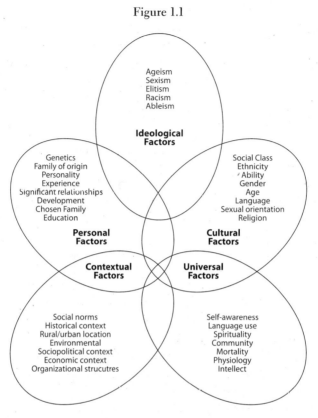

Figure 1.1 draws on the metaphor of a kaleidoscope to illustrate the dynamic and fluid intersection of these elements within each individual. A kaleidoscope is described in the Merriam Webster's Online Dictionary (2008) as "1: an instrument containing loose bits of colored material (as glass or plastic) between two flat plates and two plane mirrors so placed that changes of position of the bits of material are reflected in an endless variety of patterns; 2: something resembling a kaleidoscope: as a: a variegated changing pattern or scene … b: a succession of changing phases or actions … c: a diverse collection" (p. 4). The coloured materials represent the various elements of cultural identity as they tumble, mix together, and reform over time and context. The mirrors represent the various lenses each woman applies in defining the complex image of self that results from the mix. The message of the kaleidoscope is that no matter how many colours are added or how they are mixed together, it is impossible to create a combination of cultural identity factors that does not result in a beautiful, unique, and valuable woman.

Full appreciation of the range of factors that may impact identity can lead to a "seemingly insurmountable complexity" because the list of diversity factors and combinations of factors appears endless (Ludvig, 2006, p. 246). Each woman internalizes various elements of culture from the five factors to form her own cultural identity, which evolves, shifts, and is recreated in different contexts and different times throughout her life. It is this multi-dimensional and ever-changing culture of the individual that becomes significant at the psychological level (Popadiuk & Arthur, 2004). This complexity and idiosyncrasy presents a challenge for both the practice of counselling and for ongoing research (Ludvig). However, the alternative of focussing only on one or two factors or ignoring the impact of cultural identities altogether serves to support the status quo and to reinforce the marginalization of many Canadian women.

The Intersection of Multiple Domains

One of the core tenets of intersectional feminist frameworks is that women's experiences are multi-faceted and must be viewed holistically and inclusively (Morris & Bunjun, 2007). Many women hold several non-dominant statuses that shape their unique sense of cultural identity. It is in careful attention to the intersectionality among these factors that the multiple and sometimes paradoxical cultural identities of individuals can be understood, honoured, and addressed in the counselling process (Brown et al., 2005; Justin, 2005; Mahalingam & Leu, 2005; Pope-Davis & Coleman, 2000; Silverstein, 2006; Valentine, 2007).

As the coloured beads in the kaleidoscope shift, a new, unique pattern emerges. Ludvig (2006) defines *intersectionality* as "the merging and mingling of multiple markers of difference" (p. 246). No single identity factor (class, ability, gender, ethnicity, sexual orientation, etc.) functions in isolation (Wiegman, 2000). Each component of an individual's identity is interconnected and interdependent on the others, and each individual experiences and manages multiple identities in a unique way (Justin, 2005; Valentine, 2007).

Integrating feminist, LGBT, and multicultural models involves working with the complexity of cultural identity (Brown et al., 2005; Lowe & Mascher, 2001). Reid (2002) refers to the shift required as moving to a "complexity paradigm." Silverstein (2006) warns us that "without sensitivity to this complexity, professional psychologists are at risk for supporting patriarchal practices that masquerade as cultural norms" (p. 24). They also risk supporting the illusion of the "unidimensional woman" (Brown et al.), which serves to marginalize the many women who do not fit this picture.

Experiencing multiple cultural affiliations may dramatically alter the meaning and significance of any one cultural factor to the individual (Valentine, 2007). Cultural identities are not static entities that can simply be added incrementally to one another and measured accordingly (Ludvig, 2006). People do not experience gender and class separately, for example; they are simultaneous and interconnected (Valentine, 2007). The experience and construction of gender itself may differ once class, ethnicity, or other socio-cultural identity factors are added to the mix (Valentine; Mahalingam & Leu, 2005; Williams & Barber, 2004). I noted in the introduction to the chapter how my own experience and expression of gender identity has been shaped in recent years by coming out as a lesbian.

Simultaneously holding different cultural identities may mean not just multiplicity but also conflict and dissonance (Lowe & Mascher, 2001; Rivière, 2004; Valentine, 2007). Flexibility and a tolerance for ambiguity are needed on the part of both the counsellor and the client(s) because of the potential for conflicts and tensions among various cultural identities (Barcinski & Kalia, 2005). Diversity and flexibility in our definitions of health and of healthy outcomes of identity management are also required (Collins & Arthur, 2005b). For example, in some literature on LGBT issues, "living out" is seen as the target of healthy identity development. However, when viewed within the complexity of multiple cultural affiliations and multiple influences on identity management, more variation in what we consider expressions of healthy lesbian identities is required (Collins & Oxenbury, 2005; Lowe & Mascher). For women from certain ethnic groups, for example, the social costs of coming out to family may heavily outweigh the benefits; it is important that their choice to remain closeted about one aspect of their cultural identity be understood within this context and validated as a healthy alternative.

Some authors speak of the emergence of a "third space," which represents existence in the borders between cultural identities that results from the "blending" of various cultural factors (Barcinski & Kalia, 2005; Justin, 2005). This merging of identities has been termed "hybridity" (Bhabha, 1990). This concept allows for fluidity across a range of potentially "contradictory social contexts" (Justin, 2005, p. 368). Those with hybrid identities participate simultaneously in more than one cultural world or move between these worlds (Barcinski & Kalia). Many first- and second-generation immigrants find themselves in this position as they move between traditional cultural contexts and the dominant culture, creating a new blended identity.

Experiencing multiple cultural affiliations also amplifies and complicates the experience of cultural oppression (Valentine, 2007). The multiple oppressions experienced by women of colour, for example, may be difficult for women who hold white privilege to understand (Bowman et al., 2001). In parallel with the analysis of multiple cultural identities, feminists of colour emphasize the importance of analyzing multiple and intersecting oppressions (e.g., sexism, racism, heterosexism) (Barret et al., 2005; Valentine; Zerbe Enns et al., 2004). Not only must multiple factors be examined, but this analysis must be free of bias in terms of the relative importance of one form of oppression over another (Bowman et al.).

Appreciation of Within-Group Differences

The focus on cultural identity provides a reminder that within-group differences are often just as significant as between-group differences. Those writing in the area of queer theory or lesbian feminism emphasize the importance of "appreciating the diversity among those with marginalized sexualities" (Zerbe Enns et al., 2004, p. 416). Similarly, women may experience more differences in values and world view within a particular ethnic community than across communities when gender is factored in (Bowman & King, 2003). Immigration and globalization have also contributed to a blurring of boundaries, which challenges traditional definitions of cultural differences (Barcinski & Kalia, 2005). Justin (2006) speaks to the intergeneration tensions within ethnic communities in Canada based on differences in age and level of acculturation. Women with disabilities also represent a group with huge variability, based on the nature of the disability as well as the intersections of class and ethnicity (Brown et al., 2005). In some cases, neither gender nor ethnicity may be as significant to the individual client as socio-economic status, ability, or other identity factors (Bowman & King).

The invisibility of certain cultural identities for some women further complicates the discussion of identity development (Lowe & Mascher, 2001). Women of colour may pass as white; lesbians, bisexuals, and transgendered women as heterosexual; women with invisible disabilities as physically or mentally able-bodied. In addition, degree of visibility may differ across various contexts, resulting in an experience of being perceived as *other* that is different from the experience of women who are consistently labelled as *other* based on visible characteristics (Lowe & Mascher). For example, lesbians are often assumed to be heterosexual and are treated as heterosexual, until they choose to identify their difference. As a result, they may experience *otherness* in contexts where they are *out* versus contexts where they remain *closeted.*

Any theoretical perspective that assumes homogeneity on one factor precludes attention to, and sometimes the predominance of, other factors (Bowman et al., 2001). The end result is that many women will be excluded and marginalized in the discussion. The same principle applies to practitioners within various streams in psychology: "Presorting women as feminists and multiculturalists creates stereotypes that preclude seeing women as multidimensional" (Bowman et al., p. 790). There is a fear that the solidarity of women of colour, for example, will be threatened if their differences in experiences are fully embraced; however, to remain silent about these divisions is a barrier to true solidarity among women (Suyemoto, 2006).

Attention to Context

It is also important to attend to the contexts or social locations in which each woman interacts because they impact the expression or experience of her cultural identities (Barcinski & Kalia, 2005; Brown et al., 2005). Women's cultural identities are historically and socially situated (Morris & Bunjun, 2007); they fluctuate and transform over time and context (Barret, 2005; Justin, 2005; Lowe & Mascher, 2001; Mahalingam & Leu, 2005; Valentine, 2007). This is akin to repositioning the kaleidoscope to absorb a different light, moving it back and forth to reveal the effect of changing context on the images produced. To fully appreciate the pattern that emerges at any point in time, counsellors must understand how both past and present forces impact the individual or community (Morris & Bunjun).

Postmodern feminist perspectives emphasize the importance of situated or contextual identity development and identity management (Valentine, 2007; Zerbe Enns et al., 2004). Justin (2005) uses the term *situational ethnicity* to refer to the impact of context on the expression of personal identities for women of colour. Collins and Oxenbury (2005) differentiate between personal identity and group identification to emphasize the continual process of negotiation between lesbians and their social contexts. The expression of gay identity within individualistic versus collectivist cultures, for example, may differ significantly (Lowe & Mascher, 2001). Historical and social contexts may also have a dramatic effect as the dominant discourse and its associate misrepresentations of various cultural relations shift over time. Personal circumstances as well as social, historical, and physical contexts must all be considered (Barcinski & Kalia, 2005; Morrow et al., 2006).

As counsellors, it is important to recognize that particular identities or components of identities may be more or less salient in different contexts (Rivière, 2004). Gender may not be the primary factor in a woman's experience of socio-cultural oppression (Williams & Barber, 2004), and her experience may change over time and in different contexts. One identity may unsettle, overshadow, disappear, or be rejected in different situations and at different times (Valentine, 2007). Certain factors, such as spirituality, may be also more salient to women of certain cultural groups than others (Bowman & King, 2003).

This does not mean that there is no continuity in each woman's experience and expression of cultural identity (Barcinski & Kalia, 2005). Rather, each individual is a "whole embedded in the sea of social relations" (Barcinski & Kalia, p. 106). Zerbe Enns and colleagues (2004) note the importance of attending to the movement of various social identities from foreground to background as contexts change. The key question for both counselling practice and research is: What identities are being expressed or given import by a particular woman in a particular context and under particular conditions? (Collins & Arthur, 2005b; Valentine, 2007; West, 2005)

Rejection of Essentialized, Fixed Identities

A woman's identity is not a fixed or stable concept but rather fluid and interactive as each woman finds herself moving between the different contexts of her life (Barcinski & Kalia, 2005; Lowe & Mascher, 2001; Ludvig, 2006). Essentialist assumptions about gender, ethnicity, sexual orientation, and other identity factors simply do not reflect an appreciation of the nuances associated with intersections of social identities and experiences of power and oppression (Gustafson, 2005; Lowe & Mascher; Mahalingam & Trotman, 2007). There are no *pure* identities when multiplicity, within group diversity and intersecting and hybrid identities, are factored in (Mahalingam & Leu, 2005).

Setting up exclusive and binary identity markers—male/female, white/of colour, heterosexual/homosexual—serves to reinforce power structures and inequalities since these categorizations are not value neutral (Ludvig, 2006; Mahalingam & Leu, 2005). This is especially true when identity is defined from the *outside*, according to these false dichotomies (Lowe & Mascher, 2001; Ludvig, 2006). While biology may play a direct role in some areas, the meaning and value attached to a particular dimension of identity are socially defined, as are the consequences of that identity affiliation within the larger systems of power in society (Brown et al., 2005). Removing these labels from the social context in which they emerge renders them meaningless (Barret et al., 2005).

Creating the Space for Self-definition

The theory and practice of psychology would be less complex if we were able to categorize women into tidy and mutually exclusive categories. However, it is the complexities of women's experiences and identities that offer us the opportunity to more fully integrate the wealth of knowledge and applied practice experience within these various streams.

The way in which women, individually and collectively, view their own cultural identities and the meaning they make of these factors in a given social context is more significant than their visible group affiliations (Reynolds & Constantine, 2004). Culture and identity, therefore, are both personally and contextually constructed (Barcinski & Kalia, 2005; Gustafson, 2005). The concepts of multiplicity, intersectionality, and hybridity all come with a recognition of the personal agency of each woman in reacting to and acting upon the contexts of her life to shape her own identity as well as the realities of her cultural community(ies) (Barcinski & Kalia). Self-definition then becomes core to respecting and valuing each individual's cultural identities.

The implications of this image of cultural identity as a fluid and dynamic kaleidoscope of factors unique to each women will be explored in more detail in later sections. What is clear from this discussion is that a welcoming space must be created for each client to explore her "unique constellation of identity dimensions and life circumstances rather than having her ... choose one aspect of identity on which to focus in counselling" (Morrow et al., 2006, p. 234).

IMPACT OF DOMINANT DISCOURSES ABOUT POWER AND PRIVILEGE

The discussion of cultural identities cannot occur without reference to the multiple sources and systems of oppression that women face, or we risk failing to balance our belief in the power of women to define and shape their own identities with the constraints and barriers imposed by the power-laden contexts of their lived experiences (Valentine, 2007). Speaking of being black and female in Canada, Rivière (2004) points to the complexity and interactivity of the resulting "multiple cycles of oppression" (p. 223). Her self-definition cannot be understood apart from careful consideration of these external forces.

Counsellors must be prepared to assess not only the relative meaning and importance of various cultural identities but also the multiple layers of oppression experienced by each woman they encounter (Israel, 2003; Lowe & Mascher, 2001). Robinson (1999) provides a unique model for exploring multiple identities that includes overt exploration of the interaction of various identities with the dominant discourses related to sexism, heterosexism, racism, ableism, and class elitism. "Making visible our psychological identity development as positioned in a society that differentially allocates privilege" (Lowe & Mascher, p. 759) pushes the profession to a new level of acknowledging the impact of context on cultural identity. It also ensures that we do not lose site of the negative social meanings associated with particular social locations (Gustafson, 2005).

It is important to explore how these dominant discourses themselves change over time (Lowe & Mascher, 2001). We have witnessed various waves of revolt, mobilization, and shifts in the social status of woman, ethnic minorities, and more recently members of the LGBT community. Historical shifts, such as the recent legalization of gay marriage in Canada, may have a significant impact on identity development for members of non-dominant populations (Lowe & Mascher).

There must also be a balance between releasing our hold on separate categorizations of identity and retaining our commitment to fighting against social oppression based on group affiliation (Razack, 1994; Valentine, 2007).

Some perceive the loss of political edge as a risk involved in re-evaluating the interconnectiveness and complexity of women's cultural identities (Lowe & Mascher, 2001). It is difficult to label and analyze systems of power and oppression without reference to generalized categories of experience (Morris & Bunjun, 2007). However, these common sources of oppression based on external categorization also lead to similarities in experience among members of specific groups (Brown et al., 2005). It is these similarities of experience that generate the will and energy to actively oppose the cultural oppression of non-dominant populations, which is a foundational principle of both feminist and multicultural movements.

Self-reflexivity as a Means of Disrupting Power Relations

A central concept in both the feminist and multicultural literatures is that of self-reflectivity. Suyemoto and Liem (2007) identify self-awareness and reflexive practice as a foundation for cultural sensitivity and competence. Gustafson's (2007) "absent presence of whiteness" (p. 155) refers to a lack of consciousness of the impact that dominant group membership has on the way in which practitioners position themselves and their view of the world. Recognizing the complexity, intersectionality, social location, and fluidity of client cultural identity still leaves counsellors at risk of relating to clients in a way that reproduces the dominant discourses as they seek to *know* the culture of the other rather than engage in a reflexive process that allows them to discern the social meanings and privileges associated with their own identities. This unintentional enactment of sexism, racism, and other cultural biases (Suyemoto & Liem) disrupts the therapeutic process and creates additional harm.

White, heterosexual, able-bodied feminist counsellors must actively choose to examine their subjectivity and biases precisely because these factors remain centred as normative, both within society and within the dominant discourses in psychology (Collins & Arthur, 2005b). Even the option to ignore these factors is part of what Gustafson (2007) terms the "entitlement of choice and subjectivity" (p.156). Such critical consciousness includes not only cognitive and affective awareness but also manifestation of behavioural changes by relinquishing personal and professional power and privilege to fully engage with the client in a collaborative way (Pitner & Sakamoto, 2005). Reflective practitioners engage in a dialectic process of thought and action (praxis) that actively shapes their professional actions and decisions (Collins, Arthur, & Wong-Wylie, in press).

As noted throughout this chapter, critical reflection on the impact of culture must also extend beyond the individual counsellor to the theoretical frameworks, the standards that guide professional practice, and the institutional and social contexts in which we work. Many of the models and measures of multicultural counselling focus primarily on counsellor cultural competence as it is expressed in the context of the counselling relationship and fail to extend the boundaries of professional competence to organizational, community, and socio-economic or political levels of practice or intervention (Williams, 2007).

The Transformative Power of Relationship

In addition to emphasizing the social and political systems and ideologies that impact cultural identities, particularly for women on the margins, feminist models of development provide an important reminder that it is in and through relationships that women experience the reality of these broader influences and come to understand and define themselves (Jordan et al., 1991). Birrell and Freyd (2006) note that "although oppression is often institutionalized at societal levels, it is necessarily enacted in the context of interpersonal relationships" (p. 52). From the perspective of relational cultural theory, a reflexive and culturally competent counsellor has the opportunity to engage in mutually empathic and empowering relationships with clients that offer the potential to examine and transform the relational disconnections that develop over a lifetime of marginalization and culture oppression (Birrell & Freyd; Comstock et al., 2008; Jordon & Walker, 2004). At a broader level, these same relational processes form a foundation for bridging the disconnections that have evolved over time among women in psychology (Walker, 2004). It is my hope that by starting from the experiences of women on the margins and centralizing their lives in both multicultural and feminist theories and research, new connections will emerge that serve to enhance the practice of psychology overall.

IMPLICATIONS FOR THE THEORY AND PRACTICE OF COUNSELLING PSYCHOLOGY: PLACING CULTURE IN CENTRE STAGE

Counsellors are encouraged to use the concept of the kaleidoscope as a framework to explore with each woman the various elements of cultural identity that are salient to her particular presenting concerns and to carefully attend to the implications of counsellor–client differences in cultural experiences and affiliations in developing a trusting and respectful therapeutic relationship. Full awareness of the complexity of negotiating multiple cultural identities leads to an appreciation of the resiliency, strength, and competence of these women (Justin, 2005). For the counsellor, "what is important to competence is appreciation of the broad brush strokes that may enhance our understanding of particular groups combined with the unique, colourful, idiosyncratic experiences and self-definition of individual clients" (Collins & Arthur, 2005b, p. 48).

Treating "culture" as something that applies only to certain non-dominant or marginalized groups in society has made it difficult to integrate feminist and multicultural theory into the mainstream of psychological theory and practice (Silverstein, 2006). Recognizing the centrality of cultural identities to all individuals brings gender and ethnicity, feminism and multiculturalism into the forefront. It also provides momentum for shifting other components of identity, those that continue to be marginalized even within these movements, fully into these dialogues—social class, ability, sexual orientation, age, religion, and immigration status (Brown et al., 2005; Evans et al., 2005). The result promises to be more inclusive theory and practice, both in feminist and multicultural fields, and a uniting of these movements to impact mainstream psychology (Brown et al.; Evans et al.; Silverstein).

Any theory is severely limited if it cannot account for the diversity of human experience (West, 2005). "All people participate in culture(s) and each person's cultural experience has validity" (Williams & Barber, 2004, p. 396). Cultural identity directly impacts every client, every counsellor, and the relationships between them (Collins & Arthur, 2005a). Both the theory and practice of mainstream counselling and psychology must, therefore, be *culture-infused* (Arthur & Collins, 2005b). This approach facilitates application of the "tenets of feminism and multiculturalism to *all* clients, all people" (Williams & Barber, p. 395).

A philosophical shift in our understanding of human beings is required so that variability is recognized as the norm of human experience, and it is the richness of this diversity that informs our holistic understanding of human nature and human psychology (Barret et al., 2005). This requires that we give up the tendency to define difference against one standard—male, heterosexual, white, able-bodied, and so on (Barret et al.). We must also recognize that each woman is the expert on her own experience and self-identification (West, 2005). The ultimate goal of integrating the feminist and multicultural streams and infusing them more fully into mainstream psychology is to ensure that as a profession, we "more fully consider and comprehend the intersection of multiple sociodemographic variables in the lives of a broad range of culturally-diverse individuals" (Reynolds & Constantine, 2004, p. 356). From this increased understanding, then, we are able to more effectively meet the needs of all our clients.

At the same time, we must recognize that there are "systems of exclusion and privilege" (Gustafson, 2005, p. 9) that interpret these differences in ways that have dramatic effects on the lived experiences of our clients. Silverstein (2006) asserts that the social justice agenda is what inextricably links feminism and multiculturalism. Reynolds and Constantine (2004) argue that to really transform the profession of psychology and bring together the feminist and multicultural movements, it is important to move beyond first-order change, the integration of new information, to second-order change, which "fundamentally alters the structure and practices of a system" (p. 352). The latter leads to changes in core values and assumptions, which then drive theory and practice. One consequence would be a shift within the profession beyond a focus on individuals and groups to social activism, which requires us to expand our definition of both professional roles and the boundaries of professional practice to include education, consultation, advocacy, and social change (Arthur & Collins, 2005a; Lowe & Mascher, 2001; Whalen et al., 2004).

The starting place for transformation is the person of the counsellor. Self-awareness and reflexive practice are essential to fully appreciate other people in the breadth and depth of their personal cultural identities (Collins & Arthur, 2005b; 2007). Central to that self-awareness is careful examination of our own non-dominant and privileged statuses (Lowe & Mascher, 2001). In both feminist and multicultural movements, much of the writing about the complexity of multiple identities comes from women who themselves are positioned at the intersections of non-dominant ethnicity, race, or sexual orientation (Barret et al., 2005; Evans et al., 2005). It is equally or perhaps more important for those women and men who speak from positions of privilege to openly examine their own cultural identities and the implications they hold for both theoretical orientations and applied practices (Barret et al.; Lowe & Mascher).

This chapter has emphasized the need to engage with women on the margins in a way that fully appreciates their cultural identities. However, personal and professional transformation is possible only when researchers, practitioners, and theorists hold a mirror up to their own unexamined identities and dominant positioning (Gustafson, 2007). In-depth exploration of cultural identity—from a position of complexity and multiplicity—offers both practitioners and clients the opportunity to more fully "reconcile the privileged and oppressed parts of ourselves" (Lowe & Mascher, 2001, p. 771).

REFERENCES

Adair, V.C. (2005). Class absences: Cutting class in feminist studies. *Feminist Studies, 31*(3), 575–603.

American Psychological Association. (1998). *Guidelines for psychotherapy with lesbian, gay, and bisexual clients*. Retrieved April 15, 2002, from http://www.apa.org/divisions/div44/guidelines.html.

American Psychological Association. (2002). *Guidelines on multicultural education, training, research, practice, and organizational change for psychologists*. Retrieved September 15, 2003, from http://www.apa.org/ pi/multiculturalguidelines.pdf.

American Psychological Association. (2003). *Guidelines for psychological practice with older adults*. Retrieved September 15, 2003, from http://www.apa.org/practice/Guidelines_for_Psychological_Practice_with_Older_Adults.pdf.

Anderson, J., Perry, J., Blue, C., Browne, A., Henderson, A., Khan, K.B., et al. (2003). "Rewriting" cultural safety within the postcolonial and postnational feminist project. *Advances in Nursing Science, 26*(3), 196–214.

Arredondo, P., & Glauner, T. (1992). *Personal dimensions of identity model.* Boston: Empowerment Workshops.

Arredondo, P., & Perez, P. (2006). Historical perspectives on the multicultural guidelines and contemporary applications. *Professional Psychology: Research and Practice, 37*(1), 1–5.

Arredondo, P., Toporek, R., Brown, S.P., Jones, J., Locke, D., Sanchez, J., et al. (1996). Operationalization of the multicultural counseling competencies. *Journal of Multicultural Counseling & Development, 24*, 42–78.

Arthur, N., & Collins, S. (2005a). Expanding culture-infused counselling in professional practice. In N. Arthur & S. Collins. (Eds.), *Culture-infused counselling: Celebrating the Canadian mosaic* (pp. 151–212). Calgary, AB: Counselling Concepts.

Arthur, N., & Collins, S. (2005b). Introduction to culture-infused counselling. In N. Arthur & S. Collins. (Eds.), *Culture-infused counselling: Celebrating the Canadian mosaic* (pp. 3–40). Calgary, AB: Counselling Concepts.

Barcinski, M., & Kalia, V. (2005). Extending the boundaries of the dialogical self: Speaking from within the feminist perspective. *Culture & Psychology, 11*(1), 101–109.

Barret, S.E., Chin, J.L., Comas-Diaz, L., Espin, O., Greene, B., & McGoldrick, M. (2005). Multicultural feminist therapy: Theory in context. *Women & Therapy, 28*(3/4), 27–61.

Bhabha, J. (1990). The third space. In J. Rutherford (Ed.), *Identity: Community, culture, difference* (pp. 207–221). London: Lawrence & Wishart.

Birrell, P.J., & Freyd, J.J. (2006). Betrayal and trauma: Relational models of harm and healing. *Journal of Trauma Practice, 5*(1), 49–63.

Bowman, M.L. (2000). The diversity of diversity: Canadian-American differences and their implications for clinical training and APA accreditation. *Canadian Psychology, 41*(1), 230–243.

Bowman, S.L., & King, K.D. (2003). Gender, feminism, and multicultural competencies. In D.B. Pope-Davis, H.L.K. Coleman, W.M. Liu, & R.L. Toporek (Eds), *Handbook of multicultural competencies in counseling and psychology* (pp. 59–71). Thousand Oaks, CA: Sage.

Bowman, S.L., Rasheed, S., Ferris, J., Thompson, D.A., McRae, J., & Weitzman, L. (2001). Interface of feminism and multiculturalism: Where are the women of colour? In J.G. Ponterotto, J.M. Casis, L.A. Suzuki, & C.M. Alexander (Eds.), *Handbook of Multicultural Counseling* (2nd ed., pp. 779–798). Thousand Oaks, CA: Sage.

Brown, L.S., Reipe, L.E., & Coffey, R.L. (2005). Beyond color and culture: Feminist contributions to paradigms of human difference. *Women & Therapy, 28*(3/4), 63–92.

Canadian Institute for the Advancement of Women. (2006). *Intersectional feminist frameworks: An emerging vision.* Ottawa, ON: Author. Retrieved November 12, 2008, from http://www.criaw-icref.ca/IFF/The IFFs- An Emerging Vision.pdf.

Coleman, H.L.K. (2004). Multicultural counseling competencies in a pluralistic society. *Journal of Mental Health Counseling, 26*(1), 56–66.

Collins, S., & Arthur, N. (2005a). Enhancing the therapeutic alliance in culture-infused counselling. In N. Arthur & S. Collins. (Eds.), *Culture-infused counselling: Celebrating the Canadian mosaic* (pp. 103–149). Calgary, AB: Counselling Concepts.

Collins, S., & Arthur, N. (2005b). Multicultural counselling competencies: A framework for professional development. In N. Arthur & S. Collins. (Eds.), *Culture-infused counselling: Celebrating the Canadian mosaic* (pp. 41–102). Calgary, AB: Counselling Concepts.

Collins, S., & Arthur, N. (2007). A framework for enhancing multicultural counselling competence. *Canadian Journal of Counselling, 41*(1), 31–49

Collins, S., Arthur, N., & Wong-Wylie, G. (in press). Enhancing reflective practice in multicultural counseling through cultural auditing. *Journal of Counseling & Development.*

Collins, S., & Oxenbury, J. (2005). Counselling lesbians. In N. Arthur & S. Collins. (Eds.), *Culture-infused counselling: Celebrating the Canadian mosaic* (pp. 415–450). Calgary, AB: Counselling Concepts.

Comstock, D.L., Hammer, T.R., Strentzsch, J., Cannon, K., Parsons, J, and Gustavo, S. (2008). Relational-cultural theory: A framework for bridging relational, multicultural, and social justice competencies. *Journal of Counseling & Development, 86,* 279–287

Daya, R. (2001). Changing the face of multicultural counselling with principles of change. *Canadian Journal of Counselling, 35,* 49–62.

Dossa, P. (2008). Creating alternative and demedicalized spaces: Testimonial narrative on disability, culture, and racialization. *Journal of International Women's Studies, 9*(3), 79–98.

Evans, K.M., Kincade, E.A., Marbley, A.F., & Seem, S.R. (2005). Feminism and feminist therapy: Lessons from the past and hopes for the future. *Journal of Counseling & Development, 83,* 269–277.

Fassinger, R.E. (2004). Centralizing feminism and multiculturalism in counseling; Introduction to the special section. *Journal of Multicultural Counseling and Development, 32,* 344–345.

Fassinger, R.E., & Richie, B.S. (1997). Sex matters: Gender and sexual orientation in training for multicultural counseling competency. In D.B. Pope-Davis & H.L.K. Coleman (Eds.), *Multicultural counseling competencies: Assessment, education and training, and supervision* (pp. 83–110). Thousand Oaks, CA: Sage.

Fouad, N.A., Gerstein, L.H., Toporek, R.L. (2006). Social justice and counselling psychology in context. In R.L. Toporek, L.H. Gerstein, N.A. Fouad, G. Roysicar, & T. Israel, (Eds.), *Handbook for social justice in counselling psychology: Leadership, vision, and action* (pp. 1–16). Thousand Oaks, CA: Sage.

Gustafson, D.L. (2005). Transcultural nursing theory from a critical cultural perspective. *Advances in Nursing Sciences, 28*(1), 2–16.

Gustafson, D.L. (2007). White on whiteness: Becoming radicalized about race. *Nursing Inquiry, 14*(2), 153–161.

Hansen, N.D., Petitone-Arreola-Rockwell, F., & Greene, A.F. (2000). Multicultural competence: Criteria and case examples. *Professional Psychology: Research and Practice, 31*(6), 652–660.

Ho, D.Y.F. (1995). Internalized culture, culturocentrism, and transference. *The Counseling Psychologist, 23*(1), 4–24.

Israel, T. (2003). Integrating gender and sexual orientation into multicultural counseling competencies. In G. Roysircar, P. Arredondo, J.N. Fuertes, J.G. Ponterotto, & R.L. Toporek (Eds.), *Multicultural counseling competencies 2003: Association for Multicultural Counseling and Development* (pp. 69–78). Alexandria, VA: America Counseling Association.

Ivey, A.E., D'Andrea, M., Bradford Ivey, M., & Simek-Morgan, L. (2002). *Theories of counseling and psychotherapy: A multicultural perspective*. Boston: Allyn & Bacon.

Jordan, J.V. (1997). *Women's growth in diversity*. New York: Guilford Press.

Jordan, J.V., Kaplan, A.G., Miller, J.B., Stiver, I.P., & Surrey, L. (1991). *Women's growth in connection*. New York: Guilford Press.

Jordan, J.V., & Walker, M. (2004). Introduction. In J. V. Jordan, M. Walker, & L.M. Hartling (Eds.), *The complexity of connection* (pp. 1–8). New York: Guilford Press.

Jordan, J.V., Walker, M., & Hartling, L.M. (2004). *The complexity of connection*. New York: Guilford Press.

Justin, M. (2005). Counselling members of non-dominant ethnic groups. In N. Arthur & S. Collins (Eds.), *Culture-infused counselling: Celebrating the Canadian mosaic* (pp. 361–385). Calgary, AB: Counselling Concepts.

kaleidoscope. (2008). In *Merriam-Webster Online Dictionary*. Retrieved November 12, 2008, from http://www.merriam-webster.com/dictionary/kaleidoscope.

Kymlicka, W. (1997). *Immigrants, multiculturalism and Canadian citizenship*. Retrieved October 1, 2003, from http://www.pearson-shoyama.ca/Hot_Button/immigran.htm

Lowe, S.M., & Mascher, J. (2001). The role of sexual orientation in multicultural counseling: Integrating bodies of knowledge. In J.G. Ponterotto, J.M. Casis, L.A. Suzuki, & C.M. Alexander (Eds.), *Handbook of multicultural counseling* (2nd ed., pp. 755–778). Thousand Oaks, CA: Sage.

Ludvig, A. (2006). Differences between women? Intersecting voices in a female narrative. *European Journal of Women's Studies, 13*(3), 245–258.

Mahalingam, R., & Leu, J. (2005). Culture, essentialism, immigration and representations of gender. *Theory & Psychology*, 15(6), 839–860.

Mahalingam, R., & Trotman Reid, P. (2007). Dialogue at the margins: Women's self-stories and the intersections of identities. *Women's Studies International Forum*, 30(3), 254–263.

Miller, J.B., (1987). *Towards a new psychology of women* (2nd ed.). Boston: Beacon Press.

Mollen, D., Ridley, C.R., & Hill, C.L. (2003). Models of multicultural counseling competence. In D.B. Pope-Davis, H.L.K. Coleman, W.M. Lui, & R.L. Toporek (Eds.), *Handbook of multicultural competencies in counseling and psychology* (pp. 21–37). Thousand Oaks, CA: Sage.

Morris, M, & Bunjun, B. (2007). *Using intersectional feminist frameworks in research: A resource for embracing the complexities of women's lives in the stages of research.* Ottawa, ON: Canadian Institute for the Advancement of Women. Retrieved November 12, 2008, from http://www.criaw-icref.ca/IFF/Final layout of report with front cover.pdf

Morrow, S.L., Hawxhurst, D.M., Montes de Vegas, A.Y., Abousleman, T.M., & Castaneda, C.L. (2006). Toward a radical feminist multicultural therapy: Renewing a commitment to activism. In R.L. Toporek, L.G. Gerstein, N.A. Fouad, G. Roysircar, & T. Israel (Eds.), *Handbook for social justice in counseling psychology: Leadership, vision, and action* (pp. 231–247). Thousand Oaks, CA: Sage.

Munley, P.H., Lidderdale, M.A., Thiagarajan, M., & Null, U. (2004). Identity development and multicultural competency, *Journal of Multicultural Counseling and Development*, 32, 283–295.

Neville, A. (2005, April). *Gender-based analysis: Building blocks for success—Report of the Standing Committee on Status of Women.* Retrieved July 23, 2007, from http://cmte.parl.gc.ca/Content/HOC/committee/381/fewo/reports/rp1778246/feworp02/03-cov2-e.htm.

Pedersen, P. (2001). Multiculturalism and the paradigm shift in counselling: Controversies and alternative futures. *Canadian Journal of Counselling*, 35(1), 15–25.

Pitner, R.O., & Sakamoto, I. (2005). The role of critical consciousness in multicultural practice: Examining how its strength becomes its limitation. *American Journal of Orthopsychiatry*, 75(4), 684–694.

Popadiuk, N., & Arthur, N. (2004). Counseling international students in Canadian schools. *International Journal for the Advancement of Counselling*, 26(2), 125–145.

Pope-Davis, D.B., & Coleman, H.L.K. (2000). *The intersection of race, class, and gender in multicultural counseling.* Thousand Oaks, CA: Sage.

Razack, S. (1994). What is to be gained by looking white people in the eye? Culture, race, and gender in cases of sexual violence. *Signs: Journal of Women in Culture and Society*, 19 (4), 894–921.

Reid, P.T. (2002). Multicultural psychology: Bringing together gender and ethnicity. *Cultural Diversity & Ethnic Minority Psychology*, 8, 103–114.

Reynolds, A.L., & Constantine, M.G. (2004). Feminism and multiculturalism: Parallels and intersections. *Journal of Multicultural Counseling and Development, 32*, 346–357.

Rivière, D. (2004). Adventures of a black girl in search of herself: Some thoughts on Canadian feminism. *Hecate: An Interdisciplinary Journal of Women's Liberation 30*(1), 222–230.

Robinson, R.L. (1999). The intersections of dominant discourses across race, gender, and other identities. *Journal of Counseling and Development, 77*(1), 73–79.

Silverstein, L.B. (2006). Integrating feminism and multiculturalism: Scientific fact or science fiction. *Professional Psychology: Research and Practice, 37*(1), 21–28.

Statistics Canada. (2003). *Ethnic diversity survey: Portrait of a multicultural society.* Retrieved September 30, 2003, from http://www.statcan.ca/english/freepub/89–593-XIE/free.htm.

Sue, D.W. (2001). Multidimensional facets of cultural competence. *The Counseling Psychologist, 29*, 790–821.

Sue, D.W., Arredondo, P., & McDavis, R.J. (1992). Multicultural counseling competencies and standards: A call to the profession. *Journal of Counseling and Development, 70*, 477–483.

Sue, D.W., Bernier, J.B., Durran, M., Feinberg, L., Pedersen, P., Smith, E., et al. (1982). Position paper: Cross-cultural counseling competencies. *Counseling Psychologist, 10*, 45–52.

Sue, D.W., & Sue, D. (2003). *Counseling the culturally different: Theory and practice* (4th ed.). New York: Wiley.

Suyemoto, K.L. (2006). Building bridges across differences to meet social action goals: Being and creating allies among people of color. *American Journal of Community Psychology, 37*, 237–246.

Suyemoto, K.L., & Liem, J. H. (2007). Training therapists to be culturally sensitive with Asian American women clients. *Women & Therapy, 30*(3/4), 209–227.

Valentine, G. (2007). Theorizing and researching intersectionality: A challenge for feminist geography. *The Professional Geographer, 59*(1), 10–21.

Votresss, C.E., & Jackson, M.L. (2004). Reactions to the multicultural counselling competencies debate. *Journal of Mental Health Counseling, 26*(1), 74–80.

Walker, M. (2004). Race, self, and society: Relational challenges in a culture of disconnection. In J.V. Jordan, M. Walker, & L.M. Hartling (Eds.), *The complexity of connection* (pp. 90–102). New York: Guilford Press.

West, C.K. (2005). The map of relational-cultural theory. *Women & Therapy, 28*(3/4), 93–110.

Whalen, M., Fowler-Lese, K.P., Barber, J.S., Williams, E.N., Judge, A.B., Nilsson, J.E., & Shibazaki, K. (2004). Counseling practice with feminist-multicultural perspectives. *Journal of Multicultural Counseling and Development, 32*, 379–389.

Wiegman, R. (2000). Feminism's apocalyptic futures. *New Literary History, 31*, 805–825.

Weinrach, S.G., & Thomas, K.R. (2002). A critical analysis of the multicultural counselling competencies: Implications for the practice of mental health counselling. *Journal of Mental Health Counseling, 24,* 20–35.

Weinrach, S.G., & Thomas, K.R. (2004). The AMCD multicultural counseling competencies: A critically flawed initiative. *Journal of Mental Health Counseling,* 24(1), 20–35.

Williams, C.C. (2007). Mixed-method evaluation of continuing professional development: Applications in cultural competence training. *Social Work Education* 26(2), 121–135.

Williams, E.N., & Barber, J.S. (2004). Power and responsibility in therapy: Integrating feminism and multiculturalism. *Journal of Multicultural Counseling and Development, 32,* 390–401.

Zerbe Enns, C., Sinacore, A.L., Ancis, J.R., & Phillips, J. (2004). Toward integrating feminist and multicultural pedagogies. *Journal of Multicultural Counseling and Development, 32,* 414–427.

CHAPTER 2

Mom's the Word: Attachment Theory's Role in Defining the "Good Mother" by Lynda R. Ross

I came to the study of psychology later in life. As a doctoral student with two teenaged children, I was attracted to attachment theory because at a first and tertiary glance, it seemed a theory that embraced and promoted positive aspects of the human experience, primarily in its discussion and focus on the importance of relationships. Through my graduate studies and with the mentoring of feminist professors at the University of New Brunswick, I came to view psychological theory, particularly attachment theory, through a much more critical lens than that offered by traditional empiricism. For the past decade, my interest in the effects of historical, social, gender, and cultural bias on theory formulation has continued. I have a particular interest in the ways in which some psychological theories have been guarded and promoted over time, but perhaps more importantly, my interest extends to the role that psychological theory plays in the lives of women. I currently teach in the Women's Studies Department at Athabasca University, where I coordinate the University Certificate in Counselling Women and have authored courses that include The Psychology of Women; Gender, Culture, and Technology; and Violence against Women: A Global Perspective.

INTRODUCTION

As feminist counsellors, psychologists, and students of the counselling professions, it is important to understand all of the tributaries that feed the construction of the "good mother" and to uncover how particular messages from specific theories impact women's understanding of motherhood and their lives as mothers. This chapter explores how attachment theory has contributed to constructions of contemporary notions of the "good mother." Psychology and psychiatry hold privileged and powerful positions in society, influencing social beliefs and values. For decades, both of these disciplines have emphasized the critical role of "good mothering" in ensuring healthy infant, child, and adult personality development. Few would disagree that people develop and prosper in environments that are emotionally warm, nurturing, and stimulating. At the same time, most would not question the idea that people benefit from being cared for by others who are sensitive, accepting, cooperative, and available. These sentiments are so much a part of the fabric of the social norms surrounding women's roles and permeate definitions of the "good mother" that one might imagine that these mandates for women, particularly mothers, have always prevailed. "A mother is not allowed to make many good efforts but be humanly flawed; she has to be perfect, because so much is at stake—the physical and mental health of her children, for which she is assumed to be totally responsible" (Caplan, 1989, p. 69).

THE "GOOD MOTHER"

We can all conjure up images of what motherhood means to us. These images often rest in our own personal experiences of being mothered and, for some of us, in the experiences of mothering. In addition, we are confronted with an array of messages, on an almost daily basis, that promote idealized as well as demonized stereotypes of mothers. On the one hand, we expect mothers to be protective, nurturing, and self-sacrificing; and on the other, mothers are presented as domineering, overly protective, and responsible for all the ills that befall their children (Matlin, 2008). Mandates for the "good mother," originating from academic and scientific sources, are often co-opted and then translated for women by an influential popular media. In an article for *The Independent* entitled "Monstering of the Modern Mother," Sophie Goodchild (2007) recently reported that "[i]t seems that everything a woman does these days comes in for criticism from an army of child-rearing gurus, government campaigners and healthcare experts who are only too ready to wag the finger and dish out blame" (p. 56). Paradigms supporting notions of the "good mother" are continually shaped and reshaped by gendered assumptions, culture, and the context of the historical moment in which motherhood is being examined. This focus on the "good mother" in contemporary society has been facilitated by a variety of conditions. Professional, government, and media organizations have given it legitimacy by funding research that supports accepted current understandings. Academic journals and educators disseminate information that enhances established ideas about the "good mother" and promotes these ideas as a legitimate way to understand women's role in child rearing. As segments of the general populace embrace the paradigm's central beliefs, it gains legitimacy. All of these circumstances, accelerating for more than half a century, are apparent when looking at the role attachment theory has played in informing contemporary views of the motherhood.

Today's mothers are without a doubt confronted with conflicting and competing "expert" information about how to achieve the status of the "good mother." Advice and self-help books on mothering abound. With a few notable recent exceptions (e.g., Gillies, 2007; Miller, 2005; O'Reilly, 1999; Schäfer, 2006), little academic attention was given to researching aspects of motherhood from mothers' perspectives. In their absence, definitions of the "good mother" relied on the interpretation and application of theories developed by so-called experts. Although advice regarding the minutiae of what constitutes "good mothering" on a day-to-day basis has changed substantially over the years (e.g., Couture, 1947; Douglas, 2001; Spock, 1961), the underlying beliefs about what it means to be a "good mother" have remained remarkably stable. Definitions resting in gendered and essentialist assumptions have worked in concert with psychological and psychoanalytic theories—like attachment theory—to lay the groundwork for and promote notions of the "good mother."

Discourse surrounding the social construction of motherhood is not new. Indeed, one might wonder why we need to keep revisiting this issue when most of us would likely agree that there is nothing innate about women's interests in mothering nor in their desire to mother. Of course, this is not the same as saying that some women do not desire or are not keenly interested in mothering. What it is saying is that women are not genetically programmed to mother. Further, achieving the "good mother" status does not involve genes but instead a set of socially prescribed and ever-changing rules—rules that have not only been developed and defined by "experts" but guarded and promoted by social norms. Since Hollingworth (1916) examined the social construction of motherhood in her article *Social Devices for Impelling Women to Bear and Rear Children* almost 100 years ago, feminist research has refuted notions that naturally tie women to motherhood and has convincingly argued for its socially constructed nature as well as delineating the consequences of such constructions to women's lives (e.g., Caplan, 1989; Cowdery & Knudson-Martin, 2005; Hare-Mustin & Broderick, 1979; Houseknecht, 1979; Kaplan, 1992; Russo, 1979; Thurer, 1994). Hollingworth (1916) advised that "at the very outset ... we should consent to clear our minds of the sentimental conception of motherhood and look at the facts" (p. 19). She concluded that "it seems very clear that 'the social guardians' have not really believed that maternal instinct is alone a sufficient guaranty of population. They have made use of all possible social devices to insure not only childbearing, but child-rearing. Belief, law, public opinion, illusion, education, art, and bugaboos have all been used to re-enforce maternal instinct" (p. 28). Today, in Canada and elsewhere, Hollingworth's list could comfortably be modified by adding the use of so-called scientific evidence as a way to rein-force notions of "maternal instinct." [1]

When it has been politically, economically, and socially convenient, and when progressive feminist discourse surrounding gender and motherhood are seen to support a broader social need, these views gain some acceptance; when inconvenient, it seems that society lapses back into essentialist notions on both counts. A recent Canadian article, for example, published in the *Walrus* laments the decline in males entering Canadian universities (Coates & Keen, 2007). The authors note how "certain shibboleths of the past have fallen by the wayside. For one, the notion of man-as-provider has largely given way to two-earner families and an even greater degree of independence on the part of young women" (p. 60). Feminist discourse has not always been successful in affecting change in the ways motherhood is understood. Ironically, the recent and growing emphasis on fatherhood can be used, albeit incidentally, to inform the social constructionist perspective of motherhood. Perlesz (2004) writes in response to arguments surrounding the necessary role that fathers have to play in their children's upbringing—particularly their male offspring. Although not the direct intent of such articles (e.g., Deutsch & Saxon, 1998; Riggs, 2005), the emphasis on fathers as necessary caregivers does suggest that if fathers can "mother," then mothering should not be seen as an exclusive or essential role that resides within women's domain. Instead, in stressing the importance of father figures in parenting, these articles imply that mothering is a role to be fully shared with male partners.

ATTACHMENT THEORY ROOTED IN "MATERNAL DEPRIVATION"

Attachment theory has played a prominent role in shaping understandings of what it means to be a "good mother" and in turn, what "good mothering" means in terms of child development. Much of the discourse surrounding "good mothering" from an attachment theory perspective is rooted in an analysis devoid of class, sexuality, and race. This void stems in part from its historical location in a time when gender, sexuality, class, and race were largely absent from the construction of any theory. The roles for mothers prescribed by attachment theory could only conceivably be met by some groups of women, those who had not only the financial means (although not necessarily the emotional desire) but also the cultural and social supports necessary to do so. And thus, the "good mother" ideal could not technically be achieved by those residing outside the boundaries of what was socially or culturally possible for them. Although early on, without its broad analysis, the theory promoted the "good mother" as if it were a universal essential construct, in later years, empirical efforts were made to include class and race in the study of mothering practices on child development. More will be said about these empirical efforts in the next section of the paper.

In April 1948, the Social Commission of the United Nations resolved to study the needs of homeless children—"children who were orphaned or separated from their families for other reasons and need[ed] care in foster homes, institutions or other types of group care" (United Nations Economic and Social Council, 1948, pp. 28–29). Dr. John Bowlby took on this major task. The results of his inquiries were first published by the World Health Organization (WHO) in 1951 as a monograph entitled *Maternal Care and Mental Health*. It seems curious that a study designed to look at the needs of homeless children resulted in a monograph entitled *Maternal Care*, with two main sections called *Adverse Effects of Maternal Deprivation* and *Prevention of Maternal Deprivation*. The concept of maternal deprivation, however, was not born out of research Bowlby conducted for the WHO; instead, it represented an evolving theory that began taking shape a decade or so before Bowlby's research was commissioned.

Bowlby was a medical doctor and qualified as a child analyst in 1937. He worked in a variety of psychiatric settings until 1945 and then spent the next 26 years of his working life as Consultant Child Psychiatrist, the Director of the Department for Children and Parents, and Deputy Director at the Tavistock Clinic in London. For almost the same length of time, Bowlby retained a position as Consultant in Mental Health for the WHO (Holmes, 1993). During the early years of his career, Bowlby published a number of articles in which he linked his ideas about juvenile delinquency to maternal deprivation (e.g., Bowlby, 1938–1950). He also worked with a research group whose focus was on children who had been placed in different settings, including tuberculosis sanatoriums, fever hospitals, and residential nurseries, following separation from their mothers (Smith, 1995). James Robertson was an important member of this research team. He was initially hired to "observe and describe the behaviour of young children during and after separation from the mother" (Robertson & Robertson, 1989, p. 12). In Bowlby's 1944 publication *Forty-four Juvenile Thieves*, the affectionless characters of the young delinquents were attributed to extreme maternal deprivation as a consequence of prolonged periods of separation. As the researcher intimately involved with observing infants' and young children's responses to separation, Robertson disagreed both publicly and privately with Bowlby's conclusions regarding the effects of maternal deprivation. Robertson noted that Bowlby's analysis was "based on inferences from his therapeutic work; there were no first-hand observations on the processes of separation/deprivation" (Roberston & Roberston, p. 12). In regards to infant and child psychological well-being, Robertson consistently held that the context under which separation occurred as well as the circumstances in which the separation existed were at least as important, if not more so, than period of separation from the mother itself. [2] Nonetheless, "maternal deprivation" became the phrase of the day and set the agenda for attachment theorizing for the next five decades.

During World War II, unprecedented numbers of women worked outside of the home. "Between 1939 and 1944 the female labour force in Canada increased by almost 70%, from a total of 639,000 in 1939 to 1,077,00 in 1944" (Gleason, 1999, p. 53). It seems no small coincidence that a theory tied to maternal deprivation and reiterating the importance of consistent and continuous mothering to infant psychological well-being should come to the fore at a time when large numbers of women had, however temporarily, broken free of the household boundaries. Gleason notes how in Canada following the war, "[t]he employment of returning servicemen nonetheless took precedence over the new-found opportunities for women. Therefore, it is not surprising that in order to preserve the social order, women were told by social engineers, such as psychologists, that they needed to be good wives and mothers in order to fit normally into post-war life" (p. 53). Gauvreau (2004) also highlights the difficulties Canadian women faced as a function of the roles that were ascribed to them. "[O]n the one hand, wives and mothers were suspected of 'Momism,' of creating a matriarchy within the nuclear family if they fulfilled their role as emotional nurturer too well; on the other, they were frequently criticized for neglecting their children if they assumed what were defined as 'masculine' roles by seeking paid employment outside of the home" (Gauvreau, p. 397). And, more pointedly, in relation to attachment theory, Dally (1982) has pointed out how Bowlby's "emphasis on 'separation' is fundamental to the subtle idealization/denigration of mothers" (p. 90).

The fifties were rife with warnings to mothers about the harmful effects of non-maternal child care on infant development (Etaugh, 1980). Bowlby (1952a), in the republished WHO report, wrote:

> For the moment it is sufficient to say that what is believed to be essential for mental health is that the infant and young child should experience a warm, intimate, and continuous relationship with his mother (or permanent mother-substitute) in which both find satisfaction and enjoyment.... It is this complex, rich, and rewarding relationship with the mother in the early years, varied in countless ways by relations with the father and with siblings, that child psychiatrists and many others now believe to underlie the development of character and of mental health. A state of affairs in which the child does not have this relationship is termed "maternal deprivation" (p. 11).

As a result of his investigations into the plight of institutionalized children, Bowlby (1952a) reached the conclusion that the child's relationship to his mother "is without doubt in ordinary circumstances by far his most important relationship during these years" (p. 13). Depriving the child of maternal care, concluded Bowlby, "may have grave and far-reaching effects on his character and so on the whole of his future life" (p. 46). Bowlby warned if, during their first three years, infants lacked the opportunity to form an attachment to a mother figure, were deprived of their mother figure for even brief periods of time, or were changed from one mother figure to another, the result would produce "affectionless" children with "psychopathic characters." Bowlby's position advocated that

> just as the baby needs to feel that he belongs to his mother,
> the mother needs to feel that she belongs to her child and
> it is only when she has the satisfaction of this feeling that
> it is easy for her to devote herself to him. The provision
> of constant attention day and night, seven days a week
> and 365 in the year, is possible only for a woman who
> derives profound satisfaction from seeing her child grow
> from babyhood, through the many phases of childhood,
> to become an independent man or woman, and knows
> that it is her care which has made this possible (p. 67).

Although Bowlby acknowledged that mothering might sometimes go awry, he attributed poor mothering primarily to mothers who themselves had been the objects of poor mothering. During later years, Bowlby (e.g., 1988) does concede that the emotional support the mother receives for herself while parenting is important in predicting her parenting behaviour. From his earlier works, "support" was conceived in the following way:

> [The] child's relation to his mother ... is without doubt
> in ordinary circumstances by far his most important
> relationship during these years. It is she who feeds and
> cleans him, keeps him warm, and comforts him. It is to
> his mother that he turns when in distress. In the young
> child's eyes father plays second fiddle and his value
> increases only as the child's vulnerability to deprivation
> decreases. Nevertheless, as the illegitimate child knows,
> fathers have their uses even in infancy. Not only do they
> provide for their wives to enable them to devote them-
> selves unrestrictedly to the care of the infant and toddler,

but, by providing love and companionship, they support
her emotionally and help her maintain that harmonious
contented mood in the aura of which the infant thrives
(Bowlby, 1952a, p. 13).

From the WHO report came a flood of reviews, popularized articles, and
another book—*Child Care and the Growth of Love*—designed for the "ordinary
reader who is apt to shy away from a page bristling with references and figures,
with unfamiliar words and names which convey nothing to him. Yet the matter of this report very closely concerns the welfare of our whole society. So it
has seemed worthwhile to produce a version of the report, abridged and to
some extent simplified for general reading" (Bowlby, 1990/1953, p. 7).[3] The
simplified report was published in 1953 and reprinted several times over the
years with only minor changes and additions, with the last edition reprinted in
1996. Bowlby also published many brief articles in popular British magazines.
Articles like "Mother Is the Whole World" emphasized an idealized role for
mother and boldly directed mothers in ways to achieve the "good mother"
status (Bowlby, 1952b).[4] For example, a typical statement by Bowlby (1952b)
tells mothers that "the first rule in helping your toddler to grow into a happy
and stable youngster able to get on well with others is to look after him yourself,
'for better or for worse, in sickness and in health ...' during his first three years"
(p. 30). Similar articles, for example, "They Need Their Mothers," with sub-
titles such as, "At last science has to admit that mother-love is all important to
young people" (Bowlby,1952c),[5] emphasized the scientific basis underlying the
"good mother." Early advice columnists were beginning to use Bowlby's ideas
to inform their counselling. In an article entitled "When Parents Part," Joseph
Brayshaw (1952), the General Secretary for the British Marriage Council,
responded with the following to a distressed husband whose wife had left him
and who confessed that he had been tempted to "steal his son back": "Modern
research, such as that conducted by Dr. John Bowlby, has shown that the part-
ing of young children from their mothers is a frequent cause of emotional
troubles when the child grows up" (n.p.).[6] In response to the question "Should
a woman with children take a job?" which appeared in the *London Chronicle*
on April 23, 1952 (d), John Bowlby answered in the following way:

Research into the effects of daily separation is less
advanced [than research into longer term separations],
but it looks as though this experience often has a blunt-
ing effect on children's development. They become
apathetic and less responsive, after an early period of
distress. Sometimes a happy, easy child of two or three

will become extremely difficult and develop phobias. I know of one two-year-old girl who, taken by her mother to a day nursery by bus, after a few weeks developed a fear of all buses and screamed with terror whenever she entered one.... There can be no doubt that daily separations sometimes produce emotional disturbances and difficulties between mother and child (n.p).[7]

Although the theory received little criticism early in its advocacy, one detractor commented how Bowlby's own enthusiasm for attachment theory helped in its promotion, noting that "[n]ot everyone will agree that a child's capacity for love depends so much on what happens to him in the first two years of life, but no one can fail to be impressed by Dr. Bowlby's devotion to his theory and by the energetic way in which he expounds it" (Sarmiento, 1953, n.p.).[8] The findings discussed in both the WHO report and in the popularized *Child Care and the Growth of Love* were based on studies of the mental health and development of children who had been institutionalized, investigations into the early histories of adolescents and adults who had developed psychological illnesses, and follow-up studies of the mental health of children deprived of their mothers for a variety of reasons in their early years. Another critic noted that

it would have been desirable to analyze critically the methodological limitations of these studies.... [I]t should be noted that the majority of the studies are based on circumstances of extreme deprivation resulting from prolonged stay in an institution.... Bowlby does not distinguish sharply between the effects of separation, of deprivation, and of institutionalization.... [W]e need to consider also how individual differences among infants may influence the degree or nature of personality damage.... [W]hat is the effect on the child of the kind of mothering he has had before being separated from his mother or mother-substitute (Yarrow, 1953, p. 85).[9]

Another critic observed that

there is one major error in Dr. Bowlby's argument, however. Removal of a child from its mother cannot be accomplished except by placing it somewhere else. It is just as logical to blame the circumstances and actual

> experiences suffered by children under the cold and
> inhuman atmosphere of some institutions to which they
> are sent and the continuing inhumanity of our society
> towards deprived children, as to blame everything on the
> deprivation of the mother (Yudkin, 1953, n.p.).[10]

Scientific language and common sense permeated Bowlby's writings. While the idea of maternal deprivation and its relationship to the "good mother" and more importantly to healthy child development was convincing to a large portion of the populace, others, like Hilde Bruch (cited in Mead, 1954) were very concerned that Bowlby's emphasis on maternal deprivation was "a new and subtle form of antifeminism in which men—under the guise of exalting the importance of maternity—are tying women more tightly to their children than has been thought necessary since the invention of bottle feeding and baby carriages" (p. 271). In the end, the appeal of explaining psychopathology using notions of maternal deprivation had more to do with the social conditions of the time than with scientific findings. From its inception, attachment theory, with its notion of "maternal deprivation," was a major influence on the now almost commonplace view that "good mothering" involves selfless, consistent, and continuous care, and that adherence to its proscriptions will lead to children's healthy personality development. One of the main criticisms has been Bowlby's overemphasis on the single factor of maternal deprivation as the primary causal agent for children's emotional and mental disorders (Andry, 1962; Lebovici, 1962; Wootton, 1962). Mead (1954, 1962) also repeatedly pointed out the ethnocentricity inherent in attachment theory. From studies of the Kibbutzim system in Israel and the Hutterites, she noted that "neither of these bodies of data suggests that children do not thrive and survive under conditions of group nurturing" (Mead, 1962, p. 50). The exclusivity of bond between mother and child, supported by Bowlby's early theorizations, demanded a society in which women were expected not only to be full-time mothers, but to do so in a completely selfless manner (Kaplan, 1992). And women were expected to mother as if it were the most important and satisfying job in the world. This view was shared by others at the time. Notably, Donald Winnicott's view of the "good-enough" mother highlighted the importance of the mother-infant dyad and a "'primary maternal preoccupation' as a necessary state for infant health" (Appignanesi, 2007, p. 286).

ENTER EMPIRICISM AND THE EARLY WORK OF MARY AINSWORTH
Beyond references to early ethological studies and observations of special groups of children living under exceptional circumstances, Bowlby's early

attachment theory, although popular, could be considered fairly speculative from a scientific perspective. For its first two decades, the theory was without the support of empirical evidence. It was not until the work of Mary Ainsworth and her colleagues that so-called scientific methods were designed to assess the relationships between those maternal characteristics outlined by attachment theory as defining the "good mother" and the infant attachment behaviours that were thought to result from "good mothering." In 1969, Ainsworth and her colleague Wittig developed the Strange Situation, an experimental procedure. Set in a controlled laboratory space resembling a bare living room and containing a standard set of toys, chairs, and monitoring equipment, the procedure permitted the scientific assessment of an infant's reaction to separation from his or her mother.

> The basic concept is that a child who can use his mother as a secure base for exploration can move away from her freely, and yet tends to return to her on his own initiative from time to time, to play at her feet or to make brief contact before moving off again (Ainsworth, Bell, & Stayton, 1971, p. 34).

One-year-old infants and their mothers were brought into the Strange Situation where, during brief periods of separation and reunion, the responses of the infants to maternal separation were recorded. As a result of these recorded behaviours, infants were categorized into one of three attachment-style groups: insecure-avoidant, secure, or insecure-anxious-ambivalent. Using a sample of 14 "family-reared, white, middle-class" (Ainsworth, Bell, & Stayton, 1971, p. 22) infant-mother pairs, Ainsworth and Wittig (1969) reported a high degree of congruity between the data that resulted from the Strange Situation and the infant classification results from their longitudinal study with the same mother-infant pairs conducted over a one-year period. These authors concluded that the 20-minute procedure produced reliable and valid assessments of the nature of the infant-mother relationship, and furthermore, the procedure was less expensive and time consuming than the longitudinal research (Ainsworth, Bell, & Stayton, 1971).

In fact, while the entire Strange Situation episode is designed to last a maximum of 20 minutes, the majority of attachment behaviour coding is done during two reunion episodes with the mother. These two reunion episodes cover a six-minute period. In cases where infants appear to be unduly stressed, the time in separation is shortened or terminated altogether, reducing the amount of time available for coding. Ainsworth, Bell, and Stayton (1971) replicated the earlier Strange Situation findings, this time using a sample of 23 "white, middle-class" (p. 21) mother-infant pairs. Four dimensions of maternal behaviour were added to the design in order to assess the relationship between maternal behaviour and infant attachment style. Each of the four maternal behaviours was measured on a single nine-point scale and included dimensions of acceptance-rejection, cooperation-interference, accessibility-ignoring, and sensitivity-insensitivity. The results of these studies were used as empirical support for earlier attachment ideas that mothers who were sensitive to their babies' signals tended also to be accessible, cooperative, and accepting. Theorizing revolved around the evolutionary, biological, and universal nature of the attachment drive and its primacy in shaping and organizing infant attachment behaviours, with a focus on how individual differences in maternal behaviours affected infant development. Although Ainsworth (1967) had conducted initial mother-infant observations in Uganda, the focus remained on explaining individual differences through a simple analysis of maternal characteristics that neglected the important contributions of class and culture in explaining those behaviours. In regards to mothering, Ainsworth, Bell, and Stayton (1971) offered the following two hypotheses:

> [A] disharmonious or unsatisfactory relationship with his mother evokes insecurity in the infant—an insecurity which generally manifests itself in heightened proximity and contact seeking as well as a low threshold to separation distress; such insecurity is commonly labelled separation anxiety; and that since rejection entails a history of painful experiences associated with contact and with contact-seeking, an infant who is conspicuously rejected not only experiences the insecurity evoked by a disharmonious relationship with his mother but also experiences conflict between heightened proximity and contact-seeking and a desire to avoid proximity and contact—a conflict engenders the development of defensive reactions. These defensive reactions channel the baby's activity towards independent play, which absorbs him and allays his insecurity and at the same time blocks his proximity-seeking behaviour (pp. 46–47).

The results of these early studies established three infant attachment styles that, to date, remain effectively unchallenged. These early studies also provided the empirical evidence establishing the causal link between maternal behaviour and the development of secure or insecure infant attachment behaviour. Above all, the Strange Situation, like the theory it was designed to evaluate, assumed the primacy and importance of the mother-infant relationship. It only measured the interactions between mothers and their infants, in an extremely artificial situation. At the time, there was little concern about the highly complex and limiting nature of the categories to which the infants were assigned, the potentially small number of measurable infant behaviours given the limited time available, or the small number of infants used to design and test these categories. Also, little concern was paid to the effects that the Strange Situation setting might have had on the mother's behaviour, nor to the impact of the infant's own characteristics on their reactions in the Strange Situation.

Many investigations followed from these initial studies, extending from the early 1970s to the present. In 1972, Bell and Ainsworth's study of crying in the context of infants' attachment behaviour concluded that mothers who were unresponsive to their infants' signals, as well as being generally insensitive or interfering, were more likely to have infants who were "fussy, demanding and difficult to control" (p. 1187). The only control variables used in this study were birth order, sex of infant, and activity level. Some years later, Gewirtz and Boyd (1977) criticized Bell and Ainsworth's (1972) findings, largely on methodological grounds, specifically the inter-correlated nature of the measures used to justify their results. Gewirtz and Boyd maintained that Ainsworth and her colleague's conclusions were unjustified. Ainsworth and Bell (1977) later responded to this criticism by asserting the appropriateness of their analytic procedures given their small sample size and maintained that their interpretation of results was, in fact, legitimate. By the time Gewirtz and Boyd (1977) had voiced their concerns, Ainsworth and her colleagues (e.g., Ainsworth, Bell, & Stayton, 1974; Ainsworth, Blehar, Waters, & Wall, 1978) were already involved in other studies using the same measures and the same procedures. Ainsworth continued to look at crying, not only as a proximity-seeking behaviour, but as the foundation for communication. As such, Ainsworth and her colleagues framed early infant crying behaviour as the basis for both competence and socialization, concluding that infants' trust in their mothers was a necessary prerequisite under which they would venture forth to explore the world. They saw the responsibility for the delicate balance between infants' attachment and exploratory behaviours as residing with a mother's responsiveness to her infant's crying. Further, Ainsworth, Bell, and Stayton (1974) concluded that socialization was also facilitated by mothers' responsiveness. They asserted that infants who exhibited socially appropriate behaviours were supported by the type of mother who, "[a]lthough she did not deliberately attempt to train her baby, her transactions with him nevertheless facilitated his acquisition of socially desirable mode of behaviour" (p. 107).

On the basis of a very few early empirical studies, a detailed picture of the relationship between maternal caregiving and infant attachment was taking shape. The picture, painted with a scientific brush, was of a competent, adventurous, socially responsive, communicative infant who would cry less and be generally easier to handle for those "good mothers" willingly committing themselves to selfless parenting. In 1978, Rajecki, Lamb, and Obmscher published an extensive theoretical overview of the infant attachment literature. They concluded that the theories at that time did not accord completely with documented attachment phenomena. Specifically, ethological theory could not account satisfactorily for the formation of infant attachment bonds to inanimate objects. Nor could the Bowlby-Ainsworth theory adequately address attachment formations in situations of maltreatment. They maintained that in abusive relationships, infants are impelled to form attachment bonds regardless of the adult's responsiveness to them. A heated debate followed the publication of their overview. Some researchers defended both the attachment construct and the evidence generated to support it. Masters (1978), for example, stated emphatically that "differences of opinion may prevail regarding the precise nature of the concept or processes by which it operates, but the most heinous crime of all is to even consider that the concept itself is faulty, either in substance or usage" (p. 452).

Those on the other side of the argument pointed to critical omissions in attachment theory, which included ignoring the context in which the infant forms attachments (Gunnar, 1978), omitting cultural factors impacting infant development and parenting practices (Wolff, 1978), and failing to appreciate the theory of cognitions effecting human attachment (Kovach, 1978). In response to Rajecki, Lamb, and Obmscher's (1978) article, Cairns (1978) posed the following question: "Why hasn't research over the past decade led to an elimination of the original statements, or at least to their drastic revision and extension?" (p. 441). In response to his own question, Cairns offered this suggestion:

> The problem remains that "attachment" has been reified—despite protests to the contrary—so that a descriptively useful but theoretically vague idea has been assigned a role of nuclear importance in the explanation of psychopathology and the effects of early experience. The empirical basis for the reification and for the linkage between early social preferences and later personality disruption remains highly speculative (p. 441).

In spite of criticism, attachment theory largely continued to ignore cultural, class, contextual, and cognitive dimensions. The studies that followed the early works of Ainsworth and her colleagues elaborated upon and added to the list of maternal qualities associated with insecure infant attachment. The fundamental question guiding research in attachment continued to be one that asked What is it that mothers do, or do not do, to effect secure or insecure attachment in their infants? At the same time, the research began extending beyond short-term developmental effects towards the long-term influences on children of both the "good" and the "bad" mother. Researchers are now beginning to question the appropriateness of Ainsworth and her colleagues' conceptualizations of the links between maternal sensitivity and infant security when examining caregiving behaviours in different socio-economic groups and cross-culturally (Posada, Carbonell, et al., 2004; Posada, Jacobs, et al., 2002; van IJzendoorn & Kroonenberg, 1988). To date, there has been no clear resolution to this issue: Some advocates of attachment theory provide evidence for greater differences in infant attachment patterns within, compared to between, cultures (e.g., Behrens, Hesse, & Main, 2007; van IJzendoorn & Kroonenberg), while other researchers continue to challenge the theory's cross-cultural relevance (e.g., Rothbaum, Pott, Azuma, Miyake, & Weisz, 2000). What is clear is that cultural and class differences are evident in both the processes leading to and the classification of infant attachment styles (e.g., Broussard, 1995; Leyendecker, Lamb, & Scholmerich, 1997). Mothering practices, more generally, have been shown to vary cross-culturally (Bornstein et al., 1998), and poverty has been linked to an increased risk for poor attachment outcomes (Sroufe, Egeland, Carlson, & Collins, 2005).

ATTACHMENT THEORY—PAST TO PRESENT

John Bowlby's attachment theory was formulated to explain the processes surrounding the mother-infant bonding experience, as well as the consequences to the child resulting from that process. The theory was bound by a number of assumptions, originally placing sole responsibility for child rearing in the hands of women in general, mothers in particular. Bowlby, like many other theorists in the mid-twentieth century, assumed that women mother instinctively, are biologically suited to child rearing, and are best able to perform tasks surrounding the raising of children. Although attachment theory has been revised to reflect contemporary views of parenting—expanding definitions of attachment figures to include other primary caregivers—the theory in its original form continues to influence psychology and the now almost commonplace view that the "good mother" remains the most critical person responsible for healthy child development. Bowlby's influence in the fields of psychiatry and psychology through his prolific writing—with publications numbering in the hundreds—about attachment and loss continued until his death in 1990.

Attachment theory has played a prominent role in shaping understandings not only about infants' interactions with their primary caregivers, but also about the course and consequences of intimate human relations across the lifespan. Initially developed to explain behavioural and emotional responses of infants to their mothers (Ainsworth, 1962, 1967, 1978; Bowlby, 1952a, 1958, 1964), the contemporary theory now claims to account for the nature and quality of enduring affectional bonds over a lifetime (Ainsworth, 1985, 1989; Bowlby, 1969, 1973, 1977, 1980).

Attachment Styles—Good Outcomes for the "Good Mother"

Attachment theory carefully defined the role of attachment figures in affecting both short- and long-term infant emotional adjustment outcomes. As with the infant attachment styles defined by Ainsworth and her colleagues, the language used to describe the ways all individuals approach and function in intimate relationships has come to be framed in terms of attachment styles or, more recently, the dimensions—avoidance and anxiety—underlying those styles (e.g., Brennan, Clark, & Shaver, 1998). Attachment styles are described in the psychology and psychiatric literature as largely unchangeable, personality-type characteristics that remain constant over time and between different attachment relationships. Main (1985) used the three infant styles isolated and refined by Ainsworth and her colleagues (1978) as a basis to describe adults in their attachment relationships (Main). Hazan and Shaver (1987) extended work done by Main and talked about attachment patterns specific to adult romantic relationships. Following these researchers, Bartholomew and Horowitz (1991) proposed four different adult attachment styles based on two underlying dimensions—one describing the self in relationships and the other describing significant others in relationships. Combining aspects of self and other, the resulting categories included a secure style describing people who feel worthy and lovable and who expect all others will be accepting and responsive; a preoccupied style describing those who feel themselves unworthy of love, while at the same time seeing others as trustworthy and accepting; a fearful style combining negative feelings of the self with negative feelings about others; and finally a dismissing style describing those who have positive feelings about themselves but expect all others to be untrustworthy and rejecting. What is significant about each of the categorizations appearing in the literature, including Bartholomew and Horowitz's, is not the particular definitions, but the implication that an individual's single style, dependent primarily on the early mother-infant relationship, remains relatively static over the life span and between attachment relationships. As such, the "good mother" retains responsibility, not just for early infant bonding experiences, but for the quality of their offsprings' attachment tendencies and hence their intimate relationships across their lifespans.

Internal Working Models—Our Cognitive Relationship Maps of Self and Other

Attachment "styles," or "dimensions," represent the measurable outcomes—in infancy, childhood, adolescence, and adulthood—of the effects mothering. One of the ways in which scientific credibility has been added to the theory is through operationalizing the mechanism that is responsible for those outcomes. As such, the styles described above have become rooted in notions of Internal Working Models (IWMs). IWMs are proposed as the mental representations, or cognitive maps, responsible for organizing perceptions, expectations, memory, knowledge, behaviours, and affects about the self and about others in all attachment relationships (Bowlby, 1969). They are hypothesized to store, transmit, and manipulate knowledge about the relationship world, as well as the skills and abilities needed by the self to function in that world. They are thought to impact on an individual's ability to make effective plans in negotiating her or his relationship environment. Whereas the role of attachment figure(s) is to provide a secure base, the overarching goal of an individual's attachment system is to maintain or regain proximity (real or imagined) to the attachment figure(s). The attachment system's goal, guided by IWMs, is to preserve or restore an individual's sense of security or well-being when the individual feels threatened. In order for IWMs to be usefully exploited, Bowlby suggests that not only must they be built on experience but they "must be extended imaginatively to cover potential realities" (1969, p. 81).

In keeping with the definitions of attachment styles that rest in the theory, there are two significant parts to IWMs: one that relates to the attachment figure and the other to the self. Some of the key features informing the development and application of IWMs as they relate to attachment figure(s) include notions of what kind of person the attachment figure is, where they might be found in times of need, and how they might be expected to respond when called upon for help (e.g., Bowlby, 1973). In psychoanalytic terms, a "good object," reformulated by Bowlby, describes an attachment figure who is imagined as being accessible, trustworthy, and ready to help when called upon; conversely a "bad object" is someone whose accessibility is uncertain, or who would likely be unwilling to respond helpfully, or, in all likelihood, someone who would respond in a hostile way to any security-seeking behaviour. Key features of IWMs related to the self include notions of how acceptable or unacceptable individuals feel they might be in the eyes of their attachment figure(s). An IWM of the self has been described by Bowlby as a construct parallel to that of "self-image" or "self-esteem." When IWMs are well adapted, their "unconscious" nature is not problematic; when IWMs are not well adapted, efforts "to change them may be arduous, frustrating, and not always very successful" (Bowlby, 1980, p. 55). "Once adopted, moreover, and woven into the fabric of the working models, they [attitudes about self, attachment figures, and the interactions between self and attachment figures] are henceforward never to be seriously questioned" (Bowlby, 1973, p. 203). "Good mothers," as "good objects," are held largely responsible for their offsprings' positive IWMs; "bad mothers," as "bad objects," for negative IWMs.

THE DIRECTION OF ATTACHMENT THEORY TODAY

On the basis of a theoretical articulation about the self and attachments figures, and their roles in creating IWMs, early empirical work in attachment focussed primarily on infant patterns, which were evaluated almost exclusively within the infant-mother relationship (e.g., Ainsworth & Bell, 1974, 1977; Ainsworth, Bell, & Stayton, 1971, 1974; Ainsworth et al., 1978). Although research now takes a more balanced approach, acknowledging the effects of other important relationships in the development of infant attachment patterns (van IJzendoorn & de Wolff, 1997), the theoretical premise informing current studies remains the same. Attempts to understand relationships from an attachment perspective continue to rely almost exclusively on Bowlby's initial theorizing about IWMs and on Ainsworth's early conceptualizations and measurements of infant attachment styles. More and more, attachment work is focussed in the areas of social dysfunction and psychopathology. Relational research still tends to use attachment orientations to explain individual differences in partner selection and differential break-up rates (e.g., Collins & Read, 1990; Kirkpatrick & Davis, 1994; Latty-Mann & Davis, 1996). Attachment styles have also been used to predict the quality of intimate romantic relationships (Keelan, Dion, & Dion, 1994; Scharfe & Bartholomew, 1995) as well as to explain abusive romantic partnerships (Dutton, Saunders, Starzomski, & Bartholomew, 1994). Most recently, adult attachment security has been linked to psychopathology, including specific psychiatric concerns such as obsessive-compulsive disorder (Myhr, Sookman, & Pinard, 2004), borderline personality disorder (Holmes, 2003), depression (Davila, Steinberg, Kachadourian, Cobb, & Finchman, 2004), deliberate self-harm (Gratz, Conrad, & Roemer, 2002), and sexual dysfunction (Gentzler & Kerns, 2004; Schachner & Shaver, 2004). In earlier times, mothers were blamed for childhood diseases such as asthma and autism, as well as psychiatric disorders such as schizophrenia (Appignanesi, 2007). From the most recent version of the *Diagnostic and Statistical Manual of Mental Disorders* (DSM-IV-TR: American Psychiatric Association, 2000), we continue to see manifestations of insecure infant and childhood attachments used as diagnostic criteria for a number of the Axis I and II disorders, and with the diagnosis of reactive attachment disorder in childhood

(American Psychiatric Association, 2000). Attachment theory today is still used as a rationale to affect social and political agendas, as well as to inform attitudes about partner abuse, freedom to work, and universal day-care, all of which affect the lives of many women. Mothers are still being held largely responsible for attachment outcomes in their offspring—outcomes such as those described in the DSM. These outcomes are more far-reaching and have greater negative implications for the practice of motherhood than when the theory was initially developed.

CONCLUSION

Attachment theory, originally formulated to explain processes and consequences of infant bonding, is bound by a number of assumptions that placed responsibility for child rearing in the hands of women. Bowlby believed that infants formed a single, principle, infant-adult attachment bond. Once formed, the bond was thought to provide the basis for the IWMs that are used to define all subsequent attachment relationships. In Bowlby's view, infant separation from the mother-figure—maternal deprivation—was the main pathogenic agent responsible for negative aspects of infant personality development. Bowlby assumed that women instinctively mother, are biologically suited to child rearing, and are best able to perform the tasks of raising children. Bowlby did not question the role of the infant in the formation of attachment bonds, nor the role played by others. Many of the attachment researchers have been either directly (i.e., Ainsworth) or indirectly (i.e., Main, Shaver, Hazan, Bartholomew) involved with Bowlby. While some claim that "[a]ttachment theory [is] firmly rooted in a scientific perspective" (Holmes, 2003, p. 524), Bowlby's work on attachment, especially his early work, could hardly be considered "scientific." In the late 1970s, the construct was operationalized in such a way that it offered the potential for measurement and evaluation, with research focussed on proving, rather than disproving, the efficacy of the theory. The shift of attachment theory into the realm of psychopathology, effectively intensifying and multiplying women's responsibilities for the psychological outcomes in child rearing, suggests the need for a continued caution before uncritically accepting any psychological theory that burdens women further through expanding the construction of the "good mother."

ENDNOTES

1 As well, contemporary definitions of the "good mother" are largely incongruent with the roles that many women play in Canadian society today. In 2003, according to Statistics Canada (2004), women accounted for 47% of the employed work force.

The likelihood that women were employed increased dramatically as educational levels rose. Seventy-four per cent of women with a university degree and 69% with a college certificate or diploma were employed in 2003 (Statistics Canada).

2 For example, in a letter to Bowlby, dated 25 November 1971, in regards to an ongoing discussion about an article James and Joyce Robertson are preparing for publication, James Robertson notes "Although our findings are not in accord with certain of your theories, this makes no problem for us." In another letter dated 7 February 1972, Robertson notes: "In light of our ample firsthand data it is inconceivable to us that you can hold to the theory of grief and mourning in infancy and early childhood." In this same letter, Robertson draws Bowlby's attention to his " failure to distinguish between separation, deprivation, and separation plus deprivation." These letters were retrieved from the PP/BOW Collection of Papers at the Wellcome Library for the History of Medicine and Understanding Medicine, London UK; File PP/ BOW/B.3/25.

3 This quote is taken from the "Preface to the first edition," published in 1953, which was reprinted in the 1990 edition of *Bowlby's Childcare and the Growth of Love.*

4 Article retrieved from the PP/BOW Collection of Papers at the Wellcome Library for the History of Medicine and Understanding Medicine, London UK; File PP/ BOW/A.4/1.

5 Ibid.

6 Ibid. Page numbers not given.

7 Ibid. Page numbers not given.

8 Ibid. Page numbers not given.

9 Ibid.

10 Ibid. Page numbers not given.

REFERENCES

Ainsworth, M.D. (1962). The effects of maternal deprivation: A review of findings and controversy in the context of research strategy. *World Health Association, Geneva, Health Papers, 14,* 97–165.

Ainsworth, M.D. (1967). *Infancy in Uganda: Infant care and the growth of attachment.* Baltimore MD: John Hopkins.

Ainsworth, M.D. (1978). The Bowlby-Ainsworth attachment theory. *Behavioural and Brain Sciences, 3,* 436–438.

Ainsworth, M.D. (1985). Attachment across the lifespan. *Bulletin of the New York Academy of Medicine, 61,* 792–812.

Ainsworth, M.D. (1989). Attachments beyond infancy. *American Psychologist, 44,* 709–716.

Ainsworth, M.D. & Bell, S. (1974). Mother-infant interaction and the development of competence. In K. Connelly & J. Bruner (Eds.), *The growth of competence* (pp. 97–118). London: Academic Press.

Ainsworth, M.D., & Bell, S. (1977). Infant crying and maternal responsiveness: A rejoinder to Gewirtz and Boyd. *Child Development, 48*, 1208–1216.

Ainsworth, M.D., Bell, S., & Stayton, D. (1971). Individual differences in Strange-Situation behaviour of one-year-olds. In H. Schaffer (Ed.), *The origins of human social relations* (pp. 17–57). London: Academic Press.

Ainsworth, M.D., Bell, S., & Stayton, D. (1974). Infant-mother attachment and social development: Socialisation as a product of reciprocal responsiveness to signals. In M.Richards (Ed.), *The integration of a child into a social world* (pp. 99–135). London: Cambridge University Press.

Ainsworth, M.D., Blehar, M., Waters, E., & Wall, S. (1978). *Patterns of attachment: A psychological study of the strange situation.* New York: John Wiley & Sons.

Ainsworth, M.D. & Wittig, B. (1969). Attachment and exploratory behaviour of one-year-olds in a strange situation. In B.M. Foss (Ed.), *Determinants of infant behavior IV* (Vol. 4, pp. 113–136). London: Methuen.

American Psychiatric Association. (2000). *Diagnostic and statistical manual of mental disorders, (4th ed.), text revision.* Washington DC: American Psychiatric Association

Andry, R.G. (1962). Paternal and maternal roles and delinquency. In Deprivation of maternal care: A reassessment of its effects, *World Health Association, Geneva, Health Papers, 14*, 31–44.

Appignanesi, L. (2007). *Sad, mad and bad: Women and the mind-doctors from 1800.* Toronto: McArthur & Company.

Bartholomew, K., & Horowitz, L. (1991). Attachment styles among young adults: A test of a four-category model. *Journal of Personality and Social Psychology, 61*, 226–244.

Behrens, K., Hess, E., & Main, M. (2007). Mothers' attachment status as determined by the adult attachment interview predicts their 6-year-olds' reunion responses: A study conducted in Japan. *Developmental Psychology, 43*(6), 1553–1567.

Bell, S., & Ainsworth, M.D. (1972). Infant crying and maternal responsiveness. *Child Development, 43*, 1171–1190.

Bornstein, M., Haynes, O.M., Azuma, H., et al. (1998). A cross-national study of self-evaluations and attributions in parenting: Argentina, Belgium, France, Israel, Italy, Japan, and the United States. *Developmental Psychology, 34*(4), 662–676.

Bowlby, J. (1938). The abnormally aggressive child. *The New Era*, (Sept.–Oct), 230–234.

Bowlby, J. (1939). Hysteria in children. In H. Milford (Ed.), *A survey of child psychiatry* (pp. 80–84). London: Oxford University Press.

Bowlby, J. (1940a). The influence of early environment in the development of neurosis and neurotic character. *International Journal of Psycho-Analysis, 21*, 154–178.

Bowlby, J. (1940b). Psychological aspects. In R. Padley & M. Cole (Eds.), *Evacuation survey: A report to the Fabian Society* (pp. 186–196). London: George Rutledge & Sons.

Bowlby, J. (1944). Forty-four juvenile thieves: Their characters and home life. *International Journal of Psychoanalysis, 25*, 1–57 & 207–228.

Bowlby, J. (1947a). The therapeutic approach in sociology. *The Sociological Review*, 39, 39–49.

Bowlby, J. (1947b). The study of human relations in the child guidance clinic. *Journal of Social Issues*, 3(2), 35–41.

Bowlby, J. (1949). The study and reduction of group tensions in the family. *Human Relations*, 2(2), 123–128.

Bowlby, J. (1950). Research into the origins of delinquent behaviour. *British Medical Journal*, 11, 570.

Bowlby, J. (1951). Maternal care and mental health. *Bulletin of the World Health Organization*, 3, 355–534.

Bowlby, J. (1952a). *Maternal care and mental health 1ˢᵗ edition*. World Health Organization, Palais Des Nations, Geneva.

Bowlby, J. (1952b). Mother is the whole world. *Home Companion*, January 17, 29–30.

Bowlby, J. (1952c). They need their mothers: At last science has to admit that mother-love is all-important to young people. *Family Doctor*, 2(7), 350–352.

Bowlby, J. (1952d). Should a woman with children take a job? The mother who stays at home gives her children a better chance. April 23, *News Chronicle London*, n.p.

Bowlby, J. (1958). The nature of the child's tie to the mother. *International Journal of Psychoanalysis*, 39, 350–369.

Bowlby, J. (1964). Note on Dr. Lois Murphy's paper 'Some aspects of the first relationship.' *International Journal of Psychoanalysis*, 45, 44–46.

Bowlby, J. (1969). *Attachment and loss: Vol. 1., Attachment*. New York: Basic Books.

Bowlby, J. (1973). *Attachment and loss: Vol. 2., Separation: Anxiety and anger*. New York: Basic Books.

Bowlby, J. (1977). The making and breaking of affectional bonds. *British Journal of Psychiatry*, 130, 201–210.

Bowlby, J. (1980). *Attachment and loss: Vol. 3., Loss, sadness and depression*. New York: Basic Books.

Bowlby, J. (1988). *A secure base: Parent-child attachment and healthy human development*. New York: Basic Books.

Bowlby, J. (1990/1953). *Child care and the growth of love*. London: Penguin Books.

Brayshaw, J. (1952). When parents part. August 4, *Daily Herald London*, n.p.

Brennan, K., Clark, C., & Shaver, P. (1998). Self-report measurement of adult romantic attachment: An integrative overview. In J.A. Simpson & W. S. Rholes (Eds.), *Attachment theory and close relationships* (pp. 46–76). New York: Guilford Press.

Broussard, E. (1995). Infant attachment in a sample of adolescent mothers. *Child Psychiatry & Human Development*, 25(4), 211–219.

Cairns, R. B. (1978). Beyond attachment? *The Behavioral and Brain Sciences*, 3, 441–442.

Caplan, P. (1989). *Don't blame mother: Mending the mother-daughter relationship*. New York: Harper & Row Publishers.

Coates, K., & Keen, C. (2007). Snail males: Why are men falling behind in universities while women speed ahead? *The Walrus, 4*(2), 58–63.

Collins, N., & Read, S. (1990). Adult attachment, working models, and relationship quality in dating couples. *Journal of Personality and Social Psychology, 58,* 644–663.

Couture, E. (1947). *The Canadian mother and child.* Ottawa: King's Printer and Controller of Stationary.

Cowdery, R., & Knudson-Martin, C. (2005). The construction of motherhood: Tasks, relational connection, and gender equality. *Family Relations, 54,* 335–345.

Dally, A. (1982). *Inventing motherhood: The consequences of an ideal.* London: Burnett Books Ltd.

Davila, J., Steinberg, S., Kachadourian, L., Cobb, R., & Fincham, F. (2004). Romantic involvement and depressive symptoms in early and late adolescence: The role of a preoccupied relational style. *Personal Relationships, 11,* 161–178.

Deutsch, F., & Saxon, S. (1998). The double standard of praise and criticism for mothers and fathers. *Psychology of Women Quarterly, 22,* 665–683.

Douglas, A. (2001). *The mother of all baby books: An all-Canadian guide to your baby's first year.* Toronto: John Wiley & Sons Canada Ltd.

Dutton, D., Saunders, K., Starzomski, A., & Bartholomew, K. (1994). Intimacy-anger and insecure attachment as precursors of abuse in intimate relationships. *Journal of Applied Social Psychology, 15,* 1367–1386.

Etaugh, C. (1980). Effects of nonmaternal care on children: Research evidence and popular views. *American Psychologist, 35*(4), 309–319.

Gauvreau, M. (2004). Conclusion: The family as pathology-psychology, social science, and history construct the nuclear family 1945– 1980. In N. Christie & M. Gauvreau (Eds.), *Mapping the margins: The family and social discipline in Canada, 1700–1975* (pp. 381– 407). Montreal & Kingston: McGill-Queen's University Press.

Gentzler, A., & Kerns, K. (2004). Associations between insecure attachment and sexual experiences. *Personal Relationships, 11,* 249–265.

Gewirtz, J., & Boyd, E. (1977). Does maternal responding imply reduced infant crying? A critique of the 1972 Bell and Ainsworth report. *Child Development, 48,* 1200–1207.

Gillies, V. (2007). *Marginalised mothers: Exploring working-class experiences of parenting.* London: Routledge.

Gleason, M. (1999). *Normalizing the ideal: Psychology, schooling, and the family in postwar Canada.* Toronto: University of Toronto Press.

Goodchild, S. (2007). Monstering of the modern mother. *The Independent,* May 20, 56–57.

Gratz, K., Conrad, S., & Roemer, L. (2002). Risk factors for deliberate self-harm among college students. *American Journal of Orthopsychiatry, 72,* 128–140.

Gunnar, M. (1978). How can we test attachment theories if our subjects aren't attached? *The Behavioural and Brain Sciences, 3,* 447–448.

Hare-Mustin, R., & Broderick, P. (1979). The myth of motherhood: A study of attitudes toward motherhood. *Psychology of Women Quarterly*, 4(1), 114–128.

Hazan, C., & Shaver, P. (1987). Romantic love conceptualized as an attachment process. *Journal of Personality and Social Psychology*, 52, 511–524.

Hollingworth, L. (1916). Social devices for impelling women to bear and rear children. *The American Journal of Sociology*, 22(1), 19–29.

Holmes, J. (1993). *John Bowlby & attachment theory.* London: Routledge.

Holmes, J. (2003). Borderline personality disorder and the search for meaning: An attachment perspective. *Australian and New Zealand Journal of Psychiatry*, 37, 524–531.

Houseknecht, S. (1979). Timing of the decision to remain voluntary childless: Evidence for continuous socialization. *Psychology of Women Quarterly*, 4(1), 81–96.

Kaplan, M. (1992). *Mothers' images of motherhood: Case studies of twelve mothers.* London: Routledge.

Keelan, J., Dion, K.L., & Dion, K.K. (1994). Attachment style and heterosexual relationships among young adults: A short-term panel study. *Journal of Personal and Social Relationships*, 11, 201–214.

Kirkpatrick, L.A., & Davis, K.E. (1994). Attachment style, gender, and relationship stability: A longitudinal analysis. *Journal of Personality and Social Psychology*, 66, 502–512.

Kovach, J.K. (1978). Attachment: A general theory or a set of loosely-knit paradigms. *The Behavioural and Brain Sciences*, 3, 451–452.

Latty-Mann, H., & Davis, K. (1996). Attachment theory and partner choice: Preference and actuality. *Journal of Social and Personal Relationships*, 13, 5–23.

Lebovici, S. (1962). The concept of maternal deprivation: A review of the research. *World Health Association, Geneva, Health Papers*, 14, 75–95.

Leyendecker, B., Lamb, M., & Scholmerich, A. (1997). Studying mother-infant interaction: The effects of context and length of observation in two subcultural groups. *Infant Behavior & Development*, 20(3), 325–337.

Main, M. (1985). *An adult attachment classification system: Its relation to infant-parent attachment.* Paper Presented at the Biennial Meeting of the Society for Research in Child Development, Toronto, Canada.

Masters, J.C. (1978). Implicit assumptions regarding the singularity of attachment: A note on the validity and heuristic value of a mega-construct. *The Behavioral and Brain Sciences*, 3, 452.

Matlin, M. (2008). *The psychology of women, 6th edition.* Australia: Thompson Wadsworth.

Mead, M. (1954). Some theoretical considerations on the problem of mother-child separation. *American Journal of Orthopsychiatry*, 24, 471–483.

Mead, M. (1962). A cultural anthropologist's approach to maternal deprivation. *World Health Association, Geneva, Health Papers*, 14, 45–62.

Miller, T. (2005). *Making sense of motherhood: A narrative approach*. Cambridge: Cambridge University Press.

Myhr, G., Sookman, D., & Pinard, G. (2004). Attachment security and parental bonding in adults with obsessive-compulsive disorder: A comparison with depressed outpatients and healthy controls. *Acta Psychiatrica Scandinavica, 109*, 447–456.

O'Reilly, A. (1999). Inaugurating the Association for Research on Mothering. *Mothering and Motherhood, 1*(1), 7–15.

Perlesz, A. (2004). Deconstructing the fear of father absence. *Journal of Feminist Family Therapy, 16*(3), 1–29.

Posada, G., Carbonell, O., Alzate, G., & Plata, S. (2004). Through Columbian lenses: Ethnographic and conventional analyses of maternal care and their associations with secure base behavior. *Developmental Psychology, 40*(4), 508–518.

Posada, G., Jacobs, A., Richmond, M., Carbonell, M., Alzate, G., Bustamante, M., & Quiceno, J. (2002). Maternal caregiving and infant security in two cultures. *Developmental Psychology, 38*(1), 67–78.

Rajecki, D.W., Lamb, M.E., & Obmscher, P. (1978). Toward a general theory of infantile attachment: A comparative review of aspects of the social bond. *The Behavioural and Brain Sciences, 3*, 417–464.

Riggs, J.M. (2005). Impressions of mothers and fathers on the periphery of child care. *Psychology of Women Quarterly, 29*, 58–62.

Robertson, J. & Robertson, J. (1989). *Separation and the very young*. London: Free Association Books.

Rothbaum, F., Pott, M., Azuma, H., Miyake, K., & Weisz, J. (2000). The development of close relationships in Japan and the United States: Paths of symbiotic harmony and generative tension. *Child Development, 71*(5), 1121-1142.

Russo, F.N. (1979). Overview: Sex roles, fertility and the motherhood mandate. *Psychology of Women Quarterly, 4*(1), 7–15.

Sarmiento, D. (1953). The importance of mother-love: Child care and the growth of love by John Bowlby. June 13, *Tablet London*, n.p.

Schachner, D., & Shaver, P. (2004). Attachment dimensions and sexual motives. *Personal Relationships, 11*, 179–195.

Schäfer, A. (2006). *Breaking the good mom myth: Every mom's modern guide to getting past perfection, regaining sanity, and raising great kids*. NY: Wiley.

Scharfe, E., & Bartholomew, K. (1995). Accommodation and attachment representations in young couples. *Journal of Social and Personal Relationships, 12*, 389–401.

Smith, J. (1995). Introduction to the readers aid. *PP/BOW List of Papers in the Contemporary Medical Archives Centre at the Wellcome Institute for the History of Medicine*, compiled by Jennifer Smith, May, 1995.

Spock, B. (1961). *Dr. Spock talks with mothers: Growth and guidance*. Boston: Houghton Mifflin Company.

Sroufe, L., Egeland, B., Carlson, E., & Collins, W. (2005). *The development of the person: The Minnesota study of risk and adaptation from birth to childhood.* New York: The Guilford Press.

Statistics Canada. (2004). Women in Canada: Work chapter updates 2003. Housing, Family and Social Statistics Division, 23 pp. (accessed November 14, 2005). http://www.statcan.ca/english/freepub/89F0133XIE/89F0133XIE2003000.pdf.

Thurer, S. (1994). *The myths of motherhood: How culture reinvents the good mother.* NY: Penguin Books.

United Nations Economic and Social Council. (1948). *Economic and social Council. Official Records: Third Year, Seventh Session. Supplement No. 8.* Report of the Social Commission, NY, 28–29.

van IJzendoorn, M., & Kroonenberg, P. (1988). Cross-cultural patterns of attachment—a meta-analysis of the strange situation. *Child Development, 59*(1), 147–156.

van IJzendoorn, M., & de Wolff, M. (1997). In search of the absent father—meta-analysis of infant-father attachment: A rejoinder to our discussants. *Child Development, 68,* 604–609.

Wolff, P.H. (1978). Detaching from attachment. *The Behavioural and Brain Sciences, 3,* 460–461.

Wootton, B. (1962). A social scientist's approach to maternal deprivation. *World Health Association, Geneva, Health Papers, 14,* 63–73.

Yarrow, L. (January, 1953). When a child is deprived of mothering: A comment on John Bowlby's 'Maternal Care and Mental Health.' *The Child, 17*(5), 84–85.

Yudkin, S. (1953). The pelican in her iconoclasm. October 16, *Schoolmaster London,* n.p.

CHAPTER 3

Male Violence against Women and Girls: What Feminist Counsellors Need to Know to Begin Their Work with Women by Charlene Y. Senn

My feminist consciousness was developed within the vibrant feminist movement in Calgary, Alberta, in the early 1980s. I was a founding member of the Calgary Women's Health Collective (which is now a feminist therapy collective) and was involved in a number of activist projects related to violence against women during that time. I took with me the passion and enthusiasm for gender justice I developed in my grassroots feminist community as I became a feminist social psychologist and researcher. My early research explored the role and impact of violent, sexist, and dehumanizing pornography in women's lives. I have also investigated sexual abuse against people with intellectual disabilities, predictors of male sexually coercive behaviour, and a number of other issues related to feminism and violence against women and girls. My most recent research has been in developing and evaluating feminist rape resistance education for women in university. I am currently a professor in the Applied Social Psychology and Women's Studies programs at the University of Windsor and remain active in my community, working toward an end to male violence against women and children.

INTRODUCTION

Violence against women and girls is commonplace in Canadian society. The best statistics from random sample studies tell us that if a woman has not directly experienced male violence, then another woman in her life probably has: a woman in her family, the woman one seat in front of her in the classroom, the woman next to her in line at the grocery store or doctor's office, or the woman sitting next to her in the therapist's waiting room. And not included yet are all the women who have also been affected by hearing about or watching the harm done to friends, daughters, mothers, sisters, neighbours, or co-workers. It is because this violence and its effects are so ubiquitous that women's counsellors would be negligent if they did not adequately inform themselves about it. This chapter is only a beginning and cannot stand in for the deeper investigation and professional development that counsellors should do, but it does provide an overview of some key issues and knowledge that will serve as a guide for further study on the topic.

In this chapter, I will briefly present the statistics on male violence against women in Canada and a summary of the health effects of various forms of male violence against women and girls. This information provides a sense of the scope of the problem and the damaging impact on women's lives. The last half of the chapter provides an analysis of the ways feminist perspectives on violence against women and girls differ from more mainstream approaches to the topic. Counsellors need a feminist framework to provide women in their personal and professional lives with the best possible support.

THINKING ABOUT THE EFFECTS OF VIOLENCE[1] AGAINST WOMEN ON WOMEN'S HEALTH

Any textbook chapter is too short to give a full view of the field, and this one is no exception. By necessity, it must focus on a limited number of forms of male violence against women and girls and leave out others. The focus here will be on child sexual abuse, abuse of women by male intimate partners, and sexual assault, because these are the most common experiences talked about by the women who enter counselling. The chapter will also explore the effects on adult women even when the abuse occurred in childhood. But as the United Nations (UN) definition below demonstrates, the extent and scope of violence against women globally goes far beyond these few. If you begin to see women who have experienced torture in their home countries, Aboriginal women whose communities have been devastated by state-sanctioned violence for gen-erations (see Smith, 2005), women who are experiencing sexual harassment at work or school, or any other type of violence against women, I encourage you to educate yourself using feminist literature on those topics. According to the UN, violence against women is

> any act of gender-based violence that results in, or is likely
> to result in, physical, sexual, or psychological harm or suf-
> fering to women, including threats of such acts, coercion
> or arbitrary deprivation of liberty, whether occurring in
> public or private life ... to encompass, but not be limited to

> ... physical, sexual and psychological violence occurring
> in the family, including battering, sexual abuse of female
> children in the household, dowry related violence, marital
> rape, female genital mutilation and other traditional[2] prac-
> tices harmful to women, non-spousal violence and violence
> related to exploitation; physical, sexual and psychological
> violence occurring within the general community, includ-
> ing rape, sexual abuse, sexual harassment and intimidation
> at work, in educational institutions and elsewhere; traffick-
> ing in women and forced prostitution; and physical, sexual
> and psychological violence perpetrated or condoned by
> the state, wherever it occurs (United Nations, 23 February,
> 1993 Resolution No. A/RES/48/104).

In childhood, girls are physically abused and neglected at rates similar to boys. However, they are four times as likely to be sexually abused as boys, and the abuser is most likely to be a parent (44% of all cases) or someone else known to them (Canadian Centre for Justice Statistics, 2004), specifically a father or stepfather. While estimates are very hard to come by and depend on the definition used, somewhere between one in four to five girls (for severe forms) or one in two girls (for all forms) will be sexually abused before they turn 16 (National Clearinghouse on Family Violence, 2006; 2007; Canadian Panel on Violence Against Women, 1993).

Child sexual abuse obviously has many immediate negative effects on girls, but it has also been definitively linked to a variety of serious psychological effects in adulthood such that it is considered "a general risk factor for the development of later psychological disturbance" (Neumann, Houskamp, Pollock, & Briere, 1996, p. 11). These disturbances include symptoms of "anxiety, anger, depression, revictimization[3], self-mutilation, sexual problems, substance abuse, obsessions and compulsions, dissociation, post-traumatic stress responses and somatization" (p. 13). The connections between child sexual abuse and post-traumatic stress (discussed in more detail in Chapter 7) and revictimization are particularly strong. Physical health impacts are also more recently being found. As with most of the physical health effects of violence against women, these are postulated to be the effect of long-term traumatic stress. For example, "link[s] between child maltreatment [including sexual abuse] and cardiovascular disease was especially strong for women, with maltreated women having a nine-fold increase in cardiovascular disease compared to nonmaltreated women" (Kendall-Tackett, 2007, p. 119).

In adolescence and adulthood, girls and women continue to be at high risk for violence at the hands of men they know. The most conservative statistics show that approximately 7% to 8% of women will be physically or sexually assaulted within a five-year period by a partner (Johnson, 2006) and that as many as one in four Canadian women will be assaulted by an intimate partner in her lifetime (Canadian Panel on Violence Against Women, 1993). Younger women (under 35), including adolescents, are at the highest risk of being abused by a male partner (Canadian Centre for Justice Statistics, 2004). Criminal harassment or what is more commonly known as stalking is related to abuse of women by men within intimate relationships. In over 20% of the cases reported to Statistics Canada, the stalker was a partner or ex-partner, and these men are considered by many researchers to be the most dangerous of all stalkers (Johnson).

Over 40% of physical assaults by male partners will result in physical injuries (Johnson, 2006). In the worst cases, women are killed. Between 1979 and 1998 in Canada, 1468 women were murdered by their male partners (Statistics Canada, 2000). Of homicides that are solved by the police, 50% of all women murdered are "killed by someone with whom they had an intimate relationship at some point, either marriage or dating" (Statistics Canada, 2006). It is important for counsellors to know that the risk of death or serious injury for women is more elevated when she is leaving or has left a relationship with a physically, sexually, and/or psychologically violent man. Physical violence often increases or begins after women have separated from their male partners (Johnson). Safety plans are therefore critical, and feminist counsellors have an integral role to play in ensuring that every woman who is experiencing abuse at the hands of an intimate partner prepares one. The strategies, such as opening a bank account in her own name at a different bank than the one she uses with her partner and keeping a spare set of keys for the house and car and originals or copies of important documents (e.g., bank accounts, car ownership, insurance, health cards, custody agreements) with a close friend or family member, are fairly simple and yet can make a real difference if the woman is forced to leave her home without her purse or basic essentials. Many websites provide sample plans with fill-in-the-blank formats or helpful checklists (e.g., http://www.shelternet.ca/en/women/making-a-safety-plan/, http://www.pcawa.org/rp1.htm, http://www.ncadv.org/protectyourself/SafetyPlan_130.html). An excerpt from the ShelterNet safety plan is provided in Appendix A at the end of this chapter.

Women who are assaulted report immediate effects of the abuse such as having problems sleeping, being fearful for their children and themselves, feeling confused and ashamed, and suffering from anxiety attacks, depression, and lowered self-esteem (Johnson, 2006). Women whose partners are currently abusing them are more likely to have unwanted pregnancies and to be subjected to higher risks of sexually transmitted diseases due to their partners' high-risk sexual behaviours, such as not using condoms and non-monogamy (Coker,

2007). Other effects are directly related to the doubling of risk for abuse during pregnancy (Chrisler & Ferguson, 2006). These effects include higher rates of "preterm labor, vaginal bleeding, severe nausea, severe vomiting, dehydration and kidney infection and /or UTI [urinary tract infection]" compared to women who are not abused (Sharps, Laughon, & Giangrande, 2007, p. 110). Not surprisingly, a higher frequency of miscarriages has also been found in some studies (Chrisler & Ferguson).

In the longer term, women who have been battered by their male partners have higher rates of suicidal thoughts and attempts, depression, and post-traumatic stress, as well as being more likely to develop alcohol or drug dependence or abuse (Golding, 1999). These experiences are also related to poorer health and chronic disease (Coker et al., 2002). Emotional and psychological abuse have the same negative long-term effects as does physical abuse, with the exception of those produced by physical blows (e.g., Coker et al., 2002; Coker, Smith, Bethea, King, & McKeown, 2000). There is evidence, however, that once women are able to escape the abuse, many of these harmful effects begin to diminish so that in time women no longer have higher rates of depression or Post-traumatic Stress Disorder (PTSD) (Golding).

Based on in-depth interviews conducted by highly trained female interviewers, two-thirds of all Canadian women will, in their lifetimes, have had an experience that meets legal standards of sexual assault (Canadian Panel on Violence Against Women, 1993). This legal definition includes any touching with a sexual purpose without consent (Canadian Criminal Code, Sections 271, 272, 273). Using a more conservative definition of forced intercourse, between 25% (surveys, Statistics Canada, 2000) and 40% (interviews, Canadian Panel on Violence Against Women) of women will be raped in their lifetimes. When attempted sexual assaults are included, the prevalence of sexual victimization goes over 50%. The vast majority (81%) of these sexual assaults are committed by men who are known to the victim. For example, 50% of women who are physically assaulted by their male partners are also sexually assaulted by them (Canadian Panel on Violence Against Women).

While physical injuries from sexual assault are less common than people often expect [Center for Disease Control (CDC) estimates of 36% cited in Chrisler & Ferguson, 2006; 11% Statistics Canada, 1993], there are obvious immediate health risks for women, such as unwanted pregnancies, sexually transmitted diseases including HIV and Hepatitis C, and other physical consequences of the assault (Koss, Heise, & Russo, 1994). In both the short and long term, psychological health risks are also evident, including but not limited to intrusive memories, depression, suicidal ideation, lack of sexual enjoyment, anxiety, fear, and PTSD (Brener, McHahon, Warren, & Douglas, 1999; Koss, Aurelio, & Prince, 2002; Wingood & DiClemente, 1998). In fact, some authors have suggested that "there may be something unique to the experience of sexual assault that increases the likelihood of women developing PTSD" (McFarlane, 2007, p. 129). Research is just beginning to document how these psychological effects can translate into higher risk for seemingly unrelated physical health problems as well (World Development Report 1993, cited in Koss et al., 1994). Rape victimization has also been linked to a detrimental impact on self-protective health behaviours, including inability to negotiate safer sex (Wingood & DiClemente), increased cigarette smoking, and, when demographic characteristics are controlled, drinking and driving, and heavier alcohol and drug consumption (Brener, et al.).

By this point, it should be clear that the proportion of women who have been victims of violence against women is very high. If we include the women who are sexually harassed by an employer or co-worker and the girls and women who have had obscene phone calls, been forced to view violent pornography, been flashed by strangers, sexually accosted, or groped in public places, and experienced street harassment or other forms of violence against women, then most women have directly experienced it. Further, most women have had more than one experience. The effects of these types of violence are magnified by knowing the perpetrator (e.g., Temple, Weston, Rodriguez, & Marshall, 2007; Martin, Taft, & Resick, 2007), which is the condition under which most male violence against women takes place.

All women are at risk of male violence against women, but some women are at higher risk than others. Research is clear that women who are exposed to male perpetrators through unsafe living and working conditions, who are given less credibility (and hence the chance that men will prosecuted for the crime is lower), and who are more dependent on others for survival are generally at a higher risk. Women exploited in prostitution (Farley & Barkan, 1998; Nixon, Tutty, Downe, Gorkoff, & Ursel, 2002), women with mental disabilities (i.e., mental illness or intellectual impairment) and physical disabilities (Sobsey, 2000), Aboriginal women (Johnson, 2006; Smith, 2005), and women who are poor, particularly those in unstable housing (Kennedy, 2005), are all at higher risk of male violence, particularly physical and sexual assault. Immigrant women in Canada are actually at lower risk of violence by male intimates than non-immigrant women (Johnson); however, where vulnerability or dependence is increased through sexist refugee or sponsorship arrangements (e.g., deportation of a woman if she is sponsored by her husband and the marriage ends), the effects of ongoing abuse and subsequent feelings of powerlessness would likely be magnified (Canadian Panel on Violence Against Women, 1993; Dasgupta, 2002). Further, Canadian random sample surveys underestimate violence against all marginalized women since they are conducted in the two official languages and by phone, which rules out women without stable housing, phone service, and English or French language proficiency (e.g., see MacLeod & Shin, 1994). Moreover, the experiences of lesbian or bisexual women will be mixed in with all of the Statistics Canada studies since questions about same-sex partner abuse were not included in any of surveys to this point. Estimating the prevalence of abuse of lesbians by their female partners is very difficult, as random samples are impossible and selective samples are notoriously bad for estimating prevalence. However, it is clear that physical and psychological abuse of women by their lesbian partners does occur (see Ristock, 2002 and in this collection for the best Canadian research available) and that the effects of the abuse are likely to be complicated by issues of homophobia (internalized and external) (Rose, no date).

Counsellors of marginalized women need to explore and understand each woman's unique social and economic location in order to best address her experience of male violence, which may well be strongly influenced by racism, classism, and other vectors of oppression. Without an "intersectional" framework (Crenshaw, 1989; 1991), feminist counsellors, particularly but not exclusively those who are from the dominant groups (i.e., white, middle-class, heterosexual), can miss or ignore issues of utmost importance to women's ongoing safety and healing. All feminist therapists should do anti-oppression training (anti-racist, anti-classist, anti-ableist, and anti-homophobic) when possible and should read as much as they can in the feminist literature on abuse within marginalized communities (e.g., Smith, 2005 for Aboriginal women) so that they are better prepared to deal with the violence experienced by the diverse women who come to see them without their own cultural baggage and ignorance getting in the way. This is critical if issues of abuse are to be handled sensitively and well.

THE LITANY OF HARMS AND THE AVERAGE WOMAN

Given this startling prevalence of the problem of male violence against women, it is important that feminist counsellors take the time to acknowledge that *most* women who have these experiences resist the experiences, deal with the aftermath as best they can, have positive intimate relationships, create and/or work productively inside and outside the home, continue raising or go on to raise their children, are active in their communities, and are a source of support for others. They are only temporarily victims—they resist, survive, and thrive and sometimes even go on to be counsellors for other women, to protest against violence against other women or girls, or to fight other social justice battles.

It is also important to remember that there is no one way of being affected, and a lack of obvious long-term effects means nothing in particular about the woman or her experience. While all of the effects listed earlier are average group differences between abused and non-abused women, this does not mean that all women who were abused in a particular way will have the same symptom or pattern of symptoms. For example, only approximately 25% of women suffer from the effects of sexual assault years later (Hanson, 1990). As Briere and Jordan (2004) suggest, counsellors should "intervene with each woman based on her own specific clinical and social situation, as opposed to making assumptions that certain symptoms or problems are present and, therefore, that an assault-specific treatment is indicated" (p. 1267).

But violence perpetrated against women does affect them psychologically, emotionally, and physically usually for at least a year and for that sizeable minority long after the acts have taken place. While all forms of violence against women are notoriously under-reported to police (e.g., estimated 10% of all situations for sexual assault) and some women never tell anyone, most women tell friends or family members. Further, of all the sources of support women could access, they seek medical assistance (for abuse and non-abuse related issues) (Campbell & Lewandowski, 1997; Koss, Koss, & Woodruff, 1991) and assistance for mental health concerns frequently (Golding, 1994). It is critical that the people who they turn to for support truly understand the phenomenon of violence against women, or the consequences can be disastrous. What is known is always changing, so even if a counsellor has some background, it is absolutely necessary to keep seeking out information, learning, and thinking about these issues throughout her or his career.

Next, I will explore how feminism and a feminist perspective has shaped the way male violence against women is understood and the unique contributions and critical features of a feminist approach to counselling women and girls who are the survivors of male violence.

CONTRASTING A FEMINIST FRAMEWORK WITH THE MAINSTREAM IN PSYCHOLOGY, SOCIAL WORK, AND OTHER DISCIPLINES

It was feminists who first brought issues of male violence against women to the surface and demanded public acknowledgement and discussion. In Canada, the United States, and Britain in the late nineteenth and early twentieth century, primarily middle-class white women were concerned about violence against single women working in cities, wives, and children. They often masked their battles in so-called "purity" and temperance campaigns to prohibit alcohol consumption and prostitution or in struggles for divorce, but underneath their arguments were concerns about the safety of women and children (Gordon, 1988). In the second wave, beginning in the 1970s, women in Canada[4], the United States, and Britain spoke publicly about male violence against women, naming many forms for the first time (e.g., wife battering, child sexual abuse, sexual harassment, wife rape) and stating what is now obvious: that male violence against women is common and must be stopped. They started rape crisis centres and battered women's shelters, held Take Back the Night marches, engaged in various forms of activism, and encouraged women to talk to each other about their experiences (Pierson, 1993). The consciousness-raising groups of this period were politically motivated and were part of feminist organizing (Kravetz, 1978), but they were also in many ways what some people would now call high-quality peer support groups with a more consciously political agenda (Kravetz, Maracek, & Finn, 1983). While topics discussed were wide-ranging across varied aspects of women's oppression, male violence was necessarily a key feature of many of them. Feminist therapy grew out of these experiences and was originally seen as an extension of them (Enns, 1993; Maracek, 2000).

The success of the grassroots women's movement at naming male violence against women and forcing society to face the realities of many women's lives eventually led mainstream psychologists, social workers, and counsellors to realize that they must begin to deal with these issues. Much of this work originated with feminists within these disciplines who were part of both worlds, grassroots feminism and mainstream disciplines (Enns, 1993). Feminist books and articles burgeoned and knowledge expanded. But at some point, mainstream approaches without feminist principles at their core began to dominate disciplinary discussions of violence against women, and at this point in history, most of the workshops, books, and journal articles on sexual assault, child sexual abuse, and particularly woman abuse, do not have a feminist core. This has led to several trends that have turned back the struggle to end violence against women. Feminist counsellors should know about these trends, which have been strongly critiqued by feminists. Once formal training is completed, counsellors need to be able to sort through the knowledge being presented in various disciplines, professional development, and general reading to identify which knowledge is most beneficial to the women in their practice.

One of the major successes of the feminist movement was to provide a label for the experiences women were having but were unable to talk about to others. So-called problems at work were named "sexual harassment," and while there is a long way yet to go, workplace and human rights policies were then written, and with greater and lesser success, enforced. What was often described as "wifely duty" was more accurately named "marital rape," and with much struggle, exemptions in the Criminal Code for husbands were eliminated[5]. Some "problems" in marriages (and later in all heterosexual intimate relationships) were named "wife battering," and later "woman abuse" or "wife assault." "Rape," with its focus on sexual intercourse and on the sexual nature of the crime, was renamed "sexual assault," to highlight its violent nature. While there are issues with some of these labels that feminists continue to debate (e.g., Verberg, Wood, Desmarais, Kalra, & Senn, 2000), everyone who heard these terms knew who was being hurt and by implication who was doing the hurting.

As the so-called helping professions took over these discussions, the labels often shifted in the literature (DeKeseredy & Schwartz, 2001). For example, as the field grew, battering of women by men became "domestic violence," "family violence," and more recently, "interpersonal violence" (IPV). The identity and gender of the perpetrator and victim becomes masked when these terms are used in media and academic reports. The negative effects of even small changes in language on people's perceptions of the responsibility and blame ascribed to perpetrators and victims have been well documented (e.g., Lamb & Keon, 1995), so these are not small concerns. Concurrently, the feminist perspectives underlying the work also began to disappear. At a conference I recently attended on women's health, this lack of care in labelling was taken to a whole new level when the term "women with IPV" was used in scientific presentations in the same way that "women with diabetes" is used. Where is the onus on the male perpetrator when this is used? This slippage of responsibility is to some extent inevitable unless feminist counsellors are vigilant about their own use of language and terms, and ensure that they call their colleagues on these inappropriate usages when they are heard or read.

Naming and labelling may seem to be a trivial issue at first, but it is fundamental to the feminist political struggle to end violence against women and to the work of healing. If a woman cannot name what happened to her, then she cannot see herself as similar to other women who have had the same experience. How could she find them? She cannot read about the issue in a library because she does not know what to look up; she cannot go to the appropriate services designed for women who have been hurt in the ways that she has been hurt; she cannot decide whether she should leave the man who is hurting her or whether she needs to stay and try to fix the problems in her family or domestic situation. And society has definitely not reached a place where people do not need to worry about terms any more. For example, even with all of the feminist work done over the years and what seem to be improvements in knowledge about issues of violence against women, an evident lack of confidence and knowledge regarding labelling is still found in research and teaching on sexual assault. Most young women who have had experiences that meet legal definitions of sexual assault do not name their experiences as rape or sexual assault, and so while affected the same way emotionally as women who do, they do not approach sexual assault centres or other related services, nor do they report their experiences to the police (Koss, 1992). When a counsellor sees women in her counselling centre or private practice or talks to other women in her life, providing them with a possible label for their experiences is a big step towards dealing with what happened. And in those situations, gender-neutral labels that mask who did what to whom are not a step forward.

Another example of the power of language is the progression of terms feminists use to describe those who have been hurt by male violence. "Victims" have become "survivors," and then for some, "warriors," to highlight that victim status is tempo-rary and that women are engaged actively to overcome what has been done to them. This was not a trivial change in terminology and affected many women positively. In fact, a search of the web for the terms *survivor* and *warrior* shows that they have been widely adopted and adapted by women in their personal blogs and discussions beyond the experiences of male violence to include, for example, women's battles against breast cancer and the medical profession's treatment of them.

People within mainstream psychological, social work, and medical practice, as well as feminists, approach the harms of male violence against women in many different ways. Mainstream perspectives range widely. For some, it is apparently presumed that a good counsellor (or medical doctor or other professional) can deal with any issues that arise in clients' lives, without specialized training. This belief exists even though many instances have been documented where untrained counselling staff have failed dismally in their contacts with women who have been abused (e.g., Saunders, Holter, Phal, & Tolman, 2006). Some workplaces have recognized this reality and have tried to educate traditionally trained social work-ers, psychologists, and counsellors with more knowledge about particular forms of violence against women (Saunders, et al.). This is an uphill battle since most universities and other training programs still do not provide any regular training in graduate school for these issues (Campbell, Raja, & Grining, 1999).

Some professions have tended to endorse diagnosis (the collecting of reports of mental health "symptoms" with the objective of correct diagnosis) of women who have experienced male violence. It is thought that correct diagnosis leads to selecting appropriate treatment, even though many experts have pointed out that there is no one specific treatment, even for PTSD (Briere & Jordan, 2006). This focus on diagnosis acts to locate the "problem" within the individual woman rather than in the society or in the man or men who abused her. In psychiatry and psychology particularly, an overwhelming focus on symptoms stemming from abuse and diagnosis has been extremely problematic.

> Feminist therapists have had a dual focus: to critique the mental health establishment and to develop innovative forms of treatment.... Recognizing that psychiatric diagno-ses are potent means of social control, they have vigorously opposed psychiatric diagnoses that are sexist, heterosexist, homophobic, or racist ... (Maracek, 2000, p. 473).

Feminist therapists (and other feminists) have "reframed 'symptoms' as 'cop-ing skills'" (Burstow, 2003, p. 1295) and as the evidence of the harm of violence against women. They work to empower women to recognize those harms and work to heal and to thrive, with or without a therapist. Early feminists and feminist therapists believed that women's feminism and political action, generally (Enns, 1993; Mander & Rush, 1974) and on violence against women particularly, was a very powerful way to reclaim power that was lost and to heal (Mies, 1983). Consciousness-raising groups linked to groups of feminists organizing on various issues (fighting pornography, lobbying for changes to rape laws, etc.) fit into this pattern. Some feminists created resources that survivors of violence could use to work through issues on their own (e.g., Bass & Davis, 1988). Others recognized that assistance from a feminist therapist or other women's service provider (e.g., sexual assault counsellor, shelter worker) would sometimes be preferable. But always, these guidelines for therapy/healing included education on the issues from a feminist perspective, connecting women with other women in their communities (Enns, 1993), and had the goal of social transformation (Maracek, 2000). There is, as Enns suggests, still debate about the extent to which women who are actively dealing with the consequences of male violence should be encouraged to be activists. However, when the issues are those in which isolation from other women is a tactic of abusive men and sometimes result in non-disclosure and shame (such as child sexual abuse and woman abuse), these feminist strategies of encouraging connections between women should definitely be considered.

Figure 3.1 Power & Control Wheel

As alluded to earlier, many feminist therapists go beyond work with their own clients to expose the harms of mainstream practices more generally. Diagnosis has been the subject of the most vigorous feminist critiques. The worst of these diagnoses have been ones that are obviously woman-blaming, particularly Self-defeating (masochistic) Personality Disorder[6] and Borderline Personality Disorder[7] for sexual abuse survivors (Briere, 1992; Shaw & Proctor, 2005). Feminists like Paula Caplan (Pantony & Caplan, 1991) fought these types of diagnoses with often creative and persuasive responses. Caplan (1991a, 1991b) very publicly proposed that a Delusional Dominating Personality Disorder be added to the *Diagnostic and Statistical Manual* (DSM) for male batterers and other men "with rigid masculine socialization" (Pantony & Caplan, 1991, p. 120) to make the sexism in the Self-defeating Personality Disorder diagnosis more visible. It was due to these feminist struggles that the Self-defeating Personality Disorder was not converted to a full-fledged diagnosis and included in the DSM, however, a number of clinicians are still using it (evidenced by Google searches in the summer of 2007). Protests about Borderline Personality Disorder have reduced over the past decade (for an exception see Shaw & Proctor, 2005), although the issue of diagnosing a woman as having a personality disorder when the very symptoms used to determine the diagnosis are almost identical to those experienced by sexual abuse survivors is still patently problematic. Pro-feminist psychologist John Briere continues to point this out in his speeches and writings on diagnosis and treatment of child sexual abuse (Briere, 1992).

Some diagnoses/labels, such as the Battered Woman Syndrome (BWS; Walker, 1984) and Post-traumatic Stress Disorder (PTSD), originally used for male soldiers but now applied to women who have experienced violence by men, are not perhaps so obviously problematic. They do label the violence as a trauma, a term feminists were using themselves (Burstow, 2003), and acknowledge the source of symptoms in the male abuser's behaviour. However, there are still problems for women and other victims of violence in these diagnoses. While it is beyond the scope of this chapter to itemize all the issues feminists have with BWS and PTSD, I will attempt to provide the flavour of these critiques.

Elizabeth Comack (2002) has focussed her critiques of BWS on an analysis of legal proceedings in which BWS was used as a defence for women who have killed the men who abused them. She points out that while the diagnosis and its use as a defence is sometimes successful in getting women acquitted, it fails because it is still focussed on answering the question of why the woman "didn't just leave," a question that ignores the entire context of her experience. In the end, then, the diagnosis still "serves to *individualize, medicalize,* and *depoliticize* an abused woman's experiences.... In the process, abused women are transformed into victims—not so much of their male abusers as of their own dysfunctional personalities" (italics in original, Comack, p. 281).

Bonnie Burstow (2005) has crystallized the critique of PTSD in her article "A Critique of Posttraumatic Stress Disorder and the DSM." This article is highly recommended for anyone who is considering using the diagnosis or concept. Burstow suggests that while PTSD has been changed due to feminist concerns—the original wording required that the trauma be "outside the range of human experience" (DSM-III-R, 1987, p. 250)—fundamental problems remain. The most powerful of these critiques is that many of the "symptoms" listed (e.g., "efforts to avoid thoughts, feelings, or conversations associated with the event," "hypervigilance," etc.) are in fact ways that women cope with what has happened to them. She acknowledges that while "this way of coping can and does frequently lead to problems—sometimes extreme problems—it does make sense; and there are times when it is wise and even necessary" (Burstow, p. 433). Symptoms in the DSM are, by definition, things that are undesirable and, as a result, Burstow points out that some "leading trauma therapists" have "instructed practitioners" to "try to eradicate the symptoms, whether through drugs or other means" (p. 433–434). However, a woman's hypervigilance may in fact be a completely reasonable reaction to the realities of violence against women (Burstow). Is it really a good idea to remove women's accurate perception of danger and her coping skills?

As Maracek (2000) says, one of the features of "most, if not all" feminist therapies is "a commitment to conceptualising clients' difficulties and distress in social and cultural context" (p. 4 73). There is no type of feminist therapy or counselling where this is more important than when working with women who have experienced male violence. Whether or not Comack's or Burstow's arguments are found convincing, diagnosis as a practice places the problem of male violence against women within the woman who has experienced it (Burstow, 2005). If something becomes a disorder or a syndrome, is it not then easier to think that something is wrong about the woman (and not society) and needs to be fixed? Feminists will continue to debate diagnoses and other labels assigned to women who have experienced violence. Many feminist therapists refuse to diagnose the women they see (Burstow, 2003), and others only use diagnoses when forced to by the requirements of women's health insurance. No feminist should ever use diagnostic labels unselfconsciously.

This chapter has only touched the surface of feminist knowledge on violence against women and girls and how a feminist perspective provides a unique capacity to assist survivors of male violence without pathologizing them. The strengths of a feminist approach to counselling women who are survivors of male violence are many. But as Enns (1993) suggests, just because a counsellor is a feminist does not mean she/he is a feminist therapist/counsellor. Feminist counsellors are informed about the gendered nature and the extent and variety of violence perpetrated against women and girls in the culture. They do not look for individual explanations for women's experiences (e.g., in personality or behaviour), but rather look to the social context (e.g., one that supports violence against women, makes it hard for women to disclose and be believed, puts some women at increased vulnerability due to poverty, immigration status, disability, or marginalization, etc.) and at the male perpetrator when assigning responsibility for the violence. Feminist counsellors see "symptoms" as the evidence of harm, but they acknowledge differences in women's perceptions of their experience and their coping and survival skills. Above all, feminist counsellors provide a safe environment in which women can continue to cope, survive, grow, and thrive.

ENDNOTES

1 Whenever "effects" of violence are presented, the best data available is used, usually from meta-analyses or random sample studies. Reliance on single studies especially with clinical samples is inadvisable as negative effects tend to be overstated.

2 Many feminists have criticized definitions like this one for the inclusion of "traditional" cultural practices such as genital female mutilation while Western cultural practices such as widespread mutilation of women's bodies through breast implants and more recently, cosmetic labiaplasty, are not. [See Wilson, T.D. (2002). Pharaonic circumcision under patriarchy and breast augmentation under phallocentric capitalism: Similarities and differences. *Violence Against Women*, 8(4), 495–521 for one feminist perspective on this issue.] Despite this problem, the UN definition is one of the best and most comprehensive available at the current time.

3 Revictimization is the term used in the mainstream literature to describe the situation where sexual abuse or assault in one time-period is followed by another sexual abuse or assault experience by a different perpetrator. This term has become the focus of research and discussion that appears to suggest that victimized women are in some way through their behaviour "inviting" later attacks. Catherine MacKinnon's (1982) description of women as having "disabled resistance" as a direct effect of the abuse they suffered is preferable because it makes woman-blaming explanations less likely. See her article "Feminism, Marxism, method, and the state: An agenda for theory" in *Signs*, 7(3), pp. 515–544.

4 Judy Rebick's (2005) chapter, "No means no: Resistance to male violence" in her book *Ten Thousand Roses: The making of a feminist revolution* (Penguin: Toronto) is highly recommended.

5 It should be noted that not all American states have eliminated this exemption and everywhere it is extremely difficult to convict husband rapists.

6 Self-defeating Personality Disorder is a pervasive pattern of self-defeating behaviour, beginning by early adulthood and present in a variety of contexts. The person may

often avoid or undermine pleasurable experiences, be drawn to situations or relationships in which he or she will suffer, and prevent others from helping him or her, as indicated by at least five criteria, which include, "not being able to accept help from others, "choos[ing] people" who disappoint or badly treat them and "reject[ing] people" who would treat them well, "engaging in excessive self-sacrifice" and being unable to experience or acknowledge pleasure (DSM-III-R, 1987).

7 Borderline Personality Disorder is defined by "instability of interpersonal relationships, self-image, and affects, and marked impulsivity beginning by early adulthood and present in a variety of contexts" (DSM-IV-TR, 2000, p. 710) and must meet five of nine criteria, which include "chronic feelings of emptiness," "severe dissociative symptoms," emotional instability, "recurrent suicidal behaviour, gestures or threats or self-mutilating behaviour," etc. (p. 710).

REFERENCES

American Psychiatric Association. (1987). *Diagnostic and statistical manual of mental disorders, third edition, revised.* Washington, D.C.: Author.

American Psychiatric Association. (2000). *Diagnostic and statistical manual of mental disorders: DSM-IV-TR.* Washington, D.C.: Author.

Bass, E., & Davis., L. (1988). *The courage to heal: A guide for women survivors of sexual abuse.* New York: Harper & Row.

Brener, N.D., McMahon, P.M., Warren, C.W., & Douglas, K.A. (1999). Forced sexual intercourse and associated health risk behaviours among female college students in the U.S. *Journal of Counseling and Clinical Psychology, 67*(2), 252–259.

Bricre, J.N. (1992). *Child abuse trauma: Theory and treatment of the lasting effects.* Newbury Park: Sage.

Briere, J., & Jordan, C.E. (2004). Violence against women: Outcome complexity and implications for assessment and treatment. *Journal of Interpersonal Violence, 19*(11), 1252–1276.

Burstow, B. (2003). Toward a radical understanding of trauma and trauma work. *Violence Against Women, 9*(11), 1293–1317.

Burstow, B. (2005). A critique of posttraumatic stress disorder and the DSM. *Journal of Humanistic Psychology, 45*(4), 429–445.

Campbell, J.C., & Lewandowski, L.A. (1997). Mental and physical health effects of intimate partner violence on women and children. *Psychiatric Clinics of North America, 20*(2), 353.

Campbell, R., Raja, S., & Grining, P.L. (1999). Training mental health professionals on violence against women. *Journal of Interpersonal Violence, 14*(10), 1003–1013.

Canadian Centre for Justice Statistics. (2004). *Family Violence in Canada: A Statistical Profile 2004.* (Report No. 85-224-XIE). Ottawa, Ontario: Statistics Canada.

Canadian Panel on Violence against Women. (1993). *Changing the Landscape: Ending Violence, Achieving Equality.* Ottawa, Ontario: Ministry of Supply and Services Canada.

Caplan, P.J. (1991a). How *do* they decide what is normal? The bizarre, but true, tale of the DSM process. *Canadian Psychology*, 32(2), 162–170.

Caplan, P.J. (1991b). Delusional Dominating Personality Disorder, *Feminism & Psychology*, 1(1), 171–174.

Chrisler, J.C., & Ferguson, S. (2006). Violence against women as a public health issue. *Violence and Exploitation against Women and Girls Annals of the New York Academy of Sciences, vol. 1087, Issue 1, pp. 235–249.*

Coker, A.L. (2007). Does physical intimate partner violence affect sexual health? A systematic review. *Trauma, Violence, & Abuse*, 8(2), 149–177.

Coker, A.L., Davis, K.E., Arias, I., Desai, S., Sanderson, M., Brandt, H.M. et al. (2002). Physical and mental health effects of intimate partner violence for men and women. *American Journal of Preventative Medicine*, 23(4), 260–268.

Coker, A.L., Smith, P.H., Bethea, L., King, M.R., & McKeown, R.E. (2000). Physical health consequences of physical and psychological intimate partner violence. *Archives of Family Medicine*, 9(5), 451–457.

Comack, E. (2002). Do we need to syndromize women's experiences? The limitations of the 'Battered Woman Syndrome.' In K.M.J. McKenna, & J. Larkin (Eds), *Violence against women: New Canadian perspectives* (pp. 277–284). Toronto, Canada: Inanna.

Crenshaw, K. (1989). Demarginalizing the intersection of race and sex: A black feminist critique of antidiscrimination doctrine, feminist theory and antiracist politics. *University of Chicago Legal Forum*, 139–167.

Crenshaw, K.W. (1991). Mapping the margins: Intersectionality, identity politics, and violence against women. *Stanford Law Review*, 43, 6, 1241–1299.

Criminal Code, R.S.C. 1985, c.46, s.231(6).

Dasgupta, S.D. (2002). A framework for understanding women's use of nonlethal violence in intimate heterosexual relationships. *Violence against Women*, 8(11), 1364–1389.

DeKeseredy, W.S., & Schwartz, M.D. (2001). Definitional issues. C.M. Renzetti, J.L. Edleson, & R. Kennedy Bergen (Eds.), *Sourcebook on violence against women* (pp. 23–34). London: Sage Publications.

Enns, C.Z. (1993). Twenty years of feminist counseling and therapy: From naming biases to implementing multifaceted practice. *The Counselling Psychologist*, 21(1), 3–87.

Farley, M., & Barkan, H. (1998). Prostitution, violence, and posttraumatic stress disorder. *Women & Health*, 27(3), 37–49.

Golding, J. (1994). Sexual assault history and physical health in randomly selected Los Angeles women. *Health Psychology*, 13, 130–138.

Golding, J.M. (1999). Partner violence as a risk factor for mental disorders: A meta-analysis. *Journal of Family Medicine*, 14(2), 99–132.

Gordon, L. (1988). 'The powers of the weak': Wife-beating and battered women's resistance. In *Heroes of their own lives: The politics and history of family violence, Boston, 1880–1960* (pp. 250–257). New York: Viking.

Hanson, R.K. (1990). The psychological impact of sexual assault on women and children: A review. *Annals of Sex Research, 3,* 187–232.

Johnson, H. (2006). *Measuring Violence against Women: Statistical Trends 2006.* (Report No. 85-570-XIE). Ottawa, Ontario: Ministry of Industry, Statistics Canada.

Kendall-Tackett, K.A. (2007). Inflammation, cardiovascular disease, and metabolic syndrome as sequelae of violence against women: The role of depression, hostility, and sleep disturbance. *Trauma, Violence, & Abuse, 8*(2), 117–126.

Kennedy, M. (2005). *Woman Abuse: Exploring the Connections to Women's Experience of Mental Health and Homelessness.* London, Ontario: Centre for Research on Violence against Women and Children, The University of Western Ontario.

Koss, M. P. (1992). The underdetection of rape: Methodological choices and their effects on incidence estimates. *Journal of Social Issues, 48*(1), 61–75.

Koss, M.P., Aurelio, J.F., & Prince, R.J. (2002). Cognitive mediation of rape's mental, physical, and social health impact: Tests of four models in cross-sectional data. *Journal of Consulting and Clinical Psychology, 70*(4), 926–941.

Koss, M.P., Heise, L., & Russo, N.F. (1994). The global health burden of rape. *Psychology of Women Quarterly, 18,* 509–537.

Koss, M.P., Koss, P.G., & Woodruff, W.J. (1991). Deleterious effects of criminal victimization on women's health and medical utilization. *Archives of Internal Medicine, 151,* 342–347.

Kravetz, D. (1978). Consciousness-raising groups in the 1970s. *Psychology of Women Quarterly, 3*(2), 168–186.

Kravetz, D., Maracek, J., & Finn, S.E. (1983). Factors influencing women's participation in consciousness-raising groups. *Psychology of Women Quarterly, 7*(3), 257–271.

Lamb, S., & Keon, S. (1995) Blaming the perpetrator: Language that distorts reality in writing about men battering women. *Psychology of Women Quarterly, 19,* 209–220.

MacLeod, L., & Shin, M.Y. (1994). *"Like a Wingless Bird ..." A Tribute to the Survival and Courage of Women Who Are Abused and Who Speak Neither English nor French.* (Report No. H72-21/110-1994E). Ottawa, Ontario: National Clearinghouse on Family Violence.

Maracek, J. (2000). Feminist therapy. In L. Code (Ed.), *Encyclopedia of feminist theories* (pp. 473–474). London: Routledge.

Mander, A.V., & Rush, A.K. (1974). *Feminism as therapy.* New York, NY: Random House.

Martin, E.K., Taft, C.T., & Resick, P.A. (2007). A review of marital rape. *Aggression and Violent Behavior, 12*(3), 329–347.

McFarlane, J. (2007). Pregnancy following partner rape: What we know and what we need to know. *Trauma, Violence, & Abuse, 8*(2), 127–134.

Mies, M. (1983). Towards a methodology for feminist research. In G. Bowles, & R.D. Klein (Eds.), *Theories of women's studies* (pp. 117–139). London: Routledge & Kegan Paul.

National Clearinghouse on Family Violence. (2006). *Child Sexual Abuse.* (Report No. H72-22/2-2004E). Ottawa, Ontario: Government of Canada.

National Clearinghouse on Family Violence. (2007). *Fact Sheet: Child Sexual Abuse.* (Report No. H72-22/2-1997E). Ottawa, Ontario: Health Canada.

Neumann, D.A., Houskamp, B.M., Pollock, V.E., & Briere, J. (1996). The long-term sequelae of childhood sexual abuse in women: A meta-analytic review. *Child Maltreatment,* 1(1), 6–16.

Nixon, K., Tutty, L., Downe, P., Gorkoff, K., & Ursel, J. (2002). The everyday occurrence: Violence in the lives of girls exploited through prostitution. *Violence against Women,* 8(9), 1016–1043.

Pantony, K., & Caplan, P.J. (1991). Delusional dominating personality disorder: A modest proposal for indentifying some consequences of rigid masculine socialization. *Canadian Psychology,* 32(2), 120–133.

Pierson, R.R. (1993). The politics of the body. In R.R. Person, M.G. Cohen, P. Bourne, & P. Masters (Eds.), *Canadian women's issues. Volume I: Strong voices Twenty-five years of women's activism in English Canada* (pp. 98–122). Toronto: James Lorimer & Company.

Power and Control Wheel. Domestic Abuse Intervention Project, Duluth, Minnesota.

Ristock, J. (2002). *No more secrets: Violence in lesbian relationships.* Routledge: New York.

Rose, S. (no date). *Lesbian partner violence fact sheet.* Web site: URL http://www.musc.edu/vawprevention/lesbianrx/factsheet.shtml.

Saunders, D.G., Holter, M.C., Pahl, L.C., & Tolman, R.M. (2006). Welfare workers' responses to domestic violence cases: The effects of training and worker characteristics. *Families in Society: The Journal of Contemporary Social Services,* 87(3), 329–338.

Sharps, P.W., Laughon, K., & Giangrande, S.K. (2007). Intimate partner violence and the childbearing year: Maternal and infant health consequences. *Trauma, Violence, & Abuse,* 8(2), 105–116.

Shaw, C., & Proctor, G. (2005). Women at the margins: A critique of the diagnosis of borderline personality disorder. *Feminism & Psychology,* 15(4), 483–490.

Smith, A. (2005). *Conquest: Sexual violence and American Indian genocide.* Cambridge, MA: South End Press.

Sobsey, D. (2000). Faces of violence against women with developmental disabilities. *Impact: Feature Issue on Violence against Women with Developmental or Other Disabilities,* 13(3), 2–3.

Statistics Canada. (1993). *The Violence against Women Survey.* Ottawa, Ontario.

Statistics Canada. (2000). Family violence in Canada: A statistical profile 2000. Canadian Centre for Justice Statistics, No 85-224-XIE.

Statistics Canada. (2006). Violence against women in Canada ... by the numbers. Ottawa, Ontario.

Temple, J.R., Weston, R., Rodriguez, B.F., & Marshall, L.L. (2007). Differing effects of partner and nonpartner sexual assault on women's mental health. *Violence against Women, 13*(3), 285–297.

United Nations. (1993). A/RES/48/104, Declaration on the Elimination of Violence against Women. Resolved at 85th plenary meeting, 20 December 1993.Available from: http://www.un.org/documents/ga/res/48/a48r104.htm Retrieved August 8, 2007.

Verberg, N., Wood, E., Desmarais, S., Kalra, M., & Senn C.Y. (2000). Is "date rape" a gender neutral term? Gender differences in survey respondents' written definitions of date rape. *Canadian Journal of Human Sexuality, 9*(3), 181–190.

Walker, L. (1984). *The Battered Woman Syndrome.* New York: Springer.

Wingood, G.M., & DiClemente, R.J. (1998). Rape among African American women: Sexual, psychological, and social correlates predisposing survivors to risk of STD/HIV. *Journal of Women's Health, 7*(1), 77–84.

Appendix A. Excerpt of Sample Safety Plan from ShelterNet.ca (http://www.shelternet.ca/en/women/making-a-safety-plan/)

WHAT IS A SAFETY PLAN?

Making a safety plan involves identifying the steps you can take to increase your safety and helps to prepare you and your children in advance for the possibility of further violence.

This plan was adapted from information provided in several Domestic Violence/Woman Abuse Safety Plans. In particular, we have referred to plans developed by the Peel Committee Against Woman Abuse, Kathy Cawthon, Metropolitan Nashville Police Department and Women's Community House.

MY PERSONAL SAFETY PLAN

While I do not have control over my abuser's violence, I can make myself and my children safer by planning actions that will help us deal with the abuse. I will use this plan as a guide and reminder to help me find ways to be safe. If I am concerned that my abuser will find a printout, I will write the points I believe apply to me on a separate piece of paper and hide it in a safe place.

I will review and update this plan on a regular basis so that I will be ready in case my situation changes.

WHAT I CAN DO BEFORE A VIOLENT INCIDENT

If I believe my partner will be violent, there are a number of things I can think about in advance.

I CAN PREPARE TO LEAVE BY DOING SOME OF THE FOLLOWING THINGS:

I will keep a suitcase, box or bag _____where I can get to it quickly and easily. In it, I will keep as many of the following items as I can:

- An extra set of keys for the apartment or house and vehicle

- Small bills and change for taxis and telephone calls

- Identification papers - passport, social insurance card, birth certificates, immigration papers, citizenship card, aboriginal status card

- Driver's licence and registration

- Health cards and children's immunization records for myself and my children

- Divorce and custody papers

- Restraining orders, peace bonds, any other court orders

- Bank books, cheque book, credit cards, mortgage or loan papers

- Lease/rental agreement, property deed, business or partnership agreements, rent or mortgage payment receipts

- Address book

- Photograph of my (ex) partner to help identify him/her

- A list of other items I can pick up later

I can keep my purse, wallet, personal identification, keys and other emergency items _____ in case I have to leave suddenly.

I can open a separate bank account in my name at _____. I will request that any statements be sent to _____ so that my abuser doesn't see them.

I can also check to see how much money is in our joint account in case I need to remove half the money quickly. If my abuser knows my account or PIN,

I will _____.

I can help my children escape by telling them _____
____. I will teach them the number of the local police _____ and other emergency numbers such as _____.

I will review and revise my safety plan every _____.

WHAT I CAN DO DURING A VIOLENT INCIDENT

I must be able to think and act quickly in order to keep myself and my children safe during a violent episode.

Here are some things I can do to increase my safety.

I can make sure I can grab my clothes and/or my children's clothes quickly by _____. If my abuser asks me what I'm doing, I will tell him/her_____.

I trust _____ and _____ to tell them about my situation. I will use the code word _____ to let them know I am in danger and to contact police immediately.

I can use the code word _____ with my children so that they can protect themselves during a violent incident.

I will look in each room and figure out the best way to escape. I will try to stay out of places such as the bathroom and kitchen if there is no outside exit. I will also try to avoid places where weapons such as knives or guns are kept.

On the main floor, the best way to get out is _____

On the second floor, the best way to get out is _____

In the basement, the best way to get out is _____

I will use my judgment and intuition. If the situation is very dangerous, I should consider _____ to calm down my abuser. I will remember that my first priority is to keep myself and my children safe.

I will review and revise this safety plan every _____

The Safety Plan continues on the website with more detail on:

My Child(ren)'s Safety
What Can I Do When I Am Living In A New Place
Safety In My Neighbourhood
How I Can Increase My Safety At Work
Safety With A Court Order
Taking Care Of My Emotional Well-Being
Safety for Women in Special Circumstances (Rural Women, Women with Disabilities, Immigrant Women

Hitting Like a Girl[1]: An Integrated and Contextualized Approach to Confronting the Feminist Dilemma of Women's Use of Violence by Susan Le Blanc

I am a faculty member and adult basic education instructor at Capilano University. I hold a master of arts: Integrated Studies graduate degree with dual specialization in work, organization, and leadership and equity studies from Athabasca University. My bachelor of arts undergraduate degree, from York University, is in women's studies. I was born and raised in Montreal, and my partner, Michael, and I currently make our life together in Squamish, raising our three children: Katelyn, 10, Maxwell, 9, and Samantha, 5. I have a passion for knitting, reading, and time with my family at our island getaway off the Sunshine Coast of British Columbia.

INTRODUCTION

This chapter was inspired, in the course of the last eight years, by my experience as a mother accompanying my children to playgrounds and community programs, and overhearing those caring for children state that "boys will be boys" as an explanation for boys' aggressive behaviour. This statement symbolizes the dominant ideological discourse surrounding aggression. It is understood as normal male behaviour and, in terms of gender, this is a double standard that separates male and female behaviour on the basis of aggression.

Male aggression has a long history of validation and social reward. Over the last 30 years, socially denouncing specific kinds of male violence against women has significantly increased. Although "one of the achievements of feminist analysis over the last three decades has been to recognize the ways that domination silences and hides the coercive and violent outcomes of power" (D'Cruze & Rao,

2004, p. 499), women currently have no history that legitimizes their own use of violence.[2] The standardized, ideological framework for understanding violence is not gender neutral but entrenched in masculine experience.

Limiting the study of violence against women to wife abuse or male spousal violence denies the complexity of the relationships between violence and women. It ignores the many ways in which women find themselves related to their unique experiences and understandings of violence in general, as well as violence against women in particular (McHugh, Livingston, & Ford, 2005). The underlying ideological links between domestic, public, and global violence against women need to be more forcefully explored and moved to the forefront of mainstream thought and public agendas, and extended to academic disciplines resistant to ideological change.

Patriarchy and its history are relevant to understanding male as well as female uses of violence. The legacy of patriarchy[3] not only serves to maintain and perpetuate the subordinate status of women, it also helps to explain women's violence as acts of defence and resistance. Patriarchy is one part of a contextualized puzzle that informs the study of gendered violence. A complete understanding of gendered violence ought to include the study of the use of violence by women (McHugh et al., 2005). The study of gendered violence within a feminist framework must include a contextualized examination of what we know about female violent behaviour. Drawing on existing literature, this chapter explores women's use of violence in intimate partner relationships and informs a more purposeful argument against the misrepresentations of female violence. Consistent with a minority of authors, I posit that the study of female violence has the potential to inform how we approach the prevention of violence against women (Barron & Lacombe 2005; Downs, Rindels, &Atkinson, 2007; Johnson, 2006; McHugh et al., 2005; Muftic & Bouffard, 2007; Swan & Snow, 2006).

A BRIEF HISTORY OF PATRIARCHY IN CIVILIZED SOCIETY

Historically, civil societies defined citizenship in terms of the military service of men, as defenders of home and territory (Lister, 1997). For men, the yardstick of citizenship was measured in terms of the number of battles fought and combat-readiness. Publicly, men served the state, and privately, they ruled their home and family. "A wife had no legal existence and therefore no responsibility, the husband was liable for her debts and had to answer for her misbehaviour; therefore he had the right to chastise her" (Gies & Gies, 1978, p. 30). Women occupied a formally subordinate status to men, namely to their brother(s), father, and husband. Women were excluded from the category of citizenship, the full pursuit of its rights and public obligations, and as such, full human agency (Lister). Public life was the formal purview of men, while domestic work and child care the vocational relegation of women. Within the family, the negotiation of basic needs or welfare tended "to fall to women" (Lister, 1997, p. 26).

During the medieval period, there were women who more formally occupied the public sphere[4]. For example, Cantor (1994) speculates that during the time of the Roman Empire "perhaps 10 percent of the female urban population of the empire were licensed prostitutes" (p. 37). It is unclear if women entered prostitution as an alternative to marriage or were forced into prostitution. There is sufficient evidence to conclude that life as a woman—wife or prostitute—was an oppressive existence for the vast majority. It is certain that women of this era had no viable option for being economically independent of men in order to meet their basic human needs. During the era of the rise of the Christian church,[5] women "were regarded as machines for the gratification of men" (Cantor, p. 71), with mental capacities assumed to be on par with "children, or mental defectives" (p. 167). St. Ambrose is said to have "raise[d] the position of women somewhat above utter degradation" (p. 71) in allowing certain women to serve the Christian church as nuns. These positions were reserved for "high-born wealthy Frankish women … who chose not to marry (or remarry)" (p. 120). Noting that "the nunnery thus became a favourite family charity [of the noble class]" (p. 120), Cantor credits these nuns for beginning, in spiritual terms, the feminist tradition. Avoiding patriarchal marriage with a symbolic marriage to God is perhaps an early example of feminist resistance. These women, however, were still dependent upon men, as they were forced to rely on the continued support of their wealthy male relatives while living in the nunneries.

At any given time, and within any given "nation-state," citizenship and non-citizenship cannot be described in terms of an absolute dichotomy, but rather would be better represented on a continuum (Lister, 1997). Although patriarchy has traditionally informed law, and societies are traditionally patriarchal,[6] historical examples of individual noble women who commanded more status than the majority of men do exist. However, within individual classes and cultures, women universally were ascribed less value and were defined as a subclass in relation to their male counterparts (Johnson, 1997; Kimmel, 2000; Lerner, 1986; Lorber, 2000). In many ways, women's well-being was determined by the men in their lives and their subordination formalized through their dependency on men. Law afforded men the individual right and, as dominant group members, the responsibility to ensure women adhered to their subordinate status. Women's well-being hinged on the mercy of the men in their lives. Although no state laws regulated the private sphere, Gies and Gies (1978) partly credit fifteenth-century marriage doctrine as evidence contributing to men's continued domination over women:

> When you see your wife commit an offence, don't rush at
> her with insult and violent blows: rather, first correct the
> wrong lovingly and pleasantly, and sweetly teach her not
> to do it again.... But if your wife is of a servile disposition
> and has a crude and shifty spirit, so that pleasant words
> have no effect, scold her sharply, bully, and terrify her.
> And if this still doesn't work ... take up a stick and beat
> her soundly ... not in rage, but out of charity and concern
> for her soul (Sienese *Rules of Marriage*, pp. 47–48) [7].

Men ruled their homes, their women, and their children. They used their
judgment to govern the use of brutality, or the threat of same, to maintain
patriarchal order.

THE LEGACY OF PATRIARCHY

In the nineteenth century, beginning around the time of the industrial revolution, the market economy and employment to a large extent replaced the role
of the military in defining active citizenship status (Lister, 1997). Women's
social value still depended on their domestic reproductive skills[8] and their
sexual reproductive performance. In terms of the history of women, it is
important to note that "throughout the ages, until antisepsis and improvement
in obstetrical techniques arrived in the nineteenth century, childbirth was a
mortal hazard" (Gies & Gies, 1978, p. 5). The *Nurses Handbook of Obstetrics*[9]
(Zabriskie & Eastman, 1943) illustrates the "magnitude of maternal mortality
in the United States during a 96-year period [1846 to 1942] as compared with
mortality of [male] soldiers" (p. 5) [10]: More than one million women died in
maternal related events, compared to the 850,000 American soldiers who died
in battle (Zabriskie & Eastman). Approximately a century past the historical
mark of "improved obstetrics" noted by Gies and Gies, Zabriskie and Eastman
found that women still had a greater chance of dying in pregnancy or during
childbirth than men did serving in war. When we place these statistics in the
context of what defined citizenship historically, it exposes the obscene lack
of gender parity in valuing and honouring what men risked in their duty to
society as compared to what women risked in childbirth.

Today, in Western terms, most patriarchal laws have been repealed, and
yet the legacy of patriarchy remains (Johnson, 1997). There is a vast and long
history of women who have risked violence and the threat of social ostracism
by working to bring about measures of transformatory[11] change in citizenship
status for women, without which many women of today would find themselves
differently positioned. Traditional patriarchal resisters, or feminist activists,

were often women members of the dominant class. In 1929, a most-notable legal achievement by[12] and for Canadian women was the Supreme Court of Canada Appeal decision to include women in the definition of *persons* under the British North America Act (Munroe, 2008). Although a full treatment of the history and contribution of these activist women is outside the scope of this chapter, what is of present importance is that the incremental gains women have secured through history are not universal, but rather are dependent upon class, race, culture, political affiliation, religion, disability, sexual orientation, beauty, education, and economic status, for example. Understood as socially constructed and as a social institution, gender is resistant to change: "[R]ebellions have altered gender norms, but so far they have rarely eroded the statuses" (Lorber, 2000, p. 108). Globally, most economic and political power remains in practice the relative purview of men, and a legacy of patriarchy. The most extreme reminder of the patriarchal legacy is male violence.

> Male violence inside and outside the home, together with
> the fear it creates, serves to undermine women's position
> as citizens. If women cannot move and act freely in the
> public sphere and/or are intimidated in the private sphere
> because of the threat of violence, then their ability to act
> as citizens is curtailed (Lister, p. 113).

THE FEMINIST DILEMMA

Violence against women forms a unifying contemporary feminist theme (D'Cruze & Rao, 2004). What contemporary feminist theorizing argues is that the magnitude of violence against women is one of the most ghastly symptoms of dominant male ideology. As a socially oppressive women's issue, violence against women represents a literal, as well as symbolic, expression of male power. Violence against women in the form of both sexual assault and wife battering is a global social issue (Weldon, 2002). In political contexts, "activists and governments from more than 180 countries have identified violence against women as an issue of literally vital importance" (Weldon, p. 1162). Conversely, whether deliberate or by default, women are cast as victims or potential victims of violence. Within this construction, violent behaviour is defined as unfeminine or unwomanly. Feminists have been reluctant to address the topic of female violence (McHugh et al., 2005). The distance feminists maintain from the study of female violence can be understood as a strategy to avoid fuelling further anti-feminist rhetoric. However, in retaining a one-dimensional approach to women and violence, the victim default status often ascribed to women serves to maintain the traditional feminine gender stereotype of girls and women as weak and in need of protection (Rozee, 2004). This reluctance by feminist scholars to engage the study of violent women has also, unintentionally, invited a proliferation of research that has been used to serve anti-feminist claims that male and female aggression in heterosexual intimate partner relationships occurs with equal frequency. Later in this chapter, I return to address this issue.

VIOLENCE AGAINST WOMEN AND PUBLIC WILL

State-sanctioned action to combat violence against women relies on legal deterrents directed at men. In contrast, the vast majority of social efforts and services directed at women are reactive and occur in the aftermath of actual violent events. Victim service referrals follow police interventions or are sought by women themselves after determining they have endured abuse long enough. Based on the knowledge and experience I gained as a peace officer from 1988 to 1990 in Alberta and as an elected local community women's centre board member from 2001 to 2003 in British Columbia, and as Muftic and Bouffard (2007) find in their review of coordinated community response programs to domestic violence (see "Criminalizing the Victim," later in the chapter), most prevention programs and services come into play only after violence has occurred and represent efforts to reduce recidivism and/or continued victimization. Grassroots public campaigns serve to educate and raise understanding about violence against women in an effort to stop violence before it starts. To some degree, these campaigns do serve to keep the issue of violence against women on the public agenda, but have not managed to eradicate its occurrence. These strategies reflect, in different ways, public understanding of violence against women as dysfunctional acts that individual men engage in, rather than as a systemic, social problem that is intimately related to recreating and maintaining the subordinate status of women. The social issue of violence against women has become myopically focussed on individual men as social misfits, women as powerless victims, and is reduced to discussions of pathology and treatment. The onus to combat and prevent violence against women lies not with the state, the public, or individual men, but defaults to women to make use of inadequate, limited, or non-existent social service supports to escape, remove, or protect themselves from harm's way.

Although male violence has been theorized from a variety of perspectives that focus on males as perpetrators, when narrowing the study to domestic violence, the study becomes dislocated from the spectrum of cultural and public violence against women. Other acts that become disassociated from the broader topic of violence against women include, for example, selective abortion of female fetuses, pornography, prostitution, and the trafficking of women and girls. To illustrate this dissociation, we can examine one state's response to prostitution. In the industrialized country of the Kingdom of the Netherlands, prostitution is legal. It could be argued that the political will of this nation made the decision to regulate the sex trade industry as a recognized profession and extend labour rights to women (and men) who make the choice to work in this industry. The problem is that "choice" is only relative in the presence of viable alternatives and in the absence of coercion. The point that coercion is victimization is not lost on the Dutch government and is acknowledged in their 2007 parliamentary coalition agreement (Netherlands, p. 35). Choice is a theme that permeates the lives of many women in terms of their social relationship to men and in securing basic needs for themselves and their children. If, for example, we examine a woman's choice between exchanging an economically dependent life with one violent man for the economic independence derived by sexually serving an endless parade of men, perhaps a woman's odds of certain abuse will be mitigated. It is a perversely patriarchal delusion to argue that prostitution is a *free choice* for women. Given the economically and socially subordinate position of women in society, arguments framing prostitution as women's choice are misplaced.

Calls for action to combat male domestic violence against women are often translated by the state into policy that suggests male violence is both a crime and an illness. The state readily adopts this model, as evidenced by naming court mandated prevention programs "treatment programs." Evolutionary theorists argue that aggression is a trait innate to men and that the privacy of the patriarchal family—as opposed to the once-communal living, with other women offering women protection—makes women more vulnerable to abuse (Campbell, 2002). Explaining male violence as either an illness or an evolutionary imperative masks the underlying gender ideology and serves to reinforce traditional male behaviour. It facilitates a sidestepping by state and society from critically addressing the systemic and problematic oppression of women and its underlying causes. It privileges patriarchy to explain male violence as illness or as a consequence of the natural behaviour of men. Such explanations also discourages an examination of patriarchy as the cause of violence against women. Amnesty International Canada (2007) describes violence against women and girls as "the world's most pervasive human rights violation," (p. 1) which contradicts the notion of attributing male violence to factors associated with illness, but it could at the same time appear as support for a theory of innate male aggression. However, in appropriate historical or cultural settings, male violence has been accepted, anticipated, and condoned through both an adherence to patriarchal ideology and traditional understandings of masculinity. Furthermore, theories of aggression suggesting that male aggression is innate fail to account for the number of men in society who are not violent, either with each other or with women. Treating male violence against women as an illness or innate behaviour serves to perpetuate violence against women, as well as its underlying patriarchal ideology.

Studying violent males, and female victims of male violence, is necessary work. However, limiting study to the former approach serves to establish and maintain a one-dimensional victim status for women. The irony is that women have been positioned to receive protection funded, defined, and delivered by the dominant gender group. It is an ideological legacy of patriarchy to understand men as protectors, the gender that benefits most from dominant ideology. Therefore, the root cause of violence against women, anchored within dominant ideology, also serves to perpetuate violence against women. Violence is not envisioned as behaviour that is in the repertoires of average women, as it is outside the stereotypical and patriarchal definition of the feminine. Compounding the problematic victim status of women is the apparent reluctance on the part of feminist scholars to address female use of violence. What that has served to do is to leave the study of female violence to those factions of society that wish to use women's violence as a venue to discredit feminist claims.

MEASURING AGGRESSION AND THE CLAIMS FOR GENDER SYMMETRY

Fiebert (2004) makes the bold statement that "women are as physically aggressive, or more aggressive, than men in their relationships with their spouses or male partners" (p. 140). In his examination of 155 academic works addressing heterosexual intimate partner violence, Fiebert's conclusions serve to contradict notions that violence in intimate relationships is a gendered issue. Fiebert's claim that women are equally capable of aggression is not where my critique of his work lies. What is problematic is that he has based his claim in quantitative terms in the absence of qualitative discussion. Furthermore, Fiebert never defines what constitutes aggression in relation to his claim of gender symmetry in intimate partner violence.

Reviewing Fiebert's (2004) annotated bibliography reveals that 69 of the 155 works cited refer to the Conflict Tactic Scale (CTS) as the research tool used to gather aggression data. Valid criticism of the CTS has been offered by researchers based on how this test counts a slap or a shove, although potentially intimidating and injurious to one's pride, as equivalent to more severe acts of violence that require medical attention and hospital stays for grievous bodily harm (McHugh et al., 2005). Further, the CTS fails to capture the context of aggressive acts. In addition, Downs et al. (2007) note how "act-based measures of violence undercount men's violence by failing to include sexual violence" (p. 29). If researchers want to measure how frequently men and women in intimate partner relationships resort to aggression, then they need to clearly define what constitutes aggression, as well as place it in its context. Simply counting and drawing conclusions about gendered differences or similarities based on these counts is not acceptable. As a final criticism, quantitative researchers employing the CTS fail to explore gender differences related to "motives" and "women's development of self-protection strategies" (Downs et al., 2007, p. 29).

CONTEXTUALIZING WOMEN'S USE OF VIOLENCE

As previously stated, the vast majority of practical intimate-partner violence research fails to develop in a contextualized manner. I found only one research study specific to contextually examining women's use of violence during intimate partner violence: Research findings of Downs et al. (2007) led the authors to theorize a framework for understanding women's use of violence when faced with intimate partner violence in terms of "self-protection" strategies. Their research participants are women drawn from two main sources: domestic violence support group programs and substance use disorder programs. Through the course of their research, they found that women used a variety of self-protection skills during incidences of intimate partner violence. Downs et al.'s analysis reveals that "women typically used physical means only after the non-physical means were clearly not helping her protect herself" (p. 39). Further, these authors found that "[w]omen described using different physical means of self-protection, but most of the acts they described involved pushing a partner away from them or throwing something at a partner. A few women reported hitting their partner back or kicking their partner" (p. 32–33).

Specific to the self-protection framework mentioned above, Downs et al. (2007) identify three distinct self-protection strategies, consisting of those that are non-physical, physical, and a combination of both physical and non-physical. Non-physical acts of defence include talking, a call or threat of a call for help, fleeing the scene, compliance with a violent intimate partner's requests, and faking a more severe injury than was actually sustained (Downs et al.). The sub-sample of women from the domestic violence support group program reported using non-physical defence twice as often (57.1% of incidents) as women from the substance use disorder treatment program (26.4% of incidents). In terms of physical defence, Downs et al. found that for both sub groups of women studied, 23% reported resorting to this means of defence when trapped by their partner in a room that had only one exit. Both samples reported that this kind of defence was most often met with a response of greater violence from their partner (Downs et al).

The third self-protection strategy identified by Downs et al. (2007) employs both non-physical and physical means of defence. Combined strategies were sometimes used in response to continuing incidences of violence over the course of time—hours or days (Downs et al.). In one scenario, a woman can be yelling at her partner to stop his violent acts or yelling for help, while at the same time, in an attempt to lessen the blows, the woman could elect to "grab her partner while he [is] punching her" (pp. 36–37). These physical acts by women would be counted as aggression on the CTS. This combination of methods of defence was reported more frequently by women from the substance use disorder program sample, at a rate of 24%, compared to the almost 18% reported by the women in the domestic violence support group program (Downs et al.).

In the course of their research, Downs et al. (2007) also found that women reported initiating violence with their partners: less than 3% by the women in the domestic violence support group program and just over 20% by the women from the substance use disorder treatment program. The contextual examples supplied by the Downs et al. are disturbing. They describe women's reports of violence as "preemptive strike[s]" in "anticipation" of threatened violence or in recognition of "indicators of his impending violence," based on a women's history of abuse with the same partner (Downs et al., p. 38). There is an unmistakable terror associated with what these women describe as leading to their use of violence. I now turn to research that focusses on the quantitative work that "distort women's use of violence by not differentiating between its offensive and defensive use" (Downs et al., p. 41).

THE BACKLASH OF THOSE TOO MANLY TO CRY

In an eloquent massage of domestic violence statistics, Fontes (1998) crafts an argument that "domestic violence is far from a gender-specific event" (p. 7). An advocate of the CTS and a voice for abused men, Fontes's lengthy article concludes that "men and women [in intimate partner relationships] are assaulting each other at nearly the same rate" (p. 37). Categorizing feminism as "sexist feminist dogma," Fontes explicitly blames feminists for ignoring male victims of domestic violence, stating that "although feminists have indeed helped many women, they have done so at the expense of men" (p. 34). He posits that the reason feminists suppress the domestic-victim status of men is to maintain an administrative monopoly over funds earmarked for domestic violence programs, for as Fontes states, "where attention goes, money flows, and where money flows, programs grow" (p. 40).

Fontes (1998) rejects the argument that patriarchy is the cause of domestic violence because "over the past fifty years our patriarchal system has been watered down in our American culture, perhaps more than most countries, and yet domestic violence cases have not gone down dramatically as one would suspect" (p. 39). Yet Fontes readily employs patriarchal masculine gender stereotyping to argue that male victims of domestic violence have a disadvantaged status. According to Fontes, men feel they cannot come forward and be taken seriously, as they are expected to be "self-sufficient," "strong," and act as "protectors." A man who asks for help, expresses his needs, and requires protection from violent women " cannot protect himself or his children. He is a **WIMP** and is not a true man"[13] (p.32). He also notes that "[f]or a man to admit he is a victim of spousal abuse is a very shaming thing" (p. 40). What is implied by Fontes's reasoning is that men do not want to be equated with the devalued (patriarchal) characteristics women are thought to embody and the lack of value women command in society. Fontes contradicts his claim that American patriarchy is on life supports by resting his argument on adherence to patriarchal gender values and stereotypes—a legacy of patriarchy.

GENDER ASYMMETRY IN SPOUSAL VIOLENCE AND HOMICIDE

The Canadian Centre for Justice Statistics' *Family Violence: Statistical Profile 2006* clearly contradicts claims of gender symmetry (Orgrodnik, 2006a). In 2004, "84% of spousal violence victims [were] women, while the remaining 16% [were] male victims" (Mihorean, 2006, p. 19). Mihorean further reports that "there has been no change in the level of reporting by victims of spousal violence to the police from 1999 and 2004" (p. 19). For 2004, based on the incidences of domestic violence reported to police, women are five times more likely than men to be victims (Orgrodnik, 2006b, p. 13). Further, as applicable to 2004 and based on solved homicide crimes, women are also five times more likely than men to be murdered by their partner (Kolawski, 2006, p. 52).

A number of factors give meaning to who is most at risk of spousal homicide. Noting that for both men and women, the rate of spousal homicide has declined over the 10-year period studied, risk factors for spousal homicide include marital status, age, employment status, alcohol and drug use, history of domestic violence, and criminal history (Kolawski, 2006). Undifferentiated by gender, common-law spousal status coincided most strongly with spousal homicide, representing 39% of spousal victims, while only 14% of the population lived in common-law relationships during that same period (Kolawski). Although not inversely related to rates in the general population, separations were also represented in large portions of spousal homicides, with 35% committed against martially separated partners (Koloawski). Of the common-law spousal status victims, 56% were under the age of 25 years old (Kolawski). In Canada, being young and in a common-law spousal relationship, followed by being separated or divorced, places a person most at risk for spousal homicide.

Unemployment, for both female victims and accused males, coincides strongly with spousal homicides. Borrowing from a 1994 Ministry of Supply and Service report, Kolawski (2006) identifies that "both low income and violence limits women's independence and makes it difficult for her to leave an abusive partner upon whom she maybe economically dependant" (pp. 53–54). Although not cited as causal, "alcohol and drug use [is] common in spousal homicides" (p. 54) by both victims and accused: "[In] spousal homicides that resulted from an argument, 78% of accused persons and 72% of victims had used drugs and/or alcohol" (p. 54). A history of domestic violence preceded 65% of spousal homicides, with "[f]emales accused of spousal homicide ... more likely than males accused of homicide to have experienced a history of family violence" (p. 55). In regards to spousal homicide as a culmination of other criminal behaviour, Kolawski states that "all precipitating incidents of sexual assault, criminal harassment, kidnappings, break and enter or other property crimes that lead to [spousal] homicide were perpetrated [by men] against female victims" (p. 55).

PATRIARCHAL SPIN ON GIRL VIOLENCE

Barron and Lacombe (2005) address public opinion that suggests girl violence is "rampant" in Canada. In reviewing applicable crime statistics published by Statistics Canada, they find that "the number of girls charged for murder and attempted murder has been constant for the past twenty years and that such charges are infrequent" (Barron & Lacombe, p. 52). Barron and Lacombe posit that public hype followed on the well-publicized 1997 British Columbia murder of a teenaged girl named Reena Virk. The police investigation led to evidence of criminal involvement by seven young women and one young man, all also teenagers at the time of the murder of Virk. Six of the accused young women were treated by the court as young offenders: They were charged, found guilty, and sentenced with some variation of the lesser-to-murder charge of assault (CBC, 2005). The two remaining teens, Kelly Ellard and Warren Glowatski, age 15 and 17 respectively at the time of their involvement in Virk's death, were both treated by the courts as adults and charged with second degree murder (CBC). While the scope of this chapter is about women's use of violence rather than girls', Reena Virk's murder is relevant not simply because two of the criminally accused youths were treated as adults, but primarily in view of the aftermath of this horrific crime: The case provides evidence that patriarchy is alive and directing mainstream study and discourse about girls' use of violence (or women's, as the patriarchal use is interchangeable) and influencing decisions as to what to do about it.

Using a social constructionist framework, Barron and Lacombe characterize this public opinion about girl violence as "moral panic" created about and projected on violent girls. Barron and Lacombe demonstrate how this "nasty girl" social construction locates the problem with the girls in the breakdown of the family, as well naming them as a factor contributing to it. Commenting on the media attention to this purported problem, Barron and Lacombe note that "acts of girl violence are not new; rather, the attention paid to them is novel" (p. 54). Kimmel (2000) argues that the real issue of youth violence is statistically located as "a problem of young *men* and violence" (p. 9). Violence, on the one hand, is equated with being male, and male continues to define the social norm; on the other, since violence has been normalized as male behaviour, it takes on an invisible character and leads to accusations against "feminist[s] for causing girls to become violent in vain imitations of boys" (Kimmel, p. 9). Girls who behave violently are characterized as "emulating their male counterpart" (Barron & Lacombe, p. 56). The irony of this double standard is that the high incidence of violent behaviour normalized for boys (and men) is on some level acceptable; whereas the relatively low incidence of violent behaviour by girls (and women) is regarded as a gender abrogation commanding an inordinate level of negative attention and public demands for action.

Media, public opinion, and government (state) have a tendency to defer to "experts." What Barron and Lacombe (2005) reveal is lacking in the analysis of female violence is the "considerable impact of structural factors, including institutional racism, and economic and social inequality in the life of young female offenders [and girls and women in general] and their victims" (p. 58). The backlashes against feminism that follow public outcry play out at the government level through preparation of policies to address assumed issues of girl violence. This leads to enlisting the support of social agencies, such as public schools, for the "identification of girls at risk [of offending]" (p. 60). Barron and Lacombe posit that this has the potential to create irrational fears and a need "to bring them [girls] into line with socially approved desires and identities, and in the process, ensure the good functioning of the family and the schools" (p. 62). Further, they note that perceived "girl power" (p. 65) rather than violence accounts for the real "social anxiety" (p. 65) and suggest that "moral panic over the statistically insignificant Nasty Girl is a projection of a desire to retrieve a patriarchal social order characterized by gender conformity" (p. 65).

CRIMINALIZING THE VICTIM

Continuing with the theme of state policy response to gendered violence, Muftic and Bouffard (2007) examine gender differences in coordinated community response (CCR) programs to domestic violence. These programs originated in the United States in the 1980s (Muftic & Bouffard). Following women's successful lobby to have domestic violence placed on the public agenda came the response in the form of directives for mandatory police arrest policies[14], restraining orders, aggressive prosecution, advocacy, and treatment programs (Muftic & Bouffard). Under CCR programs, coordination of service delivery, protection, and prosecution occurs between the police, courts, and treatment agencies (Muftic & Bouffard). Muftic and Bouffard focussed their research on a sample of 201 arrestees convicted of "heterosexual relationship" (p. 54) domestic violence. The sample consists of a sub-sample of 131 men collected over a one-year period beginning in 2003, and 70 women collected over three years beginning in 2001 (Muftic & Bouffard). It was necessary to reach back an additional 24 months for the women "to garner a large enough subsample of female offenders" (Muftic & Bouffard, p. 54). In addition to gender asymmetry in rates of offending, researchers found significant gender differences in terms of demographics and criminal history. Most notable demographically is that women convicted of domestic violence had higher unemployment rates and were more often in co-habiting rather than in formally married relationships with their intimate partners (Muftic & Bouffard). Conversely, convicted men showed higher employment rates and were more often formally married to, separated from, or divorced from their intimate partner (Muftic & Bouffard). Few of the convicted women had previous criminal offences, whereas convicted men had a high percentage of previous convictions for domestic violence as well as other offences (Muftic & Bouffard). Convicted women were most likely arrested as part of a dual-arrest situation[15] as compared to their male counterparts (Muftic & Bouffard).

Focussing their research on the type of treatment convicted male and female domestic violence offenders were referred to, Muftic and Bouffard (2007) found that "men received a majority of the components of the CCR model" (p. 49). As part of the CCR program upon conviction, the criminal court process determines treatment referrals aimed primarily at reducing the risk of recidivism. With no significant gender-based difference, one-quarter of the research sample received no court mandated treatment referral. The striking difference was that convicted men were most often referred to a 24-week domestic violence treatment program: This program was unavailable to convicted women. Instead, convicted women were most often referred to a five-hour anger management program or to individual counselling (Muftic & Bouffard). Overall, compared to men, women were found to have a higher rate of completing their court mandated treatment (Muftic & Boufffard).

CCR programs were designed with male offenders and female victims in mind. Failing to take into consideration factors such as power differences between men and women based on gender, culture, economics, and physiology signals an inappropriate "one-size-fits-all approach to domestic violence" (Muftic & Bouffard, 2007, pp. 66–67). Men more often use violence to control, whereas there is evidence that women use violence to protect themselves and their children (Muftic & Bouffard). As discussed by Muftic and Bouffard within the framework of a CCR program, equating self-defence as violence against abusive partners places women at risk of having their citizenship criminalized. Further, court-mandated referrals to anger management treatment programs for women living in abuse relationships are counter-productive (Muftic & Bouffard). As Muftic and Bouffard point out, women do not need to learn to restrict their emotions, as directed by anger management treatment programs; abused women need to be empowered.

DISCUSSION

The institution of gender has served to maintain the social, political, and economic order of patriarchy for millennia. We still have to escape the legacy of patriarchy and the ideologies that serve to maintain and recreate it. Women have not yet reached full citizenship status. Women's voice and representation in legislatures across Canada and the world ranges from non-existent to token, and approaches critical mass in only a very few jurisdictions (Black, 2003; Lovenduski & Norris, 2003; Savoie, 2007; Trimble & Arscott, 2003; Weldon, 2002). The political realm is where laws get made and economic and social policies are influenced. This is where the public takes the stage to answer or ignore the calls of social justice. There is growing global awareness that violence against women is a social issue of importance. But the awareness of violence against women remains tempered within the legacy of patriarchy—the ideological underpinnings that for so long sanctioned the use of male violence against women.

Society is currently unable or unwilling to embark upon the project of addressing, in full and more meaningful ways, how ideology acts as the barrier to transformative change for women. The feminist chrysalis around exploring women's use of violence has only begun to crack. Perhaps the fear society has of critically addressing its own ugly ideology has something in common with feminists' aversion to examining women's use of violence. But feminists must continue to come forward and address a very real and ignored part of women's experience. Women are human and capable of aggression and violent behaviour. Women's use of violence contradicts the one-dimensional victim status we have imposed on women in relation to violence. We risk harming women by both avoiding the reality of women's use of violence and by leaving the study of it to those that conduct their work from an androcentric perspective. No research is free of bias or political interest, and this fact presents another reason that the exploration of women's use of violence requires a feminist framework and a contextualized analysis. For example, of the 28,000 spousal violence incidents reported in Canada for the year 2004 (Ogrodnik, 2006b), it would be meaningful to know what portion of the 16% perpetrated by women represents women fighting back against intimate partner abuse. We need not abandon current social efforts that respond to violence against women, but we need to recognize and allow for an expanded study of gendered violence that includes contextualized studies of violence done by women and men and use it to inform, update, modify, and build upon what is currently labelled as prevention of violence against women.

ENDNOTES

1 "Hitting Like a Girl" is a sarcastic play on the sexist sport or physical prowess insult offered to males when they perform badly at bat in baseball or lose in a physical altercation. It captures the androcentric and derogatory perspective of appreciating female physical capabilities, lends evidence that the standard of measure is male, and serves as a reminder of the continued infantile reference of women as girls throughout their lives.

2 The feminist project of the last 30 years or so to capture women's roles, political action, and importance in history is vibrant (Gies & Gies, 1978; Lerner, 1986, 1993; Rowbotham, 1973).

3 My use of the concept of legacy of patriarchy is borrowed from the work of Johnson (1997). The idea of linking patriarchy to women's acts of violence is inspired by the works of Lorber (2000), Kimmel (2000), and Lerner (1986, 1993).

4 Women are also said to have entered the public sphere to trade or secure from within the economy basic needs such things as food and fabric for clothing (Cantor, 1994).

5 It cannot be understated how integral a role formal religion played historically in terms of education and politics (Cantor, 1994), but such an exploration is outside the scope of this chapter.

6 This paper does not argue or claim that patriarchy originated in the Middle Ages. There are various points in pre-civilized human history that are argued to have accounted for the creation of patriarchy, and one that I favour links the origins of patriarchy to the trading or "commodification" of women (Lerner, 1986).

7 I was unable to secure a primary or secondary source for this quote, but because it is so powerful in meaning, I feel compelled to include it. As such, it is offered in this chapter as basically a fourth-hand quote from the referenced authors who cite this quote from the secondary source: Cherubine de Siena, *Regola della vita matrimonial*. Bologna, 1888, pp.12–14, cited in Not in God's Image, Ed. Julia O'Faolain and Lauro Martines. New York, 1973, p. 177 (Gies & Gies, 1978).

8 A Marxist understanding of domestic reproduction is implied as domestic duties related to the daily reproduction of workers and students including the care needs of children, elderly, and ill family members—with an aging population, the latter is increasingly a responsibility downloaded to women.

9 My late mother left me this book. It was required reading during her nursing training in the 1940s.

10 During this time period, U.S. soldiers participated in four wars, namely the Mexican, Civil, Spanish-American wars, and World War I (Zabriskie & Eastman, 1943).

11 "Transformatory" is a term I was first introduced to in an Athabasca University graduate course. It refers to ways we organize and make decisions while addressing underlying ideology that acts as a barrier to change (Oseen, 2005).

12 The five Alberta women credited with the victory in the Persons Case are: Emily Murphy, Henrietta Muir Edwards, Nellie McClung, Louise McKinney, and Irene Parlby (Munroe, 2008).

13 Bold and underlined formatting emphasis is as it appears in the referenced source.

14 In the 1980s, Canadian police also instituted a family violence mandatory arrest policy (Orgrodnik, 2006b).

15 Dual arrest refers to police arresting both parties of a domestic violence complaint. Both parties are assigned the dual identity of accused and victim. In the Canadian legal context, this amounts to a consenting fight between two people and fails to meet the *Criminal Code of Canada* elements of domestic assault in terms of successful court prosecution.

REFERENCES

Amnesty International Canada. (2007). Stop violence against women. Retrieved September 10, 2007, from http://www.amnesty.ca/stoptheviolence/.

Barron, C., & Lacombe, D. (2005). Moral panic and the nasty girl. *Canadian Review of Sociology & Anthropology, 42* (1), 51–69.

Black, J.H. (2003). Differences that matter: Minority women MPs, 1993–2000. In M. Tremblay, & L. Trimble (Eds.), *Women and electoral politics in Canada* (pp. 59–74, refs. pp. 227–248). Don Mills, ON: Oxford UP.

Campbell, A. (2002). *A mind of her own: The evolutionary psychology of women.* Oxford: Oxford UP.

Canadian Broadcasting Corporation of Canada. (2005). "The Murder of Reena Virk: A Timeline." CBC News Online. Retrieved November 11, 2008, from http://www.cbc.ca/news/background/virk/.

Canter, N. (1994). *The civilization of the middle ages* (revised ed.). New York: Harper-Perennial.

D'Cruze, S., & Rao, A. (2004). Violence and the vulnerabilities of gender. *Gender & History, 16* (3), 495–512.

Downs, W.R., Rindels, B., & Atkinson, C. (2007). Women's use of physical and non-physical self-defense strategies during incidents of partner violence. *Violence Against Women, 13* (1), 28–45.

Fiebert, M.S. (2004). References examining assaults by women on their spouses or male partner: An annotated bibliography. *Sexuality & Culture, 8*(3–4), 140–177.

Fontes, D.L. (1998). Violent touch: Breaking through the stereotype. Elk Grove, CA: Author. Retrieved February 11, 2007, from http://www.dgp.utoronto.ca/~jade/safe/essays/vtbreak.pdf.

Gies, F., & Gies, J. (1978). *Women in the middle ages.* New York: Harper & Row.

Johnson, A. (1997). *The gender knot: Unraveling our patriarchal legacy.* Philadelphia: Temple UP.

Johnson, M.P. (2006). Conflict and control gender symmetry and asymmetry in domestic violence. *Violence Against Women, 12* (11), 1003–1018.

Kimmel, M. (2000). *The gendered society.* New York: Oxford UP.

Kowalski, M. (2006.). Spousal homicides. In L. Orgrodnik (Ed.) *Family Violence in Canada: A Statistical Profile 2006.* Statistics Canada and Canadian Centre for Justice Statistics Catalogue no. 85-224-X1E. Ottawa. pp. 52–58. Retrieved February 11, 2007, from http://www.statcan.ca/english/freepub/85-224-XIE/85-224-XIE2006000.pdf.

Lerner, G. (1986). *The creation of patriarchy.* New York: Oxford UP.

Lerner, G. (1993). *The creation of feminist consciousness: From the middle ages to eighteen-seventy.* New York: Oxford UP.

Lister, R. (1997). *Citizenship: Feminist perspectives.* New York: New York UP.

Lorber, J. (2000). The social construction of gender. In T.E. Ore (Ed.), *The social construction of difference and inequality: race, class, gender, and sexuality* (pp. 106–113). Mountain View: Mayfield P.

Lovenduski, J., & Norris, P. (2003). Westminster women: The politics of presence. *Political Studies, 51,* 84–102.

McHugh, M., Livingston, N., & Ford, A. (2005). A postmodern approach to women's use of violence: Developing multiple and complex conceptualizations. *Psychology of Women Quarterly, 29* (3), 323–336.

Mihorean, K. (2006). Factors related to reporting spousal violence to police. In L. Orgrodnik (Ed.) *Family Violence in Canada: A Statistical Profile 2006.* Statistics Canada and Canadian Centre for Justice Statistics Catalogue no. 85-224-X1E. Ottawa. pp. 19–28. Retrieved February 11, 2007, from http://www.statcan.ca/english/freepub/85-224-XIE/85-224-XIE2006000.pdf.

Muftic, L.R., & Bouffard, J.A. (2007). An evaluation of gender differences in the implementation and impact of a comprehensive approach to domestic violence. *Violence Against Women, 13*(1), 46–69.

Munroe, S. (2008). Person's Case: A milestone in the history of Canadian women. Canada Online. Retrieved November 4, 2008, from http://canadaonline.about.com/cs/women/a/personscase.htm.

Netherlands, Parliament. (2007). *Coalition agreement between the parliamentary parties of the Christian Democratic Alliance, Labour Party and Christian Union.* Retrieved August 16, 2009 http://www.government.nl/dsc?c=getobject&s=obj&objectid=94058.

Orgrodnik, L., Ed. (2006a). *Family violence in Canada: A statistical profile 2006.* Statistics Canada and Canadian Centre for Justice Statistics Catalogue no. 85-224-X1E. Ottawa. 78 p. Retrieved February 11, 2007, from http://www.statcan.ca/english/freepub/85-224-XIE/85-224-XIE2006000.pdf.

Orgrodnik, L. (2006b.). A 10-year spousal violence data file: 1995 to 2004. In L. Orgrodnik (Ed.) *Family violence in Canada: A statistical profile 2006.* Statistics Canada and Canadian Centre for Justice Statistics Catalogue no. 85-224-X1E. Ottawa. p. 11–17. Retrieved February 11, 2007, from http://www.statcan.ca/english/freepub/85-224-XIE/85-224-XIE2006000.pdf.

Oseen, C. (2005). *Master of Arts Integrated Studies 611 Transformatory Organizing Course Guide.* Athabasca: Athabasca University.

Rowbotham, S. (1973). *Hidden from history.* London: Pluto Press.

Rozee, P.D. (2004). Women's fear of rape: Causes, consequences, and coping. In J.C. Chrisler, C. Golden, & P.D. Rozee (Eds.), *Lectures on the psychology of women* (3rd ed.) (pp. 276–291). New York: Random House.

Savoie, D. (2007). In the house: On the status of women. Retrieved June 25, 2007, from http://www.denisesavoie.ndp.ca/page/44.

Swam, S.C., & Snow, D.L. (2006). The development of a theory of women's use of violence in intimate relationships. *Violence Against Women, 12*(11), 1026–1045.

Trimble, L., & Arscott, J. (2003). *Still counting: Women in politics across Canada.* Toronto: Broadview.

Weldon, S.L. (2002). Beyond bodies: Institutional sources of representation for women in democratic policymaking. *The Journal of Politics, 64*(4), 1153–1174.

Zabriskie, L., & Eastman, N.J. (1943). *Nurses Handbook of Obstetrics* (7th Ed.). Philadelphia: Lippincott Co.

The Political as Personal: Socio-cultural Factors Informing Feminist Practice

Stocker (2005) reminds us of the ethical drive behind feminist therapy that has found expression in critiquing and discovering alternatives to therapeutic frameworks that have commonly reflected patriarchal norms within societies. For Stocker, being a feminist is not a matter of simply following rules or doing our duty. She stresses the obligation for a moral charactering, acting correctly and truly seeing the world and its habitants, both without illusion or despair. She suggests this as one of the principle goals of feminist practice. Porter (2005) reminds us of the common themes that flow through the works of influential feminist theorists who "have struggled to move beyond gender as a dichotomous category to expose the impact of all forms of oppression on women, and to describe women's development, growth, and dilemmas in all of their complexity and depth" (p. 148). This attention to context, complexity, and diversity has been articulated by the authors in the previous section of this collection. These themes continue here with specific and personalized examples about how context informs and impacts different women's lived realities in different ways.

This section opens with *A Word Is Worth a Thousand Pictures: Counselling with Metis and First Nations Women.* In this chapter, Cathy Richardson reminds readers of the need to be mindful of the broader context that brings Aboriginal and Metis women to counselling. At the forefront of her discussions are notions of both "the colonial container" and the importance that language plays in replicating the dominant relationships evident in colonization. Throughout Richardson's analysis of violence against Aboriginal women, she shows how language is often used to promote ongoing destabilization and victim blaming. Conversely, the author discusses how appropriate language can be used to clarify violence and resistance for women, while at the same time work as a mechanism to hold perpetrators accountable for the harm they have done. The case of an Aboriginal woman named Lily, who was subjected to "state-imposed racialized violence in British Columbia" is shared in detail in order to highlight the impact of racism on Aboriginal women's experiences of violence. In concluding her chapter, Richardson talks about ways of working with clients that invite their safety and dignity and that also allow them to develop workable responses to violence, while still providing opportunities for resistance.

In *Aboriginal Women and Post-traumatic Stress Disorder: Implications of Culture on Therapy and Counselling Practices*, Kathy Bent draws on Aboriginal research methodologies and, like many of the other authors in this collection, highlights the need to situate our analyses within the contexts of issues being explored. Bent looks at the social contexts that inform childhood experiences and how, for many Aboriginal peoples, these childhood experiences are tied to later suffering in adulthood, specifically in terms of relationship problems, parenting issues, and career choices. All these psychological concerns disrupt Aborignal women's ability to lead satisfying lives. Her chapter focusses on Post-traumatic Stress Disorder (PTSD) and its relationship to Aboriginal women who have both experienced and witnessed family violence. In a broader sense, the author highlights the need for contextualizing and reconceptualizing psychological "disorders" to accommodate cultural differences. Bent argues for Aboriginal-centred counselling theories and practices and suggests the need for closer examination of the criteria that are currently used to define mental health concerns and to describe Aboriginal women's lived realities.

Discussions of trauma continue in *Considerations in Counselling Children and Adult Survivors of Childhood Traumas: Community, Context, and Inter-subjective Resiliences*. Here, Marie Lovrod uses Chong's (2006) poignant account of the experiences of Kim Phuc, "the girl in the picture," to illustrate important issues underpinning feminist counselling practice that focuses on childhood trauma. Like Bent (in the previous chapter of this section), Lovrod expands on notions of relational webs and the critical role they play in helping survivors make meaning of and from traumatic events. She calls for a more inclusive understanding of how past and present remembered experiences affect treatment strategies and well-being, particularly as our cultural frames of reference are becoming more diverse. Drawing on theories of evolving experiences of embodiment, Lovrod's discussion goes beyond the individual and offers an analysis that supports the idea that memory requires community. As such, she asks for a collective understanding and investment in developing effective approaches that can inform therapies for healing from trauma.

Gina Wong-Wylie and Shelly Russell-Mayhew focus on other socio-cultural influences and pressures, those that demand women's and girl's bodily perfection. Their chapter, *No "Body" to Blame? Embodiment: Socio-cultural Influences on Girls and Women,* presents a critical analysis of embodiment using personal examples to examine the way internalized embodiment issues subsequently result in depression, low self-esteem, obesity, disordered eating, and other weight-related issues. Wong-Wylie and Russell-Mayhew revisit major feminist influences, such as Friedan's (1963) critique of the "good woman" from *The Feminine Mystique,* to highlight how societal values and definitions of what it means to be a good woman can lead to psychological problems. Like Wolf (1990), the authors discuss how, despite the fact that women have reclaimed an identity apart from domesticity, social control continues to be maintained by the age-old ideology of feminine beauty. Wong-Wylie and Russell-Mayhew note how, even in the face of feminisms' evolution, pressures to conform to societal standards of beauty and womanhood persist. Embodiment, as an organizing schema bringing these larger contextual issues together, is used as a framework to shed light on factors counsellors should be aware of in working with today's girls and women.

In the final chapter of this section, *Is Being a Lesbian a Queer Thing to Do?,* Bonita Decaire and Deborah Foster continue with reflections on difference. They highlight monumental changes in Canada that have seen lesbians adopting, accessing fertility clinics, marrying, experiencing rights and privileges previously only afforded to heterosexual women, and benefitting from the amendment of discriminatory laws and policies. In light of these changes, these authors discuss how attitudes towards lesbians have not progressed at the same pace, especially in small towns and rural areas of Canada. The authors look at how continued discrimination and heteronormativity lead lesbians to seek counselling services. They debate discourses suggesting lesbians be considered as similar to gay men, discussing how non-heterosexual individuals are often conveniently grouped into an ever-expanding group labeled as "queer." Decaire and Foster argue that queer labelling fails to recognize issues that are unique to women and more specifically to lesbians in Canada.

REFERENCES: SECTION II

Chong, D. (2006). *The girl in the picture: The story of Kim Phuc, the photograph and the Vietnam War.* Toronto: Penguin.

Friedan, B. (1963). *The feminine mystique.* New York: Dell Publishing.

Porter, N. (2005). Location, location, location: contributions of contemporary feminist theorists to therapy theory and practice. *Women & Therapy,* 28(3/4), 143-160.

Stocker, S. (2005). The ethics of mutuality and feminist relational therapy. *Women & Therapy,* 28(2), 1-15.

Wolf, N. (1990). *The beauty myth.* Toronto: Random House.

CHAPTER 5

A Word Is Worth a Thousand Pictures: Counselling with Metis and First Nations Women by Cathy Richardson[1]

"Words," said the colonialist writer Rudyard Kipling (1923), "are the most powerful drug used by mankind." In my therapeutic work counselling Metis and First Nations clients, I too have discovered the power of words to help or to harm. Words can be used to soothe, to liberate, to create psychological freedom and a sense of well-being. They can also be used to perpetuate domination, to minimize or mutualize violence, and to cast Aboriginal clients as deficient and less worthy. In writing about other people, it is important that I identify my own location in this work, both professionally and culturally. I am a Metis woman, family therapist, clinical supervisor, and child welfare advocate. I was born in Coast Salish territory on Vancouver Island; my ancestry is Cree, Gwich'in, Dene, English, and Scottish, as well as a mix of some European tribes. I am influenced by a history of colonialism, the Canadian Indian Act, and the harm both have caused Indigenous people in Canada. My professional engagement takes place at the intersection of counselling, human rights, and social justice. I have found that recovery and well-being relate directly to the justice, or lack of it, experienced both in the immediate and in the broader sense after a person has been harmed. This chapter draws on my experience in practice and the integrated wisdom of my teachers (clients and mentors), combined with my doctoral research on Metis cultural survival and family history, to offer perspectives on counselling with Indigenous women.

INTRODUCTION

Throughout my formal learning process, I was amazed to realize that neither social justice nor resistance to oppression are presented for consideration in most counselling and therapy textbooks. I also came to realize that many counselling methods did not adequately address the issues of violence or safety for the clients I was seeing, and they often paid little attention to the person's social context. Some of my best teachers were Indigenous women in the most marginalized of situations who showed me that mainstream theories often did not apply to their reality. I soon understood two things: one, that I could not work in ways that failed to take into account that violence is always accompanied by resistance; and two, that eliciting responses to violence must become a main focus of my counselling practice.

When I refer to resistance, I am suggesting a broad scope of action that protests against mistreatment in many ways—with gestures grand or subtle, flagrant or delicate—and facilitates the reassertion of personal dignity. Therapist Allan Wade (1997) describes these acts of resistance in the following way:

> Virtually any mental or behavioural act through which a person attempts to expose, withstand, repel, stop, prevent, abstain from, strive against, impede, refuse to comply with, or oppose any form of violence or oppression, from disrespect to overt abuse, or the conditions that make such acts possible, may be understood as a form of resistance. Further, any attempt to preserve or reassert one's dignity, to imagine or establish a life based on respect and equality on behalf of one's self or others, including any effort to redress the harm caused by violence or other forms of oppression, represents a de facto form of resistance (p. 25).

For me, such gentle acts as shedding tears or shuddering in the witnessing of cruelty constitute resistance and indicate an orientation to something better.

Like bell hooks, I see in theory "a location for healing" (1994, p. 59). Working with colleagues Allan Wade and Linda Coates has helped me to envision a better way of doing therapy, based on concern for complex social issues and the ongoing colonization of Indigenous Canadians. As well, co-workers from the Indigenous specialization in the School of Social Work at the University of Victoria have helped to hone my analysis in relation to ongoing colonial violence. This focus on Indigenous justice and wellness also considers issues of spirituality and culture, as well as Indigenous ways of healing, belonging, and connection to ancestors and land. This orientation also involves helping mothers to find their children who have been taken by the state, as well as working with people who are fighting to save their land from ecological destruction. Post-colonial psychiatrist Frantz Fanon (1963) reminds us that "for a colonized people the most essential value, because the most concrete, is first and foremost the land: the land which will bring them bread and above all dignity" (p. 44). Working in culturally appropriate ways that attend to what Metis corrections worker Lucie Draybie (2000) calls "fire illness"—the spiritual pain and emptiness that comes from being removed from the land—is foundational for counselling in Indigenous communities. (L. Draybie, personal communication on a tour of William Head Institution, Metchosin, BC, 2000.).

In this chapter, I outline a number of ideas and practices related to the importance of language use in therapy with Aboriginal women. I describe the "colonial container," a site of violence against and negative social responses to Aboriginal women, and where most therapy takes place. I discuss the resistance of these women to the various forms of violence against them in Canada, while paying attention to the ongoing efforts to keep this violence invisible. For example, the rape of Native women has continued more or less unchecked since the time of contact and has not been publicly identified as a major social concern.[1] This issue links to the "colonial code of relations," an imposed Euro-superiority as well as a linguistic device known as the "four operations of language," meaning that language is used to 1) conceal violence, 2) conceal resistance, 3) shift responsibility away from the perpetrator and 4) blame victims (Coates & Wade, 2004). These four operations are most often found together and are activated through linguistic constructions such as the missing perpetrator, euphemisms, romanticization/eroticization, nominalization (turning verbs into nouns) and mutualizations. Later in the chapter, I share the case of Lily, [2] to whom I provided counselling after she experienced violence and mistreatment in various forms. Then I propose a way of working therapeutically that invites a greater sense of safety and dignity. Here I emphasize the importance of accurate language use to clarify violence, elucidate resistance, contest victim-blaming, and hold perpetrators accountable for stopping their violence.

THE CREATIVE POWER OF WORDS

Like laying the track as we walk, the social world is brought into being through words. Reality is constructed in ways that benefit some people at the expense of others, and discourse—the use of words with a particular "spin" and embedded assumptions—advances particular agendas. For example, in Canadian historical accounts, the terms "discovery," "settlement," and "surrender" are used to describe colonial processes of land theft, rape, and forced child removal (Coates & Wade, 2007). These examples of colonial discourse evoke noble pioneers and brave settlers, while Indigenous people are portrayed as less than human, or as animals (Fanon, 1963). Accounts of European settlement portray a picture far removed from the genocide that accompanied the British imperial project in Canada and across the globe (Adams, 1989, 1995; Anderson, 2000; Annett, 2002a; Annett, 2002b; Campbell, 1973; Government of Canada, 1996; Logan, 2001; Monture-Angus, 2001).

The story that is portrayed in a thousand pictures depicting the history of this land we call Canada celebrates the righteous triumph of the colonial project: diverse people and cultures living in apparent equality and democracy. But even the most clear and compelling snapshot captures only a moment frozen in time. Without any identifiable context other than what the viewer imposes on the view, discourse and the particular of world view may lead the viewer to assume that the subjects act on an equal field of play. A therapist observing the scene may then impose a set of assumptions, construing the client as having equal access to resources and opportunities. In the discourse of New Age, we hear talk of one's ability to manifest "unlimited happiness, love, health, and prosperity" if only one knows "the secret" and visualizes appropriately.[3] This linguistic currency tends to offer over-generalized panaceas, telling us that violence against us happens for a reason, that our wounded bodies attract more suffering, that everything is as it was meant to be, and that God never gives us more than we can handle. Still, people die from violence, from overdose, from suicide in the aftermath of state-imposed violence such as residential school imprisonment. Borrowing from religious and New Age discourse, therapists sometimes talk with Aboriginal clients about the importance of forgiveness, even though premature forgiveness may compromise their safety and open the door to more violence.

In reality, Aboriginal clients experience a disproportionately high level of violence compared to European Canadians; when the violence is disclosed, they encounter social and judicial responses that are primarily negative (Andrews, Brewin, & Rose, 2003; Annett, 2002b; Coates, 1997; Coates & Wade, 2004; Coates & West, 2003; Donalek, 2001; Todd & Wade, 1994). Without appropriate attention to Canada's historical context, we may assume that our clients have had benign experiences, that their dignity has been held intact, and that they possess relative social influence that could be applied to stopping violence and racism. Building on these initial assumptions, the therapist may then apply psychological or social science theories based on how people might behave in a benign world—theories that state that an individual bears some responsibility for creating her or his social condition, such as that of a person who is "internally oppressed" (Freire, 1993), "co-dependent with their abuser" (Cermak, 1986), or even attracting a reality of violence and colonization:

> Colonization has always been based upon the existence of
> need and dependency. Not all people are suitable for being
> colonized; only those who feel this need are suitable. In

almost all cases where Europeans have founded colonies
… we can say that they were expected, and even desired, in
the unconscious of their subjects (Mannoni,[4] 1950, as cited
in Macey, 2000, p. 188).

When viewing the Aboriginal client out of context, the therapist runs
the risk of "replicating dominance" (Reynolds, 2006) and causing further
degradation. Todd and Wade (1994) document the "parallel objectifying
practices" of colonization and psychotherapy. Language plays an integral part
in replicating dominance and colonial forces. Indigenous educator Marie
Battiste (2000) notes that linguists believe that differences in the ways that
language is used by indigenous compared to European or North American
peoples may lead to "sociolinguistic interference" (p. 192), which constitutes
yet another tool for assimilation. It is therefore critical for the therapist to
have an informed view of how colonial forces operate and how language
holds them in place.

Linda Coates and her colleagues have shown in micro-detail the ways in
which colonial reality is reproduced in Canadian courts in cases of physical
and sexualized violence (Bavelas & Coates, 2001; Coates, 1997; Coates, Todd,
& Wade, 2003; Coates & Wade, 2004; Coates & West, 2003). Their research
demonstrates how language casts victims as deserving and perpetrators as troubled or misunderstood. State-imposed violence against Aboriginal clients is
difficult to contest when professionals use language that mutualizes, obscures,
suppresses, and conceals violence while casting the victims as "complainers"
or "women who seek it."[5] Contesting the use of language that perpetuates
domination and reproduces the idea of client deficiency involves swimming
heartily against the stream, particularly as we are swimming in a "colonial
container."

THE COLONIAL CONTAINER AS A CONTEXT OF VIOLENCE AGAINST ABORIGINAL WOMEN

Violence in Canada, particularly violence against Aboriginal people, takes
place within a specific context that I describe as a "colonial container." Within this container sit the top-down structures of colonial relations, including
a framework of British laws, Eurocentric practice, and systemic racism. The
colonial container is, for some, difficult to see. That the accurate history of
colonization has been made invisible is perhaps one of the greatest victories
of the colonial project. As part of a landscape of colonial success, many of the
violent acts against Indigenous people throughout history have been wiped
off the whiteboard and placed deliberately outside of the mainstream view.[6]

The colonial container is imbued with a particular world view, as well as structures and practices that privilege some and disadvantage others. Battiste (2000) refers to this world view as "cognitive imperialism" or "cultural racism" (p. 192), noting that "confronting cultural racism in Canada is a difficult task because cultural racism cannot be contained to any one portion of the state" (p. 195). The colonial container includes structures such as the legal system, the education system, Indian and Northern Affairs Canada, corporations, the armed forces, the police, the medical system, and an array of social services based on the needs of European Canadians or on what non-Aboriginal politicians refer to as "the national interest" (British Columbia Human Rights Commission, 2001; CERD Report Ad Hoc National Network, 2002; Department of Justice Canada, 2008; Dylan, Regehr, & Alaggia, 2008; Furniss, 1999; Government of Canada, 1996; Health Canada, 1999; Littlebear, 2000; Matthews & Lewis, 1995; Native Women's Association of Canada, 2007b). When Aboriginal people are taken out of context of the colonial container, they are seen as less worthy of the rights, goods, and services promised by society. In fact, many Indigenous people are criticized for demanding their rights as laid out in the British North America Act, in which the federal government promised to preserve Aboriginal rights in perpetuity.

When non-Aboriginal Canadians are oblivious to colonial history, to the treaties and rights of Aboriginal Canadians, they are more likely to assume negative opinions of and aggressive positions toward Aboriginal people. Then, when an Aboriginal person is harmed, often she is seen as a deserving victim, as if she brought the harm upon herself (Coates, Todd, & Wade, 2003; Coates & Wade, 2004; Richardson & Nelson, 2007; Strega, 2004; Strega, Callahan, Rutman, & Dominelli, 2003; Wade, 1995).

Inside the colonial container, acts of violence such as the 15,000 cases of sexual abuse perpetrated by the Church against Indigenous children (G. Oleman, November 23, 2007, personal communication at a provincial Aboriginal cultural sensitivity training, Vancouver, BC) are supported by the structures of colonial relations, structures that do not defend equality, justice, or fairness. Gerry Oleman of the Indian Residential School Survivors Society identifies "5 Rs" as the source of violence against Indigenous people: racism, religion, residential school, reserves, and the R.C.M.P. (G. Oleman, November 23, 2007, personal communication). Yet these forms of violence have not been viewed as a major therapeutic consideration in mainstream psychotherapeutic training, just as the colonial container is not seen as a source of unwellness.

When viewed out of context of the colonial container, acts of violence are often misconstrued as violence between individuals. For example, in her analysis of the court proceedings in the murder of First Nations woman Pamela George, Sherene Razack (2002) writes:

> Colonial violence … has not only enabled white set-
> tlers to secure the land but to come to know themselves
> as entitled to it. In the men's encounter with Pamela
> George, these material (theft of the land) and sym-
> bolic (who is entitled to it) processes shaped both what
> brought Pamela George to the Stroll and what white
> men from middle-class homes thought they were doing
> in a downtown area of prostitution on the night of the
> murder. These processes also shaped what sense the
> court made of their activities (p. 129).

Life and death in the colonial container means that a foundation of colonial discourse is operationalized to the detriment of Aboriginal people, who have been stripped of their wealth and dignity in Canada and other nations. Of particular relevance to therapeutic work with Aboriginal women are "failure to protect" laws, which blame Aboriginal mothers for the violence enacted upon them and endorse that blame through the state removal of their children (Strega, 2004; Strega et al., 2003). Aboriginal mothers are held accountable both for male violence and for poverty; many mothers have had their children removed for no other reason than that they were poor. The colonial devaluing of Aboriginal people is manifested in child welfare practices where Aboriginal children are given to "specialist" caregivers, moving them from Aboriginal communities to white, Euro-Canadian families and communities (Carriere, 2007; Green, Kovach, Montgomery, Thomas, & Brown, 2007; McGillivray, 1997; Richardson & Nelson, 2007). Violence is central to most child welfare situations.

Violence against Aboriginal Women
First Nations women are subjected to violence more than any other group of women in Canada (Ministry of Community Services & Minister Responsible for Seniors' and Women's Issues, 2005; Monture-Angus, 2001). Aboriginal women report spousal assault at a rate three times higher than non-Aboriginal women, and they are significantly more likely than non-Aboriginal women to report the most severe and potentially life-threatening forms of violence, including being beaten or choked, having a gun or knife used against them, or being sexually assaulted (Statistics Canada, 2006). Frequently, Aboriginal women are battered, raped, and sexually violated from the time of childhood. One study by Corrections Canada (1990)discovered that, unlike non-Aboriginal women, their experience of violence is not incidental (that is, it is not one rape or one battering by one partner, or one incest event experienced with one relative).

128

Many women from isolated communities report anecdotally the ritualized gang rape of young women as they enter puberty (Burnet, 1994; Kaufman et al., 2007). In many cases, community lawlessness or lack of attention to sexualized violence means that Aboriginal women are victimized by both Aboriginal and non-Aboriginal perpetrators (Amnesty International, 2004).

An Ontario study found that eight out of 10 Aboriginal women had experienced violence in their relationships. Of these, 87% were physically injured and 57% were sexually abused. An estimated 75% to 95% of women in some Northern Aboriginal communities have been physically abused (Health Canada, 2005, cited in Peel Committee Against Woman Abuse, 2005).

To escape from violence, poverty, and other negative situations, many Aboriginal women leave their communities for urban centres, where they must fend for themselves or raise their children without traditional forms of support. In these situations, they become susceptible to scrutiny from child welfare authorities (Sinclair, Bala, Lilles, & Blackstock, 2004).

An estimated 500 Aboriginal women have gone missing or been murdered in Canada over the past 30 years (Native Women's Association of Canada, 2007a). Rarely are their disappearances covered on the nightly news, nor do they provoke search parties or national alerts. Aboriginal women aged 25 to 44 are five times more likely than other Canadian women of the same age to die of violence (Indian and Northern Affairs Canada, 1996, cited in Amnesty International, 2004). Metis poet Marilyn Dumont (1993) acknowledges the pervasiveness of violence against Aboriginal women in Canada in her ode to Helen Betty Osborne, who was murdered by four white men in 1971:

> Betty, if I set out to write this poem about you
> It might turn out instead
> To be about me
> Or any one of my female relatives (...) (p. 20)

Violence against First Nations and Metis women includes not only interpersonal violence but racism, unequal access to goods, services, and Canadian justice, and the violence of the state, as for example, at Kahnawake in the summer of 1990 (Monture-Angus, 2001). At Kahnawake, local Mohawk residents resisted the expansion of a golf course onto their sacred lands. This resulted in the Oka crisis. During this infamous event many Mohawk residents were attacked in their cars by non-Indigenous people who were throwing bottles, rocks and sticks, while trying to leave the village to seek safety, supplies or medical assistance. Mohawk writer Patricia Monture-Angus (2001) articulates most eloquently the complex violence perpetrated against Aboriginal women:

My experience of violence transcends my gender and also includes my experience of the state. When the experience of Aboriginal women is fully understood on these terms, it seems to make little sense to report on the incomplete statistical evidence that documents that eight out of ten Aboriginal women currently live in situations of overt physical violence—the violence of their male partners (p. 13).

Individual perpetrators:	Colonial agents have:
Isolate victims (separate them from family members, friends, and community)	Isolated victims (e.g., in residential schools, on reserves, in institutions)
Take control of the household money	Taken control of wealth through colonial expansion (e.g., taking land, minerals, oil, knowledge, animals, etc.)
Use surveillance; control who she sees and talks to	Used surveillance as a tool of control (e.g., Roberts, 2002)
Use interrogation	Used interrogation
Use insults, criticism, character assault, and victim-blaming	Used insults, criticism, negative racial stereotyping, decontextualized and victim-blaming accounts of individual suffering
Use unpredictability and threats, undermine dignity	Used unpredictability and threats to withhold income and rights for non-compliance
Use alcohol irresponsibly and as a post-assault excuse for the violence	Introduced alcohol, enacted racist laws around alcohol use in conjunction with attacks on families and dignity, then later blamed Aboriginal people for erratic alcohol use
Administer beatings with precision to hide bruises and conceal damage	Administered beatings with precision (often in jails)
Use rhetorical strategies to avoid responsibility (e.g., "I am proficient, you are deficient")	Used rhetorical strategies to avoid responsibility (e.g., colonial discourse of "I am proficient, you are deficient"; "the Indian problem")
Do harm in private spaces rather than in front of witnesses	Killed people in custody, abandoned people in sub-zero temperatures in fields
Circumvent the law in order to instill fear and perpetuate violence	Circumvented and changed laws to perpetuate state violence
Use psychological rationalizations to explain their behaviour	Used psychological rationalizations to explain their behaviour

Focusing on incidents of violence, abuse, and racism disguises the utter totality of the experience of violence in Aboriginal women's lives. And a chilling similarity is found between the violence enacted by individual perpetrators upon their victims and the violence enacted by colonial agents against Aboriginal people in Canada (see table below, Richardson & Wade, 2007, built upon Todd & Wade's 1994 parallel objectifying practices).

THE COLONIAL CODE OF RELATIONS AND NEGATIVE SOCIAL RESPONSES TO ABORIGINAL WOMEN

Indigenous people around the globe have been characterized as deficient in terms of a colonial code of relationship (Wade, 1995). Wade articulates this code as follows:

1) I am proficient

2) You are deficient, therefore I have the right to

3) Fix you, diagnose you, change you, intern you

4) For your own good.

This code of relating is embedded in the helping discourses of various human services. On these terms, and despite the best efforts of social workers and advocates to undermine these structures, child protection systems separate women from their children because, in the reality of the colonial container, psychology is used as a tool to identify some people as healthy and others as ill and therefore less deserving. Many Aboriginal women who come for counselling report that they have experienced a series of negative social responses in their lives, including when they have disclosed being victimized, and that these responses often create more hardship than did the initial acts of violence.

Negative Social Responses

A negative social response to violence is when someone does or says something to minimize it, to blame or to silence the victim, to rationalize the actions of the perpetrator, or to mutualize the victim's responsibility in the violent interaction. Negative social responses can be blatant (e.g. "What were you doing in that part of town?" or "Maybe your skirt was too short") or more subtle statements implying that the victim attracted the violence for spiritual purposes, that it mirrors something inside her or reminds her of previous issues. Children who disclose violence or incest are sometimes told to keep quiet, that the perpetrator is a respectable member of the family or the community who would not do such a thing. A victim's reputation is often undermined by those supporting the perpetrator's or the family's reputation. Often victims are left alone to doubt their sanity, betrayed by people they trusted. Abused Aboriginal mothers frequently have their children removed because beaten mothers are treated as unfit under "failure to protect" child welfare laws (Strega, 2004; Strega et al., 2003).

Such negative social responses undermine the well-being of Aboriginal women after they experience violence; they contribute to ongoing suffering; and they are seldom brought to public attention as a social or human rights issue. As noted on the Canadian Department of Justice website, "there is virtually no literature or research that explains the high rate of Aboriginal victimization on a general level." However, "[t]here are a few theories that attempt to explain the high prevalence of family violence in Aboriginal communities" (Aboriginal Nurses Association of Canada & Royal Canadian Mounted Police, 2001, cited in Department of Justice Canada, 2008, para. 2). To find these theories, one may need to ask Aboriginal women themselves, or study Indigenous or post-colonial writings that document the complex, ongoing violence that is both so apparent and so invisible, depending on who is looking on.

Recently, however, therapeutic and mental health research has documented some of the important connections between violence, disclosure, and Post-traumatic Stress Disorder (PTSD). For example, Brewin, Andrews, and Valentine (2000) conducted a meta-analysis of 14 separate risk factors for PTSD in trauma-exposed adults and found lack of social support to have the strongest weighted average effect. In a subsequent study, Andrews, Brewin, and Rose (2003) noted the following about women victims of violent crime:

> [They] were more likely than men to report negative responses from family and friends. This difference in the level of negative responses appeared to explain the gender difference in PTSD symptoms 6 months postcrime. These findings suggest strongly that routine assessment of negative support and attempts to counter it, for example by including partners and relatives in the therapeutic process, could significantly improve PTSD outcomes, particularly for women" (Andrews et al., p. 426).

The findings of Campbell, Ahrens, Sefl, Wasco, and Barnes (2001) concur that many people who disclose harm receive negative responses from their family and friends and experience additional distress. Given the detrimental impact of negative responses on survivors' well-being, they argue that "victims may be well advised to assess the probable reactions of their friends and family members." In other words, "selective disclosure may be imperative for survivors" (Campbell et al., p. 300).

Resistance Is Ubiquitous

The concept of resilience has gained a lot of currency in the helping professions. Noting that some child victims of violence appear to "survive and even thrive in adverse circumstances" (Duryee, 2003, p. 153), psychologists have tended to view an individual's ability to bounce back as a personal trait rather than acknowledging the importance of social support. Duryee argues: "It is the redundancy of support, the safety nets in place in the various domains of a child's life (home, school, community), that provides for good adjustment, or resilience" (p. 153). Howard, Dryden, and Johnson (1999) further contend that labelling children as resilient "can be as dangerous and misrepresentative as labeling others 'at risk' in deficit models. Resilience ... is not a discrete quality that children either possess or do not possess" (p. 310).

What may be more helpful than notions of pathology or resilience is to consider that victims invariably resist violence and other forms of abuse (Burstow & Weitz, 1988; Coates, Todd, & Wade, 2003; Haig-Brown, 1988). Wade (1997) contends that "alongside each history of violence there runs a parallel history of prudent, determined, and often creative resistance" (p. 23). The manner in which victims resist depends on the unique combination of dangers and opportunities present in their particular circumstances. Victims typically take into account that any act of defiance will cause perpetrators to become even more violent. Consequently, open defiance is the least common form of resistance (Burstow & Weitz; Kelly, 1988; Scott, 1990). In extreme circumstances, the only possibility for resistance may be in the privacy afforded by the mind: the prayers that are uttered silently or the longing for safety and comfort.

It is important to note that women may not recognize their own resistance to violence, often because they have not been asked about it by investigating officers, medical professionals, lawyers, or therapists. Too frequently, a victim's resistance is recognized or treated as significant only when it succeeds in stopping or preventing the perpetrator's violence. This is an entirely inappropriate criterion. The point of resistance is not to stop violence, for if one could stop an abuser with more power, the violence probably would not occur. The point of resistance is to preserve one's dignity and spirit and to maximize safety as much as possible, both during and after the assault. Victims resist in myriad ways that may not succeed in stopping the violence but nevertheless are profoundly important as expressions of dignity and self-respect. Helping them to discover, dignify, and respect their resistance is an important goal of counselling.

LILY: A CASE STUDY IN DIGNITY

As a counsellor, I sit in the privileged position of listening to the stories of many people. When Lily told me her story, my mind wanted to go to the astounded place of asking her, "What country was this?" "What era was this?" Amazingly, Lily's story happened quite recently on British Columbian soil. Lily partici- pated in preparing an accurate account of her experiences. She offers her story in hopes that it will help others, both counsellors and clients, to prevent and heal from racialized and sexualized violence. Lily and Angel are the names Lily herself chose to protect her privacy and that of her daughter, who was six at the time. This is what happened to them.

Lily was a woman who paid a lot of attention to safety. She had learned from a young age that it isn't safe to tell people you are Aboriginal, particularly if they are not Aboriginal themselves. When one is Metis, this telling is even more precarious because you sometimes "get it from both sides," as they say. Lily's mother had admonished her for "telling" and had made it clear that "this is not something we do." So, being an undisclosed Metis, Lily was careful to choose situations that were safe, particularly now that she had her daughter, Angel.

One day, Lily was invited to a barbecue by a woman she had recently met at work. Before she agreed to attend, Lily went over in her mind her standard safety check: "Who will be there?" "What kind of people are they?" "How much alcohol will be served?" "Is it safe to bring my daughter?" She even asked her workmate about her use of medications, which she recalled from an earlier conversation. Lily was assured that her friend only used the meds to help her fall asleep. The answers she received were satisfactory, so Lily decided she would go. Before she did that, however, she apprised a friend who was staying with her of the details of the proposed eve- ning out, reviewing her safety check with him.

When the time came to go, Lily placed Angel in her jeep and drove to the gathering. There, she spent the evening in the company of a small number of people: her colleague, the colleague's partner, and his friend: a next-door neigh- bour who arrived later on, around 10 p.m. They talked, ate, and laughed, without a particular focus on alcohol or intoxicants. Lily put Angel down to sleep on a bed; soon after, Lily's workmate announced that she too was tired and was going to bed. The woman invited Lily to spend the night if she wanted to, and Lily decided she would. She was about to go to bed when the tone of the evening changed, suddenly and dramatically.

Lily started to feel unsteady and incoherent: "woozy." She realized much later, upon reflection, that something had been placed in her drink. At that point, the workmate's partner began an intensive assault on Lily, one that would last for hours. He hit, punched, kicked, dragged, and hurt her in innumerable ways. There is a period for which Lily has no recollection, a black hole in her experience. "What did he do to me?" she wondered, after the more dreaded question: "Is my daughter safe?"

After the brutal attack, Lily was barely able to walk. She remembers asking the man several times. "Please just let me take my daughter and go home!" Finally, there was an opening. Heartbroken, battered, and bleeding, Lily managed to collect her daughter, make her way to her jeep, start it, and back out of the yard. Under command of Lily's broken wrists and blood-filled vision, the jeep lurched ahead a small distance, hit the train tracks at an unfriendly angle, and crashed, all under the cruel gaze of the perpetrator.

Lily and Angel remained in the jeep until an ambulance arrived some time later. When the ambulance drivers and police removed her from the wrecked vehicle, Lily said, "See that man back there, standing in the window? He just assaulted me!" She told the police that the man looking out of the window had beaten her up and that she needed to get away from him.

The authorities did not believe Lily, nor did they act on her allegations. Before she could even begin to piece together the night's events, Lily was immersed in a second nightmare, this one at the hands of her "helpers." She found herself locked in a jail cell at the local RCMP detachment. She received no medical help for days. Her consistent panicked requests to know the whereabouts of her daughter were met with silence or crude remarks by the officers. She heard the words "drunken squaw" and other derogatory and racist formulations of her experience. Eventually, Lily was told that she was being charged with impaired driving, despite the fact that drinking was not what had impaired her that evening.

When Lily finally was offered medical attention, the hospital had been forewarned that she was an Aboriginal woman charged with impaired driving. Her profile had been created and she was treated accordingly. Still, Lily treated her "helpers" with the respect they did not accord her. She was patient, believing in the possibility of changing racist attitudes through kindness.

It was two weeks before someone finally told her that her daughter was in a foster "home." On the other side of the colonial divide that separates Aboriginal children from their mothers, Angel thought her mother was dead, and no one told her differently. She was placed in the child welfare system to "save" her from her Aboriginal mother. Now the state had Lily as well. A good mom, she was nevertheless criminalized and imprisoned.

When Lily was finally permitted to see her daughter, they cried in each other's arms. Lily was left with her injuries, her pain, an impaired driving charge, and the indignity she met at virtually every turn, but at least she had her daughter—metaphorically, that is, because Angel was not returned to her right away. She remained in the foster home for six weeks while Lily was investigated. Unlike her offender, Lily had to prove that she was a responsible human being. She continued to co-operate, demonstrating calm hopefulness because, she thought, "This must all be a mistake that will be cleared up soon. This is Canada, after all."

I am grateful to Lily for her courage in sharing her story, for her commitment to helping others, and for teaching about grace, dignity, and generosity of spirit in relation to her tormentors. Once again, I marvel at the depths of human capacity for healing and creative resistance to injustice. Throughout her ordeal, Lily maintained her dignity and her faith in goodness. She became clearer in her relationship to spirit, to her inner guidance, to her sense of connection with all that is. Though she was told she had low self-esteem and other psychological deficiencies, Lily contested these formulations over time and shed the labels placed on her by "helping" professionals and racist law enforcement officers. She went on to live well, to exist on her own terms, and to find love.

Lily did not get a conviction for the man who broke several of her bones, who cut her face, kicked her stomach, and violated her to the maximum of his limited creativity, perhaps with help from a neighbour, while his girl-friend slept, drugged by sleeping pills. These kinds of violent incidents are often referred to as "he said, she said" stories. Aboriginal women often do not see justice in these cases. Offenders are innocent until proven guilty; many remain unaccountable due to various obstacles that exist in the judicial system. Compounding the situation is the difficulty victims face in accessing legal services, even legal aid, in the midst of ongoing governmental cutbacks and neo-conservative fiscal agendas.

In such cases, counselling can take the powerful form of *witnessing* the client's experiences of violence or injustice, offering the positive social response that is so important in the process of disclosure and that can make the difference in the client's future well-being (Brewin et al., 2000). When clients like Lily are acknowledged for their resistance—their determination, hope, and generosity toward others who have done wrong—they are spared the ongoing stigmatization and frustration of further negative social responses. When working with an Aboriginal woman who has experienced violence, a counsellor can hold a space of safety, dignity, justice, and acknowledgement of pre-existing abilities. Like Leonardo da Vinci's Vitruvian man, helping professionals can hold back the walls that oppress and restrain people. The counselling room can be one of many pockets of resistance for Aboriginal women like Lily, a space where they can exist on their own terms and be supported to care for their children in cultural ways without unhelpful state interference—a temporary social place where they can be central rather than marginal. By pressing outward against the walls of the colonial container, we may create a space for people like Lily and Angel to breathe and to express more fully their dreams.

WORKING WITH ABORIGINAL WOMEN

Lily is not the only Aboriginal woman to carry a story about not being believed or helped in the aftermath of violence. When I am speaking to Lily or to a woman in a similar situation, I can do a few things to try to be helpful. First, I can attend to her safety and to restoring her dignity after the violence that others failed to acknowledge. Every degrading and hurtful act may erode a person's sense of hope. Seeking to actively restore dignity may serve as a counterbalance to despair. To do this, I may ask Lily, with her permission, to tell me about earlier encounters with professionals in the times immediately after she disclosed the violence. If she shares positive accounts, I may then learn what was most helpful and what could be helpful now. If she shares a negative account, I may learn from that, too, and prevent myself from offering unhelpful assistance. Then I may seek to know how Lily reacted to these negative social responses. In so doing, I am learning about and reflecting aloud on her capacity, her pre-existing ability, and her history of resistance to mistreatment. I am listening for the words she selects to then check whether this is her word, one that she adopted for convenience, or one that was imposed on her at some point. Women who have been victims of violence sometimes find they are better received when they use the discourse of the trade, the language that has been applied to them by human service professionals. For example, a woman says, "I have been in a series of abusive relationships." If this phrase is left uncontested, the client leaves with the experience that the abuse was mutual and that she was a co-perpetrator. I can then clarify: "Does that mean you have been in a number of relationships where you and your partner abused each other?" "No," the client replies. "I was in relationships where my partner was violent to me." [7]

Danet (1980) contends that there are no impartial accounts: "All accounts of violence influence the perception and treatment of victims and offenders. Where there is violence, the question of which words are fitted to which deeds is crucial" (p. 189). Linda Coates might say it is imperative that we "fit words to deeds" (Danet, 1980) and clarify who is doing what to whom before we can have judicial justice or social justice. Her research shows that obscuring violence serves to perpetuate it, to excuse it, and to discourage perpetrators from becoming accountable for it. The same can be said about the violence of the state. Token acts of restitution create a public snapshot of a government that cares and that seeks to apologize and compensate for past wrongs. Meanwhile, the 500-year attack on Aboriginal people continues, with the violence largely erased from public consciousness. When the problem cannot be seen, there is nothing to apologize for or to change.

To keep victims safe from ongoing violence, it is important to acknowledge that violence is deliberate on the part of perpetrators. From extensive research and clinical work, it is clear that perpetrators use a number of strategies to circumvent and suppress victims' resistance to violence (Richardson & Wade, 2007).

AN INTERVIEWING ACTIVITY TO ESTABLISH SAFETY

When beginning an interview, it is important to attend to safety. Safety is best invited into the room as a tangible presence. It can be invoked by some of the following questions:

1. Before we begin, I'm wondering if I may ask a few questions about safety. For example, I'd like to ask you if you have ever been in a situation similar to this one, and if you have been, how that went.

2. When you were in that situation, what kinds of things did you experience that let you know that you either felt safe, unsafe, reasonably safe, or safe enough to talk to someone?

3. Is there anything you are experiencing right now that might help you to notice how much safety you sense in this moment?

4. Think about sharing your experiences with me, and then think about what that might feel like next week. Does that thought help you to assess what you might be comfortable sharing with me?

5. Is there anything else about this situation that makes you think it might be okay to go ahead with this conversation? What risks might be involved in having this conversation today?

6. Are there any kinds of agreements we should make before we start, like an understanding that you can stop anytime or only share what feels safe? How might you let me know if you want to stop or change the subject?

Questions like those that follow are helpful to assess positive and negative social responses that the client may have received in the past:

1. Have you ever fired a helping professional who was unsupportive by, for example, not showing up for an appointment or not returning to the professional after the first meeting? What was it about that helping experience that didn't work for you?

2. Before we start talking about what happened to you, I'm wondering if this is the first time that you have ever shared this information with anyone? If not, who else knows about this?

3. And when you told them about this experience, what happened? What did they say or do?

4. What was it like for you to tell about this event?

5. What decisions did you make about sharing information? What did you notice about other people's responses?

6. Who else did you tell? Was there variety in the responses you received? Was there any kind of consensus about you? Did you think that people misunderstood or understood your experience?

7. Was anyone particularly positive or supportive at that time? If so, what was that person like? What things did she or he do that you found to be helpful, kind, or appropriate?

8. What kind of response would have been the most helpful and supportive at that time? What would be most helpful now?

9. What would you recommend to someone who is in a position to hear about moments that might be embarrassing, difficult, or painful for people?

This safety-oriented, dignity-based approach to therapeutic work has been influenced greatly by the ideas and practices of Allan Wade and Vikki Reynolds and by the research Linda Coates has conducted on judicial responses to violence. Response-based ideas have provided me with a liberatory framework that is non-pathologizing and respectful of the lives of regular people who do remarkable things in the quest to preserve their humanity. Vikki Reynolds's therapeutic work, including the "supervision of solidarity" (2006), has been instrumental in creating safety, both for clients who have experienced torture and for therapists needing support in their work. To protect client confidentiality, therapists are not permitted to share the details of their clients' lives, identities, and experiences, which makes it challenging to bring public attention to the acts of cruelty and deliberate violence that women experience. We end up "privatizing pain" and thus keeping the secrets of violent perpetrators and those who do harm. Reynolds believes that "burnout" and "compassion fatigue" are linguistic misnomers and that we are harmed not by our clients but by isolation and by being prevented from naming the injustices we witness. She encourages supervision sessions that invite therapists to experience membership in a "community of concern" and to organize their work around social justice and the ethics of human rights. Through these types of supervision practices, therapists are energized by honouring stories of resistance and by joining with clients against violence.

When we use language to expose violence and its deliberateness, clarify victims' resistance, and clarify perpetrator responsibility (Coates & Wade, 2004), we move towards disassembling stereotypes and inaccurate notions of the passive victim. In fact, whenever humans are subjected to mistreatment, they resist in some way (Wade, 1997), and their resistance is a sign of their capacity, their humanness, and their spirit. When working therapeutically with clients, in addition to asking about what was done to them, I ask how they responded to each particular incident of being "acted upon" (Wade, 2007). If we ask a woman, "What did you do?" without the proper spirit of inquiry behind the question, we may find ourselves blaming her for not doing enough. Alternatively, the woman might think we are trying to mutualize the violence and blame her for "her part" in the attack. Most women will say they did not do anything, that they could not. When asked the therapeutic question, "*How* did you do nothing?" a rich, descriptive account of resistance (in terms of thinking, feeling, sensing, intuiting, praying, etc.) is likely to follow. The matching of acts that were done to a woman with her responses to those acts creates a to-and-fro account of interaction where the brutality of the acts is clarified by the intensity of the response. While contesting euphemisms, generalizations, stereotypes, and self-blaming phraseology from popular psychology, I may assist Lily and other women to recognize their energy, skill, and intellect—as well acknowledge their own willingness to step into partial responsibility when they are in fact blameless. Indigenous women, as well as all other citizens, have a right to live in safety, with respect and dignity.

Through attention to the precision of words, we may learn who did what to whom and what kind of restoration might be required in order for the client to feel better. Just as words lay the tracks, they may also liberate a client from the self-blame imposed as a result of the negative social responses she received after she disclosed violence. Words help to forge a path of ethical resistance based on acts, "the small acts of living" (Wade, 1997) that are often unrecognized because they are internal, subtle or spiritual, perhaps not visible to the outside world. Responses that evoke values, commitments, preferences, and justice represent a longing for better relationships and a world where people live in dignity. A word can produce a thousand pictures of a better world.

ACKNOWLEDGEMENTS

Heartfelt thanks to "Lily," who agreed to share her experience with the hope of helping others. I would also like to thank to Allan Wade, Linda Coates, and

Vikki Reynolds, who inspire me endlessly in this work and continually offer new ways to align with clients spiritually and linguistically in a spirit of solidarity. I also thank the Cowichan people, on whose territory I live as a visitor.

ENDNOTES

1 Feminist and Indigenous scholars (e.g., Anderson, 2000; Monture-Angus, 2001; Razack, 2002), filmmakers (Welsh, 2006), anti-racism educators (Elliott, 2006) as well as Amnesty International (2004) and Native Women's Association of Canada (2007a) have documented the high incidents of sexualized violence against Aboriginal women in Canada, including the issue of women forced into "sex for money" for reasons of economic marginalization. Cherokee activist and scholar Andrea Smith (2005) documents the use of sexual violence as a tool for colonial domination in the United States. While this topic is not discussed at length in the chapter, it is important that therapists understand the pervasiveness of sexualized violence against Indigenous women and understand the reasons why it is so often unreported to authorities.

2 "Lily" is a pseudonym used to preserve her family's privacy in the aftermath of professional racism and mistreatment in British Columbia.

3 *The Secret*. Retrieved April 6, 2009 from http://www.thesecret.tv/.

4 The intimate relationship between colonialism and psychiatry, and, by extension, the helping professions, is demonstrated in the quote by Octave Mannoni, a psychiatrist who worked in Madagascar before and after the French suppressed the rebellion of 1949, killing an estimated 90,000 Malagasies. Absent from Mannoni's theory is any mention of the land theft that ensued and the wealth accrued or lost as a result of colonization. One might think that the absurdity of the assertion quoted would be challenged in the helping professions, but that has seldom been the case, and clients are typically treated apart from the socio-political, historical context of their lives.

5 Women are blamed in many ways for the violence enacted upon them. One way this blame is articulated is through a discourse of "choice." Women are often blamed for choosing violent partners while, at the beginning of romantic relationships, perpetrators of violence do not reveal their future plans to be violent. The fact that many perpetrators begin relationships showing tenderness, attentiveness, generosity, caring, and self-sacrifice demonstrates the *deliberateness* of their behaviour. In fact, many perpetrators start relationships by expressing outrage at the past mistreatment of their new partners. They often make commitments to love, honour, and respect their new partner. In fact, if a woman was attracted to violence, she would leave the relationship when the man was *not* violent.

6 Much violence was enacted on Aboriginal people in Canada, primarily to facilitate the theft of land and resources into the hands of the colonial power. In addition to

being raped, murdered, and sexually abused on a frequent basis (Annett, 2002b), Aboriginal children interned in residential camps were electrocuted, shaved, cut, had their tongues pierced by pins, were whipped, degraded, humiliated, and purposely exposed to tuberculosis and small pox while inoculations were withheld. The Royal Commission on Aboriginal Peoples (Government of Canada, 1996) documents that former head of Indian Affairs Duncan Campbell Scott was made aware of the 50% death rate in the so-called schools. His response was that this is how Canada is dealing with "the Indian problem." Indeed, Scott was following standard Victorian beliefs about empire and race, agreeing with Charles Lyell (1832, cited in Crosby, 2004) that "if we wield the sword of extermination as we advance, we have no reason to repine the havoc committed" (p. ix).

Fundamentally, Canadians need to know that a cultural genocide was perpetrated. The Indigenous population of North America was reduced from 10 million people at contact to 250,000 by the year 1900 (Thornton, 1986, cited in Duran & Duran, 1995, p. 28). Canadians need to know that the government, churches, and mining and logging companies played an active role in the theft of commonly held Aboriginal wealth into the hands of a particular class of Europeans. We need to know that race-based legislation through the Indian Act still separates Indian people today into a group considered inferior to both white Canadians and immigrant Canadians. We need to know that a 1951 change to the Indian Act enabled the state to apprehend Native children en masse (Huntley & Blaney, et al., 1999; Lawrence, 2004, p. 7). While we often refer to this mass transfer of Aboriginal children into white homes as "the sixties scoop," it is still happening today. For example, on Vancouver Island, 50% of the children in the child welfare system are First Nations and Metis (Carriere, 2007).

7 The concept of mutualizing euphemisms found in everyday language and professional discourse was discussed by Dr. Allan Wade in a Victoria, BC, workshop hosted by the Aboriginal Family Therapy Centre, March 12–13, 2006. The workshop was called "Responding to Violence: Preserving Dignity and Spirit through Small Acts of Wellness" with Allan Wade, Cathy Richardson, and Vikki Reynolds as presenters. Dr. Wade shared this example and explained how women often say that they were in an "abusive relationship" or have experienced "domestic violence." When he asks, "So who was abusive?" the woman often says, "My husband abused me." By seeking clarification, the therapist learns more precisely "who is doing what to whom," and the client is then released from holding a shared burden for the violence.

REFERENCES

Adams, H. (1989). *Prison of grass: Canada from a Native point of view* (2nd ed.). Saskatoon, SK: Fifth House.

Adams, H. (1995). *A tortured people: The politics of colonization*. Penticton, BC: Theytus Books.

Amnesty International. (2004). *Stolen sisters: A human rights response to discrimination and violence against Indigenous women in Canada*. Retrieved August 25, 2008, from http://www.amnesty.ca/stolensisters/amr2000304.pdf.

Anderson, K. (2000). *A recognition of being: Reconstructing Native womanhood*. Toronto: Second Story.

Andrews, B., Brewin, C.R., & Rose, S. (2003). Gender, social support and PTSD in victims of violent crimes. *Journal of Traumatic Stress, 16*(4), 421-427.

Annett, K. (2002a). *Love and death in the valley*. Vancouver, BC: 1st Books Library.

Annett, K. (2002b). Hidden from history: The Canadian holocaust. *Nexus Magazine, 9*(2). Retrieved September 1, 2007, from http://www.nexusmagazine.com/articles/canada.html.

Battiste, M. (2000). *Reclaiming Indigenous voice and vision*. Vancouver, BC: UBC Press.

Bavelas, J., & Coates, L. (2001). Is it sex or assault? Erotic versus violent language in sexual assault trial judgments. *Journal of Social Distress and Homelessness, 10*, 29–40.

Brewin, C.R., Andrews, B., & Valentine, J.D. (2000). Meta-analysis of risk factors for post-traumatic stress disorder in trauma-exposed adults. *Journal of Consulting and Clinical Psychology, 68*(5), 748–766.

British Columbia Human Rights Commission. (2001). *Pathways to equality: Hearings on access to public education for Aboriginal people*. Vancouver: Author.

Burnet, R.W. (Producer). (1994). Heads up: A self-esteem video. [Film]. Yellowknife, NT: YWCA of Yellowknife.

Burstow, B., & Weitz, D. (Eds.). (1988). *Shrink resistant: The struggle against psychiatry in Canada*. Vancouver, BC: New Star Books.

Campbell, M. (1973). *Halfbreed*. Toronto: McLelland & Stewart.

Campbell, R., Ahrens, C.E., Sefl, T., Wasco, S.M., & Barnes, H.E. (2001). Social reactions to rape victims: Healing and hurtful effects on psychological and physical health outcomes. *Violence and Victims, 16*(3), 287–302.

Carriere, J. (2007). Promising practice for maintaining identities in First Nation adoption. *First Peoples Child and Family Review, 3*(1), 46–64.

CERD Report Ad Hoc National Network. (2002). *Report on racial discrimination against Indigenous peoples in Canada: Summary*. Report to United Nations Committee on the Elimination of Racial Discrimination. Retrieved September 9, 2008, from http://www.turtleisland.org/news/cerd.pdf.

Cermak, T. (1986). *Diagnosing and treating co-dependency*. Minneapolis, MN: Johnson Institute Books.

Coates, L. (1997). Causal attributions in sexual assault trial judgments. *Journal of Language and Social Psychology, 16*, 278–296.

Coates, L., Todd, N., & Wade, A. (2003). Shifting terms: An interactional and discursive view of violence and resistance. *Canadian Review of Social Policy, 52,* 116–121.

Coates, L., & Wade, A. (2004). Telling it like it isn't: Obscuring perpetrator responsibility for violent crime. *Discourse & Society, 15,* 499–526.

Coates, L., & Wade, A. (2007). Language and violence: Analysis of four discursive operations. *Journal of Family Violence, 22*(7), 511–522.

Coates, L., & West, K. (2003). *Representation and responsibility: An analysis of sexual assault judicial judgments.* Lethbridge, AB: University of Lethbridge.

Corrections Canada. (1990). *Creating choices: The report of the task force on federally sentenced women.* Ottawa: Correctional Service of Canada.

Crosby, A. (2004). *Ecological imperialism: The biological expansion of Europe, 900–1900.* New York: Cambridge University Press.

Danet, B. (1980). Language in the legal process. *Law & Society Review, 14*(3), 445–564.

Department of Justice Canada. (2008). *A review of research on criminal victimization and First Nations, Métis and Inuit peoples 1990 to 2001.* Retrieved September 16, 2008, from http://www.justice.gc.ca/eng/pi/rs/rep-rap/2006/rr06_vic1/p9.html.

Donalek, J. (2001). First incest disclosure. *Issues in Mental Health Nursing, 22,* 573–591.

Dumont, M. (1993). *A really good brown girl.* London, ON: Brick Books.

Duran, E., & Duran, B. (1995). *Native American postcolonial psychology.* New York: State University of New York Press.

Duryee, M.A. (2003). Expected controversies: Legacies of divorce. *Journal of the Center for Families, Children & the Courts, 4,* 149–160. Retrieved September 9, 2008, from http://www.courtinfo.ca.gov/programs/cfcc/pdffiles/149Duryee.pdf.

Dylan, A., Regehr, C., & Allagia, R. (2008). And justice for all? Aboriginal victims of sexual violence. *Violence Against Women, 14*(6), 678–696.

Elliott, J. (2006). Indecent exposure: Systemic racism today. Presentation at the Victoria Inn, Winnipeg, Manitoba, April 27.

Fanon, F. (1963). *The wretched of the earth.* New York: Grove Press.

Freire, P. (1993). *Pedagogy of the oppressed.* [Trans. M. Bergman Ramos]. New York: Continuum. (Original work published 1970.)

Furniss, E. (1999). *The burden of history: Colonialism and the frontier myth in a rural Canadian community.* Vancouver: UBC Press.

Government of Canada. (1996). *Report of the Royal Commission on Aboriginal Peoples.* Ottawa: Author.

Green, J., Kovach, M., Montgomery, H., Thomas, R., & Brown, L. (2007). Witnessing wild woman: Resistance and resilience in Aboriginal child welfare. In L. Foster & B. Wharf (Eds.), *Protecting children from neglect and abuse: A historical and analytical review of child welfare in B.C.,* (pp. 1–18). Vancouver, BC: UBC Press.

Haig-Brown, C. (1988). *Resistance and renewal: Surviving the Indian residential school.* Vancouver, BC: Tillacum Library.

Health Canada. (1999). *Discrimination, HIV/AIDS, and Aboriginal people: A discussion paper* (2nd ed.). Montréal: Canadian HIV/AIDS Legal Network and Canadian Aboriginal AIDS Network.

hooks, bell. (1994.) *Teaching to transgress: Education as the practice of freedom.* New York: Routledge.

Howard, S. Dryden., J., & Johnson, B. (1999). Childhood resilience: Review and critique of literature. *Oxford Review of Education, 25*(3), 307–323.

Huntley, A., & Blaney, F., with Daniels, R., Hall, L., & Dysart, J. (1999). *Bill C-31: Its impacts, implications, and recommendations for change in British Columbia–Final report.* Vancouver, BC: Aboriginal Women's Action Network & Vancouver Status of Women.

Kaufman, C., Desserich, J., Big Crow, C.K., Holy Rock, B., Keane, E., & Mitchell, C.M. (2007, May). Culture, context, and sexual risk among Northern Plains American Indian youth. *Social Science & Medicine, 64*(10), 2152–2164.

Kelly, L. (1988). *Surviving sexual violence.* Minneapolis, MN: University of Minnesota Press.

Kipling, R. (1923, February 15). Speech to the Royal College of Surgeons, London, England, February 14. *The Times.*

Lawrence, B. (2004). *"Real" Indians and others: Mixed-blood urban Native peoples and Indigenous nationhood.* Vancouver, BC: UBC Press.

Littlebear, L. (2000). Jagged worldviews colliding. In M. Battiste (Ed.), *Reclaiming Indigenous voice and vision,* (p. 77). Vancouver, BC: UBC Press.

Logan, T. (2001). *The lost generations: The silent Métis of the residential school system.* Winnipeg: Southwest Region Manitoba Métis Federation.

Macey, D. (2000). *Frantz Fanon: A life.* London: Granta.

Matthews, C. J., & Lewis, L. (1995). *Racism in the criminal justice system: A bibliography.* Toronto: University of Toronto Centre of Criminology.

McGillivray, A. (1997). Therapies of freedom: The colonization of Aboriginal childhood. In A. McGillivray (Ed.), *Governing childhood* (pp. 135–199). Aldershot, UK: Dartmouth Press.

Ministry of Community Services and Minister Responsible for Seniors' and Women's Issues. (2005). *Researched to death: B.C. Aboriginal women and violence.* Victoria, BC: Queen's Printers.

Monture-Angus, P. (2001). *Thunder in my soul: A Mohawk woman speaks.* Halifax, NS: Fernwood.

Native Women's Association of Canada. (2007a). *Violence against Aboriginal women and girls: An issue paper.* Prepared for the National Aboriginal Women's Summit, June 20–22, 2007, Corner Brook, Newfoundland. Retrieved August 25, 2008, from http://www.nwac-hq.org/en/documents/nwac-vaaw.pdf.

Native Women's Association of Canada. (2007b). *Aboriginal women and the legal justice system in Canada: An issue paper.* Prepared for the National Aboriginal Women's

Summit, June 20–22, 2007, Corner Brook, Newfoundland. Retrieved August 25, 2008, from http://www.laa.gov.nl.ca/laa/news/pdf/nwac-legal.pdf.

Peel Committee against Woman Abuse. (2005). *Working together to end violence against women.* Retrieved August 25, 2008, from http://www.pcawa.org/wap3.htm.

Razack, S. (2002). Gendered racial violence and spatialized justice: The murder of Pamela George. In Sherene Razack (Ed.), *Race, space and the law: Unmapping a white settler society* (pp. 121–56). Toronto: Between the Lines Press.

Reynolds, V. (2006). *Supervision of solidarity. Notes on the intersections of theory/practice.* Presentation at "Responding to Violence: Preserving Dignity and Spirit Through Small Acts of Wellness" workshop, Victoria, BC, March 12–13.

Richardson, C., & Nelson, B. (2007). A change of residence: Government schools and foster homes as sites of forced Aboriginal assimilation. *First Peoples Child & Family Review,* 3(2), 75–83.

Richardson, C., & Wade, A. (2007). *Understanding that violence is deliberate and not accidental.* Handout from "Responding to Violence: Preserving Dignity and Spirit Through Small Acts of Wellness" workshop, Victoria, BC, March 12–13.

Roberts, D. (2002). *Shattered bonds: The colour of child welfare.* New York: Basic Civitas Books.

Scott, J. (1990). *Domination and the arts of resistance.* New Haven, CT: Yale University Press.

Sinclair, M., Bala, N., Lilles, H., & Blackstock, C. (2004). Aboriginal child welfare. In N. Bala, M. Zaph, R. Williams, R. Vogl, & J. Hornick (Eds.), *Canadian child welfare law: Children, families and the state* (2nd ed.) (pp. 199–244). Toronto: Thompson Educational Publishing.

Smith, A. (2005). *Conquest: Sexual violence and American Indian genocide.* Cambridge, MA: South End Press.

Statistics Canada. (2006). *Violence against Aboriginal women.* Retrieved August 25, 2008, from http://www.statcan.ca/english/research/85-570-XIE/2006001/findings/aboriginal.htm.

Strega, S. (2004). Failure to protect. Child welfare interventions when men beat mothers. In R. Alaggia & C. Vine (Eds.), *Cruel but not unusual: Violence in Canadian families,* (pp. 650–690). Ottawa: Wilfred Laurier University Press.

Strega, S., Callahan, M., Rutman, D., & Dominelli, L. (2003). Undeserving mothers: Social policy and disadvantaged mothers. *Canadian Review of Social Policy, 49–50,* 175–198.

Todd, N., & Wade, A. (1994). Domination, deficiency, and psychotherapy. *The Calgary Participator,* 37–46.

Wade, A. (1995). *A persistent spirit. Towards understanding Aboriginal health in British Columbia.* Canadian Western Geographical Series, 31. Victoria, BC: Western Geographical Press.

Wade, A. (1997). Small acts of living: Everyday resistance to violence and other forms of oppression. *Journal of Contemporary Family Therapy, 19*(1), 23–40.

Wade, A. (2007). Presentation at "Responding to Violence: Preserving Dignity and Spirit Through Small Acts of Wellness" workshop, Victoria, BC, March 12–13.

Welsh, C. (Director). (2006). Finding Dawn [Film]. Ottawa: National Film Board of Canada.

CHAPTER 6

Aboriginal Women and Post-traumatic Stress Disorder: Implications of Culture on Therapy and Counselling Practices by Kathy M. Bent

*T*he post-traumatic stress experienced by Aboriginal[1] women in Canada has direct links to a historical context marked with political and cultural alienation brought about by the process of colonization (Royal Commission on Aboriginal Peoples, 1996). As an Anishnaabe woman with Ojibway, Irish, and French/Metis roots who is a member of the Little Black River First Nation in Manitoba, my life has not gone untouched by the intergenerational effects of colonization. These effects have largely been propelled by such legislation as the Indian Act (and its many amendments, including Bill C-31) and by the reserve, residential school, and child welfare systems. Due to these factors, family disruption has been a hallmark of much of my experience. For example, my maternal and paternal grandparents attended the residential school, then called the Catholic Mission, in Fort Alexander, Manitoba. At the Catholic Mission, my paternal grandmother learned to speak French, Latin, and English. At school, she was not allowed to speak her native Saulteaux tongue, which she spoke at home. Sadly, she died of tuberculosis at the tender age of 32. My grandparents, with the exception of my maternal grandfather, who passed away when I was eighteen, died before I was born. Therefore, like so many other Aboriginal women, I never had the opportunity to experience the continuity of family life that is derived by intergenerational influences. My life was more directly affected by the child welfare system of the 1960s and 1970s. For example, for the first five years of my life, I was raised with a mixture of Ojibwa, Metis, and Irish traditions. I remember vividly being rocked not in a cradleboard (dikinaagan) but in a swing (wewepizun), where I was tightly bound. There was always a lot going on around me, and I remember the feeling of warmth, safety, protection, and love. To this day, when I need to soothe myself, I *wrap a blanket tightly around my body (even if it is extremely hot), and I lay really still. Eventually, I am soothed and feeling stronger and better. Unfortunately, I also remember the day I was placed in a foster home during the "sixties scoop." One of the most culturally damaging aspects of colonization was a Child and Family Services assimilation practice. Aboriginal children were removed—"scooped"—from their families of origin and placed in white middle class homes. Tears still come to my eyes when I think of it, and I know it has affected me profoundly. For example, I was a single mother for most of my two daughters' lives, and I am also a proud grandmother. My daughters are both successful in their own right today, but one comment my oldest daughter has made on a number of occasions rings strongly through my consciousness: "Mom, I think you were a great mom, but I wish you would have hugged us more." I wished I had hugged my daughters more as well, because I know my spirit was alive with many of the Aboriginal values that were the federal government of Canada's target of destruction.*

Long-honoured Aboriginal values and beliefs passed down from generation to generation seem to be present in my life and Aboriginal people's lives despite the overarching issues that arise from living with Post-traumatic Stress Disorder (PTSD). In my work as a doctoral student and community researcher, I continue to have first hand experience dealing with the enormous impact of PTSD on Aboriginal women's lives. Like my own family, identity, and relationship issues, the far-reaching effects of PTSD weaving through the many realms of Aboriginal women's lives is apparent perhaps most in developing lasting and satisfying relationships with friends, family members, and significant others. This dilemma has widespread consequences because positive social relationships have been shown to ameliorate other physical, social, emotional, intellectual, and spiritual health problems.

INTRODUCTION

In 2001, there were approximately 499,605 Aboriginal women in Canada out of a total Aboriginal population of 976,305. Many of these women suffer the effects of mental health problems at disproportionately higher rates compared to other women in Canada (Dion Stout, Kipling & Stout, 2001; Statistics Canada, 2003). In the general Aboriginal population, PTSD has been reported as the most prevalent diagnosed mental health problem (Corrado & Cohen, 2003; Söchting, Corrado, Cohen, Ley, & Brasfield, 2007). One of the symptoms of PTSD is persistent avoidance of situations that remind an individual of the traumatic event(s) they have experienced. It may also involve a numbing of general responsiveness to others (American Psychiatric Association, 1994). Numbing and avoidance symptoms can be directly related to Aboriginal women's inability to experience positive intimate feelings that are necessary to form healthy, stable relationships (Mills & Turnbull,

2004). Rates of partner violence and divorce in Canada indicate that Aboriginal women's relationships with significant others can be extremely negative.

Substance abuse, major depression, dysthymia, anxiety disorders, and certain personality disorders such as borderline personality disorder are other reported mental health problems that hinder relationship development for Aboriginal women (Petchkovsky & San-Roque, 2002). Statistics that show disproportionate numbers of Aboriginal women are incarcerated or home-less, suffer from drug addictions and family violence, are prostitutes and gang members, have poor health status, fail to complete their education, and are unemployed as well as underemployed (Dion Stout et al., 2001; Kunz, Milan, & Schetagne, 2000; Public Health Agency, 2003). These factors also impede healthy relationship formation. The words of one Aboriginal woman parallel the relational experiences of many Aboriginal women:

> Well, we got married at almost 19 ah well I was 20 actually. I had 2 children, a bad marriage … mentally and physi-cally by my husband and my husband took my children away from me here when I came back to Canada and I lost it then and I became a heavy-duty drug addict. I ended up in the hospital having open heart surgery because I was an IV drug user (quote from interviews collected as part of a study by Parkes, Bent, Peter & Booth, 2008).

These negative outcomes can be traced back to the great amount of trauma and subsequent stress associated with the trauma experienced by Aboriginal women, beginning in infancy and continuing throughout their lives. The rates of PTSD in Aboriginal women are considerably higher than non-Aboriginal women due to these traumatic past experiences (Bopp, Bopp, & Lane, 2003). It is now generally accepted that a direct link between Aboriginal women's mental health problems and colonization in Canada exists. Brave Heart (1999) has referred to Aboriginal PTSD as "historical trauma" due to the strong link between the unique historical backgrounds of Aboriginal peoples and the trauma experience. As a result of colonization, Aboriginal people have experienced a legacy laced with extensive trauma and grief, which remains unresolved today (Brave Heart & DeBruyn, 1998; Macfarlane, 2005; Petchkovsky & San-Roque, 2002).

In Canada, the colonization process took place in the eighteenth century when the federal government developed and implemented systems to maintain their newly formed European colonies for economic expansion and exploitation. During this period and beyond, European values and views dominated, eventu-ally eroding Aboriginal cultural values and identity. In fact, the colonization of the Americas has been referred to as a "five-century-long cycle of European conquest, genocide ... a process which changed the face of Native America beyond all recognition" (Churchill, 1996, p. 21). To illustrate the travesty of the situation, some people have drawn a parallel between the loss of culture the American Indians and Alaskans experienced through colonization and that of individuals who lived through the Holocaust (Brave Heart & DeBruyn, 1998).

Assimilation policies (e.g. the residential school system), segregation practices (e.g. the reserve system), and legislation (e.g. the Indian Act) are examples of the colonizing systems that affected Aboriginal cultures. Family segregation was a major impact of colonization, illustrated by the words of one Aboriginal woman:

> I am Saulteaux and um ... my mother was an alcoholic and we grew up, I grew up with Foster parents, home-makers all my life ever since I was one years old and my mother passed away when I was 9 and I lived in a foster home for 4 years after that and I ended up adopted out in the United States and that didn't work out very well. I lived there for 3 years and then my Mom and Dad gave me a one-way ticket to Winnipeg so I came back and ended up in a group home again then my brother helped me get on independent living and then I lived on independent living from 16 (quote from interviews collected as part of a study conducted by Parkes et al, 2008).

The same Aboriginal woman tells of the profound consequences of Aboriginal family disruption:

> Well, I prostituted ever since I was 16 years old off and on. Here in the city [Winnipeg] and the States too to make my way across the country. Yes, quite a few times [picked up for prostitution] ... Well I will always be addicted to coke but I haven't done any of that since I went to jail ... because that almost death experience scared me ... I see a psychiatrist every week (quote from interviews collected as part of a study conducted by Parkes et al, 2008).

Colonization has indeed left its imprint. Socio-economic security and prosperity does not exist for most Canadian Aboriginal people, particularly Aboriginal women, who must deal with the dual effects of racial and gender marginalization. Aboriginal women, however, have not been dormant through-out this situation, which provides evidence of the intergenerational transmission

152

of strong cultural values and beliefs that reap characteristics of strength and resilience. For example, reporting on a national summit that took place in the spring of 2008, the Native Women's Association of Canada (2008) states that collectively native women "face common issues, common difficulties, and can find strength, understanding and assistance from one another to deal with them" (p. 6). Promotion of this train of thought shows both strength and resilience.

Furthermore, Aboriginal peoples are now taking the lead in developing healing strategies to deal with their culturally specific health problems. Promoting Aboriginal people's holistic world view and values by using their strengths is the cornerstone of these strategies. A holistic world view fosters the development of balance across the physical, emotional, intellectual, spiritual, and social realms as a way of life and a means of healing. This approach has garnered much support from Aboriginal communities and has been proven successful, as evidenced by the words of Aboriginal women who sought healing from organizations operating from an Aboriginal holistic stance. Spirituality, an integral part of an Aboriginal holistic world view, shines though in the voice of two Aboriginal women:

> Being Aboriginal or Native or Anishnaabe or Indian or whatever you want to call us, it's hard living in two worlds. The spirituality part, it's sacred to us and we have to learn it. That's what's keeping me going now (Iwasaki, Bartlett, & O'Neil, 2005, p. 981).

> I go to sweat lodges in the city. We try to take our kids. It's important to get them to understand that this is part of our heritage and our spirituality, because of how things evolved. So that they'll understand fundamentals of being good, of respecting, understanding and caring that we share at these places (Iwasaki et al., p. 981–982).

The voices of other Aboriginal women show the strength attained in honouring such Aboriginal values as humour and interconnection:

> Well, laughter is a big healer when you're down and out. My grandparents, they're gone now, and one of the things that they taught me is, when you have a problem you have to talk about it and also put a little bit of laughter in it. And it heals. Laughter is a big thing (Iwasaki et al., p. 984).

> I came to understand it wasn't because of me that all these things happened, it was because this bad thing happened to

my aunt and uncle and grandfather and great-grandfather
... all the way back ...it was being collected from the point
of European contact and being spilled out on the younger
generation each time (McEvoy & Daniluk, 1995, p. 229).

The words of an Aboriginal woman from one of the poorest neighbourhoods in all of Canada, the Downtown Eastside of Vancouver, illustrates the resilience that is so prevalent in Aboriginal communities:

Even though I am a strong woman on the outside, deep
down I'm hurting and many of us women are like that.
But we don't show it because we don't want people to
look at us like we're less than we are. It's just our way: we
walk with our head high and proud (Benoit, Carroll, &
Chaudhry, 2003, p. 824).

This chapter examines the literature on PTSD in relation to Aboriginal women's experiences with intimate partner violence, gender differences, feminist and current counselling theories and practices, and ethical dilemmas that can arise when clinicians and Aboriginal patients' worlds meet during the building of therapeutic relationships necessary for successful treatment of PTSD.

PTSD DEFINED

PTSD has been defined by the DSM-IV as a dissociative anxiety disorder that occurs as a result of exposure to life-threatening experiences and witnessing of traumatic events that pose a threat to self or others (American Psychiatric Association, 1994). According to the DSM-IV, re-experiencing the traumatic event, avoidance of reminders related to the event, and chronic anxiety are the main criteria for a PTSD diagnosis. These symptoms must also be persistent in nature and disrupt an individual's ability to function (American Psychiatric Association, 1994). The main characteristics of PTSD have the propensity to seriously affect the development of positive and healthy relationships because they lead to negative behavioural, emotional, and cognitive reactions, including the following:

- impairment in regulating affective impulses, in particular anger directed at both self and others,

- alterations in attention and consciousness leading to dissociative episodes, amnesia, or depersonalization,

- alterations in relationships with others, primarily evident by the inability to trust and enjoy emotional intimacy,

- alterations in systems of meaning, such as lost faith in existing belief systems or the value and meaning of one's unique life (American Psychiatric Association, 1994, pp. 424–429 & pp. 751–753).

A great deal of research exists on PTSD. Most of this work has focussed on men and most particularly on war veterans. Significant gender differences have been noted (Brave Heart, 1999; Vogt, 2006) with males experiencing more traumatic events in their lifetime than females (Vogt, 2006) which is not surprising given the focus on men and not women. Females are, however, more apt to develop chronic PTSD compared to males and tend to seek treatment more readily. More than half of all women residing in the United States experience traumatic events in their lives, and females are estimated to display the signs of PTSD at rates twice as high as males (Vogt, 2006). For women, these traumatic events most often encompass sexual abuse, childhood parental neglect, childhood physical abuse, family violence, and the unexpected death of a loved one. PTSD has been reported to be the most common outcome of exposure to these events, followed by depression and substance abuse.

In addition to differences in gender, PTSD has been shown to be culturally relative. Elsass (2001) assessed cultural differences related to responses associated with trauma in Colombian and Peruvian citizens. The results of this study showed that Columbians, with their individualistic backgrounds, tended to report more negative responses to trauma compared to Peruvians, who are more community minded. (Reasons for this finding are explored further in the section of this chapter on individualism and collectivism.) Cultural differences point to the need to examine factors related to the customs, traditions, and belief systems inherent to a given cultural group.

At least two forms of PTSD are discussed in the literature. In addition to PTSD as it is spelled out in the DSM-IV, complex PTSD is associated with persistent childhood and adolescent trauma delivered by a person in a position of trust. This type of trauma is especially debilitating in the absence of emotional support(Yellow Horse Brave Heart, 1998). PTSD has been differentiated from complex PTSD in that the latter arises from the experiences of multiple and prolonged traumatic events in comparison to one traumatic event (Herman, 1996), and has added outcomes of interpersonal impairment and self-destructive behaviours (National PTSD Center, 2007). Complex PTSD more aptly fits the experiences of colonized people. More often than not, they have experienced multiple traumas, and there is an intergenerational component to those experiences.

Perhaps complex PTSD has been promoted as a possible framework for assessing trauma in the Aboriginal population because it most closely captures the complex nature of multiple traumas and because it is closely related to borderline personality disorder, also associated with incidences of childhood sexual abuse (National PTSD Center, 2007). High rates of sexual abuse in childhood are reported by individuals diagnosed with PTSD (National PTSD Center, 2007), and as previously mentioned, Aboriginal women report higher rates of sexual abuse compared to non-Aboriginal women (Dion Stout et al., 2001). When a classification such as complex PTSD is used merely because it is convenient, the danger of failing to recognize major contextual and situational influences may arise. The use of diagnostic labels such as complex PTSD to understand behaviours that have grown to be almost normative creates limitations when it comes to acquiring knowledge-driven strategies to deal with problems that are largely precipitated by contextual influences rather than individual differences. For example, in many Aboriginal communities, family violence and other forms of violence that have reached epidemic proportions are other predictors of PTSD (LaRocque, 1994; Royal Commission on Aboriginal Peoples, 1996). The diagnostic category of PTSD is used to describe and understand the experiences of Aboriginal women and the trauma they experience as a result of violent actions that are generally not solely related to singular personal causes (Ristock, 1995). There is a collective element related to the trauma that must be acknowledged.

PTSD AND VIOLENCE AGAINST ABORIGINAL WOMEN

> My father had passed away in 1972, I was about 5 turning 6 years old, and after that my mother just lost it cause that was the 2nd husband she lost, and she kind of just ignored us and we were going back and forth from her community in Saskatchewan to our community in the Pas and we were just back and forth back and forth, and then she started to abuse alcohol and she would just leave us or send us back to her home community to her parents with my aunts and uncles and stuff, there was drinking and fights and stuff and most of my family came from the Residential Schools so there was a lot of anger there already. I saw my Uncle shoot my grandfather right off the doorstep, and I seen my uncle stab my aunty where she was almost bleeding to death and all the children were around, and I was the oldest about 8 or 9, and back then phones were pretty

scarce on the reserve, I think there was only about 5, so I
had to run around to phone the ambulance and we just
about lost her. Then my mom bought us back to the Pas,
and it was even worse there, you always saw men beating
up women, husbands beating up their wives and children
… and my sister and myself were sexually abused, but I
can't remember those incidents, I just can't remember, but
my sister remembers very clearly. And she tries to jar my
memory but I guess that it hurt me so much that I just
blanked it out, but I have all the symptoms of the sexually
abused, like when they talk about how they're feeling, I say
eh! That's how I'm feeling (quote from interviews collected
as part of a study by Parkes et al, 2008).

The words above are from an Aboriginal woman who participated in a study
on access to justice in Manitoba (Parkes et al., 2008). A link between traumatic
events, such as those she describes, and Aboriginal women's mental health problems has been established (Bent, 2004; Dion Stout et al, 2001; Mills & Turnbull,
2004; Royal Commission on Aboriginal Peoples, 1996). Aboriginal women have
experienced many forms of trauma (McEvoy & Daniluk, 1995). Research shows
that Aboriginal women are at far greater risk of becoming victims of homicide,
rape, and other assaults compared to non-Aboriginal women (Brownridge, 2003;
McEvoy & Daniluk; McGillivray & Comaskey, 1999; Statistics Canada, 2001).
In 1999, Statistic Canada's (2001) General Social Survey showed that 25% of
Aboriginal women were assaulted by a current or former spouse during a five-
year period. In all likelihood, this is a conservative estimate because intimate
partner violence in some Aboriginal communities is so rampant that it has
become a normal part of life (McGillivray & Comaskey). Indeed, McGillivray
and Comaskey report that "community denial of the violence, or its definition as
natural, cultural, or inevitable hinders victims from defining it as a problem that
can be helped, and complicates system response" (p. 41).

A 1991 study on wife abuse provides evidence that more accurately describes
violence against Aboriginal women in Canada (McGillivray & Comaskey, 1999).
Findings revealed that a high percentage (i.e., 75% to 90%) of Aboriginal women
in Northern communities experienced physical abuse. The rate of spousal homicide among Aboriginal women is also more than eight times higher than for
non-Aboriginal women (Statistics Canada, 2001). Health Canada (1999) reports
that the mortality rate due to violence for Aboriginal women is three times the
rate experienced by all other Canadian women. For Aboriginal women in the
24 to 44 age group, the rate is five times higher than the rate for non-Aboriginal
Canadian women (Health Canada, 1999). The Ontario Native Women's

Association (1989) found that eight out of 10 Aboriginal women have endured abusive relationships. A further indicator of the extent of the problem is the "high percentage of Aboriginal men incarcerated for crimes related to family violence in correctional facilities across Canada" (Proulx & Perrault, 2000, p. 11). To make matters worse, over the past two decades, over 500 Aboriginal women have been reported missing across Canada, and the government, law enforcement agencies, and Canadian society in general do not seem to care, as little or no attention is paid to this problem (Bennett, Blackstock, & De La Ronde, 2005). Clearly, intimate partner violence is so rampant in the Canadian Aboriginal population that some researchers have concluded that it is a severe problem that permeates entire Aboriginal communities (McGillivray & Comaskey, 1999).

The connection between intimate partner violence and PTSD has long been recognized (Vogt, 2006). Females who have experienced interpersonal violence report more PTSD symptoms than males and show evidence of slower recovery than do males (Vogt, 2006). This poses serious implications for the relational experiences of Aboriginal women, who, like their non-Aboriginal counterparts, are more likely to feel responsible for the violence inflicted upon them, because Western societal values still dictate the relationship roles of men and women. For the most part, a man is still perceived as having rightful control over a woman, especially if the woman is not financially or emotionally self-reliant. Women's roles as child-bearers and caregivers also predispose them to experiencing more severe PTSD symptoms than males because their sense of self is often deeply embedded in their ability to maintain relationships (Vogt, 2006).

Farley, Lynne, and Cotton (2005) found high rates of PTSD and lifetime histories of violence in a group of 100 Canadian prostitutes. Over 50% of the women interviewed were Canadian First Nation members, and 72% of the participants had PTSD according to the criteria set by the DSM-IV. In analyzing data extrapolated from a population health survey administered in 1991, Kirmayer, Boothroyd, Tanner, Ableson, and Robinson (2000) supported this contention. Through a secondary analysis of 1136 Cree participants, they found that being female was a major predictor of experiencing distress.

White et al. (2000) examined PTSD in relation to the everyday life of immigrant, refugee, and visible minority women. One of their goals was to identify similarities between the experiences of minority women and Aboriginal women. Only two Aboriginal women were interviewed for the study, so an adequate comparison could not be made. Not surprisingly, one of the Aboriginal woman interviewed revealed a past laden with ongoing abuse, oppression, addictions, and PTSD symptoms. Interviews were also conducted with mental health workers who stated that according to their case files, Aboriginal women sought services for PTSD symptoms at rates considerably higher than refugee and immigrant women (White et al., 2000).

Bopp et al. (2003) reported on the long-term mental health effects of complex PTSD in 127 students who had attended residential schools. In examining the health profiles of 127 students from 24 Aboriginal bands in British Columbia, Bopp et al. found that almost all of the students experienced physical, sexual, or emotional abuse at the residential school, as well as before and after attending the school. Those who had been abused prior to attending residential school revealed that most often it was family members who had inflicted abuse on them. All of the students reported being sexually abused at least once while attending the school, although many reported several incidents. High rates of physical abuse were also reported. Bopp et al. looked at details of relationship problems and found evidence of intergenerational transmission of violent behaviour committed by intimate partners or family members. As well, almost three-quarters of the participants reported that they had been physically abusive to others; over half reported that they had been sexually abusive to others. Smaller numbers of participants reported that they had inflicted emotional and psychological abuse on other people. The results of these studies support the contention that Aboriginal women face a number of serious obstacles when it comes to developing healthy relationships. For Aboriginal women, the effects of colonization and intimate partner violence lead to the development of PTSD. It is therefore imperative that a thorough understanding of Aboriginal cultural traditions be acquired by Aboriginal people and all health care providers, and in particular, it is important to examine current concepts that are used to understand minority cultures. Collectivism and individualism are two dominant cross-cultural constructs used to understand and explain cultural differences.

COLLECTIVISM VERSUS INDIVIDUALISM

Collectivism is associated with in-group harmony and interdependence, which can greatly reduce everyday stress levels by providing much needed social support and by fostering low levels of competition. In collectivistic societies, one's position is predetermined by birth, sex, and age. A person does not have to compete for a position to the same degree that an individual living in an individualistic society does. The disadvantage of collectivism is in its relation to sub-standard economies and, in some communities, corrupt government officials that may favour their own families at the expense of the collective good. Individualism, on the other hand, is related to high levels of economic development and greater competitiveness brought about by an independent focus on self over others.

These two dominant cultural constructs—interdependent versus independent modes of thinking, behaving, and constructing the self—give credence to environmental and social influences on the self that are pertinent to increasing knowledge on Aboriginal women's mental health problems. An understanding of these models can increase our understanding of aboriginal women's health problems. An interdependent self is contextually focussed and common to collectivistic societies, which emphasize the role of self to other (Markus & Kitayama, 1991). On the other hand, the independent self that is prevalent in Western cultures is thought of as "an entity containing significant dispositional attributes, and as detached from context" (Markus & Kitayama, p. 225). At the psychological level, individualism and collectivism correspond to an allocentric and idiocentric orientation (Triandis, Bontempo, Villareal, Asai, & Lucca, 1988). Research indicates that allocentrism is positively associated with social support and low levels of alienation and anomi, while idiocentrism is positively related to achievement and loneliness (Triandis, et al). At the cultural level, these constructs correspond directly to the constructs of individualism and collectivism.

The concept of individual versus collective self-orientation has been critiqued by researchers using post-structuralism, post-colonial, and critical cultural perspectives (Burman, 2005; Gustafson, 2005; Moodley, 2007; Qin, 2004). Qin, using a feminist perspective of culture and self, revealed the need to embrace differences in social aspects of self-identity based on Aboriginal women's self understanding, as opposed to grand narratives that are universal in nature. Qin proposes that "no single theory can possibly capture the truth about all women, as every truth is incomplete, partial and culture bound" (p. 307). Notwithstanding this, most Aboriginal cultures fit the description of a collectivist culture because of a reliance on the clan and tribal systems of organization.

These systems are clearly social structures that place great importance on kinship, family ties, and the collective well-being of the tribe in which the family is situated. It is fair to say, then, that Aboriginal cultures, in their unassimilated form, are collectivist and interdependent in nature. Assimilation into the Euro-Canadian culture, however, may have changed Aboriginal cultural traditions in a way that the two central constructs—interdependence and independence—cannot explain. To make matters worse, psychological research pertaining directly to Canadian Aboriginal cultures is limited. This further clouds the application of interdependence and independent constructs to aid our understanding PTSD in Aboriginal women. Thankfully, much research does exist on the debated topic of the benefits of using interdependence versus independence as constructs to aid our understanding of collectivistic cultures that may be similar to Aboriginal cultures. For example, research has been conducted cross-culturally with collectivist cultures in Asia and other countries.

The relationship between the orientations of collectivism and individualism and their impact on people's thinking patterns becomes clear when examining the cross-cultural literature related to issues of the self that correspond directly to the formation of theories that inform counselling and other therapeutic practices. Harrington and Liu (2002) looked at self-enhancement and attitudes specific to an Indigenous population, the Maori in New Zealand. Like Aboriginal women, who are a minority group in Canada, Harrington and Liu describe "the Maori as a minority people in their homeland" (p. 37). Prior to colonization, the Maori culture was collectivistic and therefore had high regard for the extended family and the greater Maori community. Individual identity was largely dependent on family ties and community relationships rather than individualistic aspects (Harrington & Liu). It has been postulated that low self-enhancement is common in collectivist cultures. *Self-enhancement* is a term used to describe an individual's view of his or her own self-worth and has been found to be positively and significantly associated with high self-esteem and subjective well-being (Kurman, 2003). According to Harrington and Liu, however, self-enhancement may not be valued by members of collectivist cultures and may even be seen as deviant. Contrary to these views, they found that both the European and the Maori participants in their study showed strong self-enhancement tendencies in the social and academic areas. These findings may reflect the influence of assimilation practices vis à vis colonization on the Maori people. To account for assimilation effects on attitudes towards self-enhancement, Harrington and Liu discuss their findings using a bicultural view of the independent and interdependent self. That is, they take into consideration that self-construal is taking place in a bicultural environment where societal forces naturally affect the formation of self. The bicultural view therefore implies that the collectivist cultures may not be as interdependent as research would indicate and vice versa: Individualistic cultures may not be as independent.

Kurman (2003) also looked at self-enhancement in collectivist cultures and included modesty as a mediating variable. An examination of self-construal, using self-construal, and self-enhancement measures was conducted with Singaporean Chinese, Israeli, Japanese, and Ethiopian students to assess the belief that low self-enhancement is a prime characteristic of collectivist cultures. As postulated, her findings indicated that collectivistic participants had lower levels of self-enhancement than individualistic participants. Like Harrington and Liu (2002), Kurman also noted that self-enhancement was positively associated with self-esteem and subjective well-being in collectivist and individualist cultures. She also discusses the possibility that cultural restrictions imposed on the self through cultural norms give way to modesty requirements that undermine the self-enhancement motive. In this vein, Kurman's findings show that the cultural differences in modesty may best explain cultural differences in self-enhancement rather than the primary focus on others common to collectivist cultures. Cultural restrictions, therefore, may be more responsible for low self-enhancement levels in collectivist cultures rather than a lack of a self-enhancement motive.

Tafarodi, Lang, and Smith (1999) examined individualism and collectivism in relation to self-esteem and asserted that "comparisons of individualist and collectivist cultures on self-esteem instruments have revealed lower scores among collectivists" (p. 621). However, like Kurman (2003), they discuss the possibility that low self-esteem scores may reflect modesty, which would be more prevalent intuitively in collectivist cultures, rather than a negative self-concept and may also be associated with a devaluing of self-enhancement, as discussed by Harrington and his colleagues (2002). Tafarodi et al. (1999) put forth the notion that individualism and collectivism may both hold certain costs and benefits. They suggest that thinking of individualism as promoting the development of self-competence or high self-esteem is an obvious benefit to individuals from a culture that values high self esteem over modesty. On the other hand, for collectivist cultures where less focus is placed on a person's individual achievements is described as inhibiting the development of high self-competence, and having lower self-esteem promotes self-liking and modesty because the individual does not stand out over and above other members of society.

Phinney and Flores (2002) have suggested that culture as a single construct should not be used to examine cultural differences when measuring and understanding psychological phenomenon. They support the identification of values, behaviours, and attitudes inherent to a given culture as a means to better understand that culture and its impact. There is a need for Aboriginal perspectives on mental health and wellness that embrace culture specific traditions and integrate those traditions into theories that guide counselling strategies (Brave Heart & DeBruyn, 1998; Chandler & Lalonde, 1998; Dumont-Smith, 1995; Kirmayer, 1994).

PTSD AND COUNSELLING THEORIES AND PRACTICES

I am almost 40. I am 39. And I recently just did time for aggravated assault and I spent close to 9 months in jail for that. Well I was very intoxicated and ... as far as I was concerned it was in self-defense but just by the wounds they determined it was aggravated assault because it was an in and out stab wound. I stabbed my best friend. Female. Well, I actually saved her life as well because I kept her from bleeding. We smoked a piece of crack and it seemed like they were ganging up on me and I blacked out and came to and I just really don't hardly remember most of it. I was really hurting then because I really didn't think that I had it in me to do something like that and that is when I went to jail (quote from interviews collected as part of a study by Parkes et al., 2008).

Race, gender, the effects of colonialism, minority status, and unequal access to societal resources that leads to underdevelopment of Aboriginal communities all exacerbate the problem of dealing with violence against Aboriginal women and PTSD. These factors are not common to most mainstream white women, for whom most therapeutic interventions are designed. Thankfully, when it comes to diagnostic strategies, the DSM-IV has included mental disorder assessment measures to detect cultural variations in symptoms and socio-demographics that influence treatment strategies for PTSD (Christensen, 2001). The most commonly used methods to treat PTSD encompass individual and group counselling (i.e., cognitive behaviour therapy, psychotherapy, etc.), drug therapy (i.e., antidepressants such as selective seratonin re-uptake inhibitors), self-care methods (i.e., meditation, yoga, etc.) and alternative therapies (i.e., hypnosis, acupuncture, herbal remedies, etc.). In treating Aboriginal people with PTSD, some researchers contend that there is still a paucity of adequate information related to the best practices to use (Shepard, O'Neill & Guenette, 2006). This calls attention to the need for more culturally appropriate practices. Culturally appropriate practices respect cultural traditions and embrace the teachings and values that coincide with those traditions (Hart, 1996, 2002). Mainstream Western values and beliefs oftentimes do not correspond to cultural notions of healing and well-being among Aboriginal groups. Failure to recognize and respect Aboriginal perspectives can result in ethical dilemmas that hinder the healing process for Aboriginal women suffering from PTSD and other mental health problems.

Willging (2002), for example, examined the relationship between mental health workers and Navajo patients within the context of clanship ties. Like other Aboriginal groups, the Navajo Nation is organized according to clan systems that are based on matrilineal lines and geographical locales. Clan systems espouse to collectivism rather than individualism. Therefore, clan members' behaviours are guided by strict rules of conduct that are based on group harmony rather than on individual needs. Willging contends that relational problems arise when non-Aboriginal mental health workers, schooled in Western traditions that are based on individualism, are unable to reconcile their Western beliefs and values with those of their Navajo patients. Promoting self-enhancement techniques to raise self-esteem may therefore prove to be useless when it comes to treating PTSD in Aboriginal people, who may be embarrassed and offended by the idea of favouring self over group enhancement. Aboriginal patients' ability to trust and disclose information necessary for a successful therapeutic process may also be affected if they feel they are not clearly understood by their therapist. This dilemma may be addressed through the delivery of education programs on Aboriginal cultural traditions to all counselling therapists.

In that vein, McEvoy and Daniluk (1995) suggest that therapists working with Aboriginal clients must realize that these clients value their extended family and community wellness over selfhood. The lack of trust many Aboriginal people have of mainstream institutions, arising from the colonization process, must also be considered when developing and delivering therapeutic responses to violence against Aboriginal women. It is imperative that therapists who offer treatment to Aboriginal clients receive education related to Aboriginal cultural traditions so, at the very least, they will have a rudimentary understanding of the cultures. In order to be more effective, they should also familiarize themselves with Aboriginal healing practices, some of which include the medicine wheel, healing and talking circles, pow-wows, sweat lodges, fasting, sun dances, potlatches and other Aboriginal healing ceremonies (McEvoy & Daniluk).

Healing techniques that give credence to the colonial experience of Aboriginal people and Aboriginal traditions are paramount to addressing inadequate Aboriginal mental health care. Hart (1996, 2002) supports this contention and has discussed and promoted the use of a sharing circle for therapeutic reasons. Heilbron and Guttman (2000) conducted a study where they examined the effects of using a sharing circle in cognitive therapy with Aboriginal women survivors of childhood sexual abuse. They report successful outcomes in that the sharing circle added a spiritual dimension that is not common in mainstream cognitive therapies. The healing process was enhanced by this Aboriginal traditional practice.

A great deal of literature exists on the important role Aboriginal cultural enrichment holds in relation to healing and the development of overall well-being (Bent, 2004; Bent, Josephson & Kelly, 2004; Chandler & Lalonde, 1998; Dion Stout, 1997; Dion Stout et al., 2001). Chandler and Lalonde found that culture played a strong role in addressing youth suicide. Communities engaged in healing practices based on cultural traditions reported reduced numbers of youth suicides. Bent et al. evaluated the cultural component of an Aboriginal cultural enrichment program and found that female adolescents who had more exposure to their Aboriginal culture had higher self-esteem compared to adolescents who did not have as much exposure to their culture. Proulx and Perreault (2000) reported favourable results in a study that evaluated the effects of a treatment program for Manitoba inmates. The treatment program was based on the medicine wheel concept and was instrumental in helping inmates deal with violent behaviours and improve relationships with their families. Dion Stout et al. (2001) examined the health disparities between Aboriginal women in Canada and found that the restoration of Aboriginal cultural healing practices was one of the most successful ways of dealing with physical and mental health issues.

Kirmayer, Brass, and Tait (2000) also promote Aboriginal cultural enrichment and argue that mental health services geared towards Aboriginal people can be improved by cultural psychiatry, which integrates cultural elements into the healing process. Promotion of community and youth empowerment has also been suggested as a means to deal with Aboriginal mental health problems (Kirmayer, Simpson & Cargo, 2003). Yellow Horse Brave Heart (1998) has also reported success with a mental health intervention, based on cultural traditions and designed to help Lakota individuals who suffered trauma associated with the colonization process. The intervention, which encouraged sharing grief experiences, consisted of increasing participants' knowledge of the trauma and its association with colonization within a traditional Aboriginal context.

Therapeutic techniques based on the lived experiences of Aboriginal women and their partners are necessary. McEvoy and Daniluk (1995) used a phenomenological approach to capture the lived experiences of child sexual abuse for six Aboriginal women. Through thematic analysis, they found that some of the themes experienced by Aboriginal women are commonly reported in the literature on non-Aboriginal women, while others were unique, including, colonization, racism, lack of social support, poor education, deprived socio-economic circumstances, repeated exposure to a wide range of violent acts, high rates of alcoholism, high rates of sexual abuse, and cultural shame (McEvoy & Daniluk). All of these circumstances form the context in which counselling theories and practices for Aboriginal women must be developed (Morrissette, & Naden, 1998). This context reflects the lived experience held by Aboriginal women who have PTSD.

CONCLUSION

A large segment of the female Aboriginal population suffers from psychological problems and disorders that disrupt their ability to lead satisfying lives in terms of relationship development, parenting, career development, and so on. The studies discussed in this chapter exemplify the problems associated with Eurocentric mechanisms to understanding cross-cultural differences in mental health problems associated with PTSD and the methods used to treat this disorder.

Regarding Western and Aboriginal world views, individualism and collectivism measurements do not always align with the characteristics of individualist and collectivist cultural groups. The task of measuring where certain cultural groups, like the Aboriginal population in Canada and other colonized groups, fit on the continuum between individualism and collectivism remains a problem. Furthermore, current conceptions of psychological problems related to trauma do not coincide with an Aboriginal world view in some cases. This has led to difficulties in coming up with adequate treatment and counselling practices. The integration of culturally appropriate Aboriginal healing techniques based on Aboriginal perspectives will inform the development of new models. Clearly, psychological effects of culture on minority and colonized populations, such as the Aboriginal women in Canada, are affected by a lack of understanding of cultural variations within a given Aboriginal group.

Although some headway has been realized in understanding the impact of culture and gender on psychological well-being and disorders such as PTSD, researchers too often ignore issues related to gender and the impact of sexism when completing examinations of ethnicity or race (Trotman Reid, 1999). Trotman Reid goes on to say that these same contentions can be applied to white feminist researchers who, in the past, have operated on the premise that all women experience oppression in the same manner. It is ludicrous to apply the same set of psychological principles and standards to the analysis of all human thinking and behaviour. For example, Dr. Rushton (2001) a psychologist from the University of Western Ontario made claims about brain size and intelligence on the basis of race. A woman with a Muslim, Middle East background has unique qualities, both biological and environmental, that set her significantly apart from a white middle-class or Aboriginal Canadian woman. Yet differences due to ethnicity or social class are still ignored, resulting in a psychological perspective representative of middle-class white women. Aboriginal women and other minority women are left out of the psychological discourse. Trotman Reid (1999) thinks this is due to a failure to adequately consider contextual influences on thinking and behaviour. A reliance on one dominant perspective limits the acquisition of knowledge, hinders the research process, and has grave consequences for Aboriginal women who must rely on therapeutic practices based on a perspective that is irrelevant to their lives.

In order to more adequately understand Aboriginal women's psychological experiences, it is important to include a feminine perspective based on how Aboriginal women view the world in the study of psychological disorders such as PTSD. Counsellor education on working with Aboriginal women must address both cultural and gender issues. Applying feminist theory within a multicultural counselling perspective may aid this endeavour. However, integrating issues particular to Aboriginal women are integral to the healing process. Once counsellors and therapists have an increased awareness of these factors, they will be better prepared to help Aboriginal women suffering from the effects of intimate partner violence and PTSD.

ENDNOTES

1 The term Aboriginal used here refers to First Nations, Non-Status, Metis, and Inuit people. However, the cultural diversity of these groups are recognized and honoured.

REFERENCES

American Psychiatric Association. (1994). *Diagnostic and statistical manual of mental disorders 4th Edition.* Washington, DC: American Psychiatric Press.

Benoit, C., Carroll, D., & Chaudhry, M. (2003). In search of a Healing Place: Aboriginal women in Vancouver's Downtown Eastside. *Social Science & Medicine. 56,* 821–833.

Bennett, M., Blackstock, C., & De La Ronde, R. (2005). *Literature review and annotated bibliography on aspects of Aboriginal child welfare in Canada.* The First Nations Research Site of the Centre of Excellence for Child Welfare and The First Nations Child & Family Caring Society of Canada. Retrieved February 1, 2006, from http://www.fncfcs.com/docs/AboriginalCWLitReview_2ndEd.pdf.

Bent, K. (2004). *Anishinaabe Ik-We Mino-Aie-Win – Aboriginal Women's Health Issues: A Holistic Perspective on Wellness.* Retrieved September 5, 2004, from http://www.pwhce.ca/pdf/abWoHealthBentFull.pdf

Bent, K., Josephson, W., & Kelly, B. (2004). Effects of an Aboriginal cultural enrichment program on adolescent mothers' self-perceptions. *First Peoples Child & Family Review, 1,* 83–100.

Bopp, M., Bopp, J., & Lane, P. (2003). *Aboriginal domestic violence in Canada.* The Aboriginal Healing Foundation Research Series. Retrieved February 1, 2004, from http://www.ahf.ca/publications/research-series.

Brave Heart, M. (1999). Gender differences in the historical trauma response among the Lakota. *Journal of Health and Social Policy, 10,* 1–21.

Brave Heart, M., & DeBruyn, L. (1998). The American Indian Holocaust: Healing historical unresolved grief. *American Indian and Alaskan Native Mental Health Research, 8,* 56–78.

Brownridge, D.A. (2003). Male partner violence against Aboriginal women in Canada: An empirical analysis. *Journal of Interpersonal Violence, 18,* 65–83.

Burman, E. (2005). Engendering culture in psychology. *Theory & Psychology, 15,* 527–548.

Chandler, M., & Lalonde, C. (1998). Cultural continuity as a hedge against suicide in Canada's First Nations. *Transcultural Psychiatry, 35,* 191–219.

Christensen, M. (2001). Diagnostic criteria in clinical settings: DSM-IV and cultural competence. *American Indian and Alaska Native Mental Health Research. The Journal of the National Center, 10,* 52–66.

Churchill, W. (1996). *From a Native son: Selected essays on Indigenism, 1985–1995.* U.S.: South End Press.

Corrado, R., & Cohen, I. (2003). *Mental health profiles for a sample of British Columbia's Aboriginal survivors of the Canadian residential school system.* Prepared for The Aboriginal Healing Foundation. Retrieved August 10, 2007, from http://www.ahf.ca/publications/research-series.

Dion Stout, M. (1997). Stopping family violence: Aboriginal communities enspirited. In J.R.Ponting (Ed.), *First Nations in Canada, perspectives on opportunity, empowerment, and self-determination* (pp. 273–298). Toronto, ON: McGraw-Hill Ryerson Ltd.

Dion Stout, M., Kipling D., & Stout, R. (2001). *Aboriginal women's health research synthesis project, final report.* Ottawa: Health Canada.

Dumont-Smith, C. (1995). Aboriginal Canadian children who witness and live with violence. In E. Peled & P.G. Jaffe (Eds.), *Ending the cycle of violence: Community responses to children of battered women* (pp. 275–283). Thousand Oakes, CA: Sage Publications.

Elsass, P. (2001). Individual and collective traumatic memories: A qualitative study of post-traumatic stress disorder symptoms in two Latin American localities. *Transcultural Psychiatry, 38*, 306–316.

Farley, M., Lynne, J., & Cotton, A. (2005). Prostitution in Vancouver: Violence and the colonization of First Nations women. *Transcultural Psychiatry, 42*, 242–271.

Gustafson, D. (2005). Transcultural nursing theory from a critical cultural perspective. *Advances in Nursing Science, 28*, 2–16.

Harrington, L., & Liu, J. (2002). Self-enhancement and attitudes toward high achievers: A bicultural view of the independent and interdependent self. *Journal of Cross-Cultural Psychology, 33*, 37–55.

Hart, M. (1996). Utilizing traditional practice methods for teaching, helping, and supporting. In S. O'Meara & D.A. West (Eds.), *From our eyes: Learning from Indigenous peoples* (pp. 59–72). Toronto: Garamond Press.

Hart, M. (2002). *Seeking Mino-Pimatisiwin: An Aboriginal approach to helping.* Halifax, NS: Fernwood Publishing.

Heilbron, C., & Guttman, M. (2000). Traditional healing methods with First Nations women in group counseling. *Canadian Journal of Counselling, 34*, 3–13.

Health Canada. (1999). *The health of Aboriginal women. One in a series of fact sheets prepared for the Women's Health Bureau.* Retrieved December 10, 2003, from http://www.hc-sc.gc.ca/english/women/facts_issues/facts_aborig.htm.

Herman, J. (1996). *Trauma and recovery: The aftermath of violence: From domestic abuse to political terror.* U.S.: Basic Books.

Iwasaki, Y., Bartlett, J., & O'Neil, J. (2005). Social coping with stress among Aboriginal women and men with diabetes in Winnipeg, Canada. *Science & Medicine, 60*, 977–988.

Kirmayer, L. (1994). Suicide among Canadian Aboriginal peoples. *Transcultural Psychiatric Research Review, 31*, 3–58.

Kirmayer, L., Boothroyd, L, Tanner, A., Ableson, N., & Robinson, E. (2000). Psychological distress among the Cree of James Bay. *Transcultural Psychiatry, 37*, 35–56.

Kirmayer, L., Brass, G., & Tait, C. (2000). The mental health of Aboriginal Peoples: Transformations of identity and community. *Canadian Journal of Psychiatry, 45*, 60–616.

Kirmayer, L., Simpson, C., & Cargo, M. (2003). Healing traditions: Culture, community and mental health promotion with Canadian Aboriginal peoples. *Australasian Psychiatry, 11*, S15-S23.

Kunz, J., Milan, A., & Schetagne, S. (2000). *Unequal access: A Canadian profile of racial differences in education, employment and income.* A Report Prepared for Canadian Race Relations Foundation by the Canadian Council on Social Development.

Kurman, J. (2003). The role of perceived specificity level of failure events in self-enhancement and in constructive self-criticism. *Personality and Social Psychology Bulletin, 29*, 285–294.

LaRocque, E. (1994). Violence in Aboriginal communities in the Royal Commission on Aboriginal peoples. *The Path to Healing.* Retrieved December 10, 2009 from http://www.phac-aspc.gc.ca/ncfv-cnivf/archives/publications/fv-abor-eng.php.

Macfarlane, D. (2005). *Mental wellness in First Nations and Inuit communities: Challenges and opportunities, an environmental scan for a strategic action plan to improve First Nations and Inuit mental wellness outcomes.* Report prepared for Health Canada's First Nations and Inuit Health Branch, Health Canada.

Markus, H., & Kitayama, S. (1991). Culture and the self: Implications for cognition, emotion, and motivation. *Psychological Review, 98*, 224–253.

McEvoy, M., & Daniluk, J. (1995). Wounds to the soul: The experience of Aboriginal women survivors of sexual abuse. *Canadian Psychology, 36*, 221–235.

MGillivray, A, & Comaskey, B. (1999). *Black eyes all of the time: Intimate violence, Aboriginal women and the justice system.* Toronto, ON: University of Toronto Press.

Mills, B., & Turnbull, G. (2004). Broken hearts and mending bodies: the impact of trauma on intimacy. *Sexual and Relationship Therapy, 19*, 265–289.

Moodley, R. (2007). Re-placing multiculturalism in counselling and psychotherapy. *British Journal of Guidance & Counselling, 35*, 1–22.

Morrissette, P., & Naden, M. (1998). An international view of traumatic stress among First Nations counselors. *Journal of Family Psychotherapy, 9*, 43–60.

National Post Traumatic Stress Disorder Centre (2007). *PTSD in men and women: Research on the HPA axis.* Retrieved August 10, 2007, from http://www.ncptsd.va.gov/ncmain/researchers/fact_sheets/fs_specific.jsp

Native Women's Association of Canada. (2008). *National Aboriginal Women's Summit - Standing Committee Presentation.* Retrieved May 1, 2008 from http://www.nwac-hq.org/en/documents/20080429HoCCommitteePresentationNAWSFinal.pdf.

Ontario Native Women's Association. (1989). *Breaking free: A proposal for change to Aboriginal family violence.* Thunder Bay, Ontario December, 1989, Retrieved August 15, 2007, from http://onwa-tbay.ca/PDF%20Files/Forms/Breaking%20Free%20Report.pdf.

Parkes, D., Bent, K. Peter, T., & Booth, T. (2008). Listening to their voices: Women prisoners and access to justice in Manitoba. *The Windsor Yearbook of Access to Justice,* 26(1), 85–119.

Petchkovsky, L., & San-Roque, C. (2002). Tjunguwiyanytja, attacks on linking: Forced separation and its psychiatric sequelae in Australia's "Stolen Generations." *Transcultural-Psychiatry, 39,* 345–366.

Phinney, J., & Flores, J. (2002). Unpackaging acculturation: Aspects of acculturation as predictors of traditional sex role attitudes. *Journal of Cross Cultural-Psychology, 33,* 320–331.

Proulx, J., & Perrault, S. (2000). The Ma Mawi Wi Chi Itata Stony Mountain project: Blending contemporary and traditional approaches for male family violence offenders. In S. Perrault & J. Proulx (Eds.), *No place for violence: Canadian Aboriginal alternatives* (pp. 99–119). Nova Scotia: Sage.

Public Health Agency of Canada. (2003). *Women's health surveillance report: A multidimensional look at the health of Canadian women.* Canadian Institute for Health Information. Retrieved August 15, 2007, from http://www.phac-aspc.gc.ca/publicat/ whsr-rssf/pdf/CPHI_WomensHealth_e.pdf.

Qin, D. (2004). Toward a critical feminist perspective of culture and self. *Feminism & Psychology, 14,* 297–312.

Ristock, J., (1995). *The impact of violence on mental health: A guide to the literature.* Discussion Paper on Health Family Violence Issues for the University of Manitoba Manitoba Research Centre on Family Violence and Violence against Women and The Mental Health Division Public Health Agency of Canada, Health Canada.

Royal Commission on Aboriginal Peoples. (1996). *Report of the Royal Commission on Aboriginal peoples. (v. 1)* Ottawa: The Commission.

Rushton, P. (2001). Is there a biological basis for race and racial differences? Insight, May 28. Retrieved December 11, 2009 from http://www.lrainc.com/swtaboo/ stalkers/jpr_insight.html

Shepard, B., O'Neill, L., & Guenette, F. (2006). Counselling with First Nation women: Considerations of oppression and renewal. *International Journal for the Advancement of Counselling, 28,* 227–240.

Söchting, I., Corrado, R., Cohen, I., Ley, R., & Brasfield, C. (2007). Traumatic pasts in Canadian Aboriginal people: Further support for a complex trauma conceptualization? *BC Medical Journal, 49,* 320–326.

Statistics Canada. (2001). *Census Aboriginal Population Profile.* Retrieved February 9, 2004, from http://www12.statcan.ca/english/profil01ab/PlaceSearchForm1.cfm

Statistics Canada. (2003). *Aboriginal peoples survey 2001– initial findings: Well-being of the nonreserve Aboriginal population.* Retrieved December 5, 2003 and modified version March 1, 2004, from http://www.statcan.ca/english/freepub/89-589-XIE/ index.htm.

Tafarodi, R., Lang, J., & Smith, A. (1999). Self-esteem and the cultural trade-off: Evidence for the role of individualism-collectivism. *Journal of Cross-Cultural Psychology, 30*, 620–640.

Triandis, H., Bontempo, R., Villareal, M., Asai, M., & Lucca, N. (1988). Individualism and collectivism: Cross-cultural perspectives on self and ingroup relationships. *Journal of Personality and Social Psychology, 54*, 323–338.

Trotman Reid, P. (1999). Poor women in psychological research: Shut up and shut out. In V. Rosemary, P. Taylor, L. Peplau, & S. DeBro (Eds.), *Gender, culture, and ethnicity: Current research about women and men* (pp. 336–352). Mountain View, CA, US: Mayfield Publishing Co.

Vogt, D. (2006). *Research on women, trauma and PTSD.* Women's health sciences division, National Centre for PTSD. Retrieved July 6, 2007, from http://www. ncptsd.va.gov/ncmain/ncdocs/fact_shts/fs_womenptsdprof.html?opm=1&rr=rrl76 5&srt=d&echorr=true.

White, J., Tutt, S., Rude, D., Mutwiri B., Cancino E., Ghosh, B., et al. (2000). *Post traumatic stress disorder: The lived experience of immigrant, refugee and visible minority women.* Retrieved August 2, 2007, from http://www.uwinnipeg.ca/admin/ vh_external/pwhce/pdf/postTraumaticStress.pdf .

Willging, C. (2002). Clanship and K'é: The relatedness of clinicians and patients in a Navajo counseling center. *Transcultural Psychiatry, 39*, 5 – 32.

Yellow Horse Brave Heart, M. (1998). The Return to the sacred path: Healing the historical trauma and historical unresolved grief response among the Lakota through a psycho-educational group intervention. *Smith College Studies in Social Work, 63*, 287–305.

CHAPTER 7

Considerations in Counselling Children and Adult Survivors of Childhood Traumas: Community, Context, and Intersubjective Resiliencies by Marie Lovrod

M*y work in childhood trauma studies grows out of an early community-based service project involving young people (ages 15 to 24) who were seeking to move through and beyond experiences of physical and sexual violence in their lives. While completing my master's degree in the late 80s in Kingston, Ontario, I became involved with a grassroots group who, in consultation with the wider counselling community, recognized that services and choices for youth in crisis due primarily to disclosing sexual abuse were extremely limited. We sought and received provincial funding to establish a safe housing project for youth, which was in operation for several years until a round of budget cuts reduced the program to a referral service. Recognizing gaps in my own education as I became part of a larger feminist community responding to these experiences, I began doctoral work to study the social mobilization of childhood trauma as a cultural and political phenomenon implicated in the formation of social systems and identities, in historical and contemporary contexts ranging from the intimate to the international. My initial research focussed on personal and social documentation in response to injustices that target children. Subsequent efforts to support youth empowerment have included directing a peer-centred diversity education program and supporting collaborations among youth groups from diverse communities. My current research partnership involves working with an organization made up of youth in government care and "aged out of the system" who seek to sustain peer and alumni networks, and ensure that public policy reflects their needs and voices.*

INTRODUCTION: SYMBOLIC CONSTRUCTIONS OF CHILDHOOD

Children are the living messages we send to a time we will not see.
—Neil Postman, *The Disappearance of Childhood*

Late in the unfolding of the American-Vietnam war, Nick Ut, a Vietnamese photographer working closely with Horst Faas of the Associated Press (Chong, 2006), captured the terror of violence in an image that coalesces around Kim Phuc, a young girl running naked, horror-stricken and in pain from a napalm blast of "friendly fire" that left her body scarred and in precarious health, and her family in a tenuous struggle for survival that lasted decades after the official "end" of the war. That instantly recognizable Pulitzer Prize–winning photograph remains one of a handful that still summons, in a breath, the insanity of the period for many who lived through it, however near or far from the firestorm that marked Kim Phuc's life and community with the trauma of war. It stands, more than 30 years later, as testimony to human suffering in political conflicts initiated outside the range of their impact and without accountability. It also represents what one can only hope is a growing collective abhorrence for the mindless injuries inflicted on those whose options, such as they may be, are so mercilessly scripted from elsewhere.

Denise Chong (2006) has traced the web of relationships and events leading up to and emerging from that afternoon of June 8, 1972, in her book *The Girl in the Picture: The Story of Kim Phuc, the Photograph, and the Vietnam War*. That volume, which emerged in the wake of Kim Phuc's eventual flight to Canada and her struggle to establish a new life for herself and her family, reveals the remarkable series of life-altering negotiations she undertook in childhood and as a young woman. Chong also looks at the various interpreters of the photograph and the story behind it—whether they were from allies or not. Her subsequent work as a peace ambassador speaks for itself.

Chong's (2006) text chronicles the persistent interest in Vietnam and beyond, from people who either feared that the "girl in the picture" had died in the battle or wanted to discover what had happened to her. She also narrates the pivotal acts of care and moments of trust and possibility that led to this particular girl child's medical treatment and ultimate survival into maturity. That Kim Phuc's life now includes but has always exceeded the meanings attributed to the photograph is self-evident; that the primary subject of the photograph is a terrified young girl has clearly played a substantial role in its enduring signifying power.

Chong's (2006) account of the photograph's rescue from the editorial cutting floor bears out this conjecture. Reviewing the negatives, Nick Ut appreciated the compelling nature of the image he had captured, but together with colleagues, initially rejected it because full frontal nudity was not allowed in the press at the time. In the final selection process, Horst Faas could not let the image go and printed it. Seeing the enlargement in Faas's hand, everyone present understood that this time, breaking the rules was the right thing to do. However, as Chong notes:

> Someone in the office remarked that the shadows on the girl's body gave the appearance of pubic hair where there was none. Faas called over a technician, telling him to bring his paintbox of white and grays. The technician set to work, and when he was done, there were compliments on his artistry and guffaws all around (p. 65).

That those guffaws were a response to the successful *de*-eroticization of the photograph reveals the gendered nature of the racialized international power dynamics the men were both attempting to neutralize yet had simultaneously articulated in their efforts to show, in image and text, the destructive effects of ongoing combat in civilian lives. While their "correction" evaded a misreading of the photograph's intent, it also clarified a range of possible interpretations that they were trying to narrow in order to make the image's message clear.

My purpose in recalling these historic events and in citing Chong's (2006) thoughtful and well-researched account of the multiple agendas informing them is to emphasize several key critical factors in approaches to feminist counselling around childhood trauma. First among them is the recognition that children and childhood, in ways that correspond to women's experiences under patriarchy, live in worlds where they are both living, breathing beings, and where they also operate as symbols in meta-narratives that exceed their immediate control or perhaps even full awareness at the time of inscription. Gender is clearly a formative factor in the signifying role that children occupy in any prevailing social order, and intersects with other categories of relationally constructed identities and affinities, including but not limited to race, class, ability, sexual orientation, ethnicity, and religious affiliation.

Many theorists, therapists and activists share this recognition. In *Small Worlds: Transcultural Visions of Childhood*, co-editor Davis (2001) argues that the child, with her inherent vulnerabilities, evolving perspectives, and capacity for growth operates as a compelling figure and salient signifier in many accounts of cross-cultural experience. The perceiving child who vanishes into the complex and more culturally mature and sophisticated adult can offer, by virtue of her misapprehensions and stark interpretations, uncanny insights that illuminate gaps and shifts in meaning-making practices as she learns to navigate across cultures, time, and space. As such, the remembered or imagined children in the accounts cited in *Small Worlds* recreate or represent disappearing but formative *pasts*, reworked through the interpretations of adults who revisit them, often with revised perspectives. The title of the collection is also a subtle reminder that apparent social distance or geographic proximity is no measure of the personal or collective impact of situated or culturally reproduced childhood experiences. As feminist theorists have long asserted, however atomized or individuated identity constructions may be, experiential meanings are negotiated along relational webs, the coincidental and expansive natures of which constantly vanish from view.

This attention to relational webs also informs another recent collection that considers the operations of the child in culture. In *Child Honoring*, activist and children's troubadour Cavoukian (2006) proposes that reorganizing social practices and policies for a sustainable *future* might well be grounded in political commitments that cherish and serve the potentials of children. In this case, honouring the situated child holds out a promise of better collective well-being in the wider *external* world. Meanwhile, historian Steedman (1995) has argued that one of the characteristic features of Western modernity is the adoption of the child and childhood as a symbol of the unconscious and/or human *interiority*. Making a related assertion, mental health professionals Apfel and Simon (1996) confirm that "the definition of childhood is problematic also because ... the child lives on inside the adult. That child may be a source of energy, vitality and hope, or conversely, of lethargy, apathy and despair (p. 4). Thus, the pasts and futures, interiors and exteriors that children have come to represent account for much of the political and psychic freight that attaches itself to them, as emblems of wider social effects and as survivors of trauma. All of these authors attend to the irreducible specificities of particular childhoods, while recognizing that present and remembered children bear the burdens of symbolic as well as inherent meanings and value in the cultures they inhabit and through which their lives and experiences come to be understood.

This ubiquitous social practice of projecting cultural scripts onto childhood in ways that mirror and depend upon gender norms as they intersect with other social constructions of human diversity lends support to the suggestion made by Helleiner, Caputo, and Downe (2001) that childhood and feminist studies need to be more fully integrated across a much wider range of disciplines. The imperative for a more inclusive and comprehensive understanding of how present and remembered childhood experiences are implicated in the treatment of both children and adults is made clear by the complex needs that clients bring to feminist counselling. Helleiner et al. further argue that both women and children operate in various spheres of public influence as targets *and* agents of actions and meanings, and affirm that "adult/child hierarchies articulate with other forms of oppression" (p. 135) in such a way that adults are inevitably positioned in relation to childhoods marked by social inequities.

Feminist counsellors are often called upon to navigate these complex terrains, with clients whose lives bear the marks of troubled pasts that increasingly traverse more than one cultural frame of reference, even if they may not have travelled far from their place of origin. In some cases, among refugee populations for example, access to individual supports may well depend on a wider community with limited resources or capacities to attend to the well-being of young people, particularly in ways that centre the perspectives of affected children and youth. Indeed, as Apfel and Simon (1996) point out, "most children in the world suffer from poverty, malnutrition and violence," under conditions where any "ideal for the dignity, well-being and unfolding of the full potential of the child" (p. 6) may be compromised by political economies that both exploit and devalue children's contributions. Even in sites where the violence of global economics and political strife has not reduced possibilities for children so profoundly, other forms of adult betrayal have similar effects. Following Berman and Jiwani (2002), Hussein et al. (2006) point out that in respect to North American childhoods "a continuum of violence exists in the lives of girls, linking individual lived realities to systematic institutional structures" (p. 56). In reference specifically to child sexual abuse, Heiman and Heard-Davison (2002) suggest that "we would benefit from more details about how ... abuse might interact with ethnicity to produce different sexual health and relational outcomes" (p. 39). Sensitivities to the imbrications of socio-cultural contexts with childhood's symbolic valences is crucial to successful counselling among children, youth, and adults who have endured traumatic childhood experiences, whether acute or "insidious" (Root, 1992).

Clearly, one of the recurring effects of children's function as symbols, both in the world and in the realms of adult imagination and memory, is that the needs of children and youth themselves can be obscured by habits of reductive interpretation and constraints upon social resources that impact the invisibility of childhood traumas and therefore how children and young people are seen and view themselves. This is familiar ground for feminist therapists. Drawing on the accumulating evidence from women's collaborative efforts to liberate themselves from cruel double binds, feminist counsellors can mobilize growing expertise about practical measures in therapy that challenge social processes of overdetermination as they play out in the remarkable levels of societal violence that conditions gender "training" in multiple contexts. The feminist counselling session, then, can make use of literal and symbolic materials both drawn from the client's own past and possessions and brought to the encounter by the therapist to create more flexible and life-affirming meanings for the trauma survivor.

That childhood is itself a ground of contested meanings, no less for the child herself than for her cultural surround, or for the adult who remembers, in no way diminishes the embodied personal experience of traumatic life events and conditions, and the need to find empowered ways to engage with them for healing. Nor does it negate the role of community in establishing possibilities for resiliencies and post-traumatic growth (Malchiodi, Steele, & Kuban, 2008). Understanding more about how children and young people experience the world as they grow up, and how the social surround places children in relation to one another and the existing societal infrastructure, is vital to helping children, youth, and women sort through and find empowered meaning as they redirect their energies toward more viable futures than those bound up in the limitations imposed by childhood trauma.

According to Steedman (1995), one of the ways childhood as a category of experience has been established in the West, beginning in the early nineteenth century, is through segregation of children into peer groups for education and social indoctrination based on age cohort and, therefore, expected mental and corporeal processes of development. With this shift in social organization of children came "child psychology, developmental linguistics and anthropometry" (Steedman, p. 7) as professions concerned with measuring the standardized growth of children. The adoption of developmental models of childhood in the West has been extrapolated to discourses on development of the nation-state and to the "infantilization of so-called primitive cultures" (Aitken, Lund, & KjØrholt, 2008), which necessarily has profound political effects on the life trajectories of individual children and their communities. Thus, in its affiliations with and resistances to its antecedents, feminist counselling as a profession is implicated in the construction of meanings that accrue to childhoods, and can participate in unpacking the metaphoric freight that infringes on the idiosyncratic and nuanced (Walkerdine, 1984) unfoldings of particular childhoods and their interpretations. James (2000) points out that because "childhood is commonly envisaged as the literal embodiment of change over time" (p. 23), children have come to represent personal pasts and collective futures, in fields that range from personal recovery to social policy. She clarifies, however, that children are also capable of making interventions in the ways their bodies are read as signs by peers and others in the cultural surround.

EMBODIED CHILDHOOD EXPERIENCE AND THE "PLURAL BODY"

There is nothing natural or a priori about these modes of corporeal inscriptions ... through them, bodies are marked so as to make them amenable to prevailing exigencies of power.
—E. Grosz, "Inscriptions and Body Maps, Representations and the Corporeal"

Attending to the specificities of experiences of childhood embodiment and growth is central to the feminist therapeutic project, and to the recognition and affirmation of the agency and formative cognitions, adaptive or otherwise, that children develop in relation to the troubling experiences that bring them, perhaps as children, perhaps as adults, to feminist counselling. Remaining aware of and present to the embodied experience of childhood in the counselling session remains a potential resource in unseating social scripts and reductive interpretations that evacuate children of self-generated meaning.

Christensen (2000) makes the profound point that while adults ascribe particular readings, notably of vulnerability and innocence, to children's bodies and thereby shape their own and children's self-images and potentials, children themselves experience their bodies in much more fluid and less superficial or metaphorically demarcated ways. She cites Frankenberg (1990), who attributes to adults the perception of a bounded and objectified "somatic" body, and to children an experience of what he terms the "incarnate" body described as

> a unity of past, present and future simultaneously experi-
> enced from inside and outside.... The perspective of the
> incarnate body lacks boundaries in both time and space
> and is permeable to the world (Frankenberg, p. 358).

Psychoanalysis posits a similar view of early childhood experience, assuming a necessary disjuncture between child and adult perceptual frames, often attributed to the operations of language, as built into the processes of growing up. For many, the transition between polymorphic incarnate experience and the parsing of the world through linguistic and other social structures operates relatively smoothly, as the child reorients to a more collectively shared world view. However, when trauma intervenes, exceeding received frames of reference (Felman & Laub, 1992), the difference between personal experience and social interpretation becomes too great, and social incoherence (Lynn, Pinter, Fite, & Stafford, 2004) can result. Davoine and Guidilliere (2004) suggest that disastrous experience creates internalization of a reductive symbolic, with signifying chains that reinforce negative interpretations and reduced possibilities for the trauma survivor herself and her sense of the world around her:

> Every catastrophe in the social order, domestic or
> organic, sets in motion a loss of trust, limited or radical,
> in the safety of the laws governing men, the universe or
> the body. Otherness undergoes an abrupt change of states.
> From guarantor of the good faith from which issue speech

> and the permanence of physical laws, the other becomes
> a surface of signs and forms to be deciphered against a
> background of devalued words (p. 64).

The experience of being bodily reduced to a target of violence or shame has the potential effect of simultaneously reducing the survivor's world view, in what Scarry (1985) has termed "the unmaking of the world," through physical and psychic pain. Part of the therapeutic task, then, is to support the client as she bridges the metaphoric frames that have undermined her well-being and sense of competence in the world, and through which she has been reduced and thereby driven to reduce others to symbols, as well. By valuing memories implicit in the experience of the body incarnate, children, youth, and adults can learn to engage fixed or intrusive traumatic memories more intersubjectively and creatively.

Christensen (2000) goes on to explain that children experience immanence through the incarnate body as temporally, spatially, and socially situated. She points out that when young children are hurt, and you ask them where, they will often identify a spatialized site of injury beyond themselves, such as the swing or the sandbox, rather than pointing to their wound. This occurs because the place in the world where their mobile body met with the immovable object, or vice versa, strikes children as the site of inflicted pain. No doubt, there are adaptive functions to this form of cognition. Small bodies need to avoid dangerous places.

Children also interpret wellness in terms of being able to do what they are accustomed or expected to, in age cohort. For children, being and doing are mutually and deeply contextual. Davoine and Guadilliere (2004) take this experience of spatio-temporal embeddedness further and point out that young children may also experience transitivism, which is the tendency to feel with another. Thus, when one child witnesses another being hit, she may cry herself. Perhaps it is this remembered capacity to feel with another child that created such public identification with Kim Phuc's pain. For some adults, though, as Christensen (2000) argues, feelings of tenderness toward children when they are constructed as victims "confirm adult power" (p. 42).

Because a child's experience of self exceeds the objectified somatic body, within a situated embodiment that depends on contextual interpretations, the early capacity for transitivism can be a resource for healing in the case of childhood trauma. Several theorists remark upon the need for a shared response to psychic and embodied pain. Davoine and Gaudilliere (2004) suggest that, in the case of traumatic experience, "[o]nly a plural body can support such knowledge" (p. 230). Feminist counsellors draw on this recognition to support their client's need for shared understanding, both in the therapy session and in the wider world, where the traumatized child or adult survivor needs to reinvigorate her web of social relationships with a sense of safety and connection, and with a realistic estimate of the dangers she will inevitably encounter as triggers to possible traumatic responses.

This point—that healing from traumatic experience requires plural relational containment—is brought home by a return to the image with which this discussion opened. In fact, Kim Phuc is not alone in the famous photograph. Her elder brother is in the foreground of the frame, equally terrified and running for his life. There are also several other children close behind her, and one being carried by two of five men dressed in combat fatigues, bringing up the rear as they escort the group of distressed children away from the dust and smoke billowing out behind them. Whatever symbolic meanings have been attached to her image at the time of its publication and since, even within the frame of the photograph, Kim Phuc's pain is visibly contextualized in family, community, and international relationships. Ultimately, she would renegotiate all of these connections and develop revised personal and publically shared interpretive frames as she consistently worked to expand her life's possibilities (Chong, 2006).

Because of the terrible burns she endured, Kim Phuc's sensory responses to heat and cold were affected in such a way that sudden onset of pain, itching, or sensations of extreme temperatures (Chong, 2006) demanded that she be willing to call on others to massage her back, to provide water or ice, or to be present to other intrusive discomforts. She also had to learn that she was not automatically excluded from romantic companionship or marriage by her embodied disfigurement. Kim Phuc's mother, whose tireless work in the noodle shop she operated kept her large family alive through a series of brutal regime changes, was concerned for her daughter's future and encouraged her to pursue schooling or become a religious novitiate as a way to secure financial independence and survival (Chong). For the woman whose gender role required the unceasing labour that forms a relentless backdrop to this story, Kim's chances of marriage seemed slight because she could not perform the demanding physical work expected of women of her social stratum. It was not until Kim went to Cuba to continue her education that she encountered the possibility that her strength of character and lovely features and ways could still be recognized as deserving of love (Chong). She learned this lesson from her young Cuban roommate, whose extended family of women immediately took Kim under their wing. In crossing cultures, Kim had traversed multiple sets of gendered expectations. She thus came to recognize their constructed nature, so that she could begin to imagine new futures for herself as a young woman whose life exceeded her injury and the inscriptions that her gender training and the press photo impressed upon it. Shortly after coming to Cuba, she met her future life partner.

This awareness of gender as a social construction, derived through peer and intergenerational relationships with a number of women in Kim Phuc's life, illustrates a significant insight for feminist therapy and provides an example of what Surrey (1991) has termed "connected learning" (p. 171). Although not formalized through a publically organized structure, Kim's capacity to learn through her relationships with other women demonstrates a significant resource in constructing therapeutic opportunities to reframe traumatic experience.

As the legacy of the photograph of her childhood distress demonstrates, Kim's capacity to navigate world views was honed in the cross-cultural conflagration of war. In order to survive, adults in her family were required to engage with American and South Vietnamese soldiers by day and the Viet Cong by night, being sure to alienate no one (Chong, 2006). Eventually, Kim would revise her spiritual affiliations, instinctively choosing a faith orientation that would affirm her conflicted feelings about the communist regime that came into power in the region when the Americans left and prepare her for a life far from her home village of Trang Bang (Chong). The new regime exploited Kim Phuc's notoriety terribly, removing her from the medical training she had long dreamed of—and which they touted as her new direction in life—in order to force her compliance in falsified interviews with journalists from both sides of the cold war, in an effort to glorify themselves (Chong). Showing determined resilience, Kim repeatedly reached out to various officials to intervene in this disruption of her education and abuse of her integrity, until she eventually succeeded in being sent to Cuba for language training.

Although driven deep into herself by the very particular experiences of physical, psychic, and social pain she endured, as time went on, Kim Phuc began to recognize her anguish as shared by other children who had suffered in the war and started to mobilize from her position as "the girl in the picture" to be an active voice for peace. In an experience in which technology operated like a recovered memory, she had the opportunity to view an archival film clip of the moment that was captured "in the picture." By the time she reached adulthood, the family's copy of the image that had made world news had been lost to the contingencies of war, along with her medical records from the Barsky burn unit, where she had spent six months recovering from her wounds and subsequent surgery (Chong, 2006). Thus, when NBC's Arthur Lord offered to show her a newsreel of that fateful afternoon, she agreed, and found herself thrown back into a newly relational sense of the pain the photograph depicted.

As the film clip unwound, she saw her grandmother run by, carrying in her arms a beloved cousin, Danh, a three-year-old boy whose burns were so extensive he did not survive. In an on-the-spot, temporally unbounded reconstruction of childhood transitivism, Kim answers her grandmother's cry to her lost cousin, "Chay did au nhu vay ne troi?" (Why didn't you run from the fire?):

In his place, Kim replies, "No, Grandma, I could not run out of the fire, not with my heels burned like that" (Chong, 2006, p. 246). Until the moment of viewing the film, Kim had been spared the vision of her grandmother's distress and her cousin's charred young body. But the moment now revealed to her why so many people identified with her image: "I know I am not the only victim of the war, but others don't have the evidence. I have the film. I have the picture, I have the body" (Chong, p. 246). Thus, Kim translated her own embodied experience into a transitive and temporally fluid frame of reference where she understood herself to experience her own pain and to connect with the pain of other children who had endured similar effects of war; she could also appreciate the invisible bonds that people who were strangers felt with her.

Of course, children were not the only ones who identified with Kim Phuc's image and the painful past it has come to represent. Adults who had been nearby, and who had been involved in the rescue of other children, often mistakenly thought that they had been the ones, to airlift Kim to safety. In fact, it was Nick Ut who brought her to Saigon, together with another wounded woman and child, in the Associated Press van (Chong, 2006). Several doctors believed that they had performed the surgery on Kim's wounds; there were so many children badly injured at the time.

The poignant case of the doctor who actually performed that surgery recalls the gender training of Kim Phuc's mother, whose life was a round of gender-scripted labour in support of her husband and children. Dr. My, who responded to nurse Lien Huong's insistence that the injured girl not be left to die, permitted American doctors to claim responsibility for her life-saving surgery because she "did not want the limelight and did not think it her role to disabuse Kim Phuc of the belief that foreigners were the ones who had helped her" (Chong, 2006). Amidst such self-effacing gender training, Kim's experience of being catapulted into the public eye of the world stage was truly remarkable, and would necessarily situate her experience in revised gender and power relations.

Kim Phuc's transformative experience of transitivism on viewing the archival film clip recalls her mother's sense of connection to the moment in the photograph, even though she was not on the scene at the time. Tung, Kim's father, brought the image home and showed it to her mother, Nu:

> Nu cried until she thought she would go blind. They put it away in a drawer of an armoire. Tung would find he could go for ten days, maybe fifteen, before he was drawn back to the image. Less often, Nu felt the same need to gaze upon it. When she did, she would ask her husband to retrieve it so that he might sit beside her as her tears flowed (Chong, 2006, p. 88).

The unresolved memories—whether through Kim's own experience of speaking for her lost cousin, her resulting identification with other trauma survivors, or her mother and father's need to revisit the image of her experience of injury—come to be shared in a "plural body," in part because it takes more than one life to contain the feelings or to understand the complex webs of relations implicated in traumatic experiences.

This account of one set of situated experiences, based in a surviving vestige of childhood transitivism, helps to explain the occurrence of both secondary and intergenerational trauma. While adults understand themselves to occupy a "somatic" body, the childhood experience of the "incarnate" body remains alive within them and is necessary to summon experiences of a "plural body" and to apprehend trauma's "address beyond itself" (Caruth, 1995, p. 11) toward future resolution and healing.

As Danieli (1998) argues in summarizing the import of the geographically dispersed and thoroughly researched cases informing the *International Handbook on Multigenerational Trauma*, there is a "solid clinical, theoretical, and empirical basis for understanding the multigenerational legacy of trauma [which] strongly suggests that it is a universal phenomenon" (p. 669). Within the same volume, Duran, Duran, Yellow Horse Brave Heart, and Yellow Horse-Davis (1998) describe the need for plural and culturally appropriate containment among Indigenous survivors of the intergenerational traumas inflicted by colonialism. They describe the effects of imperialist expansion on Indigenous peoples as a "soul wound" (p. 341). This concept reflects the perspectives of Indigenous heritages, and according to Duran et al., has been taking hold in healing responses "all over Indian country" (p. 352). They argue that this individually articulated but collectively held wound responds best to treatments grounded in "indigenous epistemology as the root metaphor for theoretical and clinical implementation" (p. 350) in part because of the misinterpretations Indigenous cultures have endured under colonialism. That transitivism or childhood experiences of plural embodiment might pose a partial explanation for the universal existence of intergenerational trauma remains consistent with the need for culturally appropriate and sensitive treatment models, because the life world of a child and her community are co-extensive and provide the first line of explanatory power in negotiating the abuses of power that inevitably characterize interpersonal and inter-communal trauma.

This does not mean that traumatic experiences cannot be understood among cross-cultural plural bodies, as Kim Phuc's experience clearly demonstrates. In fact, Duran et al. (1998) also show that the specifically Indigenous form of transitive healing they describe is related to "a similar phenomenon, *transposition* ... observed among Jewish Holocaust descendants, where the past is simultaneously experienced with the present reality" (Kestenberg, 1990).

Childhood incarnate embodiment, with its conceptual capacity to extend through time and space, provides an important context for imagining healing in feminist counselling and for understanding trauma's address to the future. Further, connected cross-cultural learning can provide invaluable insights into trauma's intergenerational and therefore plural body, if grounded in mutual respect that recognizes contemporary traces of historical traumas in the lives of subsequent generations.

CHILDHOOD TRAUMA AND THE ROLE OF BRAIN DEVELOPMENT IN ADAPTIVE THERAPIES

Children, everybody, here's what to do.... In a time of destruction, create something. A poem. A parade. A friendship. A community. A place that is the commons. A school. A vow. A moral principle. One peaceful moment.
—M.H. Kingston, *The Fifth Book of Peace*

If transitivism and transposition, as adaptive responses to trauma, are themselves effects of childhood embodiments and the need to communicate traumatic experiences, then brain development is also implicated. Because they are still growing, children's brains register experience differently than adults and store memories in ways that render creative and solution-focussed therapies more effective in response to childhood traumas. In fact, the neurosciences claim that because children's and indeed adults' brains continue forming across the life course, embodied/emotional/ contextual/material memories may require plural body engagements to sustain recall, implicitly suggesting that collective investments in healing of trauma are called for.

Karr-Morse and Wiley (1997) have reviewed a wide range of studies demonstrating that violence and neglect in childhood have marked effects on brain, and therefore social, development. Their work suggests that early investment in prosocial child development promises greater returns on social spending than criminalization of young adults and of untreated trauma survivors as social offenders. Thus, they affirm the adaptive role of transitivism in childhood and argue, in step with feminist theorists, that

> [i]n spite of our preoccupation with independence, autonomy, and self-reliance, we are born dependent on others, and we continue to need others emotionally at every stage of development. The capacity to maintain our baby desire to communicate who we are emotionally and to read this in other people is essential for healthy

184

> adult functioning with families, at school, at work, and at
> play. Emotional connections between individuals are the
> linchpin of any community's ability to maintain prosocial
> behavior, and the growing absence of those connections
> is reflected in social incompetence, estrangement, men-
> tal illness, and violence (p. 295).

Clearly, their research review implies that the feminist project of counselling women and children recovering from childhood traumas has a profound role to play in ameliorative social change.

Seigel and Hartzell (2003) suggest that in childhood brain development, experience-dependent emotive connectors that account for early transitivism and transposition evolve and are eventually "pruned" to form adaptive neurological maps of likely social formations in adolescence. These emotive connectors are precursors of and necessary to the formation of constructive communicative pathways in the brain. They go on to suggest that integration of brain functions is necessary to prosocial evolution in the growing child and maturing adult and that "[t]rauma may impair the prefrontal region's capacity for neural integration, which is fundamental to emotional recovery from traumatic events" (p. 180). According to Gussie Klorer (2008), "traumatic memories are stored in the right hemisphere, making verbal declarative memory of the trauma more difficult" (p. 43).

This, in part, is why Campbell (2003) argues for "relational remembering," based on social investments in collaborative memory. Especially in cases of systemic violence, which seeks to obscure itself behind both idealized projections and historical erasures, memory requires community. Putting this insight in another way, Rogers (2007) suggests that "the child represses what can't be received" (p. 199) in the cultural lexicons and assumptions informing the social surround. In light of this awareness, Campbell argues for an "ethics of attention" that begins with respect for rememberers of childhood pain. Rather than targeting trauma survivors with charges of "false memory" at the first blush of any imprecision in their articulations of their experiences (as has been common in cases of child sexual abuse in the West), such an ethical view operates from interdependent trust. It assumes that the trauma survivor has something important to communicate about her experience, which is relevant to everyone. Thus, a self-in-relation approach to counselling trauma survivors helps to flesh out their memories, much like reviewing the film clip did for Kim Phuc.

Indeed, as Chong's (2006) fully authorized biography so deftly illustrates, coming to understand something about how "the girl in the picture" came to be there and what she has made of her life required not only building trust with

Kim Phuc herself, "who had escaped from a communist regime where self-censorship is ingrained as a matter of self-preservation, insinuating itself even into private thoughts" (Chong, p. 343); it also demanded extensive research into political motivations and strategic organizational processes operating on both sides of the conflict in which she was caught. Sharing the insight that trauma and healing are inevitably relational, Lynn et al. (2002) affirm that "the recognition that personal tragedy reflects larger social issues is a key insight for abuse survivors. It means they no longer have to inhabit their traumatic world alone" (p. 176). Socially contextualized work with trauma survivors relocates their pain in ways that affirm agency and enable recognition of how each person, traumatized or not, can mobilize toward interpersonal and collective healing in the daily acts of care and respect that fall to whatever social position she or he occupies.

Building on analyses from the neurosciences that clarify how long-term traumatic experience interrupts communicative brain functions and development, Gussie Klorer (2008) observes that

> [u]nfortunately, one does not have to go to a Romanian orphanage or look to Vietnam War veterans to study the effects of long-term trauma. The trauma histories of some children in the foster care system ... are akin to torture.... Although some children with histories such as these have a compulsion to tell their story, more often they do not. Those for whom the abuse has gone on for a long time often *cannot* (p. 52).

In such cases, mobilizing creative therapies and client-centred and derived rituals has been found to be particularly effective, both in accessing and reinterpreting traumatic memories among children and in adults who remember childhood violence.

Rogers's (2007) therapeutic work with a child sexual abuse and intergenerational Holocaust survivor, whom she names "Ellen," draws on artistic representation and creative word play over a period of several years to access unconscious memories and interpretations that ultimately bring the relationships between sexual abuse by an outsider and a repressed family history of war trauma out into the open. Ellen experiences both psychic and social pain and withdrawal at times during the course of her treatment, together with embodied symptoms, such as "head aches, sleepwalking [and] nightmares" (p. 200). Rogers and Ellen work together to find ways to read such messages, operating as a duo of sleuths whose relationship provides a plural container for them. As Rogers clarifies, "[e]ach symptom is the body's attempt to speak what can't be known or said. The body is versatile in terms of creating symptoms because the unconscious will insist on being heard" (p. 201).

Following Lacan's (1966) assertion in *Écrits* that "the unconscious is structured like a language", Rogers (2007) comes to understand all of the elements of her creative work with Ellen as constituting a unique lexicon reflecting her client's relational milieu and her efforts to articulate her experiences of that life world. While the sexual trauma that had been repeated each generation since its brutal emergence in the Holocaust is potentially devastating to Ellen and her family, this young woman regularly demonstrates a brilliant resilience during the course of her counselling. She takes time out from her trauma work to practice developing friendships, together with engaging the adolescent risks that were scripted by her repressed family history. Ultimately, as the traumatic history she has been struggling with reaches greater visibility in the family and therefore moves toward resolution, Ellen reaches for creative expression beyond words when she takes up the cello, with its haunting sound and ranges of emotive expression. She eventually learns, as did Kim Phuc, that intimate relationships are possible and survivable, and that a life beyond trauma can be created as the story finds containment in a wider circle of responsive relations. Ellen's final contact with Rogers, at the time of writing, included her review of Rogers's account of the case, prior to publication. Ellen wrote from her college across country, where she was thriving.

Pennebaker and Stone (2004) also explore the power of "translating traumatic experiences into language" in an article that traces the "implications for child abuse and long term health" (p. 201). They found that by simply providing college students with opportunities to write about traumatic experiences for a mere 30 minutes, they could trace measurable improvements in health outcomes, particularly when students included "copious use of positive emotion words, a moderate use of negative emotion words, and an increase in the use of insight and causal words" (p. 213). The results of this research clearly indicate the communicative need that underlies traumatic experience and demonstrate that, on some level, trauma's effects, as represented by the negative wording, can be interlaced with resilience, as represented by the positive wording and indications of explanatory discernment. Too few negative words correlated with reduced health benefits, perhaps an indication of denial of trauma's impact.

Where memory is pre-verbal, however, non-verbal approaches have proven highly successful. As Rogers (2007) demonstrates in her work with Ellen, drawing and other creative modalities such as musical or dramatic expression has the built-in benefit of eschewing any pressure to tell a story that the child or remembering young woman or adult may not be ready or able to share, while leaving the intuitive right brain free to choose its mode of articulation. Creative play enables children and remembering adults to externalize pre- or non-verbal memories and may facilitate resilience and post-traumatic growth.

MAPPING INTERSUBJECTIVE RESILIENCES AND BALANCED STRATEGIES FOR SOCIAL HEALING

She had exercised the art of unfolding the creases of time in which the horrors of men try to escape the gaze of children, generation after generation.
—F. Davoine and J.M. Gaudilliere, *History beyond Trauma*

Apfel and Simon (2004) appreciate the resources and intersubjective resiliencies that children bring to and develop in response to traumatic experiences. They identify "'salutogenic,' or health promoting forces as well as 'pathogenic' or destructive ones" (p. 1) that emerge in the intersubjective possibilities mobilized by traumatic situations. Grossman, Cook, Kepkek, and Koenen (1999) expand on this point, arguing that risk and resiliency always occur in social context. They affirm that constructions of trauma and resiliency as separate or global concepts are "not as useful as an appreciation of multiple domains of both competence and risk" (p. 9). Garbarino and Kostelney (1996) concur that for childhood trauma survivors, "risk accumulates; opportunity ameliorates" (p. 45). They argue that the "quest for meaning in a seemingly arbitrary and utterly cruel world [helps] to sustain them at critical junctures" (p. 36).

Grossman et al. (1999) provide evidence of interwoven potentials for competencies and relapse in their interviews with 10 resilient women survivors of child sexual abuse. They identify several crucial future-oriented coping mechanisms among participants, including excelling in school as a way to escape the abuse at home; the capacity to recognize that there is something "wrong" with the family situation (p. 59); a willingness, when possible and where suitable boundaries can be held, to maintain ties with family members; and an intuitive ability to choose educational opportunities that would help them with recovery, sometimes prior to traumatic recall, or beginning treatment.

Kim Phuc demonstrated all of these adaptive capacities in relation to the traumatic events of the American-Vietnam war. She continually sought to find meaning in her experiences, and recognized that their willful misrepresentation for the world media was wrong. Nevertheless, she worked within the corrupt system in which she found herself to obtain a way out. She also used every opportunity for travel and education to imagine new possibilities for her future, and seized any chances that came her way. Thus, the risks she took contributed to her resiliency and the growing explanatory power she could bring to bear on her experiences. As Shohat (2002) has argued, constructive and participatory action itself can be a form of theorizing in contexts of political dominance.

Kim Phuc's escape from the narrow confines that the famous picture might have reduced her life to illustrates how constructive actions she and others undertook led to expanded possibilities, not only for Kim, but for the many people whose lives she has touched since her image was first beamed around the world. Repeatedly, danger loomed, and repeatedly, Kim instinctively reached for new ways to resist revictimization. Because early traumatic experiences lie in wait in the psyche, lingering for an opportunity to integrate greater understanding of what has happened, the development of contingent capacities for constructive agency are vital to survival. Lynn et al. (2004) argue that

> [f]rom the social-narrative perspective, the goal of intervention is to help abuse survivors achieve social coherence before they find themselves as victimized once again. They accomplish this, not by attempting to gain mastery over historic events, but by recognizing the persistent traumas of the present. Those at risk of revictimization will have to find active ways to protect themselves from current and future threats, not by narrating danger away, but by acknowledging and responding to it in concrete ways (p. 175).

Sometimes, experiences of childhood trauma are so demanding in their capacities to overwhelm circuits of meaning that they may foreclose a sense of future possibility for the survivor. For this reason, it is important that diagnostic labels not function to diminish clients to symbols of their disease, repeating the reductive readings that cultures impose on children in the first place. As Lamb (1999) points out, "[s]ick girls can't fight back; empowered girls can" (p. 139). In this regard, it is useful for feminist clinicians to keep in mind that their own lexicons are culturally and historically situated, and constantly evolving. To subvert any labelling effect, affirming the client's own perceptions of her situation, while integrating a present and future-oriented sensibility within processes of diagnosis and memory recovery, can work to expand even the smallest potentials for improvement and healing or signs of it in the contemporary moment.

Dolan (1991) outlines a wide range of solution-oriented therapeutic practices for resolving sexual abuse in particular, although the models she describes translate well across other traumas also. Approaches she affirms include but are not limited to the following: borrowing an integrated vision of self and one's potential from a trustworthy or imagined other; drawing on or beginning to imagine supportive relationships; learning to externalize markers of safety by identifying subjectively meaningful cues of risk and security; recognizing traumatic patterns and "doing something different" (p. 97); finding ways to contain and utilize dissociation constructively; and learning to recognize relapse triggers. These open-ended tools for engaging with traumatic memories and experiences help to reduce their intrusive power and stabilize a sense of competency that protects against relapse.

Building on the power of collective remembering, feminist therapy can sometimes translate the isolation of traumatic experiences into social activism for some clients, particularly for youth and adult trauma survivors. However, some caveats are important to keep in mind in relation to this possibility. As Cvetkovich (2003) argues, "activism itself can be traumatic because of its emotional intensities and disappointments" (p. 451). Keeping expectations manageable is an important function in a feminist counsellor's responses to her own and client commitments to activism. While Greene (1996) points out that youth, especially, can benefit from "an ongoing structured setting in which the young people can talk to one another about their feelings and thoughts" (p. 140), it is also a matter of respect for their integrity that children's survival needs not be appropriated to political ends which are not their own, as Kim Phuc's were by the local regime.

Efforts to repair the world need to be balanced with needs for personal well-being, a practice that feminist therapists themselves can model in relation to their own exposure to secondary trauma, if they are overworked. As Spelman (2002) has argued, repair comes in many forms and travels along the same multidimensional webs of relational meaning that traumatic disruption does. In the end, as Rorty (1989) points out, "[s]olidarity is not achieved by inquiry but by imagination, the imaginative ability to see strange people as fellow sufferers" (xvi). Here, perhaps, Kim Phuc's story converges with those of the people who have identified with her image, and with the project of feminist counselling.

More than simply a form of inquiry, feminist counselling mobilizes the creative ability to imagine healing in constructive community, based on symbolic, embodied, and cognitive creative strategies for negotiating the imbrications of trauma and resilience. It operates as a beacon of hope in environments that so often fail to prioritize and meet the needs of women and children. The Barsky unit, where Kim Phuc received the medical care that ensured her survival, served 1200 burn victims annually over a period of six years, in a context where there were at least 100,000 known to be in need of treatment (Chong, 2006). Similarly, as Carney (2008) summarizes, in Chicago where the Coalition for the Homeless estimates some 15,000 itinerant youth, 6000 of whom identify as queer, there are 100 youth-designated beds in shelters. These points of reference could be multiplied across a myriad of contexts in which feminist counsellors work. They demonstrate that contemporary social systems conspire to manufacture childhood traumas by valuing "power over" at the expense of "power to" and allocating shared resources accordingly. Feminist counsellors work together with clients and their shared communities to repair the conceptual foundations of such a fractured world, in efforts to tip the balance toward peace and possibility, one recovered moment of socially radiating survival and healing at a time.

REFERENCES

Aitken, S., Lund, R. & KjØrholt, A.T. (Eds.). (2008). *Global childhoods: Globalization, development and young people.* New York: Routledge.

Apfel, R.J. & Simon, B. (Eds.). (1996). Introduction. *Minefields in their hearts: The mental health of children in war and communal violence.* New Haven, CT: Yale University Press.

Berman, H., & Jiwani, Y. (2002). In the best interest of the girl child: Phase II report. The Alliance of Five Research Centres on Violence.

Campbell, S. (2003). *Relational remembering: Rethinking the memory wars.* Lanham, MD: Rowman and Littlefield Publishers.

Carney, M. (2008). Creating a forum: LGBTQ youth and the Home Project in Chicago. In R. Solinger, M. Fox, & K. Irani (Eds.), *Telling stories to change the world: Global voices on the power of narrative to build community and make social justice claims* (pp. 183–192). New York: Routledge.

Caruth, C. (1995). Trauma and experience. In C. Caruth (Ed.), *Trauma: Explorations in memory* (pp. 3–12). Baltimore & London: The Johns Hopkins University Press.

Cavoukian, R. (2006). Introduction: The case for child honoring. In R. Cavoukian & S. Olfman (Eds.), *Child honoring* (pp. xv–xxiii). Westport, CT: Praeger Publishers.

Chong, D. (2006). *The girl in the picture: The story of Kim Phuc, the photograph and the Vietnam War.* Toronto: Penguin.

Christensen, P. H. (2000). Childhood and the cultural constitution of vulnerable bodies. In A. Prout (Ed.), *The body, childhood and society* (pp. 38–59). New York: Saint Martin's Press

Cvetkovich, A. (2003). Legacies of trauma: Legacies of activism. In D.L. Eng & D. Kazanjian (Eds.), *Loss: The politics of mourning* (pp. 427–457). Berkeley: University of California Press.

Danieli, Y. (1998). Conclusions and future directions. In Y. Danieli (Ed.), *International handbook of multigenerational legacies of trauma: The Plenum Series on stress and coping* (pp. 669–686). New York: Plenum Press.

Davis, R.G., & Baena, R. (Eds.). (2001). *Small worlds: Transcultural visions of childhood.* Pamplona: Ediciones Universidad de Navarra (EUNSA).

Davoine, F., & Gaudilliere, J.M. (2004). *History beyond trauma*. New York: Other Press.

Dolan, Y.M. (1991). *Resolving sexual abuse: Solution-focused therapy and Ericksonian hypnosis for adult survivors*. New York, London: W.W. Norton & Co.

Duran, E., Duran B., Yellow Horse Brave Heart, M., & Yellow Horse-Davis, S. (1998). Healing the American Indian soul wound. In Y. Danieli (Ed.), *International handbook of multigenerational legacies of trauma: The Plenum Series on stress and coping* (pp. 341–354). New York: Plenum Press.

Felman, S., & Laub, D. (1992). *Testimony: Crisis of witnessing in literature, psychoanalysis and history*. New York, London: Routledge.

Frankenberg, R. (1990). Disease, literature and the body in the era of AIDS – a preliminary exploration. *Sociology of Health and Illness, 12*(3), 351 – 360.

Garbarino, J., & Kostelney, K. (1996). What do we need to know to understand children in war and community violence? In R.J. Apfel & B. Simon (Eds.), *Minefields in their hearts: The mental health of children in war and communal violence* (pp. 33–51). New Haven, CT: Yale University Press.

Greene, M.B. (1996). Youth and violence: Trends, principles, and programmatic interventions. In R.J. Apfel & B. Simon (Eds.), *Minefields in their hearts: The mental health of children in war and communal violence* (pp. 128–148). New Haven, CT: Yale University Press.

Grossman, F.K., Cook, A.B., Kepkep, S. & Koenen, K.C. (1999). *With the Phoenix rising: Lessons from ten resilient women who overcame the trauma of childhood sexual abuse*. San Francisco: Jossey-Base Publishers.

Grosz, E. (1990). Inscriptions and body maps, representations and the corporeal. In T. Threadgold & A. Cranny Francis (Eds.), *Feminine, masculine and representation* (pp. 62–74). Sydney: Allen & Unwin.

Gussie Klorer, P. (2008). Severe maltreatment and attachment disorders. In C. Malchiodi (Ed.), *Creative interventions with traumatized children* (pp. 43–61). New York, London: The Guildford Press.

Heiman, J.R., & Heard-Davison, A.R. (2004). Child sexual abuse and adult sexual relationships: Review and perspective. In L.J. Koenig, L.S. Doll, A. O'Leary, & W. Pequegnqat (Eds.), *From child sexual abuse to adult sexual risk: Trauma, revictimization and intervention* (pp. 13–39). Washington, DC: American Psychological Association.

Helleiner, J., Caputo, V., & Downe, P. (2001). Anthropology, feminism and childhood studies. *Anthropologica: Journal of the Canadian Anthropological Society, 43*(2), 135–141.

Herman, J.L. (1992). *Trauma and recovery: The aftermath of violence from domestic abuse to political terror*. United States: Basic Books.

Hussein, Y., Berman, H., Lougheed-Smith, R., Poletti, R., Ladha, A., Ward, A., & MacQuarrie, B. (2006). Violence in the lives of girls in Canada: Creating spaces of understanding and change. In Y. Jiwani, C. Steenbergen, & C. Mitchell (Eds.), *Girlhood: Redefining the limits* (pp. 53–69). Montreal: Black Rose Books.

James, A. (2000). Embodied being(s): Understanding the self and the body in childhood. In A. Prout (Ed.), *The body, childhood and society* (pp. 19–37). New York: Saint Martin's Press.

Karr-Morse, R., & Wiley. M. (1997). *Ghosts from the nursery: Tracing the roots of violence.* New York: The Atlantic Monthly Press.

Kestenberg, J.S. (1990). A metapsychological assessment based on an analysis of a survivor's child. In M.S. Bergmann & M.E. Jucovy (Eds.), *Generations of the Holocaust.* (pp. 137–158). New York: Columbia University Press.

Kingston, M.H. (2003). *The fifth book of peace.* New York: Vintage Books.

Lacan, J. (1966). The agency of the letter in the unconscious or reason since Freud. *Écrits.* Paris: Aux Editions de Seuil: 161–197.

Lamb, S. (1999). Constructing the victim: Popular images and lasting labels. In S. Lamb (Ed.), *New versions of victims: Feminists struggle with the concept* (pp. 108–138). New York: NYU Press.

Lynn, S.J., Pinter, J., Fite, K.E., & Stafford, J. (2004). Toward a social narrative model of revictimization. In L.J. Koenig, L.S., Doll, A. O'Leary, & W. Pequegnqat (Eds.), *From child sexual abuse to adult sexual risk: Trauma, revictimization and intervention* (pp. 159–176). Washington, DC: American Psychological Association.

Malchiodi, C.A., Steele, W., & Kuban, C. (2008). Resilience and posttraumatic growth in traumatized children. In C.A. Malchioldi (Ed.), *Creative interventions with traumatized children* (pp. 285–301). New York, London: Guilford Press.

Pennebaker, J.W. & Stone, L.D. (2004). Translating traumatic experiences into language: Implication for child abuse and long-term health. In L.J. Koenig, L.S., Doll, A. O'Leary, & W. Pequegnqat (Eds.), *From child sexual abuse to adult sexual risk: Trauma, revictimization and intervention* (pp. 201–217). Washington, DC: American Psychological Association.

Postman, N. (1982). *The disappearance of childhood.* New York: Vintage Books.

Rogers, A.G. (2007). *The unsayable: The hidden language of trauma.* New York: Ballantine Books.

Root, Marie P.P. (1992). Reconstructing the impact of trauma on personality. In L.S. Brown & M. Ballou (Eds.), *Personality and psychopathology: Feminist reappraisals* (pp. 229–266). New York: Guildford.

Rorty, R. (1989). *Contingency, iron, and solidarity.* London: Cambridge University Press.

Scarry, E. (1985). *The body in pain: The making and unmaking of the world.* New York: Oxford University Press.

Seigel, D.J., & Hartzel, M. (2003). *Parenting from the inside out: How a deeper self-understanding can help you raise children who thrive.* New York: Penguin.

Shohat, E. (2002). Area studies, gender studies and the cartographies of knowledge. *Social Text, 72*(20), 67–78.

Spelman, E.V. (2002). *Repair: The impulse to restore in a fragile world.* Boston: Beacon Press.

Steedman, C. (1995). *Strange dislocations: Childhood and the idea of human interiority:1780–1930.* Cambridge, MA: Harvard University Press.

Surrey, J. L. (1991). Relationship and empowerment. In J.V. Jordan, A.G. Kaplan, J.B. Miller, I.P. Stiver & J.L. Surrey (Eds.), *Women's growth in connection: Writings from the Stone Center* (pp. 162 – 180). New York: Guildford Press.

Walkerdine, V. (1984). Developmental psychology and child-centered pedagogy: The insertion of Piaget into early education. In J. Enriques, W. Hollway, C. Urwin, C. Venn & V. Walkerdine (Eds.), *Changing the subject: Psychology, social regulation and subjectivity* (pp. 152–202). London, New York: Methuen.

CHAPTER 8

No "Body" to Blame?: Socio-cultural Influences on Girls and Women by Gina Wong-Wylie and Shelly Russell-Mayhew

Offet-Gartner (2005) suggests that it is important for writers to situate themselves for their readers by providing background and context to their writing. This practice is consistent with feminist principles in that it minimizes and then dissolves an objective, formal, and removed location of the author from her or his writing, which stems from a tradition of empirical research where the scientist is valued as a neutral individual, disengaged and unbiased. Throughout this chapter, Shelly and I (Gina) weave a thread of our personal voice and experience. As a Chinese-Canadian feminist woman writing about embodiment, the act of sharing my personal and professional history resonates strongly with me. My interest in disordered eating and body image issues stems from a feminist consciousness of the central issue of embodiment for girls and women. Feminism provides a compassionate lens and a way of understanding female body image issues in our culture in a way that rightfully detracts from the "faulty individual" perspective of disordered eating problems. In my girlhood, positive and negative comments on my appearance and ethnicity reinforced the centrality of the external and reified the "body" as an organizing schema of how I experienced the world, and how I was experienced by it. In my counselling practice, I work with adolescent girls and women on issues of disordered eating, body image dissatisfaction, sexual abuse, depression, anxiety, and self-esteem. I link these issues to a socio-cultural fixation on body size and shape in assessing female worth. As a mother of two young daughters, I am even more keenly motivated to understand and be sensitive to the perils and assaults the female body faces and the importance of the material body as a site of political and personal struggle. I am also an associate professor in the Graduate Centre for Applied Psychology at Athabasca University.

My (Shelly's) interest in eating disorders and body dissatisfaction was born of my own experiences with anorexia and bulimia in my adolescent years. I became *interested and invested in feminist perspectives during my own treatment and recovery process while in undergraduate school studying psychology. As I found my own voice and worked on developing a satisfying relationship with my body, my passion for helping women with eating and body image related issues has grown. I have worked in a number of positions in relation to eating disorders with clinical, prevention, policy, and advocacy work as core experiences. I am currently an assistant professor in the Division of Applied Psychology, Faculty of Education at the University of Calgary. My research program focusses on the prevention and treatment of eating disorders, obesity, and body image dissatisfaction. Current projects include exploring social justice as an organizing lens in the understanding of eating related issues and investigating a school-based prevention program aimed at shared risk factors for eating disorders and obesity.*

INTRODUCTION

> *Gina sits across from a young woman who has come for counselling support; she confesses to Gina the pull she experiences in being adored, admired, and desired by men. As a young woman, she garners attention from men through her behaviour and appearance. She conveys that she is achieving her goals but that she is paying the price in reduced reputation and loss of respect from her female friends.*

The dilemma this client describes is one that Gina has experienced. In the moment, Gina is relating to her own anguish and that of the client's. She is grateful that she is predominately past this point in her life and is grieving that girls and women often go through a journey of self-discovery that includes measuring worth through inconsistent and fleeting terms of external validation. In the same instant, she is cognizant of the difficult work that lies ahead with this client.

> *Shelly stands in front of a room of adolescent girls facilitating experiential activities and discussions about healthy body image. An audience member discloses her struggle to lose weight, her dissatisfaction with her changing body, and her experience of herself as fat. She reveals authentically what others seem to be hiding, and other girls in the room nod in recognition and acknowledge her courage.*

196

The dilemma this adolescent describes is one that Shelly has experienced. In the moment, Shelly is relating to her own struggle as a teenager with disordered eating. She is saddened by yet another story of a female giving her power away and is hopeful for a world where women find meaning that goes beyond the experience of the body. In the same instant, she is aware of the lifelong struggle she has had in order to accept her own body.

As academics, it is one thing to theorize about cultural constructions of body and the ideologies that serve as social control for women; as women, it is another matter to personally experience them. As feminist psychologists, we, the authors of this chapter, also work with female clients to understand their "bodied" experiences of living within the culture. The intersection of multiple perspectives—those of women, academics, researchers, theorists, and counselling practitioners—culminates within this chapter. We provide a specific focus on feminist counselling interventions for girls and women around issues of female embodiment. Given that cultural influences and standards of female beauty and behaviour cannot be turned off even as we deconstruct and critique them, we cannot extract our own experiences of embodiment from the equation.

As psychologists and academics, our personal experiences of the body are not normally revealed nor discussed within the professional milieu. A paradox exists within our position as feminist academic psychologists. That is, we should not have prioritized men's attention above all else, have eating disorders in our histories, take up a lot of physical space, nor be overtly self-conscious about our bodies or appearances. We subvert and make invisible these parts of ourselves to garner respect and visibility and to meet unwritten standards of expectation. In essence, our existence is portrayed as problem free. All the while, the code of expectation and standard of behaviour and body for female academics is positioned subordinately in academic hierarchies. The proportion of women in tenure-track positions in Canadian universities is 32%, the lowest compared to countries such as the United States, Australia, the United Kingdom, and New Zealand (Canadian Association of University Teachers, 2006). Given women's under-representation in university faculties, it is no wonder that female academics feel pressure to hide parts of themselves that do not fit the confident, strong, problem-free, child-free, fat-free, and baggage-free image defining academics.

Nevertheless, as female academics and psychologists who have experienced embodiment issues, we refuse to comply with the code of silence and invisibility. Certainly, the experience of embodiment for us is not unique. Acknowledging our experiences is what allows us to relate to other women's experiences of embodiment and fuels our passion to make a difference in our own lives and in the lives of other women. We rise above protocol of invisibility in an act of consciousness-raising, and we embody this chapter by allowing these usually hidden parts of ourselves to be seen. By weaving our personal experiences throughout the chapter, we avoid "othering" women's experiences, which is criticized by some feminist researchers as objective and impersonal (Stoppard, 2000), and add subjectivity to traditional academic writing. Furthermore, positioning ourselves from a place of vulnerability and authenticity and adding personal voice facilitates a feminist process. That is, we do not divest ourselves from the experience; rather, we disclose, as a means to connect with readers, just as we might appropriately disclose personal experiences with clients. Connecting with clients and readers by showing our vulnerability may engender others to reveal hidden parts of themselves in various life contexts; likewise, it is an effort to minimize power differentials and promote egalitarian relations, which are central feminist tenets. Enns (2004) emphasizes egalitarian counselling relationships whereby the client–counsellor power dynamic should not reproduce societal power imbalances (Contratto & Rossier, 2005).

EMBODIMENT

Defined broadly, embodiment is the experience of living in one's body (Cash, 2004), which is replete with social and cultural expectations. Merleau-Ponty (1962) describes embodiment as an interconnection between body and self, and expression of how we cast the body as an intentional agent. As such, the body is an object, a target of power, and a place where social standards are inscribed (Foucault, 1979, 1980). Skarderud and Nasser (2007) echo Ricoeur (1977), who refers to the body as a cultivated text to be read, where the practices of a culture such as taboos, norms, and ideologies are inscribed and communicated. Garland Thomson (1997) aptly remarks that women are placed "within a hierarchy of bodily traits that determines the distribution of privilege, status, and power" (p. 6). Consequently, meanings circumscribed on women's bodies and the lived experiences that result occur in moment-to-moment social interactions in everyday life, sanctioned by socio-cultural constructions.

Women's embodiment involves externally driven derivations of female beauty as well as conventional feminine ideologies of the good, appropriate, and proper woman. Her status and acceptance in our culture and consequently the way she feels about herself is inextricably connected to her body (how she looks). The way in which she is embodied also extends to race, class, and sexuality, and includes her size, ability, physical health, disposition, sexual desirability, and mental health. In essence, how she thinks, acts, and looks is sanctioned by socio-cultural expectations. At the same time, qualities defined as inherently female—such as relational, emotional, nurturing, life-giving, and feminine characteristics—are given second class status in our patriarchal culture, in which independence, emotionless, distant, and masculine traits are preferred. Indeed, feminists advance that patriarchy, which limits women's access to power, is at the root of embodiment issues (Orbach, 1978).

Embodiment issues such as disordered eating and body image dissatisfaction are not a pandemic only for white, Anglo-Saxon girls and women, as is often the public portrayal. Thompson (1994) notes how women of colour, older women, impoverished women, disabled women, and lesbian women are left out of media attention and public understanding of eating issues, due to the demographics of girls and women included in the majority of disordered eating and body image research. Original perspectives on disordered eating have developed primarily through studies including girls in hospitals, clinical settings, private schools, and colleges. This contributes to skewed public perceptions of who are the most vulnerable to developing eating issues. Such a skewed focus perpetuates debilitating consequences in which minority girls and women may be misdiagnosed and mistreated by trained professionals, and these girls and women are likewise less likely to seek support because they are not legitimized as persons who suffer from body image and eating issues.

Thompson (1994) highlights the paucity of disordered eating research on marginalized women and, in response, conducts life-history interviews with 18 women including Latina, African-American, and lesbian women. Her research reveals multiracial perspectives different from media or status-quo representations of embodiment issues. Bordo (1993) also elucidates that for Black women, white beauty standards perpetuate feelings of inadequacy and insecurity over the racial characteristics of their bodies. Thompson's research not only confirmed that biased notions about race reflect racial fears and body norms, she also found that heterosexual standards and fears of homosexuality are played out and projected onto the lesbian female body. Thompson describes the complex intersection of race, class, gender, ability, and sexual orientation on embodiment issues. In doing so, she clearly identifies eating issues as not purely by-products of the societal pressure to be thin. The following section highlights embodiment issues as a struggle for girls and women to cope.

Embodying Trauma and Problems

Thompson (1994) staunchly advances that disordered eating issues are not mere signs of self-absorbed vanity and obsession, but rather ways that girls and women cope with untenable life situations. In this view, the body is a "symbolic representation of their traumas—often manifested in unwanted eating patterns and supreme dissatisfaction with appetites and bodies" (p. 12). That is, traumatic experiences may underlie many female eating problems, as they often disrupt an intact sense of one's body. Thompson remarks that not all women with eating issues are coping with trauma; however, the view that dieting, self-denial, and eating issues are survival strategies rather than direct responses to media pressures to be thin is critical (Orbach, 1978). Writing about girls suffering from anorexia, Orbach (1986) elucidates how women are trained to deny their needs and to "excel as the *good girl* who refuses to make demands on others ... her anorexia is at once an embodiment of stereotyped femininity and its very opposite" (p. 30). As a result, girls and women are disconnected from their needs and their selves as they are persistently reinforced to seek approval and validation by looking outside themselves and to attend to the needs of others to achieve it.

SOCIAL CODES FOR WOMEN

Social codes for girls and women are unwritten standards of behaviour, appearance, dress, body size, and portrayal of female norms promulgated in our culture and reinforced by praise, approval, and sense of belonging. The following section describes a ubiquitous social code regulating women's lives.

The Good Woman

The conventional feminine ideology of the "good woman" is pervasive in Western culture. This ideology creates a norm of expectation that impacts a woman's self-identity and her place and privilege in society. Cultural narratives that convey shared ideas about what it means to be female shape socio-cultural pressures that girls and women bear. These narratives play out in practices of femininity, or the domain of gendered activities that are culturally rooted (Stoppard & McMullen, 2003). Girls and women receive and internalize social messages about what it means to be a good woman. This goodness describes a moral code of behaviour linked with implicit and explicit standards about what a woman should be thinking, feeling, and doing. These expectations are promulgated within the good woman ideology and are so engrained and entrenched in our way of being that they often cease to be recognized or named. Like white privilege (Offet-Gartner, 2005), the good woman standard is normalized and exists as invisible cross-stitches that hem the frays to the pattern of our existence. The dominant stories of Western culture compare and judge female worth according to external criteria, which coerce women to look and act "perfect," to conform, submit, compete, and obey.

Betty Friedan (1963) staunchly critiques the good woman ideology in her classic text *The Feminine Mystique*. Friedan deconstructed how societal values and definitions of what it means to be a woman can pave the way for psychological distress. Internalized scripts of the good woman include cultural imperatives related to goodness. The ubiquitous good woman messages women receive are internalized and can be summarized in five predominant themes: a) to maintain a youthful, slim, attractive, and sexually appealing appearance (Dunlap, 1997; Jack, 1991); b) to ensure a man's emotional and physical needs are met (Brown, 1986; Jack; Scattolon & Stoppard, 1999); c) to prioritize nurturing and care of others to the extent of being selfless and self-sacrificing (Gilligan, 1982; Jack; Schreiber, 2001); d) to be cheerful, strong, and productive while avoiding conflict and expressions of anger (Brown, 1986; Schreiber; Simonds, 2001); and e) to be autonomous and independent, not smothering others with emotional neediness nor exhibiting vulnerability, lest it be interpreted as weakness or failure (Mauthner, 1999; McMullen, 1999). Indeed, girls and women are trained to be self-sacrificing and to meet the needs of others while ignoring or suppressing their own desires (Orbach, 1986) and emotions. As a result, a woman often feels unfulfilled and denied (which is rewarded), and she seeks legitimacy, validation, and approval through others, especially men, which hinges on the acceptability and desirability of her body.

The Good-looking Woman

Within the good woman social code is the imperative that she be sexually appealing and desirable (good looking). A good woman is not only all-giving, nurturing, patient, and selfless, she is also sexy and seductive (but not overly, lest she be judged as promiscuous). The "desirable woman" is situated within the good woman ideology, as its social codes are concomitantly the standards that women are judged against and the way in which she is affirmed. Such a dichotomy seemingly represents a tension or contradiction (good vs. bad girl); however, these conflicting messages aptly reflect the reality of the exigencies that pressure girls and women. Women, above all, are valued for how they look, and fundamental to being a "good girl" is being a "good-looking girl." From a very young age, women are seen and judged in reference to men (Malson & Nasser, 2007) and are often seen as "ornaments" (while men are judged as "instruments"). In fact, it matters little what women do as long as they look good doing it. Examining the gendered context of our culture helps us understand how females experience their bodies in a context that requires constant and vigilant negotiation.

The societal value of thinness and the Western tendency to base much of a woman's value on appearance bear tremendous significance on women's relationships with their bodies. Society teaches girls that their physical appearance is of the utmost importance (Young, 1990). Current cultural constructions of females are dictated by a social system that defines women primarily in terms of how they look and act in relation to others (good, but sexually appealing).

The current standard for female beauty is a young, white, thin woman (with breast implants), and the perpetuation of this construction in the media has extraordinary implications for the relationship women have with their bodies (Levine & Smolak, 1996). Women's unhappiness and dissatisfaction with their bodies has been linked to media exposure to ultra-thin female bodies (Harrison & Cantor, 1997; Posavac, Posavac, & Posavac, 1998; Stice & Shaw, 1994). Increased rates of dieting, weight preoccupation, eating disorders, and cosmetic surgeries are associated with society's portrayal of the thin female ideal (Harrison & Cantor; Levine & Smolak). These images promote unrealistic standards that are impossible to achieve for the average woman (Morris & Katzman, 2003; Willinge, Touyz, & Charles, 2006), and social comparisons with models and images of such impossible standards of beauty have been found to be highly correlated with body dissatisfaction (Heinberg & Thompson, 1992).

Nevertheless, exhorting pressure for thinness as the primary culprit in disordered eating issues locates the problem within the woman herself, and her "obsession" with obtaining a thin body may reinforce demeaning notions of a young naive female controlled by media images (Evans, Rich, & Holroyd, 2004). This perspective also fails to capture the complexity of girls' and women's embodied experiences and the wide range of etiological factors that influence body regulation practices of culturally diverse girls and women. Nasser and Katzman (1999) argue that, for many females, a quest for thinness is not simply a matter of "cosmetic compliance" (p. 37). Issues of globalization, immigration, acculturation, modernization, transition, and identity along dimensions of gender, race, class, ability, and sexual orientation may play a more significant role in contributing to the eating issues and body image dissatisfaction of minority women.

Indeed, racialized issues of disordered eating and body image issues cannot be overlooked. Research involving Black communities in the United States and the United Kingdom identifies girls who struggled with their racial identity and the powerful need to fit into a new society, and who hoped to become accepted and integrated through rigid dieting and adoption of prevailing cultural standards of thinness (Skarderud & Nasser, 2007). Immigration and acculturation were also seen to underpin her susceptibility to developing body dissatisfaction and weight concerns. The stress of cultural adaptation is believed to foster "acculturative stress" (Perez, Voelz, Pettit, & Joiner, 2002, p. 442) that may be projected onto eating behaviour.

Media may contribute to female body dissatisfaction, but it is not the only direct culprit. For example, Larkin and Rice's (2005) examination of "body-based harassment" for 45 Canadian adolescent girls in grades seven and eight includes weight- and shape-related teasing, and sexual and racial harassment. Body-based harassment has a direct impact on girls' body perception and practices, as girls employ various food and weight monitoring activities to deal with body dissatisfaction and to reduce body-demeaning comments. Sexism, racism, classism, and other discriminatory factors influence body-regulating behavior (Levine & Piran, 2004). The interplay of gender with class, race, ethnicity, acculturation, and ability can create different reasons for weight preoccupation and body dissatisfaction for girls (Larkin, Rice, & Russell, 1996). Through harassment, girls get the message that their bodies are potential or actual problems and may begin to experiment with harmful solutions, such as starving, binging, purging, and other attempts at body alteration unrelated to food and eating (bleaching skin, cosmetic surgery, wearing cosmetic to hide skin color). Fuller integration of culture and gender issues into analyses of eating disorders, body dissatisfaction, and weight preoccupation is imperative. To do so, researchers must take the wider context of race, acculturation, identity, and immigration into account (Nasser & Katzman, 1999; Thompson, 1994).

EMBODIMENT OF SOCIAL CODES

Strahan and colleagues (2008) underscore the widespread dominance of socio-cultural norms for ideal appearance in a Canadian study involving adolescent girls and women. They found such norms promoted women to assess self-worth strictly on appearance, which consequently increases fixation on others' perceptions of them and encourages rampant and extreme body dissatisfaction. It appears that, culturally, a woman's worth *is* her body. Her appearance *is* her value, and at the same time, her acceptance is judged against standards of behaviour of the good woman. Orbach (1986) emphasizes that with and through her body, a woman negotiates her way in the world. Her sense of herself as a desirable and attractive person to others is deeply intertwined with her self-concept, value, and worth. In this way, women's bodies are "objects/tools/weapons in the marketplace of social relations.... [A] woman's body is a feared and wanted object for both women and men" (p. 71). Undoubtedly, she is embodied. The corset was once the design used as a means to control a woman's body; now the strings that bind us are not just external but have been internalized and are based on a socio-cultural code of expectation. Women now live with a self-imposed regime of beauty practices (Hesse-Biber, 1997) and behaviour control (Stoppard & McMullen, 2003).

Issues arising from practices of femininity and social codes on how girls and women should look and act play out in different ways. Although there are myriad consequences, our focus is on depression, disordered eating, and compromised self-esteem.

Depression

In essence, the dominant Western cultural messages women receive about how to behave in relationships play an important role in embodiment. According to Jack's (1991) "silencing the self" theory of depression, women must stifle expression of their true feelings. Women become alienated from their wants, desires, feelings, and selves in an effort to nurture, please, and look after others. This often occurs without reciprocity; as such, women may feel disconnected, unsupported, and angry. Such feelings may be shut out of awareness through the internalizing cultural scripts related to goodness and may lead to psychological issues such as depression.

Feminist researchers such as Mauthner (1999) identify that women who are depressed often internalize social messages and struggle with behaving in a way that adheres to rigid social norms that dictate how she must think, act, and look. A woman who is depressed may experience a loss of herself. Then again, she may never have developed a sense of self in strident efforts to comply with expectations and standards of goodness set out for her. Time and again, female research participants, across various research studies, describe trying to live up to a certain standard of behaviour and the feelings they experience when they fall short of their aspirations. Researchers, including Jack (1991), Gammel and Stoppard (1999), Mauthner, McMullen (1999), and Schreiber (2001) find that women diagnosed with depression consistently use moral language such as *should, ought, good, bad*, and *selfish* to describe themselves and their behaviour. The conclusive finding—that women with depression use common language to judge themselves against a standard of behaviour—demonstrates how cultural messages are translated to the individual level. It also illustrates the results of an internalized message about being not good enough.

The conflict between what girls and women feel they should be doing, thinking, or feeling and what they are actually experiencing creates dissonance. This is manifested as a struggle between different parts of the self: one that reflects cultural ideals, norms, and values, and another that is informed by the woman's actual lived experiences, where she invariably falls short. Mainstream cultural constraints, pressures, and expectations are linked to depression. Depression may be a manifestation of a woman striving to become everything to everyone and, in the process, becoming less of herself. She is caught in a world in which women cannot experience "failure, nervous breakdowns, leisured existences, or anything else that would suggest that they are complex, feeling human beings" (Harris-Lacewell, 2001, p. 7).

In the same vein, these rigid restrictions and standards that may catalyze depression also lead women to project frustrations onto their bodies (Harris-Lacewell, 2001). Feminist theorists blame the assassination of women's ownership of their bodies on the gendered politics of our culture (Perlick

& Silverstein, 1994). According to theorists such as Jack (1991) and Harris-Lacewell, "feminists view the body problems that predominate among women—eating disorders, hysteria, anxiety, and depression—as expressive, embodied protests against the social reality of restrictions, devaluations, and violence directed at women" (p. 104).

Body Dissatisfaction and Disordered Eating

For many adolescent girls and women, exposure to media that portray stringently thin, idealized female images sends the message that their body size and shape is not good enough, which can lead to body dissatisfaction, dieting, and unhealthy eating behaviours (Becker & Fay, 2006; Willinge, Touyz, & Charles, 2006). Some feminists suggest that the promotion of unrealistically thin images is not accidental, as it creates a market that drives product consumption (Hesse-Biber, Leavy, Quinn, & Zoino, 2006; Kilbourne, 1994; Wolf, 1990). As such, beauty is reinforced as a commodity for purchase. With shifting beauty standards and pervasive female body discontent as the snare, the diet, fashion, cosmetic, and beauty industries hold immense power (Orbach, 1986). That is, "commercial exigencies are the motivating force for their existence, and their profits are sustained on the enormity of the body insecurity that they both identify and allege to ameliorate, while simultaneously reinforcing and amplifying this very insecurity" (p. 71).

In her classic and landmark text *The Beauty Myth*, Naomi Wolf (1990) highlights that even as women reclaimed their identity apart from domesticity, social control was maintained by the age-old ideology of feminine beauty. Wolf contends that women are operating under the realm of a "beauty myth" that works to maintain control and power over female behaviour. Wolf asserts that women are bombarded with unattainable images of beauty manufactured by the cosmetics, diet, pornography, and plastic surgery industries in order to make them feel not good enough. In essence, these industries market female dissatisfaction for economic gain. As long as women are made to feel insecure about their physical appearance and inadequate in comparison to the unattainable standards of beauty, then these industries will prosper. Aptly, Dworkin (1974) declares that

> [i]n our culture, not one part of a woman's body is left
> untouched, unaltered. No feature or extremity is spared
> the art, or pain, of improvement.... From head to toe,
> every feature of a woman's face, every section of her body,
> is subject to modification, alteration. This alteration is an
> ongoing, repetitive process. It is vital to the economy, the

> major substance of male-female differentiation, the most
> immediate physical and psychological reality of being a
> woman (p. 21).

Furthermore, as discussed earlier, body image dissatisfaction and disordered eating issues extend beyond media and the beauty industries; they are influenced by pressures, stressors, and marginalization related to race, culture, class, sexual orientation, and ability. Likewise, constant judgment and assault on girls' and women's bodies make their bodies a veritable and legitimate target to cope with life and enact problems, which results in embodiments that are not "bizarre or anomalous, but, rather ... the logical (if extreme) manifestations of anxieties and fantasies fostered by our culture" (Bordo, 1993, p. 15). Orbach (1986) poignantly articulates how anorexia is the personification of a woman's body as the site of expression for lived dichotomies that have no other outlet. Anorexia expresses "starvation amidst plenty, the denial set against desire, the striving for invisibility versus the wish to be seen- these key features of anorexia- are a metaphor for our age" (p. 24). Women with anorexia enact the contradictions of contemporary society—to be a good girl, but "bad"—through self-repudiation and a torturous and persistent expression of independence. We are embodied as the body becomes a site for mapping the ills of the culture.

Self-Esteem

Western societal prescriptions of size and beauty and pervasive messages around conventional femininity ideologies of the good woman are intricately tied to global self-esteem—the totality of thoughts and emotions regarding oneself. Self-concept is strongly rendered by an interaction between one's global self-esteem and body esteem (Goldenberg & Shackelford, 2005). Jefferson Lenskyj (2006) cites decades of research demonstrating the significant overlap between body image and self-image. In essence, body esteem arises out of a multi-dimensional experience in which females compare their appearance against personal and societal standards within different settings (home, school, and among peers) (Dubois, Felner, Brand, Phillips, & Lease, 1996). The causal relationship between appearance and self-esteem is extremely problematic. Sanctioned by external forces and saturated with a barrage of images of the ultra-thin female body ideal, girls' and women's capacity to maintain high self-esteem and high body esteem is threatened on a daily basis (Goldenberg & Shackelford).

Researchers demonstrate the powerful connection between self-esteem and physical appearance. Social comparison with fashion models and exposure to unrealistic media images of female beauty are shown to lower body satisfaction and body esteem among girls between the ages of 11 and 16 years in the United Kingdom (Clay, Vignoles, & Dittmar, 2005). Likewise, at least one in four Ontario girls ages 10 to 14 years expresses the desire to be thinner, fears being fat, and is currently attempting to lose weight; by the age of 14, these numbers increase to about one in two (McVey, Tweed, & Blackmore, 2004). Overall, researchers reveal that in Western countries, lower self-esteem and higher body dissatisfaction are more evident among females than males, despite the fact that obesity rates are higher among males. Lowery and colleagues (2005) highlight a formidable contradiction at play in female body oppression, which relates to the message about being not good enough: "Women are trying to make themselves smaller and less noticeable (in order to be noticed)" (p. 70). They also note that "[t]he body surveillance project for women is never-ending, and the rules keep changing: big breasts, small breasts, toned muscles, no muscles...." (p. 72).

Similarly, Leary and Baumeister (2000) established a connection between a female's self-esteem and her perception of how others value their relationships with her. Given the pervasive good woman message around how girls and women should behave in various social roles, there is little doubt that the good woman ideology, coupled with looks, is the template of cultural appropriateness through which a woman's worth is assessed in relationships. The Sociometer Theory (Leary & Downs, 1995) posits that when a woman interprets message cues to mean that she is valued in the relationship, her self-esteem increases; when she perceives that she is not valued, her self-esteem decreases. The Sociometer Theory contends that self-esteem is a barometer of past, present, and future perceived relational value. The following vignettes describe our personal experiences of cultural impact on self-worth and esteem.

Body Trap

> In a rural community in Alberta, Shelly's struggle with her sense of self remained hidden because, from all outward appearances, she had her "act together"—honour role student, community advocate, drama club member, volleyball captain. Yet none of this mattered unless she felt thin and pretty. She kept her self-starvation and purging a secret for seven long years as she struggled to break free from the "never good enough" trap. Words from her 17-year-old self remind her what it was like: "Wild eyes pierce through prison bars. Only glimpses of reality exist between visits. The cold cement closes in and surrounds me. I am running out of time, no room left. I have to escape, to run, to break

free from my self-built prison walls.... My sanity exists somewhere between harsh reality and hopeful fantasy. My escape exists somewhere between the prison and the open field. My happiness exists somewhere between myself and those who love me. My freedom exists somewhere between what I create and what I MUST destroy."

Shelly looks at photos of herself and sees a normal weight adolescent looking back at her. Yet she recalls at the time wishing deep within herself to be different from her average-looking self. The greatest compliment anyone could have paid her during her teen years was that she had lost weight or that she was pretty. Shelly spent immeasurable amounts of time and energy trying to alter her appearance. All because she believed her natural self was not good enough. She struggled not wanting to be that girl in a fabricated body trap.

Falling Down

In a Canadian girlhood in Montreal, sounds of ridicule emanate from schoolmates. "Chink, Chink, Chink" is chanted in indignant rhythm as little girls and boys spit on the sidewalk at Gina's feet while they chase and kick her. She cannot recall feelings in those moments, nor her immediate reactions. She must have felt powerless, confused, and helpless ... like a child falling down after being tripped. But as to the exact feelings, and how much the scrape hurt, she is uncertain. Gina likes to imagine that she is not affected by their name-calling and cruelty, that she ignores them and skips the rest of the way home, indifferent to their insults. Yet, this is not likely the case. Even through blurred memories and amidst uncertainty of immediate feelings, one message sank in loud and clear: She is different, inferior, and not accepted by these white-skinned children.

Gina searches her memory bank but cannot recall feelings about the ridicule, or remember a salient moment when she felt a certain way about herself, or about those children. Like a pot of water on a low-flamed stove, the heat slowly

*penetrates into the viscera of her soul. Their bitter words ...
their fingers pulling at the sides of their faces to imitate her
Chinese eyes ... flavours the pot and simmers it ... stewing
passively over the years ... in ways that can only be recognized
in reflection.*

*Gina recalls wishing deep within herself to be
different from "inferior" Chinese people. The greatest
compliment anyone could have paid her during her
early teen years was that she did not look or act Chinese.
She strove hard for this ... and it was not difficult since
she was immersed in Canadian culture and spoke
English without an accent. In fact, she denied any
comprehension whatsoever of the Chinese language.
Gina spent immeasurable amounts of time trying to
alter her appearance. All because she believed her
natural self was worthless. She struggled not wanting to
be that Chinese girl with scraped knees.*

The silent embodiment of others' expectations, the natural tendency for deri-
sion turned within, and the self-eclipsing and self-alienation that result are
exemplified through these stories: the war on the body and the penetrating
experience of racism and ultimate attempts to alter personal appearance. The
racial teasing about ethnically distinctive features can push women of colour
to adopt beauty norms of the dominant culture, devalue their ethnic features,
and experience identity issues, distress, and self-denigration, thereby promoting eating and body image disturbances (Iyer & Haslam, 2003).

Our stories capture the innocent yet insidious ways women succumb to
cultural imperatives and how self-esteem plummets in the wake. Indeed, "to
be in a woman's body means to live under attack" (Maine, 2000, p.144). These
experiences reveal a body consciousness connected to a verdict of unworthiness
that propels girls and women to judge themselves as fat (regardless of actual
weight and measurements) and to use their bodies emblematically as the site of
releasing or enhancing internalized pain. Orbach (1986) contends that girls and
women are forced to be obsessively engaged with mediating the effects of culturally induced body insecurity. At the same time, this "publicly sanctioned private
activity hides the deeply anguished relationship that so many women come to
have with their bodies. Women repress the knowledge of how damaging and
hurtful this obsession is" (Orbach, p. 23). Myriad counselling approaches and
interventions exist to support girls and women in this journey. We provide a few
examples in the next section to illustrate feminist counselling interventions and
approaches in working with issues of embodiment in girls and women.

FEMINIST COUNSELLING CONCEPTUALIZATIONS, APPROACHES, AND INTERVENTIONS

From a counselling perspective, working with girls and women around issues of embodiment requires mindful practice. The following section addresses feminist couselling conceptualizations, approaches, and interventions that focus specifically on embodiment in working with girls and women.

Shifting Perspectives on Eating Disorders

Feminist scholars have advanced reconceptualizations of eating disorders that shape counselling approaches in working with girls and women on issues of embodiment. This shift includes using a continuum perspective, critiquing the cultural definition of beauty, and viewing eating disorders as coping mechanisms. According to the feminist perspective, eating disorders need to be understood within a culture where 90% of women are dissatisfied with their bodies (National Eating Disorder Information Centre, 1996). Spricer (1999) contends that we exist in a culture that systematically reifies girls' and women's chronic dissatisfaction with their bodies and encourages them to view their bodies as objects to be inspected, adorned, judged, and improved upon.

Feminist conceptualizations of eating disorders provide alternatives to other models, which dichotomize normal and abnormal, and offer instead a view placed on a continuum (Brown & Jasper, 1993). In this way, anorexia and bulimia are extremes on a continuum that can include weight preoccupation, yo-yo dieting, and body shame (Brown, 1993; Scarano & Kalonder-Martin, 1994). A continuum perspective provides a larger focus, as it seems illogical to pathologize individuals at the extreme end of the continuum, while at the same time reward and praise behaviours at the lower end of the continuum (i.e., dieting and exercise for weight control) (Malson & Swann, 1999). When the entire continuum of weight preoccupation is placed within the current social context, it highlights the relationship between the development of an eating disorder and most women's preoccupation with thinness.

The feminist perspective of eating disorders as a coping mechanism (Brown & Jasper, 1993), as highlighted in this chapter, does not discount societal pressures or the discrepancy between the reality of women's lives and the representation of them in media. Researchers suggest that a woman's eating problem may start as a strategy to solve problems (Thompson, 1992), such as feeling a lack control in her life or feeling *not good enough*. Spricer (1999) depicts the internalization of pain and struggle:

> My anger fuelled my will to survive, allowing me to fight
> for myself as well as for my mother and siblings. However,

> in order to do this as a child, I unconsciously had to lock
> away my own childhood needs, my terror and my physical
> and emotional pain. These came to be stored deep inside
> my body, only to emerge, as they always do, as uncontrol-
> lable overreactions to people and events or as confusing
> physical symptoms. My emotions and unmet needs found
> their outlet in eating and my seemingly inadequate body
> became the ultimate proof of my unloveableness (p. 33).

The female body becomes the target for what is wrong in a woman's life and is "a focus that is tangible, concrete and completely socially acceptable ... body image issues are really metaphors for our unhappiness and for our desire to change" (Spricer, p. 40). Framing eating disorders as a coping mechanism broadens our understanding of how culture impacts a woman and highlights her adaptive reactions in coping with the stress and pressure to be thin, beauti-ful, and the image of the good woman. Assisting girls and women to recognize that controlling food is a logical response to a toxic culture can be a first step in breaking free from food and weight preoccupations. Viewing disordered eating as a coping mechanism in therapy means helping girls and women to make sense of themselves and find alternate coping mechanisms within a nurturing and caring relationship. Working with a client to understand the underlying struggles and assisting her in reconnecting with herself, her feelings, and her sense of worth are meaningful approaches from this perspective.

Feminist counselling approaches also include deconstructing dominant cultural messages with girls and women in session, helping them comprehend how the *not good enough* messages are internalized and played out in psycho-logical distress, and assisting them to see that they are not the problem. Like-wise, the focus is to empower clients to alter their perspectives, to, according to one woman, "shift from other people's approval or disapproval of me to my own ... and to work through the difficult rather than trying to fix our bodies when life becomes too difficult" (Spricer 1999, p. 38).

Constructivist Approaches to Counselling

Gergen (1992) emphasizes a constructivist notion that reality and truth, such as beliefs about oneself, are a matter of perspective and influenced by social and cultural processes, conventions of language (Derrida, 1976), discourse (Shotter, 1985), and issues of power (Foucault, 1979, 1980). As such, construc-tivist approaches in counselling emerge from a philosophical perspective that individuals construct meaning and understanding of experiences within social and cultural contexts. Constructivist counselling for girls and women on issues of embodiment is most fitting, given that cultural forces underpin both perspectives. Feminist counselling from a constructivist approach involves a focus on conversation as a primary mode in which understandings are embedded and new understandings can be co-created.

Narrative therapy

Narrative therapy is a socio-political orientation that can be an effective feminist counselling approach. It leads clients from feeling disembodied via embodiment of cultural ethos to feeling empowered by exposing the problem of cultural standards and expectations for women. Narrative therapy involves a postmodern conceptualization that the culture is regulated by a multiplicity of stories and that social, historical, and political ideologies intersect with these stories. Therapy with girls and women from this constructivist approach includes re-storying experiences with clients in a way that new realities are considered (Freedman & Coombs, 1996). Narrative therapists approach clients as experts in their own lives and view problems as external to the person.

Externalizing the problem is a narrative therapy intervention in which a therapist works collaboratively with a client to differentiate the client from the problem, to dialogue with the problem, and to re-story its influence on the client and in the client's life. The basic assumption in a narrative approach is that people are not the problem, the problem is the problem (White & Epston, 1990). This approach can facilitate a critique of our collective culture rather than individual weaknesses. Conceptualizing the problem as the problem and not the person seems to offer freedom to clients (Epston, 1993) as it provides a choice about rejecting or accepting the influence of the problem in their lives. For example, the problem could be named as the culture's preoccupation with judging women's worth and value in reference to her body shape and size. Discussions evolve about what impact this problem has had on the life of the client, and a focus may develop on times in her life when she may have not been influenced by this problem. Potentially, such an approach frees up space for the client to see the possibility of standing up against the problem's influence in her life. It also allows her to see that responding to her body as a culprit of the problem in a society that overvalues women's appearance is actually adaptive, albeit not healthy or effective [see White's *Maps of Narrative Practice* (2007) and Maisel, Epston, and Borden's *Biting the Hand that Starves You: Inspiring Resistance to Anorexia/Bulimia* (2004) for in-depth descriptions of narrative therapy treatment approaches for disordered eating issues].

Social Action and Social Justice

Collins and Arthur (2005) challenged counselling professionals to move beyond the feminist call of "the personal is political" towards "the professional is political." From this expanded view, counsellors advocate on behalf of girls and women to other professionals as well as empower females to bring awareness of embodiment issues to the forefront in professional counselling work. Furthermore, counsellor interventions move beyond the counselling room. A social justice approach refers to using counselling to confront imbalances of power and privilege. The purpose of social justice work is to increase a client's sense of personal power or efficacy (Kiselica & Robinson, 2001) and to advance socio-political change. To reach both goals, counsellors need to not only do great work in the counselling room but expand their work in ways that have potential to benefit women all over the world. Kiselica and Robinson "urge counsellors to identify some human condition that moves them so deeply it inspires a personal moral imperative to make this world a better place by advocating for others" (p. 396). Feminist counsellors need to address their own issues of embodiment, given that they lead the charge for the issues in the one-on-one counselling context to be seen as political and justice issues.

Liberal feminist approaches tend to espouse individual solutions and to conceptualize a universal Canadian girl who simply needs strong female role models and the "opportunity, encouragement and inspiration to become physically active" (Jefferson Lenskyj, 2006, p. 72). We miss the boat with a similar monocular view in addressing issues of embodiment. Approaching embodiment at an individual level by working towards female empowerment is important, but not enough. That is, mitigating the albatross of embodiment issues lies in examining the socio-cultural context, systems of oppression, and ideologies of beauty and behaviour standards for girls and women. A multi-dimensional perspective to viewing the complexity of the "not good enough" societal message is needed to examine systemic barriers and to promote change at the social level. Ultimately, many issues women face would be reduced if the social meanings, opportunities, and cultural conditions of women's lives changed. Feminist counsellors recognize and acknowledge embodiment as a social justice issue and advocate and fight at a systemic level for change. For example, as counsellors, we can contribute to the elimination of sexism and continually challenge ourselves and society on the hegemony of the good woman. We can advocate for socio-political change, work towards consciousness-raising, and challenge the status quo.

CONCLUSION

In this chapter, we position ourselves inside rather than above or outside the problem and allow the text to embody our experiences, which itself is a feminist act. As mentioned at the outset of the chapter, positioning ourselves subjectively within portions of the text connects us with readers and represents a parallel counselling process of disclosure. It is also a feminist act in that it reduces "othering," and it may incite others to be self-revealing and thus crumble edifices of hierarchy, promote egalitarian relationships, and minimize power imbalances. Several counselling approaches and interventions from a feminist stance are provided to illustrate how a counsellor may work with girls and women on embodiment. We conclude by weaving our voices and reflections within the closing discussion.

> *Culture suffuses and is embodied via penetrating influence of socio-cultural imperatives.*

> *Culture is embodied by internalizing scripts related to girls and women.*

Embodiment issues cannot be addressed through counselling alone, as larger social issues of inequity and promulgations of women's beauty and behaviour standards are at the root of many women's issues, such as depression, low self-esteem, and body dissatisfaction and eating disorders. We, like our clients, are on a sojourn away from embodiment of culture towards empowerment of selves. It is our pilgrimage. After all "how can we help individuals find their relationship to the context that relates so closely to their issues" unless we as counselling professionals do the same (Ivey & Collins, 2003, p. 292; Douce, 2003).

> *In our drive to get thin, we miss the gift of simply being alive.*

> *Should we be conquering the flesh or the obsession?*

> *In our drive to please others*

> *we eclipse and alienate parts of ourselves, act certain ways—to fit in.*

> *Yet, we miss out on living authentically.*

> *We realize and teach ourselves from a meaningful place within that worth based on external measures is not that important.*

Through a complex myriad of self-awareness and social consciousness

we work to strengthen within and affirm, notice, and accept ourselves for our multifarious natural shape, size, ability, race, emotions....

We can no longer blame our bodies for problems that the culture created.

We can no longer place the impetus for change on a woman and ignore the system that created the problems in the first place.

In essence, there is No "body" to blame.

REFERENCES

Becker, A.E., & Fay, K. (2006). Sociocultural issues and eating disorders. In S. Wonderlich, J.E. Mitchell, M. de Zwaan, & H. Steiger (Eds.), *Annual review of eating disorders: Part 2 – 2006* (pp. 35–64). Seattle, WA: Radcliffe Publishing Ltd.

Bordo, S. (1993). *Unbearable weight: Feminism, Western culture, and the body.* Los Angeles, CA: University of California Press.

Brown, C. (1993). The continuum: Anorexia, bulimia, and weight preoccupation. In C. Brown & K. Jasper (Eds.), *Consuming passions: Feminist approaches to weight preoccupation and eating disorders* (pp. 53–68). Toronto, ON: Second Story Press.

Brown, C. & Jasper, K. (1993). *Consuming passions: Feminist approaches to weight preoccupation and eating disorders.* Toronto, ON: Second Story Press.

Brown, L. (1986). Gender-role analysis: A neglected component of psychological assessment. *Psychotherapy, 23,* 243–248.

CAUT. (March, 2006). Women in the academic work force: How is Canada faring? *CAUT Education Review, 8,* 1–7.

Cash, T.F. (2004). Body image: Past, present, and future. *Body Image, 1,* 1–5.

Collins, S., & Arthur, N. (2005). Strengthening the Canadian mosaic through culture-infused counselling. In N. Arthur & S. Collins (Eds.), *Culture-infused counselling: Celebrating the Canadian mosaic* (pp. 513–536). Calgary, AB: Counselling Concepts.

Contratto, S., & Rossier, J. (2005). Early trends in feminist therapy theory and practice. *Women & Therapy, 28,* 7–26.

Clay, D., Vignoles, V.L., & Dittmar, H. (2005). Body image and self-esteem among adolescent girls: Testing the influence of sociocultural factors. *Journal of Research on Adolescence, 15,* 451–477.

Derrida, J. (1976). *Of grammatology.* Baltimore: John Hopkins University Press.

Douce, L.A. (2003). Society of counseling psychology division 17 of APA presidential address 2003: Globalization of counseling psychology. *The Counseling Psychologist, 31*(3), 142–152.

DuBois, D.L., Felner, R.D., Brand, S., Phillips, R.S., & Lease, M.A. (1996). Early adolescent self-esteem: A developmental-ecological framework and assessment strategy. *Journal of Research on Adolescence, 6,* 543–579.

Dunlap, S. (1997). *Counseling depressed women.* Louisville, KT: Westminster John Know Press.

Dworkin, A. (1974). *Woman hating.* New York: Dutton.

Enns,C. (2004). *Feminist theories and feminist psychotherapies: Origins, themes, and diversity.* Binghampton, NY: Haworth.

Epston, D. (1993). Internalizing discourses versus externalizing discourses. In S. Gilligan & R. Price (Eds.), *Therapeutic conversations* (pp. 161–177). New York: W.W. Norton & Company.

Evans, J., Rich, E., & Holroyd, R. (2004). Disordered eating and disordered schooling: What schools do to middle class girls. *British Journal of Sociology of Education, 25,* 123–142.

Friedan, B. (1963). *The feminine mystique.* New York: Dell Publishing.

Foucault, M. (1979). *Discipline and punish: The birth of the prison.* New York: Vintage Books.

Foucault, M. (1980). *Power/knowledge: Selected interviews and other writings, 1972–1977.* New York: Pantheon Books.

Freedman, J. & Coombs, G. (1996). *Narrative Therapy: The social construction of preferred realities.* New York: W.W. Norton.

Gammel, D., & Stoppard, J. (1999). Women's experiences of treatment of depression: Medicalization or empowerment? *Canadian Psychology, 40,* 112–128.

Garland Thomson, R. (1997). *Extraordinary bodies: Figuring physical disability in American culture and literature.* New York: Columbia University Press.

Gergen, K. (1992). Toward a postmodern psychology. In S. Kvale (Ed.), *Psychology and postmodernism* (pp. 16–30). London: Sage.

Gilligan, C. (1982). *In a different voice: Psychological theory and women's development.* Cambridge, MA: Harvard University Press.

Goldenberg, J., & Shackelford, T. (2005). Is it me or is it mine? Body-self integration as a function of self-esteem, body-esteem and morality salience. *Self and Identity, 4,* 227–241.

Harris-Lacewell, M. (2001). No place to rest: African American political attitudes and the myth of black women's strength. *Women & Politics, 23,* 1–33.

Harrison, K., & Cantor, J. (1997). The relationship between media consumption and eating disorders. *Journal of Communication, 47,* 40–67.

Heinberg, L.J., & Thompson, J.K. (1992). Social comparison: Gender, target importance ratings and relation to body image disturbance. *Journal of Social Behavior and Personality, 7,* 335–344.

Hesse-Biber, S.N. (1997). *Am I thin enough yet? The cult of thinness and the commercialization of identity*. New York: Oxford University Press.

Hesse-Biber, S., Leavy, P., Quinn, C.E., & Zoino, J. (2006). The mass marketing of disordered eating and eating disorders: The social psychology of women, thinness and culture. *Women's Studies International Forum, 29*, 208–224.

Ivey, A.E., & Collins, N.M. (2003). Social justice: A long term challenge for counseling psychology. *The Counseling Psychologist, 31*(3), 290–298.

Jack, D. (1991). *Silencing the self: Women and depression*. Cambridge, MA: Harvard University Press.

Iyer, D.S., & Haslam, N. (2003). Body image and eating disturbance among South Asian-American women. The role of racial teasing. *International Journal of Eating Disorders, 34*, 142–147.

Jefferson Lenskyj, H. (2006). "I am my body": Challenge and change in girls' physical and health education. *Proceedings of the 6th Canadian Association for the Study of Women and Education, 6th Bi-Annual International Institute*, 68–73.

Kilbourne, J. (1994). Still killing us softly: Advertising and the obsession with thinness. In P. Fallon, M.A. Katzman, & S.C. Wooly (Eds.), *Feminist perspectives on eating disorders* (pp. 395–418). New York: Guilford.

Kiselica, M.S., & Robinson, M. (2001). Bringing advocacy counseling to life: The history, issues and human drama of social justice work in counseling. *Journal of Counseling & Development, 79*, 387–397.

Larkin, J., & Rice, C. (2005). Beyond "healthy eating" and "healthy weights": Harassment and the health curriculum in middle schools. *Body Image, 2*, 219–232.

Larkin, J., Rice, C., & Russell, V. (1996). Slipping through the cracks: Sexual harassment, eating problems, and the problem of embodiment. *Eating Disorders, 4*, 5–26.

Leary, M.R., & Baumeister, R.F. (2000). The nature and function of self-esteem: Sociometer theory. *Advances in Experimental Social Psychology, 32*, 2–51 .

Leary, M.R., & Downs, D.L. (1995). Interpersonal functions of the self-esteem motive. The self-esteem system as a sociometer. In M.H. Kernis (Ed.), *Efficacy, agency, and self esteem* (pp. 123 –144). New York: Plenarium.

Levine, M.P., & Piran, N. (2004). The role of body image in the prevention of eating disorders. *Body Image, 1*, 57–70.

Levine, M.P., & Smolak, L. (1996). Media as a context for the development of disordered eating. In L. Smolak, M.P. Levine, & R. H. Striegel-Moore (Eds.), *The developmental psychopathology of eating disorders: Implications for research, prevention, and treatment* (pp. 235–237). Mahwah, NJ: Lawrence Erlbaum Associates.

Lowery, S., Robinson, S., Kurplus, C., Blanks, E., Sollenerger, S., Nicpon, M., & Huser, L. (2005). Body image, self-esteem, and health-related behaviors among male and female first year college students. *Journal of College Student Development, 46*(6), 612–622.

Maine, M. (2000). *Body wars: Making peace with women's bodies: An activist's guide*. Carlsbad, CA: Gurze Books.

Maisel, R., Epstein, D., & Borden, A. (2004). *Biting the hand that starves you: Inspiring resistance to anorexia/bulimia.* New York: W.W. Norton & Company.

Malson, H. & Nasser, M. (2007). At risk by reason of gender. In M. Nasser, K. Baistow, & J. Treasure (Eds.), *The female body in mind: The interface between the female body and mental health* (pp. 3–16). NY: Routledge.

Malson, H., & Swann, C. (1999). Prepared for consumption: (Dis)orders of eating embodiment. *Journal of Community & Applied Psychology, 9,* 397–405.

Mauthner, N. (1999). Feeling low and feeling really bad about feeling low: Women's experiences of motherhood and postpartum depression. *Canadian Psychology, 40,* 143–161.

McMullen, L. (1999). Metaphors in the talk of "depressed" women in psychotherapy. *Canadian Psychology, 40,* 102–111.

McVey, G.L., Tweed. S., & Blackmore, E. (2004). Dieting among preadolescent and young adolescent females. *Canadian Medical Association Journal, 170,* 1559–1562.

Merleau-Ponty, M. (1962). *Phenomenology of perception.* London: Routledge and Kegan Paul.

Morris, A.M., & Katzman, D.K. (2003) The impact of the media on eating disorders in children and adolescents. *Paediatrics & Child Health,* 8(5), 287–289.

Nasser, M., & Katzman, D.K.1999). Eating disorders: Transcultural perspectives inform prevention. In N. Piran, M.P. Levine, & C. Steiner-Adair (Eds.), *Preventing eating disorders: A handbook of interventions and special challenges* (pp. 26–43). Philadelphia: Brunner/Mazel.

National Eating Disorder Information Centre. (1996). *An introduction to food and weight problems.* [Brochure]. Toronto: NEDIC.

Offet-Gartner, K. (2005). Research across cultures. In N. Arthur & S. Collins (Eds.), *Culture-infused counselling: Celebrating the Canadian mosaic* (pp. 273–310). Calgary, AB: Counselling Concepts.

Orbach, S. (1978). *Fat is a feminist issue.* New York: Berkeley Press.

Orbach, S. (1986). *Hunger strike: The anorectic's struggle as a metaphor for our age.* Markham, ON: Penguin Books.

Perez, M., Voelz, Z.R., Pettit, J.W., & Joiner, T.E.J. (2002). The role of acculturative stress and body dissatisfaction in predicting bulimic symptomatology across ethnic groups. *International Journal of Eating Disorders, 31,* 442–454.

Perlick, D., & Silverstein, B. (1994). Faces of female discontent: Depression, disordered eating, and changing gender roles. In P. Fallon, M. Katzman, & S. Wooley (Eds.), *Feminist Perspectives on Eating Disorders* (pp. 77–93). New York: Guilford Press.

Posavac, H.D., Posavac, S.S., & Posavac, E.J. (1998). Exposure to media images of female attractiveness and concern with body weight among young women. *Sex Roles, 38,* 187–201.

Ricoeur, P. (1977). *The rule of the metaphor: Multi-disciplinary studies of the creation of meaning in language.* Toronto: University of Toronto Press.

Scarano, G.M., & Kalonder-Martin, C.R. (1994). A description of the continuum of eating disorders: Implications for intervention and research. *Journal of Counseling and Development, 72,* 356–361.

Scattolon, Y., & Stoppard, J. (1999). Getting on with life: Women's experiences and ways of coping with depression. *Canadian Psychology, 40,* 206–219.

Schreiber, R. (2001). Wandering in the dark: Women's experiences with depression. *Health Care for Women International, 22,* 85–98.

Shotter, J. (1985). Social accountability and self-specification. In K.J. Gergen and K.E. Davis (Eds.), *The social construction of the person* (pp. 167–190). New York: Springer.

Simonds, S. (2001). *Depression and women: An integrative treatment approach.* New York: Springer Publishing Co.

Spricer, R. (1999). Body image: A life process. In C. Malmo, & T. Suzuki Laidlaw (Eds.), *Consciousness rising: Women's stories of connection and transformation* (pp. 27–42). Charlottetown, PEI: gynergy books.

Skarderud, F., & Nasser, M. (2007). (Re)figuring identities: My body is what I am. In M. Nasser, K. Baistow, & J. Treasure (Eds.), *The female body in mind: The interface between the female body and mental health* (pp. 17–28). New York: Routledge.

Stice, E., & Shaw, H.E. (1994). Adverse effects of the media portrayed thin-ideal on women and linkages to bulimic symptomology. *Journal of Social and Clinical Psychology, 13,* 288–308.

Stoppard, J. (2000). *Understanding depression: Feminist social constructionist approaches.* New York: Routledge.

Stoppard, J., & McMullen, L. (2003). *Situating sadness: Women and depression in social context.* New York: New York University Press.

Strahan, E.J., Lafrance, A., Wilson, A.E., Ethier, N., Spencer, S.J., & Zanna, M.P. (2008). Victoria's dirty secret: How sociocultural norms influence adolescent girls and women. *Personality and Social Psychology Bulletin, 34,* 288–301.

Thompson, B.W. (1992). "A way outa no way": Eating problems among African-American, Latina, and white women. *Gender & Society, 6*(4), 546–561.

Thompson, B.W. (1994). *A hunger so wide and so deep: American women speak out on eating problems.* Minneapolis, MN: University of Minnesota Press.

White, M. (2007). *Maps of narrative practice.* New York: Norton.

White, M., & Epston, D. (1990). *Narrative means to therapeutic ends.* New York: W.W. Norton.

Willinge, A., Touyz, S., & Charles, M. (2006). How do body-dissatisfied and body-satisfied males and females judge the size of thin female celebrities? *International Journal of Eating Disorders, 39,* 576–582.

Wolf, N. (1990). *The beauty myth.* Toronto: Random House.

Young, I.M. (1990). Throwing like a girl: A phenomenology of feminine body comportment, mortality and spatiality. In I.M. Young (Ed.), *Throwing like a girl and other essays in feminist philosophy and social theory* (pp. 137–156). Bloomington, Indianapolis: Indiana University Press.

CHAPTER 9

Is Being a Lesbian a Queer Thing to Do?
by Bonita Decaire and Deborah Foster

W e are women feminist counsellors who support building and thriving in relationships. Writing this chapter has provided us an incredible opportunity to reflect on and share our thoughts, feelings, and beliefs about being lesbian, residing in a small town, being Canadian, and the notion of being queer. We see that there are tensions that exist between each new wave of feminism. This positive conflict helps all feminists to re-examine where we have been, what comes next, and what the next generation sees as emerging issues. We think that each generation needs to build on the previous and advocate for new issues that have meaning to them. We understand the first and second waves of feminism, but the third wave appears to us to be an extension of the second, and in many ways, we struggle to understand the cause(s) of the third wave. Many third wave feminists have embraced the term queer, yet as counsellors and women, we hesitate to accept queer for ourselves. In fact, the word never enters into our repertoire when we describe ourselves, our friends, or our colleagues. The current trend to accept and adopt derogatory terms is not a part of our perspective. In Canada, we acknowledge a queer political movement; however, we are concerned that while this latest history is being created, feminist lesbian history and the current oppression that exists in society towards women and more specifically non-heterosexual women, are being ignored or overwritten. Authors such as Warner (2002) have taken what has been called lesbian herstory (and gay male history) and renamed it queer history. This we find troubling. There is a need for us as feminist counsellors to stay in tune with the current struggle of next-generation feminists, accept their history and current debate, and ask more questions. We acknowledge that we have gaps in understanding, and we need to be enlightened to the next generation's plight, whilst preserving our own beliefs. In fact, we see the next generation struggle with identity as we did.

LESBIAN, QUEERS, IN CANADA ... OH MY!

The last few decades have seen monumental changes for lesbians in Canada. Lesbians in most provinces can adopt children, access fertility clinics, marry, and experience the majority of rights and privileges afforded to heterosexual women. Even though most laws and policies that were discriminatory against lesbians (and all women who enter relationships with other women) have been amended, societal attitudes towards lesbians have often not kept pace, especially in small towns and rural areas of Canada. This continued discrimi-nation and heteronormativity can lead lesbians to seek counselling services. This chapter will discuss many of the changes in Canada that have impacted lesbians over the past quarter-century as well as explore the experiences of lesbians in Canada across their life course.

This chapter will also include a discussion of what makes lesbians unique from gay men. Non-heterosexual individuals are often conveniently grouped into an ever-expanding abbreviation (LGBTTIQQ2S—lesbian, gay, bisexual, transgender, transsexual, transvestite, two-spirited, intersex, queer, questioning), which fails to recognize issues that are unique to women and, more specifically, to lesbians in Canada. Often this alphabet soup of individuals is conveniently called queer. One of the problems with the use of the term queer is that it comes out of a particular politicization of the LGBTTIQQ2S community that not all lesbians can identify with. Increasingly, articles and books are adopting the term *queer* to describe lesbians (and others in the broader non-heterosexual community) without the knowledge of the origins of the term and the issues that surround it. Second wave lesbian feminists often object to being called queer and lumped into this larger group. They feel that the term does not fit for them. It has the potential to make lesbians and their issues invisible, not unlike how the growth of gender studies in place of women's studies at post second-ary institutions has taken the focus off women. These issues will be explored further within the paper. Finally, issues related to "non-mainstream" lesbians will be discussed, including non-white, non–middle class lesbians in Canada.

WHAT IS QUEER THEORY AND LESBIAN THEORY?

[Q]ueer theory offers a less legible map than other critical approaches. Because it is not just one theory, or one formula, or even one approach, the appeal of queer theory ... has outstripped anyone's sense of what exactly it means.
—M. Warner (Ed.) *Fear of a queer planet: Queer politics and social theory* (p. 18)

The word *queer* was meant to insult. Nevertheless, today the term is becoming part of the mainstream vocabulary. Many people understand that queer theory encompasses the study of gays and lesbians; however, the two diverse histories could better be described as two separate trees. Both trees live on the same planet, most likely even the same forest, but are very different in size, shape, and stance. In our minds, they are not branches of the same tree.

Queer theorists, by their nature, object to being boxed or defined, which in itself is a bold, queer political statement. Queer theory has multiple beginnings, one of which suggests it emerged from gay and lesbian study and the discussion of whether or not some sexual behaviours were normal or deviant. In 1991, Teresa de Lauretis was attributed with coining the term *queer theory* in a feminist cultural studies journal. In 1993, Michael Warner edited a collection titled *Fear of the Queer Planet*. In the Introduction he defines queer as

> the open mesh of possibilities, gaps, overlaps, dissonances and resonances, lapses and excesses of meaning when the constituent elements of anyone's gender, of anyone's sexuality aren't made (or *can't be* made) to signifying monolithically ... The experimental, linguistic, epistemological, representational, political adventures attaching to the very many of us who may at times be moved to describe ourselves as (among many other possibilities) pushy femmes, radical faeries, fantasists, drags, clones, leatherfolk, ladies in tuxedos, feminist women or feminist men, masturbators, bulldaggers, divas, Snap! Queens, butch bottoms, story tellers, transsexuals, aunties, wannabes, lesbian-identified men or lesbians who sleep with men, or . . . people able to relish, learn from, or identify with such (p. xxvi).

Steven Seidman (1996), a sociologist, describes queer theory this way:

> Queer theory has accrued multiple meanings, from a merely useful shorthand way to speak of all gay, lesbian, bisexual, and transgendered experiences to a theoretical sensibility that pivots on transgression or permanent rebellion. I take as central to Queer theory its challenge to what has been the dominant foundational concept of both homophobic and affirmative homosexual theory: the assumption of a unified homosexual identity. I interpret Queer theory as contesting this foundation and therefore the very telos of Western homosexual politics (p. 11).

In a speech delivered on November 8, 2000, at the New York Association of Scholars on Reasoned Discourse in a Free Society, Caleb Crains summarizes queer theory. He suggests that queer theory is a utopian ideology and a confusion of two things: a kind of history and a kind of politics. He quotes Leo Bersani's book *Homos*, which implies queer theory is "de-gaying." Crains adds that Judith Butler opposes this notion, believing there is no escaping from gender or sexual orientation. Like Butler (1990), we too oppose this notion.

Probably the best known Canadian queer theorist has been Gary Kinsman. Kinsman (2001) has been using the term *queer* in a broader sense since 1996 to include more than gays and lesbians, but to also include those who "rupture heterosexual hegemony, but who would not see themselves as lesbian or gay" (p. 210). He goes on to state that queer nationalism clearly opposes an "integrationist" strategy that views gays and lesbians as just like heterosexuals, except for who they sleep with. This is in contrast with women in the lesbian movement (within the feminist movement) who clearly saw themselves as feminist women first and lesbian feminist women second. The feminist and lesbian feminist movement in Canada did not intend to set lesbians apart from other women, rather they were part of a larger sisterhood of women fighting for women's rights. The term *feminist* rarely appears in the index of books on Canadian queer issues, and the term *queer* rarely appears in Canadian feminist and lesbian feminist publications. This is not to say that a lesbian is not queer, rather that the term *queer* cannot be lackadaisically substituted for the word *lesbian* in Canadian culture.

If, after reading this, you are not clear about queer theory and think it is more of an indistinct concept, then we have described it correctly. The goals and membership are not specific, and we have tried to avoid a standard queer definition so as not to include or exclude. Unlike queer theory, lesbian theory is easier to define and understand.

Lesbian theory, like feminism, studies gender politics and the oppression of women. It also brings to the table inequalities of power and sexuality, violence against same-sex partners, and the social construction of "different" sexuality. Lesbian theory is concerned about the effects of mandatory male–female relationships and how this may impact the identity of someone not in a heterosexual relationship, as noted by Adrienne Rich in the controversial essay entitled "Compulsory Heterosexuality and Lesbian Existence" (1980). Furthermore, it asks questions about the impact of perceived roles such as butch and femme, and how these oppress lesbians.

A number of Canadian feminists have written on lesbian issues (Rebick, 2005; Ristock & Pennell, 1996). For the most part, these theorists have come out of the second wave feminist movement, which clearly talks of lesbian issues and feminist issues being intertwined. Lesbians, as part of the feminist movement, are able to "pass" as heterosexuals if it suits them. This is especially true for lesbian mothers of young children, since the terms *lesbian* and *mother* are often viewed as an oxymoron. The feminist movement, of which lesbians have always been a part, is about equality for women as a whole. On the other hand, queer women who are part of the queer movement may be able to pass as heterosexual, but clearly would never want to be seen as anything but queer, given that they see this as their defining identity, not whom they sleep with. The queer movement is about making a statement regarding a queer person's desire to operate outside of mainstream definitions of sexuality. This was not and is not the statement that the feminist movement intends to make.

THE PRIMARY DIVIDING LINE

To us, queer has multiple meanings. It seems to be multi-sexual, yet challenges heteronormativity. The popular saying "We're here and we're queer" carries the expectation that if you have an issue with alternative sexualities, then it's your issue ... deal with it. Unlike the feminists that I know, the women and men who identify as queers are not deep-rooted in the past but look to a future of multiple possibilities. In our experience they often have no identification with being a feminist or lesbian.

Sheila Jeffreys (2003) suggests a strong relationship between those who define themselves as white gay males and those who define themselves as queer. She states, "I will argue here that the political agenda of queer politics is damaging to the interests of lesbians, women in general, and to marginalized and valuable constituencies of gay men.... [T]his book is written to bring the interests of women and lesbians once more into the forefront of lesbian and gay discussion" (p. 2). Jeffreys criticized queer theory, suggesting it fails to account for sexism. Further, she suggests that queer theory privileges and naturalizes masculinity in a way that runs counter to the aims and goals of most forms of feminism. Queer theory makes women and their unique issues all but invisible again, just as gender studies does with women's studies, and history does with herstory. If, as queer theory implies, women and men are truly equal, and the differences between the sexes is a thing of the past, then queer theory is possibly the paradigm needed to distinguish different genders or sexual orientations. If one still believes, as we do, that sexism is alive and well within Canadian society, then it is clearly short-sighted to embrace a theory that does not take into account the role of sex and gender in theory and practice.

Yvette Taylor (2005), a lecturer at the University of Newcastle, contends that queer opportunities are more readily available if you are middle class and live in an urban setting. She suggests that those lesbians who are single, minimum-wage earners, or parents on benefits do not have the same opportunities for engaging in subversive practices. Taylor writes, "A queer identity may in fact only be accessible to those materially poised to occupy the position, a point reinforced in my empirical investigation of the lives of those excluded from both heterosexual privilege and the circles of the fashionably queer" (2005, para. 14). We would further this argument by saying that the same is true of disabled, non-white, or otherwise non-mainstream lesbians in Canada. They are far too busy just trying to exist within society to be able to work to subvert the dominant cultural narrative.

As lesbian Canadians, we suggest that it is possible for both queers and lesbians to coexist, but we argue that they exist as different trees in different forests, or at least a different species of tree in the same forest. There is no way that either of us as feminist lesbians can embrace the term *queer*. Perhaps it is our age or generation, but the term is not one that we use to depict ourselves. We are activists within the feminist community as well as among our colleagues in the counselling field. This, though, does not make us queer. We have no intention of rejecting the current world view, just modifying it to make it more user-friendly towards women and, more specifically, lesbians. We wonder if this generation or third wave can be both queer and feminist. Our concern lies in our lack of opportunity to pass on knowledge and inspire activism in the third or next generation. Who will be left to carry the torch if the bands we march to play such different music?

Conversely, we also see the potential usefulness of boldly marching, challenging the confines of the box, or simply asking, "box, what box?" Albeit, there are lines that divide us, just as there are some core beliefs that unite us as feminists. Yet, underneath it all, we question just how many queer women would embrace the label feminist?

WHAT BRINGS QUEERS AND LESBIANS TOGETHER?

Opposition to mandatory heterosexuality, a concept discussed by Judith Butler (1990), is one such common bond. Heterosexuality is the perceived norm, and therefore, as a mainstream social construct, it can damage the spirit, divide, control, and attempt to conquer. Heteronormativity may be a banner under which we can unite with our queer sisters. Yasmin Tambiah (1995) agrees and further challenges mandatory heterosexuality by maintaining that it leads to abuse(s) against lesbians as well as other women who refuse to act in accordance with heterosexual norms. Queers and lesbians expect fair treatment to love and desire whomever they want. They are asking or demanding justice for all genders. It *is* about sexual desire and a political statement. But is this enough to argue that we are not different tree species in the vast forest of humankind? We would say that the fundamental differences in our basic premises—rejecting mainstream values and attitudes regarding gender and sexuality versus working to modify them—make us incompatible to become even a spliced branch on one another's tree. It is the fundamental difference between fighting for equality and recognition from within (as lesbian feminists do) and fighting the fight from the outside (as queers do) that continues to keep our trees apart.

WHAT MAKES LESBIANS UNIQUE FROM GAY MEN?

*In the 70s everyone was gay; I became a lesbian as an extension of being a feminist. (Anonymous)*Without wanting to be trapped in the polarization of us versus them, fundamental differences do exist between lesbian woman and gay men, beyond anatomy. Identifying yourself as a lesbian is a political statement; it acknowledges the oppression that exists based on your sexuality. An example of this oppression becomes obvious when you look at the word *lesbian*, which can be used as an insult for a woman who is behaving outside of the expected norm or behaving *badly*. In the late 90s, We met a woman who described how she was walking down the street holding her female partner's hand, and two males slowed their car down, rolled down the window, and screamed out "lesbian." The story resonated because of the emotional impact it had on this lady. She described feeling unsafe and was not willing to risk the chance that she might be called out at again. This carried over into other parts of her life, and she became particularly cautious who she told about her same-sex partnership, and how and when she showed affection.

Although gay men experience negative attitudes, they do not experience sexism in the way that women do. Jan Bridget (1998), from the organization Lesbian Information Service, explains that lesbians are unique as we live in a sexist society. Men have power over women, including gay men. She suggests that we share the oppression of living in a heterosexist society with our brothers, but that that is the only similarity. She writes, "Lesbians face discrimination because we are women and because we are Lesbian. Like heterosexual women, we are more likely to be poorer than men; we are more likely to be in poorly paid jobs, doing childcare, or looking after an elderly parent.... Lesbians are attacked, and experience sexual harassment, whether or not our sexuality is known" (1988, Sexism section, para. 1).

One other difference between men and women can be found in what we emphasize in selecting partners and relationships. The online exercises from the book *Everyday Encounters* identify the basis of romantic attraction and gender differences in preferences for romantic partners by analyzing personal ads. Students are asked to focus on similarities and differences between the advertisements written by women and men. Wood (2001) suggests that men are more likely than women to emphasize physical attractiveness and physical qualities in prospective partners. Typically, men define themselves more in terms of career success and financial standing than women, which suggests men believe money and success are important criteria in women's and gay men's evaluations of them (research concurs). On the other hand, women are more likely than men to emphasize psychological qualities and personal characteristics in people they'd like to meet and to define themselves more in terms of physical qualities than do male authors (Chapter 11, para. 4).

Another way to say this might be to say that in general women are much more relationship focussed, while men are more career focussed. Men place much more importance on a mate's attractiveness, while women are more interested in the personality and relationship qualities. Women also have much more plasticity in their sexuality than men do. This allows women to change and modify their sexual attitudes and behaviours to suit their relationships (Hendrick, 2004). These differences create a greater dichotomy between gays and lesbians than between lesbians and heterosexual women. We would argue that lesbians have more in common with their heterosexual sisters than they do with their gay brothers.

THE EVOLUTION OF FAMILY RECOGNITION OVER THE LAST QUARTER-CENTURY

Prior to 1980, lesbians and gay men had few legal rights, provincial or federal, even though homosexuality was decriminalized in 1969. Many significant changes have occurred in Canada and have impacted lesbians over the past quarter-century: Canadian law had been moving slowly towards equality. But the momentum changed dramatically when, in the early 1980s, Bill C-242 was introduced. It called for the end of discrimination on grounds of sexual orientation. This bill, although not passed, started an important political debate in Canada (EGALE, 2004).

In February 1981, police raided four bathhouses and arrested 300 men, which inspired over 2000 gays and lesbians to march in protest in the streets of Toronto. This event, referred to as Canada's stonewall riot, had a significant impact on the gay community. Two weeks later, gay, lesbian, and straight supporters held a rally to protest police brutality, and for lesbians, it was a time to protest their unsafe and unequal treatment in Canada (EGALE, 2004).

In 1982, Section 15 was added to the Canadian Charter of Rights and Freedoms, which included equality "before and under the law" and "the right to the equal protection and equal benefit of the law without discrimination." This was seen as a victory, although it did not specify sexual orientation. It was not until 1985 that the issue of sexual orientation was included in the Charter (EGALE, 2004). From the time of the 1985 all-party Parliamentary Standing Committee on Equal Rights report *Equality for All* (Canada. Parliament. House of Commons. Sub-Committee on Equality Rights & Boyer) and the government's 1986 response *Toward Equality* (Canada Parliament, House of Commons, Sub-Committee on Equality Rights), it was clear that a review of human rights protection in Canada was needed. The following noteworthy passages are from the 1985 report *Equality for All*:

> We were shocked by a number of the experiences of unfair treatment related to us by homosexuals in different parts of the country. We heard about the harassment of and violence committed against homosexuals. We were told in graphic detail about physical abuse and psychological oppression suffered by homosexuals. In several cities, private social clubs serving a homosexual clientele were damaged and the members harassed. Hate propaganda directed at homosexuals has been found in some parts of Canada. We were told of the severe employment and housing problems suffered by homosexuals (p. 26).

> We recommend that the *Canadian Human Rights Act* be amended to add sexual orientation as a prohibited ground of discrimination to the other grounds... (p. 30).

Toward Equality, the government's response, noted that "[t]he Government will take whatever measures are necessary to ensure that sexual orientation is a prohibited ground of discrimination in relation to all areas of federal jurisdiction" (Canada Parliament, House of Commons, Sub-Committee on Equality Rights, p. 13).

Between 1986 and 1991, many of the provinces accepted that sexual orientation was included in their Provincial legislation, but it took the Supreme Court decision on the *Vriend v. Alberta* case before Alberta conceded that sexual orientation protection is implied in the human rights legislation. The Vriend case started in 1991 when Delwin Vriend was fired from his job at King's University College in Alberta because of his sexual orientation. Vriend was denied a complaint to the Alberta Individual Rights Protection Act. He took it to an Alberta court in 1992, and they ruled that orientation must be treated as a protected class under human rights legislation. Alberta appealed and won in 1994. In 1998, the Supreme Court of Canada ruled that excluding homosexuals from Alberta's Individual Rights Protection Act was a violation of the Charter of Rights and Freedoms. This decision opened the door for many other decisions that moved gays and lesbians closer to equality for all (EGALE, 2004).

In 1992, the military was affected by gay and lesbian rights. In November, federal courts changed their stance to allow homosexuals to serve in the military. In 1996, the federal government added sexual orientation to the Canadian Human Rights Act through Bill C-33. In the same year, Bill C-41, the hate crimes bill, included sexual orientation and changed the *Criminal Code* to warrant stricter penalties for crimes motivated by bias, prejudice, or hate (EGALE, 2004).

In 1999, in the case *M. v. H.*, Ontario's Family Law Act challenged the definition of spouse and the option to apply for spousal support upon the dissolve of a relationship. Following an appeal, this decision was upheld by the Ontario Court of Appeal. This landmark case was very important for lesbians, as the Supreme Court acknowledged for the first time that same-sex couples had rights and responsibilities similar to heterosexual couples (EGALE, 2004).

Two couples, Kevin Bourassa and Joe Varnell and Anne and Elaine Vautour, were the first non-heterosexual Canadian couples to register their marriage in Toronto in 2001. It took until 2003 for these marriages to be ruled legal by three Ontario Court of Appeal judges (EGALE, 2004). The Netherlands was the first country to offer same-sex marriage in 2001, Belgium was second in 2003, and Spain third in 2005. Canada joined the other nations to allow same-sex marriage on June 28, 2005 (Marriage Equality, Inc, 2007). The official nod to marriage came with a mixed reaction. Some in the lesbian community were supportive while others felt it was a heterosexual institution. Along with the privileges of marriage, it forced Canadians and the gay and lesbian community to consider issues that had never been dealt with before, such as official acknowledgment, name changes, and the social constructs of marriage. The first Canadian gay lesbian divorce petition was filed in June of 2004, just one year after the province began to recognize same sex marriage. After five days of wedded bliss, M.M. and J.H were granted the first same-sex divorce in Toronto. In 2006, the Conservatives' motion to reopen the same-sex debate was defeated. Although this was a relief to the lesbian community, it did not ease the concern that the right to marry could be taken away.

These rules are all pivotal in terms of levelling the playing field for all in Canada. Many third wave lesbian feminists and queer women do not remember a day when lesbians and gays did not have most of the rights and responsibilities of their heterosexual counterparts. On the other hand, as second wave feminists, we have fought for those rights and continue to fight for rights, including the right to earn the same wage or hold the same job as our male counterparts. The third wave and the queer movement have a solid foundation of gains as a result of the changes that the second wave has made. Second wave feminists and lesbian feminists did not have the luxury to say we would not play the game by the rules: We were unable to reject the mainstream box we were being put in. Second wave feminist were too busy just trying to be able to play in the game, regardless of the rules.

MOTHERING

A number of Canadian publications over the last 20 years have looked at non-heterosexual women and parenting, for example Nelson (1996), Arnup (1995), and Foster (2005). Interestingly, the books, articles, and websites talk about lesbian mothers, not queer mothers. Although it has been very much an anti-establishment act for a woman to get pregnant in a same-sex relationship, all the women who chose to clearly identified themselves as lesbian, not as queer. Could this be that being a mother is very much an expected female role and thus not anti-establishment? In reviewing a number of Canadian books written on lesbian motherhood (e.g. Arnup, 1995; Kropf Nafziger, 2001; Nelson, 1996) the term *queer* does not appear anywhere in the index of any of these books. This would lead us to conclude that for the most part, we are lesbian mothers not queer mothers. This again speaks to the fact that we are different trees coexisting in the forest.

ISSUES UNIQUE TO LESBIANS IN CANADA

Since 2005, lesbians (and queers) have been afforded essentially identical rights in Canada to heterosexual women. There are, however, many issues that one could say are unique to lesbians in Canada—including marriage, rights to adoption and parenting, rights to inherit property, and rights to make life decisions for a same-sex partner who is unable to make her own decisions. Today in Canada, all laws and policies should be non-discriminatory, but we know this is not always the case. For example, lesbian and gay couples in Alberta still need to meet a much more stringent set of criteria to adopt or foster a non-biologically related child as compared to heterosexuals. The policy of Alberta Children's Services is to first rule out ALL potential heterosexual matches before non-heterosexuals will be considered for placements. Even though the majority of laws and policies have changed, public sentiment in some regions has been lagging. Clearly, just because the government of Canada adopts a non-discriminatory stance does not mean that all members of the public will change their views. This is illustrated by the ongoing tensions in the religious community regarding same-sex marriage. Denominations such as Anglicans and Lutherans are currently debating whether to allow their clergy to perform same-sex marriages. The fear in the church is that if the denominations allow same-sex blessings of marriage, it will divide the church, ultimately causing some already fragile institutions to flounder further.

Yet another example is that while working as a therapist during the 90s, one of us was told by her supervisor that under no circumstances was she to allow her clients to know she was a lesbian. The rationale for this was that family therapists should have family values, not values that contravened the family. (The assumption here, of course, was that lesbians are not part of a family, nor could they create family.) She was also told that it was an election year, and if it became public that a government agency was employing a lesbian to work with families, it could become an issue in the election. Upon reflection, we realize the power that we lesbian counsellors must have—we can cause a government to fall! Clearly, this is an example of attempting to work from within to create change as a lesbian therapist. My speculation is that if I had been a queer therapist, I most likely would have said "f--- the rules. I will be who I am and tell who I wish." Clearly, this was not the stance I took. I tried to educate those around me as to why my sexual orientation should not be an issue with regards to my work as a family counsellor.

RURAL–URBAN SPLIT

When I lived in an urban centre, I held hands with my partner and strolled through the park. When I moved to a rural setting, it no longer felt right.
(Anonymous)

Life in a major centre is a lot easier when you are a lesbian. Urban life offers theatre, lounges, coffee shops, social events, and many other amenities. In our experience, it takes a lot of courage to live in a rural setting and be a single or coupled lesbian. The rural lesbian community often consists of knowing who the others are and taking delight in knowing that you are not the only one. As previous urbanites, we have found a difference in levels of community discussion about being lesbian, or raising a family in a lesbian household. People may know or suspect that you are living in a same sex partnership, yet there is an awkward silence. They just do not want to talk about it. For example, people do not ask questions like, "How is your partner?" or "Would you and your partner like to come for dinner?" We often find ourselves in a complex dilemma, as we love our lives and enjoy the peaceful solitude of the country, yet find it can be lonely.

So you may ask, "Why stay?" Why do we stay in a small community that provides little social interaction with other lesbians and couples? We stay because we love the comfort of recognizing people in the local hardware shop, the slower-paced lifestyle, the country festivals, the variety of cultures, a lifestyle that is different than the city, and a generally enhanced quality of life. We also stay because those who know about and acknowledge our relationship provide comfort beyond what we have experienced when we lived in a large urban centre. We have found it is easier to be lesbians in a small community than to be lesbians in a large gay/queer community because of the slower pace, influence of diverse cultures, and quality of life.

POPULAR MEDIA WEIGHS IN ON THE QUESTION

When evaluating the question, Is lesbian a queer thing? we wondered what viewpoint popular media, which we recognise has power to persuade, may add to the discussion. Media influences and informs (or misinforms) society about a group or population. We looked for people in the media who may identify as a lesbian and spoke about being lesbian. What we confirmed is that as Canadian lesbians, we have few role models in the media today. Pornography has glamorized lesbianism and depicted it merely as a sexual act between two women, but only while a male is closely watching. Beyond pornography, Canada has K.D. Lang, Alex Trebek, Corner Gas and Degrassi. Recently, there was a CBC nationwide competition called the Greatest Canadian. If there was a show called the Greatest Canadian Lesbian (or Queer), would we have enough candidates to fill the competition? Can an average Canadian citizen name a lesbian person that has influenced them? Our vote is probably not. Yet, there are many, many lesbians who have done great things in Canada; unfortunately some of these women have felt the need to stay closeted for fear of retribution by society at large. These women may not be famous, but they are found in many professions from doctors, lawyers, playwrights, singers, and police officers.

Currently on television, we are influenced by our southern U.S. neighbour. Shows like Queer Eye for the Straight Guy, Queer as Folk and The L Word have portrayed queer men and women and lesbians as stunningly beautiful, sexy, impeccable designers, and in very unstable relationships. Ellen DeGeneres, Rosie O'Donnell, Martina Navratilova, and Melissa Etheridge are current popular icons in the lesbian community. Does a schism exist between the realities of lesbians and/or queers in Canada compared to their media portrayals? Why are we not portrayed more commonly in popular media and able to see ourselves multiple times in our choice of media? Where is lesbian being represented or more importantly often not represented in Canada and is lesbianism still being ignored? There is a noticeable absence of lesbian information in the media although this is beginning to change. In this case, our question about whether or not being a lesbian is a queer thing was not answered, but it certainly made us aware of the lack of unrealistic views of queers and lesbians. On the whole, though, as authors, we believe many lesbians would still say they are not represented in the media, even if queer people are beginning to be represented.

LESBIAN AND GAY PUBLICATIONS

Canada has had a number of gay and lesbian newspapers and periodicals. Over the last 40 years, most of them could be called very left leaning. One particularly well known publication was the *Body Politic*, which originated in Toronto. Although the book detailing the first decade of this publication was titled *Flaunting It!* (Jackson & Persky, 1982), the term *queer* is nowhere in the book. Clearly, the second wave activists were gays and lesbians, possibly butches and femmes, but not queers. It was not until the new millennium that the word *queer* began to appear in Canadian book titles. Two of these were *Never Going Back: A History of Queer Activism in Canada* (Warner, 2002) and *In a Queer Country* (Goldie, 2001), which chronicle the history of gays and lesbians in Canada. Yet the titles of the books talk of queers. The authors of these books use the term *queer* to encompass the history of lesbians and gays, while overlooking the fact that the history of lesbians in Canada and beyond is really more about the history of the second wave feminism movement than it is about the history of the gay rights movement. As was mentioned earlier in this chapter, lesbians have had much more in common with our heterosexual sisters than we ever will with our gay brothers.

COUNSELLING THOSE WHO IDENTIFY AS LESBIANS OR QUEER

Like any diversity, being lesbian or queer is personal and political. It may affect someone's personal life, his or her identity, global acceptance, and trust, or the ability to speak freely and be authentic. The issue of being sexually different may or may not be having an impact on the problem that a person brings into counselling. Identifying how comfortable you as a counsellor feel with sexuality that is the same or different from your own is a first step to working with diverse sexual orientation. The Sexual Orientation Counselor Competency Scale (SOCCS) (Bidell, 2005) is a tool that may help you discover your own ability. By using this scale, you can rate yourself on your training, awareness, attitudes on a number of issues, beliefs, skills, knowledge and research, and values towards lesbians.

The next step might be to work on addressing the areas that you are uncomfortable with, your fears, hidden or not, and ingrained societal beliefs. It is okay to acknowledge that you do not have enough information, or that you think it is a choice, or that you do not know anyone that is lesbian or queer? We often start where the client is at, so why not start where you are at and actively pursue what you need from there. Rutter, Estrada, Ferguson, and Diggs (2008) suggest that knowledge, awareness, and skills are key to positively influencing the mental health of clients and their partners.

Another question to ask yourself is How or should I bring up the topic of sexuality? Is it important? Just turn that question around. What would your answer be if someone asked that question to you? It is our opinion that sexuality is important and does affect our lives, thus it should be an open dialogue in the counselling room. There is a power imbalance in a counselling relationship, and the client needs to know that you are open to talking about sexuality, life partners, and lifestyle. Given the power imbalance, you should be the one asking the difficult questions.

Here is an example to demonstrate the point. An acquaintance recently got a new boss. Shortly after the boss started, she asked the acquaintance into her office and asked her about what it was like to be a lesbian, about her partner, and about how she manages at work. This friend expressed enormous relief, and she said, "for once I feel included, even though I didn't realize I felt dis-included before." Because this boss was interested in her life, without being voyeuristic, she was able to talk about her life and know that she did not have to hide her relationship. As a counsellor, you should feel comfortable asking about sexuality; however, it should not dominate the conversation for your benefit. Some clients need acknowledgement that their lesbianism or queerness is important, that it affects their lives and their problems. Let the client decide how much they want to share and how important it is, but do not be afraid to ask questions related to the problem. At the same time, if you ask a question, you need to be prepared to hear any answer, not just the politically correct ones. So prepare yourself for any sort of answer to avoid having negative non-verbals.

A final point to realize is that that every lesbian or queer individual is a person *first*, before taking into account a number of other things, such as her history, family complement or situation, past and present experiences, and her sexuality and sexual orientation. Each person experiences the labels of *queer* or *lesbian* differently. Some may choose to reject the notion of labels. We are all at different stages of our journey and different levels of being "out," depending on the situation. We may be coming out repeatedly or be in fear of acknowledging our sexuality to others or ourselves. It is more important that you are focussed on the whole person, hear and acknowledge her issues, and provide support to work them out, rather than assuming that the issues brought to the counselling room somehow tie back into sexual orientation. Sexuality and sexual orientation are important, but they may not be at all important to the presenting problem that brings the woman to counselling.

MULTIPLE OPPRESSIONS

Systemic racism and oppression are alive and well in Canada's lesbian, feminist, and queer communities. Multiple oppressions exist if you are non-white, non-middle class, or of "other sexual orientation" in Canada. Not all people are affected by oppression to the same degree or in the same way. As Hutchinson (in Van Der Meide, n.d.) observed, "The coming out process ... does not automatically 'liberate' people of colour, who, by revealing their sexual orientation and attempting to integrate themselves within white gay and lesbian communities, may encounter racial hierarchy" (p. 10)."Coming out" as a LGBT (lesbian, gay, bisexual, or transgendered) or two-spirited person, however potentially liberating a process that may be, cannot erase the realities of racism and ethnocentrism. These oppressive forces are not limited to heterosexual people.

The process of coming out can mean freedom and hope for the future, but it cannot take away years of prejudice, intolerance, hostility, racism, and ethnocentrism. Over the last decade, mass media has created an ideal lesbian that most of us cannot attain. The ideal lesbian more closely aligns with the ideal heterosexual woman's body type: hairless, tanned but not dark skinned, sleek sexy hair, flawless figure. The farther you are from the ideal, the more strongly the messages of being less desirable are felt. Regardless of whether we call ourselves lesbians or queer women, it is important that those of us who are white admit to being privileged. Just as heterosexuals have privilege, white lesbians also sit in a place of privilege within society by virtue of their skin colour. It is important that white lesbians recognize how multiple oppressions can further marginalize lesbians in Canadian society. Even if you are a lesbian therapist, if you are otherwise mainstream, it is difficult to truly understand what it is like to be a lesbian from a culture where lesbianism may be viewed as sin punishable by death.

CONCLUDING REMARKS

To answer the question of whether being lesbian is a queer thing, clearly it depends. From the standpoint of women who identify with or have grown up as part of the second wave feminist movement, the answer is no. Mostly, these women identify with their feminist sisters and see themselves working to gain equal rights for all women, including lesbians. Queer women, by definition, align themselves with queer politics, which states that as queers, they do not want to be put into a box. They are who they are and do not want to be limited by a label. As counsellors, it is important not to impose a label or a political stance on women seeking your services. In summary, it is our educated opinion that lesbians may be feminists and women may be queer, and while there might possibly be some combination of the above two, most women who see themselves as lesbians are not queer.

REFERENCES

Arnup, K. (1995). *Lesbian parenting: Living with pride and prejudice.* Charlottetown, PEI: gynergy books.

Bidell, M. (2005). The Sexual Orientation Counselor Competency Scale: Assessing attitudes, skills and knowledge of counselors working with lesbian, gay and bisexual clients. *Counselor Education and Supervision, 44,* p. 267–279.

Bridget, J. (1988). *Lesbian information service annual report.* Retrieved August 11, 2007, from http://lesbianinformationservice.org/ar88.htm.

Butler, J. (1990). *Gender trouble: Feminism and the subversion of identity.* London: Routledge.

Canada Parliament. House of Commons Sub-Committee on Equality Rights. (1986). *Toward equality: The response to the report of the Parliamentary Committee on Equality Rights.* Ottawa Ontario: Communications and Public Affairs, Dept. of Justice Canada.

Canada Parliament House of Commons. Sub-Committee on Equality Rights. & Boyer, P. (1985), *Equality for all: Report of the Parliamentary Committee on Equality Rights.* [Ottawa]: Queen's Printer for Canada.

Canadian Charter of Rights and Freedoms. (1982). Section 15. In Government of Canada. Retrieved July 19, 2007, from http://laws.justice.gc.ca/en/charter/.

Crain, C. (2000). Interview with On Queer Theory. *Hermenaut 11.08.00.* Retrieved May 31, 2007, from http://www.hermenaut.com/a156.shtml.

de Lauretis, T. (1991). Queer theory: Lesbian and gay sexualities (*differences*). *Journal of Feminist Cultural Studies, 3*(2), iii–xviii.

EGALE. (2004). Outlaws & inlaws: Your guide to LGBT rights, same-sex relationships and Canadian law. Ottawa: EGALE.

Foster, D. (2005). *Growing a family? The experiences of planned two-mother families.* Unpublished doctoral dissertation. University of Alberta.

Goldie, T. (Ed.). (2001). *In a queer country: Gay and lesbian studies in a Canadian context.* Vancouver: Arsenal Pulp Press.

Hendrick, S. (2004). *Understanding close relationships.* Toronto: Pearson.

Jackson, F. & Persky, S. (1982). *Flaunting it! A decade of gay journalism from The Body Politic.* Toronto: Pink Triangle Press.

Jeffreys, S. (2003). *Unpacking queer politics: A lesbian feminist perspective*. Oxford: Polity.

Kinsman, G. (2001). Challenging Canadian and queer nationalisms. In T. Goldie (Ed.), *In a queer country: Gay and lesbian studies in a Canadian context* (209–234). Vancouver: Arsenal Pulp Press.

Kropf Nafziger, G. (Ed.). (2001). *Home truths: Lesbian mothers come out to their daughters*. Edmonton: Rowan Books.

Marriage Equality, Inc. (2007). *Get the facts on marriage*. Retrieved August 14, 2007, from http://www.marriageequality.org/meusa/facts.shtml?marriage-status.

Nelson, F. (1996). *Lesbian motherhood: An exploration of Canadian lesbian families*. Toronto, ON: University of Toronto Press.

Rebick, J. (2005). *Ten thousand roses: The making of a feminist revolution*. Toronto: Penguin.

Rich, A. (1980). Compulsory heterosexuality and lesbian existence. *Signs, 5*. (reprinted in Abelove et al. (Eds.) (2003). *The lesbian and gay studies reader* (pp. 227–254). New York: Routledge.

Ristock, J., & Pennell, J. (1996). *Community research as empowerment. Feminist links, postmodern interruptions*. Toronto: Oxford.

Rutter, P., Estrada, D., Ferguson, L., & Diggs, G. (2008). Sexual orientation and counselor competency: The impact of training on enhancing awareness, knowledge and skills. *Journal of LGBT Issues in Counseling, 2*(2), 109–125.

Seidman, S. (Ed.). (1996). *Queer theory/sociology*. Cambridge, MA: Blackwell.

Tambiah, Y. (1995). Sexuality and human rights. In Margaret A. Schuler (Ed.), *From basic needs to basic rights: Women's claim to human rights* (pp. 369–390).Washington, DC: Women, Law and Development International.

Taylor, Y. (2005). The gap and how to mind it: Intersections of class and sexuality (Research Note). *Sociological Research Online, 10*(3). Retrieved June 10, 2007, from http://www.socresonline.org.uk/10/3/taylor.html.

van Der Meide, W. (n.d.). *Literature review*. Canadian Heritage, Multiculturalism Program. Retrieved July 20, 2007, from http://canada.metropolis.net/events/Diversity/SexualOrientation_meide_e.pdf.

Warner, M. (Ed.). (1993). *Fear of a queer planet: Queer politics and social theory*. Minneapolis, MN: University of Minnesota Press.

Warner, T. (2002). *Never going back: A history of queer activism in Canada*. Toronto: University of Toronto Press.

Wood, J. (2001). *Chapter 11 Committed Romantic Relationships*. Nelson Thompson Learning. Retrieved June 19, 2007, from http://www.nelson.com/nelson/communicate/everydayencounters1e/chapter11.html.

Counselling Practice as Feminist Praxis

s discussions in the earlier chapters suggest, the ease by which women's experiences continue to be trivialized and invalidated is an ongoing concern for feminist theorists (Contratto & Rossier, 2005). Regardless of the origins and adoptions of various feminist perspectives, common themes informing feminist therapy models emerge. A number of chapters in this collection have discussed how feminist theory and practice demands an understanding that power imbalances both create and magnify women's problems. As well, other chapters in this collection have identified context in its various forms as a critical variable in deconstructing the effects on both the self and society of the inequities that arise within and between differing contexts. For all feminist therapists, therapy models informing practice are based on feminist principles advocating the "personal is political," the need to establish and maintain egalitarian relationships, and the valuing of women's beliefs and perspectives (Worrell & Remer, 2002). In relation to all of the theory and themes guiding feminist counselling practice, the overarching goal of feminist therapy is a movement toward the empowerment of women. The papers in this section continue to draw on feminist theory. However, the focus is on specific issues and strategies that can be used to inform counselling practice and, more broadly, the empowerment of women who come into practice.

Ethics and ethical decision-making are fundamentals of counselling practice. In the first chapter of this section—*Counselling Women: Ethics for Diversity and Social Justice*—Jean Pettifor and Judi Malone explore the need for ethical guidelines designed specifically to help psychologists and counsellors who work with women. With an awareness of population diversity and human rights, and an understanding of the need to pursue equality and social justice for women who seek counselling, professionals can benefit immensely from guidelines that are designed to address issues specific to women's experiences. The authors provide the background information that informed the development of the *Guidelines for Ethical Psychological Practice with Women* (Pettifor,

Malone, & Church, 2007), a document reprinted in full in the appendix of this collection. Following a discussion of the ethical principles guiding decision-making, Pettifor and Malone go through the necessary steps, adapted from the *Canadian Code of Ethics for Psychologists* (CPA, 2000), that are needed to inform ethical decision-making and practice. A series of vignettes describing conflict of interest situations between women clients and counsellors are also included in the chapter, so that readers can consider solutions that are ethical, non-sexist, and empowering in working through the kinds of dilemmas that arise in counselling practice.

Janice Ristock's *Feminist Counsellors Respond to Abuse in Lesbian Relationships: Confronting Heteronormalcy* begins with an overview of prevalent forms of physical, sexual, emotional, verbal, and financial abuse and elaborates on specific abusive behaviours that reflect the larger context of the homophobia and heterosexism that affect non-heterosexual relationships. The chapter goes on to explore issues surrounding support for survivors of abuse and the particular problems and barriers that women of diverse sexual orientations who are the victims of violence in relationships face. Acknowledging a lack theory surrounding same-sex partner abuse, Ristock's chapter reports on findings from her nationwide study of feminist counsellors in which "dominant" and "marginal" feminist discourses are used to interrogate understandings of lesbian abuse. The chapter concludes both with a discussion of the need for "more spaces and language to talk about lesbian relationships and lesbian abuse" and with the presentation of practical guidelines that can be adapted for use by both close friends as well as counsellors or services providers in working with lesbians experiencing intimate relationship violence.

In *Feminist Crisis Counselling*, Karen M. Nielsen and Ann Marie Dewhurst focus on a feminist approach to counselling women in "crisis" using a relational orientation and one that is also based in understandings of power inequities. The authors define a crisis situation as an event or series of events in which a person's ability to cope is overwhelmed. The model described by the authors can be adapted for dealing with the impact of any crisis event, whether it is an accident, act of violence, or a natural disaster. The authors consider "pain and injury" from a women centred perspective and discuss power and gender as important factors in making sense of the impact of a crisis event on well-being. They talk about assessment, the stance of the assessor, and the unique sources of trauma for women, and focus on "behaviour" rather than "diagnosis." Nielsen and Dewhurst describe how empowerment through storytelling allows client and counsellor to deconstruct crisis experiences, encouraging change that comes primarily through women's understandings of the narratives they have constructed rather than through counsellors' prescriptions.

Continuing with the importance of women's narratives, in *Telling Stories: Making Sense* Arlene Young shows how, in both counselling and research, there is power in telling stories about important life events. Perhaps equally importantly to the storyteller is the knowledge that others have heard and understood their relevance. Young highlights how actively listening to another person's story helps women make sense of their experiences. The author describes the research she has conducted on women's experiences of job loss and the significance of finding out about what it meant to the women who lost their jobs. Through examining the theory and processes of a feminist, narrative approach, Young demonstrates the importance of narrative construction in making sense of life experiences. She provides useful suggestions and strategies for adapting this approach for counsellors in their professional practice and for others to adopt in supporting a friend or family member in need.

The final chapter of this section addresses the difficult circumstances under which women do not come voluntarily into counselling or do not voluntarily engage in storytelling. In *Counselling Women Mandated to Participate in Therapy*, Ann Marie Dewhurst and Karen Nielsen identify issues that might bring women into mandated counselling and discuss feminist understandings of issues surrounding this difficult and complex situation. The authors consider women's responsibility for committing anti-social acts from a feminist perspective and identify ways to work with mandated women from a feminist, accountability framework. Dewhurst and Nielsen focus on understanding women both as perpetrators of anti-social behaviour within a feminist context as well as the contexts in which women are mandated to counselling. Strategies for supporting change where there is limited confidentiality, mandated sharing of information, required progress reporting, and collaboration with third parties are discussed in relation to women who have been mandated into counselling. The authors provide ways that counsellors can support their clients in the resolution of issues that led them to mandated treatment in the first place.

REFERENCES: SECTION III

Canadian Psychological Association. (2000). *Canadian code of ethics for psychologists.* (3rd Ed.). Ottawa: Canadian Psychological Association.

Contratto, S., & Rossier, J. (2005). Early trends in feminist therapy theory and practice. *Women & Therapy, 28*(2), 7-26.

Pettifor, J., Malone, J., & Church, E. (2007). *Guidelines for ethical psychological practice with women.* Ottawa: Canadian Psychological Association.

Worell, J., & Remer, P. (2002). *Feminist perspectives in therapy: Empowering diverse women.* N.Y.: John Wiley & Sons.

CHAPTER 10

Counselling Women: Ethics for Diversity and Social Justice by Jean Pettifor and Judi Malone

ean Pettifor, past president of the College of Alberta Psychologists, the Canadian Psychological Association, and the Psychologists Association of Alberta, and adjunct professor at the University of Calgary, has received many awards for her lifetime contributions to the discipline of psychology and community mental health, and for the promotion of professionalism and quality in human services. She has been a practitioner, teacher, consultant, and researcher, and has served in many positions within psychology organizations. Her contributions are recognized provincially, nationally, and internationally. Today, she is probably best known for her continuing work in the development of practice guidelines and for promoting a value-based ethical decision-making model for professionals.

Judi Malone is a registered psychologist who works as a counsellor and university educator. She is an existential feminist practitioner in a rural private practice with an active interest in mentoring future Aboriginal psychologists. She is active with many provincial and national psychology organizations, and her research interests include professional ethics, rural psychology, the psychology of women, cross-cultural psychology, counselling and psychotherapy, existential psychology, and disabilities.

Both authors are psychologists and committed to the development of ethics within the field of psychology. That said, this chapter is not intended to apply only to psychologists. Counselling occurs across professions (psychologists, social workers, nurses, psychiatrists) and is provided by many skilled paraprofessionals (shelter workers, crisis line operators), who bring a wealth of practical understanding and passion for women's issues to the helping professions. Throughout this chapter, psychology is used in an inclusive manner to mean the application of knowledge to the treatment of mental health concerns—what all of us do as counsellors in the helping professions.

INTRODUCTION

Why do we need special guidelines for psychologists and counsellors working with women? In this twenty-first century, professionals are increasingly aware of population diversity, the importance of human rights, and the need to pursue equality and social justice. Progress has been made in achieving equality of opportunity in Western societies, and professional codes of ethics are based on values of respect for all people, which is the antithesis of bias, discrimination, and oppression. A reality check, however, may indicate that these values are not always demonstrated in practice. In this chapter, we explore how therapists and counsellors who are not sufficiently knowledgeable of the conditions of women's lives are not competent to provide appropriate services. Counselling is especially harmful if counsellors are culture blind to both individual and societal issues. Professionals benefit from guidelines that address issues specific to women's experiences.

Here, we explore the history of ethical guidelines for psychological services with women in North America, paying special attention to the Canadian context and the *Guidelines for Ethical Psychological Practice with Women* (Pettifor, Malone, & Church, 2007) available in the Appendix of this book. We will also present steps for ethical decision-making as adapted from the Canadian Psychological Association's (CPA, 2000) *Canadian Code of Ethics for Psychologists*. Several vignettes will represent conflicts of interest between involved parties, and the reader is asked to consider solutions that are non-sexist, empowering, and that recognize the context of women's lives. Vignettes will also include situations involving immigrant women and their values from their cultures of origin. The authors will review one vignette in detail. Although the Canadian *Guidelines for Ethical Psychological Practice with Women* has been developed within a feminist context, we believe that it is relevant to professionals of most theoretical orientations and to both female and male counsellors. While one does not need to be a feminist counsellor to act in a competent and caring manner, informed and ethical practice does promotes core feminist values, such as acknowledging social factors, power differentials, and strategies for achieving gender equality (Mandell, 2005). The feminist commitment to gender equality and freedom from oppression is strong in Western societies, where these values are often seen as issues of social justice. Awareness and sensitivity are required to ensure that this commitment is more than mere words. North American counsellors need to be particularly vigilant in considering client needs and values, and in not making assumptions.

Some of these issues will be illustrated in this chapter through guidelines, questions for reflection, ethical decision-making steps, and ethical dilemmas. Reflections are provided throughout the chapter to help the reader move beyond abstract concepts of ethics to the application of ethics in actual settings. These reflections may assist the reader in addressing the context of complex human interactions. Consult the *Guidelines* in the Appendix of this book as you reflect on this first example

---

Reflection

- When affirmative action for workplace equity means recruiting women and visible minorities, is this actually another form of discrimination and oppression of those who are not women or visible minorities?

- Identify three recent personal examples of subtle gender discrimination.

HISTORY AND CONTEXT

The Universal Declaration of Human Rights was adopted shortly after World War II (United Nations, 1948). The Declaration of the International Year of Women (United Nations, 1975) provided a major impetus to North American associations to consider the circumstances of women and recommend needed changes. The American Psychological Association's (APA) Task Force on Sex Bias and Sex-Role Stereotyping in Psychotherapeutic Practice (APA, 1975) reported four clusters of sexist practices of therapists. The first was fostering traditional sex roles. Today, many women enter traditionally male occupations but with varying degrees of acceptance and success (Bagihole, 2007; Proctor & Padfield, 1999). The second sexist practice identified was bias in expectations and devaluation of women. Despite greater awareness and more stringent ethical codes, gender bias, even if diminished or more subtle, still exists in counselling (Danzinger & Reynolds, 2000; Robitschek, & Hershberger, 2005). The third was sexist use of psychoanalytic concepts. There is loud criticism that Freud was wrong about penis envy, moral inferiority, and passivity (Auld, 2002; Lax, 2005; Steiner, 1994). Finally, the fourth was responding to women as sex objects, particularly in counselling where transference can highlight feelings of attraction. A major ongoing source of professional misconduct is sexual involvement with clients (Finger, 2000). The APA task force has developed guidelines for ethical and effective psychotherapy with women (APA, 1978) that essentially countered the sexist practices it had reported. The APA Division on Counseling followed suit with *Principles Concerning the Counseling and Therapy of Women* (APA, Division 17, 1981), and included a report on models for training counsellors of women (APA, Division 17, 1981).

In 1975, CPA established a task force that produced the *Report on the Status of Women in Canadian Psychology* (Pyke, 2001; Pyke & Stark-Adamec, 1981; Wand 1977). The fervor of Canadian women psychologists in the 1970s and 80s led the CPA to adopt many guidelines with respect to women and equality. The first was: *Guidelines for Therapy and Counselling with Women* (Pettifor, Larson, & Cammaert, 1980), and the follow-up resource *Therapy and Counselling with Women: A Handbook of Educational Materials* (Pettifor, Larson, & Cammaert, 1984), both of which were developed to endorse women's equality and reduce or eliminate sex-role stereotyping of women in therapy. These were followed in quick succession by *Guidelines for Non-sexist Research* (Stark-Adamec & Kimball, 1984), and the *Guidelines for the Elimination of Sexual Harassment* (Byers & Price, 1985).

The first *Canadian Code of Ethics for Psychologists* was adopted by the Canadian Psychological Association (CPA, 1986), followed by the first companion manual, *The Canadian Code of Ethics for Psychologists: A Companion Manual* (CPA, 1988). The first principle of the *Canadian Code of Ethics*— Respect for the Dignity of Persons—emphasized the inherent worth of all persons without prejudice of personal characteristics and was stronger than the previous statement of non-discrimination.

The CPA's Section on Women and Psychology, established in 1976, flourished (Pyke, 2001). The Applied Division Newsletter, the Section on Women in Psychology Newsletter, and presentations and workshops at conventions all contributed to an awareness of the unacceptability of sexism in the profession and in society. Detailed accounts of the history of Canadian feminism in psychology can be found in articles by Pyke and Stark-Adamec (1981), Stark (2000), Pyke (2001), Boatswain et al. (2001), and Church, Pettifor and Malone (2006). This is the context in which the *Guidelines for Ethical Psychological Services with Women* (CPA, 2007), found in the Appendix of this book, were developed. Women within the APA and the Feminist Therapy Institute had parallel concerns and activities (Brabeck, 2002; Lerman & Porter, 1990; Rave & Larsen, 1995). The Feminist Therapy Institute developed the *Feminist Therapy Code of Ethics* (1987/1999), and the APA adopted the *Guidelines for Psychological Practice with Girls and Women: A Joint Task Force of APA Divisions 17 and 35* (2007).

Reflection

- In 1972, the Canadian Psychological Association (CPA) convention organizers rejected all the submissions that had a feminist orientation (Church, et al., 2006; Pyke, 2001; Stark, 2001). The

244

women involved advertised and held a successful "underground symposium" in a nearby hotel to present their papers. Could this happen today? What if women, for example, actively promoted an anti-war agenda on the grounds that women and children suffer the greatest abuses during war time?

- Humour is said to be healing. How would you respond to a male colleague on a professional committee who asks whether you are going to speak about another "broad issue" with heavy emphasis on the "broad"?

When it came to updating the *Guidelines for Therapy and Counselling with Women* (CPA, 1980), it was no longer necessary to empirically prove that sexist discrimination and oppression exist, that such behaviour is a violation of human rights and an abuse of power, or that ignorance about women's issues could result in counsellor incompetence. Today, there is greater acceptance of diversity, and it is appropriate to develop aspirational and practical guidelines to enhance the ability of professionals to be respectful, caring, and fair when working with women and diversity. The CPA (Section for Women in Psychology) and the APA (Division 17, Society of Counseling Psychology, and Division 35, Society for the Psychology of Women) recently revised their guidelines for therapy and counselling with women. In both countries, both of these committees of volunteers worked simultaneously but independently, and both adopted revisions in February 2007 (APA, 2007; Pettifor et al., 2007). The CPA document is a relatively short, user-friendly document for the busy practitioner. The APA document is long and an invaluable resource in the application of the guidelines in various work settings, and it provides a comprehensive academic bibliography. Both have expanded the scope of practice beyond the narrower historical focus on therapy and counselling to a full range of psychological practice with women (APA, 2007; Pettifor et al, 2007). This chapter focusses specifically on applying the Canadian *Guidelines for Ethical Psychological Practice with Women* to counselling and therapy with women and the range of ethical issues professional counsellors face when working with women.

These *Guidelines for Ethical Psychological Practice with Women* are linked to the four ethical principles of the *Canadian Code of Ethics for Psychologists* and are expected to be used in conjunction with those guidelines. This is meant to provide a stronger and more explicit moral foundation, as has been done with the *Guidelines for Non-Discriminatory Practice* (Crozier, Harris, Larsen, Pettifor & Sloane, 1996/2001) and the *Guidelines for Psychologists Addressing Recovered Memories* (Crozier & Pettifor, 1996/2001). These *Guidelines for Ethical Psychological Practice with Women* address the different emotional relationship concerns of women, the fact that women are more likely to seek psychological services than men, and the paucity of services specific to women's needs.

Reflection

- A therapist lost his license to practice under his legally controlled title after a disciplinary committee found him guilty of sexual intimacy with female clients. Local women were outraged when he legally continued his practice using a non-regulated professional title. Do professional guidelines for practice with women help to diminish harm? What is the role of legislation?

- Your client's treatment is paid for by a third party (e.g., insurance company, employee assistance program, managed care company). This funder limits treatment to 10 sessions, a condition that you were aware of prior to beginning counselling. By the eighth session, the client begins to disclose traumatic childhood sexual abuse that cannot be sufficiently addressed by the tenth session. How do the *Guidelines* help you in deciding what you should do?

GUIDELINES FOR ETHICAL PRACTICE

The *Guidelines for Ethical Psychological Practice with Women* (Pettifor et al., 2007) were developed to help Canadian psychologists provide competent and ethical services to women. The *Guidelines* consider issues and conditions that affect women's lives and encourage service providers to act in ways that are non-sexist and empowering and to recognize the realities of women's lives (Pettifor et al., 2007).

The structure of the *Guidelines* consists of an introduction and rationale, a description of each of the four ethical principles in the *Canadian Code of Ethics for Psychologists*, guidelines specific to each ethical principle for working with women, positive and negative examples of applying the principles, and predominantly Canadian references.

The following commentary addresses the significance of the four ethical principles of the CPA Code in the *Guidelines for Ethical Psychological Practice with Women* (Pettifor et al., 2007).

246

Principle I: Respect for the Dignity of Persons

Respect for the dignity of persons is the moral foundation for the *Guidelines*. Respect is described as valuing the inherent worth of human beings, including their autonomy, independence, and self-determination. Respect, therefore, is more than legislated rights for fair treatment in the workplace or before the courts. It is recognized that those who are most vulnerable and disadvantaged require professionals to do more to protect their rights and value their humanity. Professional codes in Western societies have traditionally focussed on the individual and on individual rights, whereas in some cultures, greater emphasis is placed on collective identity and collective well-being. These *Guidelines* include concerns for individuals, families, communities, and cultures—the larger context within which the client lives. Counsellors and therapists have a special responsibility to be sensitive to, and respectful of, people from cultures that are different from their own.

Respect is often perceived as protecting human rights and hence applying the Universal Declaration of Human Rights (United Nations, 1948). While this document is complementary, ethical guidelines and codes are intended for the use of professionals working directly with identifiable clients. The Declaration of Human Rights is a more political and legal document where signatory states and nations promise to treat their citizens with fairness, equality, and justice. The *Guidelines* are explicit about the role of the first principle:

In applying the principle of Respect for the Dignity of Persons to their psychological practice with women, psychologists ensure that they do not, wittingly or unwittingly, engage in or support any previous or existing sex-based unjust discrimination and/or oppressions (e.g., fewer choices, greater negative consequences, restrictions on personal liberty), whether these factors are based in the individual, the family, the community, or the socio-political context. Psychologists also recognize that, in addition to gender-based unjust discrimination and/or oppressions, a woman client also may be subject, or may have been subjected, to unjust discrimination and oppressions due to other diversities (e.g., race, culture, poverty). Psychologists also understand that such circumstances can increase the power imbalance in the professional relationship, and that special consideration and safeguards for protecting and promoting moral rights are increasingly warranted in such circumstances (Pettifor et al., 2007, p. 4).

Reflection

- After reading Respect for the Dignity of Persons found in the *Guidelines*, what is your initial reaction?

- What are three other words synonymous with the word *respect*?

Principle II: Responsible Caring

Part of respect is caring. Clients seeking help are, arguably, seeking care, compassion, and understanding. Unless it is based on knowledge, skills, and a commitment to be helpful, efforts to assist may actually result in harm. The description of responsible caring for women rests heavily on competence, knowledge of women's issues in society, and on self-awareness (how the counsellor's experiences may influence or interfere with their ability to help). The *Guidelines* address what it means to be competent in working professionally with women.

> In applying the principle of Responsible Caring to their psychological practice with women, psychologists understand how women's lives are shaped by their sex in interaction with their culture, nationality, ethnicity, race, religion, gender identification, relationship status, sexual orientation, physical or mental abilities, age, socioeconomic status, as well as by other personal characteristics, conditions, or statuses. Psychologists also recognize that their women clients live in multiple contexts and that, while many of these contexts give meaning and satisfaction to their lives, some experiences (e.g., poverty, violence, undue pressure to make specific choices, socialization to a primarily passive and/or submissive role, other abuses of power) are harmful to their well being. In attempting to be of benefit to women clients, psychologists understand that it is important not to pathologize such harmful effects, but rather to view and treat them as understandable responses and results. In developing and monitoring their self-knowledge with respect to their delivery of psychological services for women, psychologists are particularly sensitive to understanding how the contexts of their own lives might influence or interfere with their attempts to help and not harm women clients (Pettifor et al., 2007, pp. 6–7).

Reflection

- Read Responsible Caring found in the *Guidelines*. Feminists emphasize outside forces (social pressures, abuse of power, and oppression) as determinants of many of women's problems in life, as opposed to inside forces (intrapsychic, psychiatric, or biomedical conditions). How do you resolve this apparent conflict on the causation and appropriate treatment approaches to counselling women, specifically those with diagnoses such as depression?

- When you were a child, what did your parents hope you would become? If you think differently today about women's role in society, how did that change come about?

Principle III: Integrity in Relationships

Honesty and straightforwardness between counsellor and client is a highly valued aspect of respect in Western society. Integrity also means knowing when honesty would do harm. With integrity, conflicts between client and counsellor values are discussed openly in order to make decisions in the best interests of the client. Counsellors avoid conflict of interest and in no way exploit the client for personal convenience or gain. The counsellor requires self-knowledge in order to avoid personal bias in the professional relationship. We are often unaware of our own personal biases and must be sensitive to the views of others in both our own and other cultures. The *Guidelines* summarize this principle as such:

> In applying the principle of Integrity in Relationships to their psychological practice with women, psychologists are aware of and sensitive to the special trust issues that some women clients might have, including being distrustful or overly trustful of those in authority. Psychologists also recognize how their own biases and early socialization might affect their attitudes and actions towards their women clients, and strive to be as self-aware, objective, and unbiased as possible. When psychologists and women clients have different beliefs relative to psychological practice, the psychologist should acknowledge this and work collaboratively with the client to resolve the issue in the best interests of the client. In some instances, this may mean referring the woman to another psychologist (Pettifor et al., 2007, p.7.).

Reflection

- Read Integrity in Relationships found in the *Guidelines*. What are your feelings about issues considered controversial in society today? Examples include abortion, mixed marriages, contraceptives, wife and child abuse, child pornography, weight-loss surgery, female circumcision, hymen replacement, sex-trade work, or engagement in risky sexual practices.

- How would your experiences and feelings affect your counselling in any of these areas? Which ones would be most difficult for you?

Principle IV: Responsibility to Society

Counsellors, psychologists, and other health care professionals are trained to provide direct client services that benefit others and above all do no harm. Activities that benefit society exist on a continuum from counselling identified clients to active lobbying for major political changes in the interest of social justice (to influence issues such as racism, poverty, homelessness, sexism, family violence, illiteracy, or the sex trade). These professions are rarely trained to bring about social service policy changes; however, feminists deeply concerned with the oppressive aspects of society and the abuse of power are committed to the eradication of oppression in society. While there is still debate on how assertive counsellors should be in working for social change, the trend is for greater emphasis on activities in the name of social justice. It is wisely stated in the *Guidelines* that there are multiple ways to help improve the lives of women in society and that counsellors choose how to use their time for the collective good. According to Toporek, Gerstein, Found, Roysircar, and Israel (2006) the term *social justice* is an integral part of a counsellor's professional identity. Diverse populations who suffer from societal discrimination know that there is social injustice and have a stronger commitment to bringing about change. This commitment, for example, is found in the Feminist Therapists Code of Ethics (1987/1999).

In applying the principle of Responsibility to Society to psychological practice with women, psychologists acknowledge that their concern for the welfare of all human beings in society includes concern for the welfare of women in society, and that some psychological theory, research, and practice has distorted, ignored or pathologized women's experiences. In response, psychologists accept the responsibility to do what they can to change societal laws and structures that unjustly discriminate or lead to oppressions of women. They recognize that there are multiple avenues to improve the lives of women, and choose the most appropriate and beneficial use of their time and talents to help meet this collective responsibility (Pettifor et al., 2007).

Reflection

- Review Responsibility to Society found in the *Guidelines*. What are three ways that you could contribute to improving the collective lot of women in society today?

- Which of the following words or phrases are you more comfortable with: responsibility to society, social change agent, social activist, advocate, lobbyist, mover and shaker, catalyst for change, or social justice? Why?

ETHICAL DECISION-MAKING

Some ethical decisions are made quickly. Others require time-consuming deliberation and, when appropriate, consultation with parties affected by the problem or with colleagues and/or advisory bodies. Seeking consultation is a responsible approach to making decisions, and in doing so, all four ethical principles are to be taken into account. In circumstances where the conflict between ethical principles cannot be resolved, priority normally is given to respect for the dignity of individuals and to responsibility to society. As mentioned earlier, this ordering is culture-based and is not universal. Some dilemmas, despite a counsellor making every reasonable effort to apply ethical principles, may defy a solution that is satisfactory for everyone involved. If a psychologist acts as a matter of personal conscience, that decision is expected to be based on a decision-making process that can bear public scrutiny.

When counsellors work within specific contexts, they need to know that often there is not one clearly correct response to resolving a dilemma. Therefore, they may need to look at an ethical decision-making model as a framework for considering their ethics code, relevant guidelines, and the needs and requirements of the environment (O'Neill, 2005; Staal & King, 2000). "In order to provide appropriate and non-sexist psychological services, psychologists must be sensitive to, and knowledgeable about, individual, group, community, and socio-cultural differences. Psychological services also need to be responsive to the complex and varied contexts of Canadian women's lives" (Pettifor et al., 2007, p. 3). Guidelines for serving specific populations, such as women, assist professionals in making more-informed decisions (Lehr & Sumarah, 2004). Review the guidelines from the Appendix and reflect on how specific guidelines reflect the needs of women (Pettifor et al., 2007, p. 9–12).

In psychological practice with women, psychologists:

1. Respect, listen, and learn from women clients, particularly when a woman client's life experiences differ substantively from the psychologist's own. (Principle I)

2. Use inclusive and respectful language with women clients; label issues related to women as such (e.g., "women's issues"); use non-specific terms regarding an individual's sex when appropriate (e.g., police "officer"); and avoid language that stereotypes, demeans, or infantilizes (e.g., "girl"). (Principle I)

3. Recognize that women clients might feel in a power-down situation when working with a male psychologist, or with any "expert," be they male or female, and that the power imbalance may make it difficult for some women clients to challenge the psychologist. (Principle I)

4. When needed, take special precautions with women clients (e.g., more time, more reassurance about right to choose) to ensure that any consent for psychological services is informed and voluntary. This includes consent for services and consent for disclosure of confidential information to others who may claim the right or need to know (e.g., partners or physicians). (Principle I)

5. Understand that, with repeated exposure to traumatic events, some women cope through making what may appear to be poor lifestyle "choices" (alcohol abuse, etc.), and that it is important to avoid diagnostic labelling that may stigmatize. (Principle I)

6. Are aware of their own cultural, moral, social, and sex-based beliefs and values and how these may influence or interfere with their ability to help and not harm their women clients; for example, how their position of privilege as professionals may lead to de-sensitization regarding the realities of women clients who live in poverty. (Principle II)

7. Keep up to date regarding current research and issues related to working with women clients through continuing education

activities such as attending conferences, reading, workshops, and courses. (Principle II)

8. Are aware of how some psychological theory, research, and practice may have distorted, ignored, or pathologized women's experience, critically appraise the applicability of psychological theories and research to women, and only use those aspects that are appropriate. (Principle II)

9. Obtain supervision or consultation, or refer to another practitioner, if their beliefs and values about a woman client's particular situation (e.g., beliefs and values regarding abortion or a woman's role in child rearing) are likely to interfere in any substantive way with their ability to benefit and not harm the woman client. If appropriate, this may include collaboration with the women clients on the solution that best serves their interests. (Principle II)

10. When needed, consult with others who are more knowledgeable about, and experienced in, working with issues related to psychological services for women. (Principle II)

11. Are knowledgeable about community resources and programs for women, recognize how such community supports and programs can be helpful and empowering, and refer women clients to them as appropriate. (Principle II)

12. Recognize that women clients may live in multiple contexts and have diverse identities, and that gender inequity may be only one of many inequities with which they contend. (Principle II)

13. Assess accurately the source of a woman client's difficulties, apportioning causality appropriately among individual, situational, and socio-cultural factors. (Principle II)

14. Help women clients to become aware of the various factors that contribute to their difficulties and, where appropriate, facilitate women client's examination of their experiences of unjust discrimination and oppressions, and support them in making new choices and developing new strategies. (Principle II)

15. Take care with women clients to determine whether they have experienced physical or sexual assault, recognizing that women are more likely than men to have been victims of physical and sexual assault, including in the context of private family discord. In such circumstances, psychologists hold the view that those who are assaulted are victims of crimes and those who assault are guilty of crimes. (Principle II)

16. Where appropriate, confirm the validity of the reality, variety, and implications of unjust discrimination and/or oppressions experienced by women clients. (Principle II)

17. Are aware that some women's experiences make them more vulnerable to being sexually exploited and take special care to establish clear and safe boundaries in the current professional relationship. (Principle II)

18. Continually monitor and evaluate their competence, attitudes, and effectiveness in the delivery of psychological services for women clients, adjusting their practices as warranted. (Principle II)

19. Establish an appropriate level of trust through honest, open, and transparent communication that is considered culturally appropriate by the woman client, being careful not to subtly invalidate her questions or opinions (e.g., by not fully listening). (Principle III)

20. Establish an atmosphere of collaboration regarding all relevant decisions, including the goals of the psychological services being delivered, the risks and benefits of possible activities or interventions, any foreseeable problems, and any issues that arise, thus creating a more equal relationship by sharing power and responsibility. (Principle III)

Partial Demonstration of Ethical Decision Making Process

Vignette

You are employed as a counsellor by a government department specifically to assist welfare recipients to become self-supporting. A 50-year-old immigrant woman will have her benefits discontinued unless she looks for paid employment.

She refuses, saying that she is the only family member left in this country who can provide constant care for her 88-year-old mother. She has promised her mother that she will never abandon her in an institution, as is common in Canada. What are the issues around respect, and for whom? What should you do? The following are these authors' suggestions.

1. Who will be affected by your decision?

    The client, her mother, you, the government department, and your professional association should there be a complaint against you.

2. What are the issues to be addressed?

    Is the client presenting her situation accurately? There appears to be a clash between the needs of the client and her mother and the rules of the government department, and a cultural clash as to what is proper care for the elderly. There may be a lack of knowledge of support services in the community or a lack of services. There is a conflict for you between compassion for your client and the rules that your employer expects you to observe. Your counselling is expected to result in less tax money being spent to support the unemployed or those who do not wish to work. You begin to see your job as part of a system that is oppressive to vulnerable women, such as caregivers, the elderly, and immigrants. The principles of respect and caring appear to be compromised.

3. What about your personal feelings in this situation?

    You feel uncomfortable. You have sympathy for your client and do not like the government rules, but you want to keep your job. You do not want to see the client's mother forced into a nursing home as your own grandmother was terribly unhappy and died soon after she was institutionalized against her wishes.

4. What choices of action are available to you, and what would be the probable consequences of each? Here, we consider three choices.

    Choice One: Continue counselling for the sole purpose of placing the mother in a nursing home and assisting the client to obtain employment within a specified time period. Cut financial benefits whether or not client complies. There are no clear benefits to the client or her mother and this may actually do harm. You benefit by your continued employment, and the benefit to government and society is that less money is spent on welfare.

Choice Two: Negotiate with your supervisor for special consideration on compassionate grounds not to cut welfare payments. Subsidized nursing home placement would cost the government more than the welfare payments. Also, an immigrant woman over 50 years of age with poor language skills cannot reasonably be placed in adequately paid employment. There are benefits to all if this choice is successful, but it may not be approved. Your supervisor may have alternate ideas.

Choice Three: Explore all possibilities that might allow the client to do work at home. What are her marketable skills? Is there home care or other support services available? Are there ethnic community supports? Could the client secure employment in a nursing home in which the mother was a resident? What is the mother's health condition, and is it reasonably manageable for the client? This client appears to need community supports, not just "a job." The client benefits by continuing to care for her mother while developing marketable skills and connecting with community supports. You also benefit by you continued employment and benefitting government and society while reducing money spent on welfare.

The initial problem in this vignette is not immediately clear. Although this vignette is too brief to consider all the alternatives, it does highlight that there may be more than one ethical resolution to dilemmas. What is appropriate action in this vignette may not be in another similar situation. Ethical decision-making is problem-solving over time.

To the extent possible and within the parameters of your government position, you need to follow through with the client and address any negative consequences of the actions that you take. Through this example, you have learned a good deal about how agencies serving the public function, and about policies that are productive and problematic. You have become more sensitive to the vulnerabilities of older women and immigrant women in society. In a counsellor's professional career, there will be opportunities to contribute to changes that will increase the respect and caring that is shown to those in need.

Other Vignettes for Consideration

Counsellors work in a variety of roles, and we recognize that there is considerable diversity across Canadian women who may seek counselling services. Here we have provided a variety of vignettes for your consideration. This list only begins to identify some of the issues faced by counsellors of women. For each, ask yourself the following questions. Who will be affected by your decision? What are the issues to be addressed? What about your personal feelings in this situation? What choices of action are available to you, and what would be the probable consequences of each? Make reference to the *Guidelines* as you explore each vignette.

1. You have begun career counselling with a woman who does not appear to be taking assertive steps to gain employment. She is a recent immigrant and single mother whose education was interrupted during revolutionary strife and who has left her husband. You suggest career planning and job search strategies, but she expresses frustration and dismay at the barriers that she faces. She tells you that she is desperate to work but that she spends all her time and energy dealing with unresponsive and insensitive systems. Which guidelines are salient? [Authors' note: This example comes from an informative published study (Dossa, 2004, p. 55).]

2. One of your current clients discloses that she was traumatized by her sexual involvement with a previous therapist. She refuses to report this abuse, as she fears the implications of being questioned in an investigation. You know the name of the offending therapist, but she refuses consent for you to tell. You believe that you have a responsibility to prevent the offending therapist from exploiting more female clients. Which guidelines are salient?

3. You are on an exchange program as a counsellor in a foreign mental health clinic. A 25-year-old client tells you that seven years ago, she was raped by her cousin, and she was afraid to let her parents know. She has refused to marry because she is not a virgin. Now she wants you to help her find a doctor to perform surgery to repair her hymen. Which guidelines are salient?

4. You are an instructor in a counselling program. One of the students says that violence against women in Canada occurs

because women do not respect their proper role in the family. In the student's culture, women obey their men, and in return, their men respect and protect them. Which guidelines are salient?

5. You are counselling a woman who was previously suicidal. She is gaining self-confidence. Her husband, who has a history of violence, was recently discharged from psychiatric in-patient care and is seeing another therapist. That therapist calls you and asks you to encourage the wife to be more passive and sub-servient, as her assertiveness is aggravating the husband's illness and increasing the potential for violence. Which guidelines are salient?

6. You have been contracted by a lawyer to assess cognitive damage sustained in a car accident and to predict chances of full recovery. You know that the woman is a single mother, with little regular income, and that if her damage is severe, the lawyer can argue for a larger financial settlement. You find that her normal level of cognitive functioning was somewhat limited and that any further loss due to the accident is minimal. These are not the results that either you or the lawyer wishes to find, and the lawyer suggests omitting information on her pre-accident functioning. Which guidelines are salient?

7. You are a rural counsellor specializing in sex therapy. At the beginning of your practice, you accept only married couples as clients. Later, when you accepted unmarried couples, there is outrage from some of the community, which threatens your practice. Now a lesbian couple is seeking your help with their sexual problems. Which guidelines are salient?

8. You are a counsellor who suffered sexual abuse as a child and are now committed to bringing child molesters to justice. You have a client who exhibits many of the maladaptive behaviours that you experienced in the past, but gives no direct indication of having been abused. You wonder if she has repressed memories of abuse that you should actively try to recover. Which guidelines are salient?

9. You often provide assessments and counselling for clients referred to you from the Department of Child Welfare. The most recent refer-ral is a refugee woman who has suffered torture and loss of family in

her homeland and the desertion of her husband after immigrating. Her English is poor, and she distrusts those in authority. You are asked for an assessment, and possibly counselling, to help answer questions about possible welfare fraud, neglect of her children, and lack of parenting skills. Which guidelines are salient?

DISCUSSION AND CONCLUSIONS

What we have reviewed in this chapter is really only the beginning when we consider ethics for diversity and social justice in counselling women. We need to learn to respect all persons and to condemn bias, oppression, discrimination, and prejudice wherever it exists. Because we have not yet achieved a sufficient degree of respect, caring, and understanding of the circumstances of women's lives (and of other diverse populations), several professional organizations have developed guidelines to assist us. The *Guidelines for Ethical Psychological Practice with Women* is relevant for professionals of all theoretical persuasions and for all professional disciplines. We do not have to be feminists to be competent and ethical counsellors.

In this chapter, we reviewed the historical perspective for developing guidelines for working with women and we discussed the application in daily practice of the *Guidelines for Ethical Psychological Practice with Women* (CPA, 2007). In this twenty-first century in the Western world (and in developing countries), guidelines still have an important role to play in enhancing the competency of those who provide services with women. Ethical practice with women must encompass respect for cultural diversity, limited only by what women themselves find harmful and oppressive, and must also include agendas for social justice defined primarily by those who suffer from injustice. The oppressions of women in many parts of the world are beyond the scope of this chapter. We may have "come a long way, baby" in Western societies, but there is no room for complacency at home or abroad. The *Ethical Guidelines for Psychological Practice with Women* reminds, assists, and guides us in providing services for women that demonstrate respect, caring, and sensitivity to the context of women's lives.

REFERENCES

American Psychological Association. (1975). Report of the task force on sex bias and sex-role stereotyping in psychotherapeutic practice. *American Psychologist*, 30,1169–1175.

American Psychological Association. (1978). Guidelines for therapy with women: Task force on sex bias and sex role stereotyping in psychotherapeutic practice. *American Psychologist*, 13, 1122–1123.

American Psychological Association, Division 17. (1979). Principles concerning the counseling and therapy of women, *Counseling Psychology*, 8, 21.

American Psychological Association, Division 17. (1981). Report of the Division 17 Committee on women task force on training for counseling women. Unpublished report.

American Psychological Association. (2007). *Guidelines for psychological practice with girls and women: A joint task force of APA Divisions 17 and 35*. Washington, DC: Author.

Auld, F. (2002). How is therapy with women different? In F. Auld, M. Hyman, & D. Rudzinski (Eds.), *Resolution of inner conflict: An introduction to psychoanalytic therapy (2ⁿᵈ Ed.)* (pp. 217–236).Washington, DC: American Psychological Association.

Bagihole, B. (2007). *Women in non-traditional occupations: Challenging men, 2ⁿᵈ Ed.* London: Zed Books.

Boatswain, S., Brown, N., Fiksenbaum, L., Goldstein, L., Greenglass, E., Nadler, E. & Pyke, S. (2001). Canadian feminist psychology: Where are we now? *Canadian Psychology*, 42, 276–285.

Brabeck, M. (2002). *Practicing feminist ethics in psychology*. Washington, DC: American Psychological Association.

Byers, S., & Price, D. (1985). Summary of guidelines for elimination of sexual harassment. *Canadian Psychology*, 27, 31.

Canadian Psychological Association. (1980). *Guidelines for therapy and counselling with women*, prepared by J. Pettifor, C. Larsen & L. Cammaert. Ottawa: Canadian Psychological Association, Ottawa.

Canadian Psychological Association. (1986). *Canadian code of ethics for psychologists*. Ottawa: Canadian Psychological Association.

Canadian Psychological Association. (1988). *The Canadian code of ethics for psychologists: A companion manual*. Prepared by C. Sinclair & J. Pettifor. Ottawa: Author.

Canadian Psychological Association. (2000). *Canadian code of ethics for psychologists, 3ʳᵈ Ed.* Ottawa: Canadian Psychological Association.

Canadian Psychological Association. (2007). *Guidelines for ethical psychological practice with women*. Prepared by J. Pettifor, J. Malone, & E. Church. Ottawa: Canadian Psychological Association.

Church, E., Pettifor, J., & Malone, J. (2006). Evolving Canadian guidelines for therapy and counselling with women. *Feminism and Psychology*, 259–271.

Crozier, S., Harris, S., Larsen, C., Pettifor, J. & Sloane, L. (1996/2001). *Guidelines for non- discriminatory practice*. Ottawa: Canadian Psychological Association.

Crozier, S. & Pettifor, J. (1996/2001). *Guidelines for psychologists addressing recovered memories*. Ottawa: Canadian Psychological Association.

Danzinger, P.R., & Reynolds W.E. (2000). Age, gender and health bias in counselors: An empirical analysis. *Journal of Mental Health Counseling*, 22, 135– 145.

Dossa, P. (2004). *Politics and poetics of migration: Narratives of Iranian women from the diaspora*. Toronto, ON: Canadian Scholars' Press and Women's Press.

Feminist Therapy Institute. (1987/1999). *Feminist therapy code of ethics.* San Francisco: Author.

Finger, W.W. (2000). Avoiding sexual exploitation: Guidelines for therapists. *SIECUS Report, 28,*12–14.

Lax, R.F. (2005). Freud's views and the changing perspective on femaleness and femininity: What my female analysands taught me. *Psychoanalytic Psychology, 12*(3), 393–406.

Lehr, R., & Sumarah, J. (2004). Professional judgment in ethical decision-making: Dialogue and relationship. *Canadian Journal of Counselling, 38,* 14–24.

Lerman, H. & Porter, N. (Eds.). (1990). *Feminist ethics in psychotherapy.* New York: Springer.

Mandell, N. (2005). *Feminist issues: Race, class & sexuality.* Toronto: Pearson.

O'Neill, P. (2005). The ethics of problem definition. *Canadian Psychology, 46,* 13–20.

Pettifor, J., Larsen, C. & Cammaert, L. (1980). Guidelines for therapy and counselling with women. *Canadian Psychology, 21,* 185–186.

Pettifor, J., Larsen, C., & Cammaert, L. (1984). *Therapy and counselling with women: A handbook of educational materials.* Ottawa: Canadian Psychological Association,

Pettifor, J., Malone, J., & Church, E. (2007). *Guidelines for ethical psychological practice with women.* Ottawa: Canadian Psychological Association.

Procter, I., & Padfield, M. (1999). Work orientations and women's work: A critique of Hakim's theory of the heterogeneity of women. *Gender, Work, and Organization, 6,* 152–162.

Pyke, S. (2001). Feminist psychology in Canada: Early days. *Canadian Psychology, 42,* 268–275.

Pyke, S. & Stark-Adamec, C. (1981). Canadian feminism and psychology: The first decade. *Canadian Psychology, 22,* 38–54.

Rave, E. & Larsen, C. (Eds.) (1995). *Ethical decision making in therapy: Feminist perspectives.* New York: Guilford Press.

Robitschek, C., & Hershberger, A.R. (2005). Predicting expectations about counseling: Psychological factors and gender implications. *Journal of Counseling and Development, 83,* 457–470.

Staal, M.A., & King, R.E. (2000). Managing a multiple relationship environment: The ethics of military psychology. *Professional Psychology, Research and Practice, 31,* 698.

Stark, C. (2000). Women and Canadian psychology: Writing our pasts and our futures. *History and Philosophy of Psychology Bulletin* [Online], 12. Retrieved 30 August 2008 from http://uregina.ca/~starkc/herstory_and_canadian_psychology.html#article.

Stark, C. (2001). Psychological climate changes for women in academic psychology: Forecasts, sources, and implications. *Canadian Psychology, 42,* 286–300.

Stark-Adamec, C., & Kimball, M. (1984). Science free of sexism: A psychologist's guide to the conduct of nonsexist research. *Canadian Psychology, 25,* 23–34.

Steiner, G. (1994). Why Freud was so wrong about women: Psychoanalysis of Freud for the 21st Century. *PsycCRITIQUES , 39*(10), 979–980.

Toporek, R., Gerstein, L.H., Found, N.A., Roysircar, G., & Israel, T. (2006). *Handbook for social justice in counseling psychology: Leadership, vision, and action.* Thousand Oaks: Sage.

United Nations. (1948). *The universal declaration of human rights.* New York: Author.

United Nations. (1975). Implementation of the world plan of action adopted by the world conference of the international women's year. Retrieved 30 August 2008 from http://www.un.org/documents/ga/res/30/ares30.htm.

Wand, B. (1977). Report of the task force on the status of women in Canadian Psychology. *Canadian Psychological Review, 18,* 3–18.

CHAPTER 11

Feminist Counsellors Respond to Abuse in Lesbian Relationships: Confronting Heteronormalcy by Janice L. Ristock

> *Most people wouldn't think that abuse in lesbian relation-ships happens ... that women would do that to another woman, because women are seen as nurturers. I'm not sure how much support there is for lesbians. They have stuff for women in heterosexual relationships and you just don't feel that you fit in if you go to something like that.... Even as comfortable as I am with my sexuality, I was anxious in trying to figure out how to get the help I needed and be accepted. Like if I went to a support group for women being abused, odds are I'd be the only one there who was a woman being abused by another woman. Try to deal with that and how they're perceiving you while you try to get the help you need ... that's a huge stigma. —*Ginny

So much has changed in Canada over the last five years alone in terms of rights for gay, lesbian, bisexual, transgender, two-spirited, and queer people. Same-sex marriage has been legalized, "sexual orientation" has been added to the hate propaganda section of the Criminal Code, all provinces and territories (except Alberta) have added "sexual orientation" to their humans rights laws, and the Northwest Territories include "gender identity" in theirs. Even lesbian invisibility has been shaken if we consider the mainstream success of Ellen and her daytime talk show. Yet the opening quotation from the woman who experienced violence in her lesbian relationship in 2008 and who felt that no help was available to her reminds us that homophobia, heterosexism, and the impact of stigma are still felt. Her anxiety speaks to the fact that policy and legal changes are not enough to change culture and attitudes when confronting oppression and discrimination.

In this chapter, I provide a brief overview of what the literature tells us about violence in lesbian relationships and include some examples from my own research in which I interviewed women about their experiences in abusive relationships with other women (Ristock, 2001, 2002, 2003). I then fully describe and analyze discussions I have had with feminist counsellors about their responses to lesbian relationship violence as a way to bring to the forefront the many challenges that still exist in doing this work. I am currently Associate Dean (Research) and a professor of women's and gender studies at the University of Manitoba. I write this chapter as a white, lesbian, feminist academic and activist who has long been part of the anti-violence movement. In my critical examination of the responses to lesbian interpersonal violence, I offer my perspective not as an authoritative voice, but rather as someone who is working to try to understand the complexities of violence and the need to develop responses that address those complexities rather than oversimplify women's experiences. I have come to see heteronormalcy—the conventions, structures, and processes that assume and enforce heterosexuality as normal—as impeding our efforts to understand and respond effectively to same-sex partner abuse despite our good intentions.

WHAT DO WE KNOW ABOUT SAME-SEX RELATIONSHIP VIOLENCE?

Over the last 25 years, we have increasingly seen more public and scholarly attention to the issue of lesbian partner violence and, more broadly, to same-sex domestic violence (e.g., Irwin, 2008; Leventhal & Lundy, 1999; Lobel, 1986; Renzetti, 1992; Renzetti & Miley, 1996; Ristock, 2002, 2005). The studies done to date report wide variations in the rates of same-sex domestic violence, from 17% to 52% (Irwin; Renzetti; Ristock, 2002). The range in rates of violence reported has to do with the differing definitions of domestic violence used: Some studies only focussed on physical violence, while others included such things as emotional, verbal, and financial abuse. The non-random, self-selected samples also affected the range in rates. While we have not yet established true prevalence rates for same-sex relationship violence, all the research concurs that violence can and does happen in same-sex relationships and can take many of the same forms as heterosexual domestic violence. For example, physical abuse can include actions such as hitting, punching, slapping, biting, restraining, and pushing. Sexual abuse may involve forcing someone to have sex against her will, raping her with an object or weapon, and/or making demeaning sexual comments. Emotional abuse can include manipulation, isolation, humiliation, lying, threats to kill, threats to commit suicide, racial attacks, stalking, and intimidation. Verbal abuse may consist of insults, name-calling, constant put-downs, and yelling.

Financial abuse may also be part of the dynamic when one person creates debts, steals money, or uses money to control another person. The violence can also be lethal.

Although many of the tactics used in abusive same-sex relationships are the same as those used in abusive heterosexual relationships, there are some specific abusive behaviours that reflect the larger context of homophobia and heterosexism surrounding lesbian, gay, bisexual, transgendered, and queer (LGBTQ) relationships. These behaviours include threats to reveal the sexual or gender identity of a partner to a boss, landlord, or family member; threats to jeopardize custody of children because of a person's sexual or gender identity; threats to jeopardize immigration because of sexual orientation; and threats to reveal the HIV/AIDS status of a partner.

The diverse stories from the women that I have interviewed reflect the need to consider the varying social contexts and spaces in which violence occurs. Efforts to understand violence in lesbian relationships that ignore these contexts run the risk of treating all cases of relationship violence as equivalent and interchangeable, when that does not seem to be the case. For example, some women spoke about violence occurring in the context of rural, isolated communities where homophobia was strongly felt; others spoke about violence occurring in context of the dislocation of being a recent immigrant without any supports; while others spoke of violence occurring within their very first relationship with another woman (see Ristock, 2002, for more information about these contexts). The pattern of violence occurring in first relationships is particularly striking since it suggests that vulnerability to violence is part of the cost of living in a heterosexist society where lesbians are often isolated, unable to access meeting places, and dependent on their first lover for information about living as a lesbian. Many young women also spoke about the shame they felt in having to come out to family members or friends by telling them about their abusive relationships. For example, Wilma was twenty when she was in an abusive first relationship with another woman. After the relationship ended, her ex-partner stalked her and made harassing phone calls, including to her family and her workplace. She described how her father could not understand what was going on:

> Wilma: I think for my dad—like, some 20-year-old girl isn't very scary ... I think I couldn't really say how scared I was.

> Janice: Were there feelings of shame for you in having to tell other people what was going on?

Wilma: Yeah, there was for a long time, and that kept
me more sort of isolated with everything.... And that was
kind of some of the circumstance of my coming out.

SUPPORT FOR SURVIVORS

Unlike Wilma, some of the women that I interviewed did not tell *anyone*
what was happening because of a combination of shame, isolation, fear of
homophobic responses, not being out, and fear of retaliation from an abusive
partner. Most women that I interviewed reached outside their abusive relationships to other people to get support. They turned to friends and family
members as a primary source of support. Others felt they could not access
formal services, assuming they were only for heterosexual women (as seen in
the opening quotation from Ginny). Some turned to formal services but had
negative experiences. For example, one woman, Gio, had a physical disability
that made it difficult for her to go to an organization in person. She explained
her experience of the insularity of communities when calling a crisis line:

> I had a very negative experience when I called a crisis
> line for battered women. When I phoned there, it turned
> out to be a former friend and colleague of my partner's,
> and she didn't believe that I was involved in an abusive
> relationship with her. She started yelling at me on the
> phone.

Many recent studies similarly report on the barriers gays and lesbians experience when accessing services, such as perceived or actual homophobia and
racism, and they comment on the inability of most services to respond fully
to same-sex partner violence because of mainstream heterosexual approaches
and assumptions (Erbaugh, 2007; Russo, 2001; Simpson & Helfrich, 2005). In
addition, there are many regional disparities in the level of helpful resources
available for lesbian partner abuse. Urban areas are more likely to have gay and
lesbian resource centres, organizations for women who are victims of violence,
and more and more agencies with programs or individuals who do specific
work on same-sex domestic violence. This is not the case for smaller cities
or rural areas. Further, a lack of knowledge about same-sex partner abuse is
commonplace in formal service systems as a result of both lesbian invisibility
and heterosexism.

Several survey studies report that lesbians who do access formal services
are more likely to turn to counsellors for therapy than to call the police, use

the criminal justice system, access health care services, or turn to shelters for battered women (Girshick, 2002; Ristock, 2002; Turell, 1999). Susan Turell views the popularity of counselling in response to relationship violence as a troubling trend. In her survey of 499 ethnically diverse gay, lesbian, bisexual, and transgendered people, she asked a hypothetical question about what services are most needed for people in abusive relationships. Over two-thirds mentioned some form of counselling (i.e., individual, support groups, self-help). In Turell's view, this suggests that gays and lesbians think of relationship abuse as a personal, private issue needing an intra-psychic response, rather than seeing violence as an outcome of a social context that permits or encourages violence. Her analysis is a challenging one for service providers who in her view must educate LGBTQ communities about the public nature of domestic violence in order to lessen self-blame and encourage connections to additional resources outside of counselling.

Feminist counsellors have always held the view that domestic violence is not an individual or couple problem, but rather an outcome of a social context that supports misogyny and patriarchy (Stark, 2007). Therefore, the work of feminist counsellors is to help clients see relationship violence as something that is systemic and rooted in gender differences that are based on unequal social power. Yet, this gender-based explanation of domestic violence is clearly inappropriate for explaining lesbian partner violence. In this model, the lesbian perpetrator may have to be seen as male-like in order for the analysis to fit. For this reason, some researchers and practitioners have rejected feminist approaches and argue instead for a social-psychological model that includes an analysis of social oppression but is not gender-based (Hamberger, 1994; Merrill, 1996). This perspective focusses more on abusive behaviours in relationships, thereby equating heterosexual relationships with gay, lesbian, and bisexual relationships, while still acknowledging social oppression as a factor.

In my view, we cannot simply equate and generalize about all intimate relationships with one totalizing theory, nor can we rely on heterosexual gender-based frameworks for explaining abusive same-sex relationships (Ristock, 2002, 2005). We need to acknowledge both the similarities and differences between heterosexual domestic violence and lesbian domestic violence without using heterosexuality as the norm through which to understand same-sex relationship dynamics. In other words, we need to see the specificity of lesbian relationship violence and the distinctive needs of lesbians if we are to work against reinforcing heteronormalcy. This view is consistent with those feminists who are working to acknowledge the differing needs and experiences of women who have experienced violence and who are marginalized by the structures of race, class, gender, ability, and sexual orientation (Potter, 2008; Sokoloff & Dupont, 2005). Given these challenges, the question arises as to how feminist counsellors currently understand and respond to the issue of abuse in lesbian relationships. Many feminists in Canada are providing services specifically for lesbian partner abuse. Among the adjustments they are making to the established models of practice designed for heterosexual domestic violence are practices such as conducting couple assessment (to determine who is abusing whom in the absence of a clear gender power differential), running support groups for lesbians who have been abused, doing outreach work on building healthy relationships, and creating services for lesbian batterers (Ristock, 2005). I turn now to the discussions with feminist counsellors that I facilitated to explore their experiences and, in particular, how feminist domestic violence theory frames and shapes their responses.

FOCUS GROUP DISCUSSIONS WITH FEMINIST COUNSELLORS

I conducted eight focus group discussions with 70 feminist counsellors in six different Canadian cities (Winnipeg, Manitoba; Vancouver, British Columbia; Calgary, Alberta; Toronto, Ontario; London, Ontario; and Halifax, Nova Scotia). Participants were recruited by contacting domestic violence and LGBTQ organizations in each city for names of feminist service providers who had a reputation for doing work in this area. Telephone interviews were then conducted with potential participants to tell them about the research and to invite their participation.

Feminist research often relies on focus groups because they offer social contexts for meaning-making and involve "collective consciousness work" (Fine, 1992) to be undertaken by participants, rather than simply gathering data from them. They also allow for discourse analysis, which is useful for seeing the ways that language practices limit and shape our understandings of issues such as violence. I facilitated each focus group discussion through a dual process of affirmation and disruption (Ristock & Pennell, 1996): I asked questions in which we could gather information on the different forms of abuse, power dynamics, and patterns that counsellors had noticed, and thereby affirm the experiences of lesbians, and I raised issues that disrupted heterosexist assumptions we might hold to explain or account for this form of violence. The framework of discussion questions included items that have been debated within feminist and lesbian communities, such as how they defined violence, whether they had ever seen examples of the contested category of "mutual abuse" or shifting power dynamics, whether they considered consensual sadomasochistic relationships as abusive. Participants added to these questions, and discussions lasted from three to three-and-a-half hours. I served as both a researcher/facilitator and a participant, since I could share information from the interviews I had done with lesbians who had experienced abuse as well as share my experiences as a lesbian and a feminist who has worked in the anti-violence movement and as someone who has facilitated support groups for abused lesbians.

The focus group participants ranged in age from 20 to 63. The majority have a university degree. More than half of the participants identified as lesbian, with a third identifying as heterosexual, and a few as bisexual. The participants were, like me, mainly white but included women of colour who identified as Aboriginal, South Asian, Asian, and Black. Many of the participants worked in agencies, including shelters, battered women's services, LGBTQ organizations, family services, sexual assault centres, women's centres, and community resource centres, drug and alcohol addiction programs, and university/college counselling services. Some of the participants worked solely as counsellors in private practice. Together, they bring a range of experience in the area of domestic violence (1 to 26 years). They have worked more with heterosexual domestic violence clients than lesbians, and they have seen far fewer gay men.

Each focus group discussion was tape-recorded and then transcribed by a research assistant who also attended the discussion. I read over each transcript three or four times to identify themes and discourses. I used discourse analysis to see how meanings were made by paying attention to language and the details of focus group conversations (see Ristock, 2002, for a more complete description of my feminist materialist, discursive, reflexive approach). In this chapter, I pay attention to both dominant feminist discourses—those that feminists tend to give the status of truth; and marginal feminist discourses—those that challenge certain feminist thinking (Marecek, 1999). In focussing on the dominant and marginal discourses and the spaces in between (contradictions, areas of tension), my analysis reveals the difficulties in bringing forward complexities or counter-discourses in our understandings about lesbian partner violence. They illustrate how we rely on white, feminist heteronormative categories and constructs to think about violence, and ultimately show how these can impede our efforts to respond effectively to same-sex partner abuse. There were many assumptions of normalcy at play that circulated in the discussions. Normative frameworks exist about violence— about victims and perpetrators, about lesbians, and about feminism. Feminist counsellors in this study were struggling not simply to see lesbian abuse based on heterosexual understandings; in fact, most of the women doing this work are themselves lesbians. However, the tendency is to go back to certain standards of normalcy, certain dominant understandings that have been part of feminist theories to explain heterosexual domestic violence. In this paper, I present two normative discourses—what Jeanne Marecek calls "trauma talk" and what I call "necessary speech"—that reflect our struggles and even our inabilities to speak about those aspects of lesbian partner violence that do not fit dominant feminist understandings of relationship violence.

Dominant Feminist Discourses

Excerpts from focus group discussions are presented to illustrate the normative discourses that I have identified. (See Ristock, 2002, where I discuss trauma talk and necessary speech in the context of assessing power dynamics, organizational mandates, and running support groups.) The first example arises from a discussion about the similarities and differences between heterosexual abuse and lesbian abuse. It is clear that participants are identifying differences between lesbian and heterosexual abuse. What is also evident is that participants are often uncomfortable with discussions that explore or speculate further on differences that go against dominant feminist thinking in the area of domestic violence. For example:

> BP: I don't know if this is a good question or not, but I'm wondering if there is more insecurity in a lesbian relationship where one partner may have been in a heterosexual relationship before, and their partner fears that they'll go back to a heterosexual relationship? I am just wondering whether insecurity could have something to do with abuse, patterns of abuse.

> WW: I myself, I have stayed away from analysis in terms of "stress causes abuse."

> MN: Though it does kind of add to that emotional pressure-cooker sort of sense in the relationship. So if there is a propensity to handle problems [stress] in a physical way, it may help to release, to disinhibit that kind of response. (Pause) And I hate myself when I talk like this because I feel really strongly when I talk about perpetrators being held responsible for their behaviours. I work with tons of survivors who've been through hideously abusive experiences. Uh, I have to do some deep breathing around it because [laughter] I think it takes the onus of responsibility off the perpetrator and that really bothers me. So having said what I said, I take it back. (Focus group # 8)

The participant took back what she said because it threatened dominant feminist concepts in which we are deeply invested for good reason; that is, we hold on to views that see perpetrators as making choices to be violent and never see stress as an explanatory causal factor. The exploratory conversation that was to examine different contexts and dynamics surrounding lesbian abuse was quickly recuperated into a known and accepted normative framework where perpetrators must be held responsible—leaving details, such as the possibility that lesbian partnerships might be more vulnerable because they are not supported by heterosexist institutions and assumptions, under-analyzed. As a result, a homogenizing "trauma talk" discourse often became the authoritative and overriding sentiment in focus group discussions about the similarities and differences, which allowed people to stay focussed on the similarities of the effects of violence rather than work further to uncover and address the complexities and differences. The tendency in feminist therapy is to focus our efforts on the results of domestic violence and to assume that we know all we need to know about the causes. Marecek (1999) has identified this discourse in her interview research with feminist therapists. She defines trauma talk as a lexicon (a system of terms, metaphors, narrative frameworks) that circulates amongst feminists and others to talk about the physical and sexual abuse of women. Her interest in the trauma talk discourse is to show how therapists' language practices construct clinical realities. For some feminist therapists in her study, the trauma model has become the "sine qua non of feminism in therapy ... retelling a woman's life as a trauma narrative was both the feminist way and the one true way to tell a life. Yet even though a woman has experienced abuse, narrating her life in terms of that experience produces only one of many possible stories" (p. 170–171). Her comments are relevant for explaining the limits of trauma talk in the discussion of lesbian abuse. In focussing only on the violence and in staying with universalist feminist assumptions of what motivates the perpetrator, we can erase and ignore any dissonance between heterosexual domestic violence theory and lesbians' experience of domestic violence, and continue with our current thinking and practices.

In another example, participants in each focus group spoke about the concept of "mutual abuse" and some of the difficulties they have in defining abuse when examining different dynamics they had encountered. Again, we see an acknowledgment of differences in lesbian relationship dynamics based on what counsellors have actually heard from clients; yet the tendency is to go back to a known framework rather than make room for new and different experiences. Consider the following example:

> HY: I do think there is something called "mutual abuse,"
> but I don't call it "mutual abuse"; I call it "bad fighting"—

"bad dynamics," "power struggles"—I see it as fairly equal in terms of people being in trouble, feeling pretty powerless, pretty helpless, not knowing how to get out of that kind of recursive cycle. Where I don't think it is mutual abuse is where the other person starts hitting back, even if it is not in self-protection, even if the hitting back is out of exhaustion. I don't see that as mutual. I see those actions as speaking more to the impact of abuse and the person [victim] has been so worn out that that's what they do. In the first example, they don't talk about the impact in the same way; they were not afraid; they were not exhausted; they were not immobilized in their lives; they were not isolated from their friends; to me that's a difference [between bad fighting and abuse].

OM: I'm still pondering the question, have I seen mutual abuse and whatever that means? I think about somebody who controls all the money, and at the same time, the other person is extremely controlling and jealous. And the one who controls the money is very homophobic and doesn't want anyone to know they are lesbians so wants to keep them isolated—is that mutual abuse?

KR: Where I find the language frightening is that working in a shelter with male violence, there are a lot of people in the population who would like to say, "Hey, this happens to everyone," so they can just defuse it. So I don't want to talk about this and that's why. I don't want to lose the funding, lose the momentum. (Focus Group # 4)

In this example, we can see the force of very real contexts, like needing funds to keep shelters operating and fearing that the scale of male violence against women will be underestimated if we talk about woman-to-woman abuse. This is the context within which feminist service providers are working. Often, we rely on dominant discourses for solid strategic reasons, but this reliance shuts down or limits the thinking and theorizing that we need to do in this area. I call this tendency a reliance on "necessary speech," speech that invokes the realities of the conditions within which feminists work; in this case, the need for funding and the context of a backlash against feminism. Necessary speech describes what is required to state in order to reassert the dominant understandings that provide strong explanatory power for the extent of male violence against women. Both necessary speech and the trauma talk lexicon mentioned earlier have the unintended effect of constructing and affirming heteronormative frameworks to understand lesbian abuse. In the example above, the reassertion of dominant feminist understandings limited the possibility of exploring certain distinctions in power dynamics that might well be important in same-sex relationships (possibly equal physical size, shared gender status, a lack of fear) that make fighting back more feasible than in heterosexual relationships.

Marginal Feminist Discourses

Focus groups discussions did reveal moments where people were working against normative frameworks rather than recuperating them. This was most evident in discussions about race and sadomasochism, where counter-discourses about naming whiteness and acknowledging the possibility of consensual domination were able to emerge.

Naming Whiteness

> JW: Something I want to—it's going off topic a bit—but I want to get a sense of the women that other people work with because I know for me, my experience is primarily working with not a racially diverse group of women—primarily white women, maybe a small number of First Nations women. So I want to know who it is that we are talking about, who it is we are basing our experience on?
>
> It's a struggle and something that needs to be addressed that the women who come forward for services are usually not women of colour, and it's happening for particular reasons. I want that to be on the table when we are talking . . . our experiences are coming from which groups of women?
>
> [Many voices commenting supportively, but with tension.]
>
> People began reporting on how many women of colour they have worked with and what they have done in their practices to address diversity. (Focus Group # 6)

273

In this example, one woman presented a challenge to the group to resist centring lesbian relationships based on white, middle-class experiences, and although there was tension in the room when the issue was raised, no efforts were made to stop the conversation or change the direction to recuperate a white normative approach. Whiteness was named and marked as a category that demanded scrutiny in order to disrupt its unspoken embodiment as truth, normality, and trustworthiness. Similarly, in all of the focus groups, we had discussions about naming and defining violence in cases where there are power complexities; for example, in interracial relationships, and in relationships where there are class differences between the partners or differences in physical abilities. Feminist counsellors spoke of the limitations of binary assumptions in feminist domestic violence theories that assume all power rests with one person (the perpetrator), which is used against the powerless (the victim). This is evidence of counter-hegemonic discourses being able to be spoken. It shows there is an opening to challenge a feminist analysis of lesbian partner abuse to be able to address the interface of sexism, racism, violence, and homophobia (Kanuha, 1990; Renzetti, 1998).

Similarly, discussions on sadomasochism (S/M) revealed attempts to disrupt certain dominant feminist homogenizing views. There have been many debates within feminist and lesbian communities about how to understand sadomasochism, with some arguing that it is consensual, while others argue it is impossible for women to truly consent in a patriarchal context, and still others state that it can be an empowering way to take control and heal from experiences of sexual abuse. These issues all resurfaced when discussing the therapeutic responses of feminist counsellors to S/M. In each focus group, most of the participants were open to seeing the complexities of women's sexual practices and experiences of abuse, rather than forcing a dominant feminist ideological stance.

Consensual S/M

> AM: I did see S/M practices as being abusive, and then I changed my position as I learned more, found more out, gained more experience in the whole area ... yet on a much broader level, I still have a problem with it. Yet when I'm working with people. I have to be very open so that we can work through different layers, so that I don't totally lose them or alienate them.

> GF: How do we learn about the complexities? I think for,
> myself, I think about my own ignorance about S/M, I'm
> not part of the S/M community, and so I've needed to
> learn about different practices. I think when it gets difficult
> is when young women are learning about S/M, and who
> they learn from, and in what context, and if there has been
> power imbalances in the relationship already. And if you
> are just coming out and you are coming into S/M, who
> is teaching you about it? Is it in a context of an already
> abusive relationship, or is it in a safe relationship?
>
> AM: Those are really important questions. [group voices:
> Hmm ... hmm] (Focus Group # 3)

The movement of this discussion shows efforts made by some of the participants to encourage reflexive stances, such as asking questions about the context
of a relationship and being aware of your own limited knowledge, rather than
asserting any either/or positions about the nature of S/M and its relation to
abuse. In many of the focus groups, S/M was identified as an issue that young
queer women want to talk about. For example, in four of the six cities where
focus groups were conducted, the participants mentioned that workshops had
been held for LGBTQ youth groups on this topic, at their request. Most feminist
counsellors saw that they needed to get information and be able to create an
environment where clients can talk about marginalized sexual practices without being judged. On this issue, there was more willingness to move beyond the
usual polarization that exists between S/M feminists and anti-S/M domestic
violence activists. Participants acknowledged S/M as a sexual practice, thereby
resisting dominant feminist domestic violence theory that S/M equals abuse
(Margulies, 1999). With this counter-discourse, they could discuss the ways
that some S/M relationships can be abusive, while others can be consensual
and non-abusive. Counter-discourses in both of these examples, race and S/M,
create the possibility of moving away from homogenizing domestic violence in
abstract terms to address the specificity and multiplicity of women's lives.

The examples from focus groups discussions with feminist counsellors on
lesbian partner abuse that I have provided above reveal the normative discourses that feminist service providers both employ and at times struggle against.
The conversations reveal the investments we have in maintaining dominant
feminist discourses about relationship violence. In our discussions, feminist
counsellors often resisted counter-discourses and continued to insist on trauma
talk and necessary speech. Yet calling attention to language practices shows
how the investments in dominant feminist discourses construct and shape

reality in ways that are not helpful to women's lives—in fact, such investments often went against the very experiences of lesbians that counsellors had been witness to.

I want to comment further on the areas where counter-discourses were able to emerge. Within academic and community feminisms, there has been considerable anti-normative discussion over the last 20 years about diversity and the need to move beyond white, middle-class women's experiences, and there have been many debates about sadomasochism (although corresponding changes in the practices of social service agencies have not always resulted from these challenges). On the other hand, dominant feminist discourses remained in place during focus group discussions about the causes of violence, mutual abuse, and differing power dynamics, areas where we had far fewer exploratory discussions because of the fear of fueling a backlash against feminism from those theorists and groups who claim that feminists have created a "wife abuse industry" that victimizes innocent men and protects abusive women.

CONCLUSION

Overall, this chapter suggests that we need more spaces and a language to talk about lesbian relationships and lesbian abuse that move us beyond white, heteronormative frameworks if we are to develop truly inclusive services and appropriate therapeutic practices. For feminist counsellors, participating in a focus group was often a welcome opportunity to speak with other counsellors about the work they were doing, the dilemmas that they encountered, and the implications for therapeutic practice. Many commented that they are isolated in private practice or isolated within mainstream agencies. Creating more opportunities for discussion allows us to share new information about same-sex domestic violence and engage in a reflexive process where we can challenge our assumptions and investments in certain positions. Feminist counsellors in these focus groups do wish to develop effective responses and interventions in this area. They spoke of the lack of services for perpetrators, the barriers that exist for lesbians of colour and lesbians who are recent immigrants, and the fact that woman-to-woman abuse challenges long-cherished ideals about women's relationships with other women. But the conversations were just a beginning step in "collective-consciousness work," with some areas of discussion opening up and others shutting down. In my view, we can expand a feminist analysis of relationship violence so that we continue to recognize and prevent male violence against women, while also broadening our feminist understandings of other forms of interpersonal violence. We need to struggle constantly to find ways of working with women in the local, specific, and contextual, while de-centring heterosexuality and resisting even our own normative tendencies.

I end by offering some guidelines for responding to lesbian relationship violence. I include suggestions for counsellors and services providers, as well as for women in abusive relationships with other women and for friends who wish to offer support since, as counsellors, we too may experience abuse in our relationships or be a friend offering support in addition to working with clients in abusive relationships. The guidelines are reproduced from my book *No More Secrets: Violence in Lesbian Relationships* (New York: Routledge Press, 186–192). Although these guidelines are still limited and partial, I try to show how we might resist reproducing homogenizing narratives so that we can disrupt normalcy and in particular heternormalcy, which only limits our understandings and responses to violence in lesbian relationships.

IF YOU ARE IN AN ABUSIVE INTIMATE RELATIONSHIP WITH ANOTHER WOMAN …

You might identify as lesbian, queer, dyke, bisexual, gay, trans, two-spirited, or you might not use any of these terms to describe yourself. There are many different forms that violence in relationships can take. Some examples of abusive behaviours can include the following:

- being hit, punched, slapped, shoved, restrained, choked, or having weapons used against you;

- being raped, being forced to have sex against your will, being criticized and made to feel uncomfortable during sex;

- yelling rages, constant screaming, verbal put-downs, humiliation, racist attacks;

- being stalked, terrorized, having your sleep constantly interrupted;

- hearing threats to harm you your children or pets; threats to "out" you; threats to your immigration status; threats to commit suicide; threats to kill you—some women have been killed by their partners;

- destroying your property, throwing objects, controlling finances, creating debt, being lied to and manipulated.

You may have experienced some, many, or all of these different forms of violence. You may have experienced something not included in these lists.

277

Sometimes there is a pattern to abusive behaviours where you can almost predict when you partner will attack you, but this is not true of every situation. Sometimes the abuse gets worse over time. Sometimes the dynamics remain constant. Things may feel confusing if your partner is constantly blaming you and telling you that you are abusive, when that does not seem to be the case. The dynamics in the relationship can also feel confusing if both of you are physically fighting, and if you are fairly evenly matched in terms of size and strength. Physical fighting can include defending yourself, or an intention to hurt your partner; sometimes it can include both. Often one person in the relationship will be directing more abusive behaviours towards their partner. Sometimes the dynamics can change where one person who was being abused gains the upper hand and is now abusing. Some women who have been abused in one relationship may go on to another relationship where they become abusive. In some relationships, one person may be more physically abusive and another person more verbally and emotionally abusive. If you are both emotionally abusive, you may feel stuck in an ugly pattern where you are constantly hurting and triggering each other. All of these situations are abusive.

Sometimes people think that certain groups or types of lesbian are more likely to be abusive or be abused. These kinds of stereotypes (for example, about butch and femme women, or about women of colour) can be inaccurate and very harmful.

Violence can also occur in different contexts. You may be in your first relationship with another woman and are isolated and worried that you will not meet anyone else. You may have moved from another city or country, and do not have any support networks. You and your partner may be using drugs and alcohol, which can sometimes increase physical violence and affect your perceptions of the abuse. If you have a history of violence (including childhood sexual abuse, rape, being the victim of a hate crime), violence in the relationship can feel familiar, almost normal, even though it is not.

You need to evaluate your relationship and ask yourself some questions, such as:

Am I being physically, sexually, or emotionally threatened or abused?

Are my thoughts, movements, and actions being negatively affected or controlled by my partner?

Am I disturbed, distressed, and anxious about how I am being treated in the relationship?

Am I isolated? Do I feel hopeless and helpless? Or am I afraid?

Answering "yes" to any of these questions means you need to gain some perspective on what is happening to you in your relationship. You need to think about your own internal signals that may also alert you to physical danger. If you fear for your safety, leave the situation. Go to the nearest safe place or call a friend. If you are in physical danger, you may want to keep a bag packed with money, identification cards, house keys, and clothing. Tell someone what is happening to you. It can be a friend, a family member, a neighbour, a service provider—someone you think will be supportive of you. If you are being abused, you may feel a range of affects including shame, anger, self-blame, shock that another woman was abusive, depression, suicidal thoughts, low self-esteem, numbness, and confusion. It is important that you try to get some support.

You also need to ask yourself if you are physically, sexually, or emotionally threatening and/or abusive. You might consider the following questions:

Am I trying to control my partner, keep her to myself?

Am I constantly lashing out at her and hurting her?

Am I threatening my partner or trying to punish her?

Am I always finding fault with her, asking her to change her behaviours, to do things to please me?

Am I blaming my partner for my actions?

Do I feel out of control and in danger of hurting my partner or myself?

Answering "yes" to any of these questions is cause for concern. Take responsibility and accountability for your actions. Sometimes your actions may be intentional, and other times they may not, but they can still cause harm, and there is no excuse for them, even if you too have been abused by her or someone else. Do not blame your partner, but instead, stop your behaviours. Leave the situation or the relationship, if necessary, to stop your abusive behaviours. You are likely experiencing a combination of feelings including anger, pain, anxiety, vulnerability, and fear. You will need the support of friends and possibly the help of a counsellor to help you stop engaging in abusive behaviors.

If the dynamics feel more confusing, you may both need to go and get some support to help you figure out and stop the abusive dynamics. You may also each need some time alone or with friends to assess the situation. Your relationship might need to end. If you hope to preserve it, the abusive behaviours need to stop to enable you to rebuild a trusting, healthy relationship dynamic.

Sometimes your relationship, even though abusive, is better than other aspects of your life where you also encounter violence. Think about things you might be able to do to reduce your chances of being seriously harmed. Think about places that you can go to for some peace, safety, and time alone. Try to find a supportive person that you can talk to.

Remember: We all want violence-free relationships. There are different forms of abuse, and different types of violent relationships, but they have this in common: The abusive dynamics need to stop. You cannot control or change your partner's behaviours; you can only be in control of your own actions. The person engaging in abusive behaviours is the only one who can stop these behaviours.

GETTING HELP

Getting help can be difficult depending on where you live, what resources are available, and your own financial resources. It likely requires you to come out as being in a lesbian relationship. Friends and family members can be supportive, or can react in ways that are homophobic, or that deny and minimize your experiences. For example, some friends may say that they do not want to choose sides in your relationship or get involved in your private issue. If you encounter negative reactions, keep trying until you find someone who will listen and support you. There are also some self-help books available on violence in relationships that include specific information for lesbians as well as some website resources. You are not alone in your experiences. Sometimes writing in a journal can help you to clarify your thoughts and feelings about what is happening.

You can find out about available resources in your community by contacting women's groups, gay and lesbian organizations, and domestic violence services. In some communities, women of colour have found help through Aboriginal organizations, AIDS organizations for people of colour, and other multicultural organizations. Community resources such as these might include free services that you can access, such as crisis counselling lines, support groups for lesbians and/or women who have been abused, and shelters, as well as counselling, peer counselling and addiction programs. Fewer programs exist for women who are abusive in lesbian relationships, but there may be more general anger management programs that can be helpful. Ask services about their policies on confidentiality before you reveal your identity. Ask if they have had experience in working with lesbians and/or same-sex relationship violence. Unfortunately, social services can also be homophobic and racist in their responses. Many women have had more positive experiences in seeking the help of a counsellor. There are often feminist and lesbian counsellors who can offer support, and who will have a sliding-scale fee for women with fewer financial resources.

You may also need to call the police in some situations. They can and should be helpful in cases involving physical and sexual assaults and threats. However, sometimes the police can be unhelpful and wrongly assess the situation and/or be homophobic and/or racist in their responses, particularly in cities where they have not received any anti-homophobia, anti-racism training. If you are concerned for your safety or your life, call the police.

Overall, seeking support from someone else helps reduce your isolation and provides other perspectives about your situation so that you can get some clarity and make some decisions about your relationship.

How friends can help

If a friend who is being abused comes to you for help, you can listen to her and let her talk about what has happened. Do not offer excuses for the violence or minimize what has happened. If you suspect that a friend is being abused, express your concern and offer to help. Many women who have been abused may initially deny the abuse but later remember the supportive comment of their friend, which helps them immeasurably.

If you think someone is being abusive, tell them that their behaviour is unacceptable and work with them to get help and change their actions, even though it may be hard and your friend may be angry with you for confronting her.

If you are worried about taking sides because you know both women who are involved, or because you are unsure of the dynamics in the relationship, think about ways that you can still offer each of them some assistance in finding resources and other people to talk to. Some abusive relationship dynamics really are muddled. Don't feel that you have to decide who is the victim or who is the abuser. Offering some support is better than offering no support at all. This can include helping a woman to find housing or a safe place to stay, referring her to a counsellor, loaning her money, going with her to the police, or calling the police. Offer her opportunities to break her isolation and connect with others. Be clear about what you can and cannot offer.

Be respectful and supportive of women's decisions, even when they might not be the ones that you would make, unless the decisions are harmful or dangerous. Examine your own responses, assumptions, and feelings. If you are a lesbian, this can be a difficult issue to face. You may want to explain it away rather than acknowledge that violence does happen in lesbian relationships. If you are not a lesbian, examine any stereotypes you may hold about lesbians and other marginalized sexualities and try very hard not to let them affect your support.

Some people have become dismissive of abuse because words such as *abuse*, *violence*, and *battering* have been used too loosely to describe every conceivable situation in which someone has been disappointed or hurt or has encountered meanness or rudeness. Overusing these words trivializes the meaning of the terrible situation they describe, but if you think your friend is being abused or mistreated, take it seriously.

How counsellors/service providers can respond

Before doing this work, it is important to have done your own anti-oppression work so that you can scrutinize your own responses and change those that are based on stereotypes and ignorance. Be aware of the language that women use to describe themselves (lesbian, gay, two-spirited, bisexual, trans, queer, dyke). Some women may feel they are just in love with another woman, and will not identify with lesbian communities. Some women's primary identification may be racial or ethnic rather than focussed on sexuality. Make sure that you have posters, brochures, and materials in your workplace that convey an open and accepting environment. Provide a woman with information about your confidentiality practices. If you are a lesbian, a woman may need even more reassurances about how you will maintain confidentiality. It is equally important for you to be open to hear the stories women tell you that might challenge your feminist understandings of domestic violence. Think about your definitions of violence and make sure they do not privilege white, middle-class women's experiences. For example, challenge you perceptions of what a victim looks like. Also be aware that dichotomies of victim/perpetrator, with their underlying assumptions of innocence/evil and femaleness/maleness, can be very limiting and inaccurate when they mask or minimize harmful relational dynamics that need to be examined. For example, don't let the identification of abuse within an interracial relationship serve racist purposes by minimizing the racist comments that a white woman makes when describing the abusive behaviour of her part-ner who is a woman of colour. Similarly, be aware that women may need to learn more about each other's cultural backgrounds and perhaps about stereotypes. For example, a woman may feel threatened by a raised, excited voice that is part of a cultural norm for the other woman but not for her. You may find it helpful to read existing research, although most studies have focussed on the experiences of white, middle-class lesbians. Overall, remember that we do not know all there is to know about lesbian relationship violence.

It is important that you begin where the woman is, or even where the couple is to begin to assess the relationship's dynamics. Be aware of the differing contexts that allow violence to take hold and give it structure in a relationship. Be aware of differing dynamics that can exist between two women where, for example, fear may or may not be part of an abused woman's experience. Making a thorough and careful assessment may take a long time, but is crucial for determining the best course of action. It is important not to assume that power dynamics in a same-sex relationship are mutual just because the dynamics are complex. For example, many women who have been victimized also fight back and have strong feelings of anger. This context has to be addressed along with their feelings of self-blame and guilt. Sometimes (though not if a woman is placed at greater risk or silenced) couple counselling might be appropriate, for example, for two women with histories of sexual abuse who are triggering each other in a mesh of emotional abuse. Be willing to work with both women's abusive behaviours and women's victimization. Women who are abusive often have the fewest resources and perhaps the most to gain from counselling. Some women have had the experience of being abused in one relationship and abusive in the next. Other women have had a lifetime of violence and may need to know that they are not to blame for it, that there is nothing wrong with them or with being a lesbian, but that they are responsible for stopping their own violent actions. Be willing to address the complex interplay between women's experiences of public and private forms of violence. Acknowledge the risks that lesbians are taking in coming forward to receive help. For example, a lesbian of colour who has experienced societal racism may feel very conflicted over betraying her partner of colour to a white counsellor and talking about the violence within her relationship.

Sexual assault and sexual coercion are not uncommon forms of abuse that lesbians experience, but it can be very hard for women to talk about. Make sure that you are comfortable in exploring this aspect of abuse. It is something you may have to ask about a few times in a number of different ways, because shame and self-blame often make women reluctant to discuss this. Make sure you are comfortable asking a variety of questions, such as, Has your partner ever forced you to have sex against your will? Have you ever felt sexually violated? Have you ever felt emotionally raped or sexually coerced? Acknowledge that this can be difficult to talk about. Be aware of the difference between consensual S/M sexual practices, which are not abusive, and non-consensual sex, which is. There is a diversity of language that women may use to describe their experiences of sexual assault or sexual coercion and we need to be comfortable using that language and saying the words our clients use.

Establish supportive referral networks so you can assist women in making connections with other services or with resources in lesbian or ethnic communities. For example, consulting with lesbian therapists or addiction counsellors might be helpful in certain cases. It may be necessary to be more of an advocate for lesbians and to have reliable contacts in shelters, with the police, with lawyers. It is also important to understand the inherent racism and classism in these institutionalized systems and to forewarn and prepare women for this.

Talk with other service providers about this issue. Join or start a coalition or network of service providers. It can be very helpful to create spaces to talk about some of the issues and dilemmas in doing this work, as well as to share innovative approaches, insights, and new ideas as well as develop plans for social action.

Remember that violence in lesbian relationships is a political issue, in that it can be used against lesbians to support homophobic views that see our relationships as deviant and unhealthy. It is important, therefore, to be involved in and support all anti-oppressive efforts.

ENDNOTES

1 This research was supported by a grant from the Lesbian Health Fund of the Gay and Lesbian Medical Association and from the Social Sciences and Humanities Research Council of Canada. The revised and updated chapter is based on: Janice L. Ristock (2001). Decentering heterosexuality: Feminist counselors respond to abuse in lesbian relationships, *Women and Therapy*, 23 (3), 59-72 and Janice L. Ristock (2002). *No More Secrets: Violence in Lesbian Relationships.* (NY:Routledge Press).

REFERENCES

Erbaugh, E.B. (2007). Queering approaches to intimate partner violence. In L.L. O'Toole, M.L. Kiter Edwards & J.R. Schiffman (Eds.), *Gender violence: Interdisciplinary perspectives, 2nd edition* (pp. 451–459). New York: NYU Press.

Fine, M. (1992). *Disruptive voices: The possibilities of feminist research.* Ann Arbor, MI: University of Michigan Press.

Girshick L. (2002). *Woman-to-woman sexual violence.* Boston: Northeastern University Press.

Hamberger, L.K. (1994). Domestic partner abuse: Expanding paradigms for understanding and intervention. *Violence and Victims*, 9 (2), 91–94.

Irwin, J. (2008). (Dis)counted stories: Domestic violence and lesbians. *Qualitative Social Work 7*, 199–215.

Kanuha, V. (1990). Compounding the triple jeopardy: Battering in lesbian of color relationships. *Women and Therapy* 9, 169–184.

Leventhal, B. & Lundy, S.E. (Eds.). (1999). *Same-sex domestic violence: Strategies for change.* Thousand Oaks, CA: Sage.

Lobel, K. (Ed.). (1986). *Naming the violence: Speaking out about lesbian battering.* Seattle, WA: Seal Press.

Marecek, J. (1999). Trauma talk in feminist clinical practice. In S. Lamb (Ed.), *New versions of victims: Feminists struggle with the concept* (pp. 158–182). New York: New York University Press.

Margulies, J. (1999). Coalition building 'til it hurts: Creating safety around S/M and battering. In B. Leventhal & S.E. Lundy (Eds.), *Same-sex domestic violence: Strategies for change* (pp. 135–145). Thousand Oaks, CA: Sage.

Merrill, G. (1996). Ruling the exceptions: Same-sex battering and domestic violence theory. In C. Renzetti & C.H. Miley (Eds.), *Violence in Gay and Lesbian Domestic Partnerships* (pp. 9–22). New York: Harrington Park Press.

Potter, H. (2008). *Battle cries: Black women and intimate partner abuse.* New York: New York University Press.

Renzetti, C.M. (1992). *Violent betrayal: Partner abuse in lesbian relationships.* Newbury Park, CA: Sage Publications.

Renzetti, C.M. (1998). Violence and abuse in lesbian relationships: Theoretical and empirical issues. In R.K. Bergen (Ed.), *Issues in intimate violence* (pp. 117–128). Thousand Oak, CA: Sage Publications.

Renzetti, C. & Miley, C.H. (Eds.). (1996). *Violence in gay and lesbian domestic partnerships*. New York: Harrington Park Press.

Ristock , J.L. (2001). Decentering heterosexuality: Feminist counselors respond to abuse in lesbian relationships. *Women and Therapy*, 23(3), 59–72.

Ristock, J.L. (2002). *No more secrets: Violence in lesbian relationship*. New York: Routledge Press.

Ristock, J.L. (2003). Exploring dynamics of abusive lesbian relationships: Preliminary analysis of a multi-site, qualitative study. *American Journal of Community Psychology*, 31 (3/4), 329–341.

Ristock, J.L. (2005). Relationship violence in lesbian/gay/bisexual/transgender/queer [LGBTQ] communities: Moving beyond a gender-based framework. http://www.mincava.umn.edu/documents/lgbtqviolence/lgbtqviolence.html.

Ristock, J.L & Pennell, J. (1996). *Community research as empowerment: Feminist links, postmodern interruptions*. Toronto, ON: Oxford University Press.

Russo, A. (2001). *Taking back our lives: A call to action for the feminist movement*. New York: Routledge.

Simpson, E. & Helfrich, C. (2005). Lesbian survivors of intimate partner violence: Provider perspectives on barriers to accessing services. *Journal of Gay and Lesbian Social Services*, 18(2), 39–59.

Sokoloff, N. & Dupont, I. (2005). Domestic violence at the intersections of race, class and gender. *Violence Against Women*, 11(1), 38–64.

Stark, E. (2007). *Coercive control*. New York: Oxford University Press.

Turell, S.C. (1999). Seeking help for same-sex relationship abuses. *Journal of Gay and Lesbian Social Services*, 10(2), 35–49.

CHAPTER 12

Feminist Crisis Counselling by Karen M. Nielsen and Ann Marie Dewhurst

W e both work in private practice in Edmonton, Alberta. Each of us has a strong social justice orientation, which informs our feminist beliefs and practices, and we work primarily with people dealing with family violence. Our client group includes women, men, and children who have experienced violence directly or have perpetrated violence. We work with individuals and families that span the socio-economic spectrum of Alberta, including people who are immigrants to Canada and First Nations people.

I (Karen) was raised in post-war Britain, where I learned early the realities of sexism and classism in the British educational system. I moved on to achieve my doctorate despite those early predictions that I would do well to work rather than study. I am a registered clinical social worker and Visiting Graduate Professor at Athabasca University, tutoring and instructing courses in Women's Studies, Criminal Justice, and the Master of Arts in Integrated Studies Programme.

I (Ann Marie) was raised primarily in a "prison and pulp mill town" in Northern Saskatchewan and was one of the first women in the Canadian prairies to provide therapy to men convicted of sexual offences and incarcerated in a maximum-security prison. I have worked in a variety of forensic and institutional settings as well as in the community. I am a registered psychologist and also instruct in the Graduate Centre for Applied Psychology with Athabasca University.

INTRODUCTION

For some women, a crisis is like a large unexpected wave wiping them off their feet during what was otherwise a comfortable wade through relatively calm water. For other women, the water they wade through is rarely or never calm. They experience crisis as more like a larger-than-average wave swamping them for a time until they can get upright again. The wading skills that each woman has will depend upon her experience in the water. Women who walk in water protected by reefs may not have the same experiences and skills as women who constantly encounter the unbuffered power of the sea. If a woman has never experienced protected areas, she may not believe they exist or know how to find them.

This chapter will explore crisis intervention and how to help women who have experienced trauma, who have been swamped by an unpredicted and unpredictable event. As we discuss more fully below, the experience of trauma is gendered; therefore, we felt it important to discuss crisis intervention from a feminist perspective.

DIFFERENTIATING CRISIS AND TRAUMA

The crisis intervention model we describe below is intended for use with women who experience an isolated traumatic event (such as a car crash or a sexual assault by a stranger) and also with women who experience repeated traumas (for example, ongoing domestic violence or workplace harassment). We differentiate between crisis and trauma in our work. Trauma is an emotional shock following a stressful event, sometimes leading to long-lasting psychological effects (Cason, Resick, & Weaver, 2002). Trauma occurs when an event experienced is incompatible with a person's fundamental beliefs about the world, and they are unable to make meaning of it (Cason, et al.). Crisis is an acute response where psychological well-being is disrupted and normal coping responses have failed. It is a situation or period of time in which things are very uncertain, difficult, or painful; it is a time when action must be taken to protect against further harm (Everly & Mitchell, 1999). Crisis counselling is used to support women through the critical moment (whenever that happens in time), to help them make meaning of the crisis event and put it into a context that expands their options and supports future trauma management strategies, community connections, safety planning, or counselling needs.

TRAUMA AND CRISIS ARE GENDERED EXPERIENCES

There is an established body of literature that confirms that the experience of crisis and trauma is gendered. Simmons and Granvold (2005) summarized this literature in their study of differences in rates of Post-traumatic Stress Disorder (PTSD) diagnoses. Women are twice as likely to develop PTSD symptoms as are men, regardless of the traumatic event. They concluded that there must be more to the development of these symptoms than simple exposure to a traumagenic experience. Solomon, Gelkopf, and Bleich (2005) suggest that although women are less exposed to terror events than men, when they are, these events evoke in them a stronger sense of danger, both to themselves and for the people whom they are close to. In addition, women report signs of greater psychological vulnerability (expressed in depressive and PTSD symptoms) in comparison to men. Following trauma, men were more optimistic than women regarding their futures and had greater confidence in their ability to cope with terror events. Women tended to talk more about their feelings about terror and to check on the whereabouts of their friends and family. Solomon et al. concluded that the subjective assessment of the magnitude of the threat and one's ability to cope with it were important aspects of why these findings were gendered.

This is consistent with trauma research that suggests that cognitive schemas (or the meanings people have about the way the world works) are directly connected with their experience of trauma (Newman, Riggs, & Roth, 1997). Newman et al. suggest that the severity of trauma symptoms is related to the extent to which core beliefs and personal schemas are disrupted. Simmons and Granvold (2005) state that female trauma survivors are more likely than male survivors to view the world as dangerous; they are more likely to blame themselves for the traumatic event; and are likely to hold more negative views of themselves than men. Barbera (2003) suggests that gender socialization plays a significant role in the development of pre-trauma schemas, which in turn plays a role in how people process and recover from trauma.

Gender schemas are organized bodies of information that impart meaning to everyday experiences and guide information processing and behaviour (Welch-Ross & Schmidt, 1996). They are dynamic knowledge structures, and the content of gender schemas varies depending on one's culture and experience (Barbera, 2003). As Bem (1981) points out, gender is one of the most important categories for organizing internal and external information. Developmentally, schemas are learned very early through direct and indirect observation (Martin & Halverson, 1981). Later on, they are maintained and reinforced by family, school, peer group, work setting, and media (Martin, Ruble, & Szkrybalo, 2004). Once formed, gender schemas become a lens through which individuals process information and strongly influence thoughts, feelings, and behaviours (Bem, 1994).

Simmons and Granvold (2005) state that gender socialization plays a significant role in the development of pre-trauma schemas, which also affect how women process and recover from trauma. According to the social psychology literature on gender schemas, girls develop their self-schemas in a societal context of gender-based oppression, which includes discrimination, violence, harassment, and sexual objectification of women. The realities of the differences in victimization rates for women suggest that women's environment is both more dangerous and perceived as more dangerous by women. This has an impact on women's experiences and understandings of crisis events and the resulting trauma. Therefore, given how gender-based pre-trauma schemas are correlated with the experience of trauma, the earlier that gender-based interventions occur in the crisis intervention process, the more likely a woman is to get her needs met and to have the severity of trauma experienced reduced.

Bronwyn Davies (1989) challenges the fixed nature of gender schemas and suggests that the telling and retelling of personal stories can change the way women produce social and psychological realities. She supports women in challenging the traditional dichotomy of male/female, where female is tightly linked to being helpless, vulnerable, and in need of rescue. We can empower women to consider aspects of their experiences that may or may not fit with the female stereotype. For example, we can support a woman in identifying elements of her crisis story where she was either actively or passively resistant to the harm being perpetrated against her. We can help her bring forth a muted element of her experience upon which she can build her preferred story in which she survives the crisis and moves forward.

CRISIS FOCUS

In reviewing the crisis intervention literature, we could find no explicit reference to a feminist crisis intervention model. If, as postmodernists imply, theory determines what we see (Hansen, 2006), having no explicit model based on feminist theory is concerning. If feminist principles are not clearly integrated into the model, the likelihood that the issue will be seen from a feminist perspective is low.

Gilliland and James (1997) suggest that what occurs immediately after the crisis event influences how the crisis is processed. A person may possess the skills, ability, and supports that allow her to process the crisis event without experiencing trauma. She may do this with or without professional support. Another alternative is that a person does not have the skills or supports to adequately process the crisis, but manages to push her experience from conscious awareness or uses a variety of coping strategies to keep the traumatic impact at bay (e.g., working hard, drinking, etc.).

A person may revisit the traumatic experience when a triggering event occurs. Gilliland and James (1997) describe this as a "transcrisis state," where a new experience triggers a return to the affective and cognitive experience of a previous crisis or trauma. They further identify "transcrisis points," which can occur within a transcrisis state. These points occur when a client experiences other dimensions of their problem or they are trying to come to grips with new developmental stages. Transcrisis points prompt therapists to shift out of managing trauma symptoms and shift back into crisis management.

CRISIS AND A FEMINIST PERSPECTIVE

Crisis counselling focusses on assessing strengths, identifying existing coping skills, and developing new ones (Gilliland & James, 1997). Gilliland and James describe how crisis theory has been expanded to include social, environmental, and situational factors involved in the trauma. However, their theory remains gender neutral. Feminist crisis counselling recognizes that women's experiences of crisis must be understood within the broader socio-political contexts of their lives.

Feminists acknowledge gender inequality (Biever, DeLasFuentes, Cashion, & Franklin, 1998). Their therapeutic interventions have a social action component where the primary emphasis is to improve the conditions of women's lives. Feminist therapists focus on developing awareness of gender roles, stereotypes, and sexism. Clients come to appreciate the socio-political context of their behaviour, and therapists encourage nurturance from other women and self nuturance, with the therapeutic goal of empowerment and self-efficacy. The therapeutic relationship is non-authoritarian and collaborative (Biever et al.). Finally, in our experience as feminist therapists, we have noted that those with the most power in situations often have influence on how events are construed and therefore are able to define what constitutes a crisis. For example, a woman is battered by her husband, but he defines her crisis response as hysterical and "crazy." We hear her repeat his words when she arrives for "counselling." Her crisis has been defined as a personal flaw rather than as a reaction to his violence.

In our practice, we regularly hear the pre-trauma schemas in women's accounts of being sexually assaulted. We hear stories of self-blame, for example, "It's my fault because … I invited him up for a drink," or "I went to his place," or "I shouldn't have gone out alone." Women who have been battered often make statements such as, "I should have just shut up and he wouldn't have hit me," or "I should have kept the kids quiet." These are examples of women taking responsibility for the actions of others, an expression of the gender role of "facilitator" that is part of their pre-trauma schema. Women are often expected to "make things work" in their families and community as a whole, even when they don't have the power to do so.

FEMINIST CRISIS COUNSELLING

Our work is guided by three feminist counselling principles: a) an egalitarian relationship, b) the personal is political, and c) the value of the female perspective (Worell & Remer, 1996). We are also influenced by constructivist (Cottone, 2007) and postmodernist theories that are reflected in narrative therapy (White & Epston, 1990), good lives models (Ward, Mann, & Gannon, 2007), and Aboriginal ways of healing (V. Whelan, Aboriginal elder, personal communication, August 10, 2006). We are assuming that the crisis responder using this framework has previous training in basic counselling skills and in the use of more general crisis intervention models.

There are four basic phases to our approach to feminist crisis counselling (see Table 12.1). Although it looks like a linear approach, it is not; in reality, it is more like a spiral. Women move back and forth, up and down and through the stages, until they have done what they need to do.

There are two goals for the Exploration Phase. The first one is to support the woman in defining the crisis in a woman-centred way. The second goal is to help her externalize the problem and to introduce a discussion of the relevant socio-political aspects of her situation. Externalizing the problem is a narrative therapy strategy in which the person and the problem are separated so that the problem becomes the focus of what needs to be changed, not the person (Freedman & Coombs, 1999). In the Normalizing Phase, we work with the woman to reframe her experience in feminine context. The goal of the Affirmation Phase is empowerment. In the Action Phase, our goal is to support the woman in making the transition toward well-being.

Exploration Phase

In this initial part of the intervention, the woman is invited to describe her crisis experience. We use reflective listening skills to support her telling her story, especially her descriptions about the worst part of the experience, paying particular attention to her affective, cognitive, and behavioural responses to the crisis event. Kaminer (2006) reports that describing the feelings, thoughts, behaviours, and sensory experiences associated with the trauma in a way that helps the survivor to organize and name her experience is central to the recovery process of crisis survivors. In our work, we prompt women to use their own words, and through the use of deconstructive questions, we learn about their beliefs and values related to what they have experienced in the crisis. It is important for us to listen for the elements of the crisis experience that were "the worst part" for her. This demonstrates our respect for the uniqueness of her experience and does not privilege our beliefs about what might be the source of her crisis (Strong & Sutherland, 2007). In this phase, we also explore her safety in relation to the crisis incident and her external context. We support her in exploring safety in the larger context of her life, not just in terms of the cessation of the crisis incident. For example, a woman who has been sexually assaulted by a stranger may face a new crisis event in telling her intimate partner if that person has a pattern of being jealous or aggressive. This egalitarian and ethical practice respects the dignity of the woman and ensures that the therapist's understanding of the issues do not override the woman's own expertise in her life.

Table 12.1: Feminist Crisis Counselling

Stage	Goals Related to Feminist Principles	Process	Intervention Strategies
Exploration Phase: part one	Define the crisis in a woman-centred way	Listening for her experience	<ul><li>prompt her to tell her story in her own words</li><li>use reflective listening and summarizing skills</li><li>listen for her sense of what was critical and/or traumatic</li></ul>
Exploration Phase: part two	Understand the problem in its socio-political context through externalization of the problem.	Understanding her perception of the crisis and its meaning to her. Separating the person from the problem.	<ul><li>listen for links to operating schemas</li><li>ask her to describe the current context of her life (her environmental context and the supports/influences/pressures active in her life)</li><li>use narrative externalization strategies</li><li>explore her safety in relation to the crisis incident and her external context</li><li>deconstructive questioning re-politicizes internalized, oppressive beliefs</li></ul>
Making-Meaning Phase	Reframe her experience in feminist context	Re-conceptualization of her experience	<ul><li>use of metaphor</li><li>narrative strategies</li><li>reframing skills</li><li>deconstructive listening</li><li>consciousness raising</li><li>reframing symptoms</li></ul>
Affirming Phase	Empowerment	Assessing resiliencies and barriers	<ul><li>affective responding</li><li>cognitive responding</li><li>physiological responding</li><li>previous successful experiences in coping with past crisis</li><li>transcrisis points</li><li>interpersonal supports or barriers (friends, family, co-workers, etc.)</li><li>access to relevant resources (financial, physical needs, child-care needs, etc.)</li></ul>
Action Phase	Transition to well-being	Examine alternatives and resources	<ul><li>plans for immediate action (ensure physical safety, intervention of medical practitioners or police) plans for longer term (referrals to supports, counselling, etc.)</li></ul>

A woman's experiences in life before the crisis are a part of her pre-crisis schema and will influence her post-crisis reactions. For example, Street, Gibson, and Holohan (2005) found that women who had experienced childhood traumas were more likely to report trauma-related guilt and use avoidance coping strategies after being abused by their intimate partners than women who did not have childhood trauma. Previous traumatic losses were found to increase the suffering for the person experiencing a new traumatic loss (Mercer & Evans, 2006).

The current context of a woman's life (i.e., the environmental context and the supports, influences, and pressures active in her life) will also influence her post-crisis reactions. For example, Bell, Goodman, and Dutton (2007) found that the economic independence of women entering a shelter for battered women was a significant factor in the degree of depression they experienced after a one-year period. Nielsen (2004) found that women who had been battered and who had established support systems were able to overcome barriers and held hopeful orientations toward the future.

At this stage of crisis counselling, the woman will usually describe herself and her actions during the crisis in negative ways. For example, she may offer the story of "her failure" or "her shame." One of the basic assumptions of narrative theory is that for every negatively focussed dominant story, there is an empowering alternative story available and possible. The role of the therapist is to open up space so that the client is able to develop an alternative story (Morgan, 2000; Winslade & Monk, 2001). By using reframing, deconstructive questioning, listening, and reflective listening to highlight strengths while learning about the woman's current context and her experiences in life before the crisis, the counsellor begins the process of opening up this space and helping her to build an empowering, alternative story. These interventions can help her shift her focus and emphasize elements that support well-being. They also demonstrate our respect for her by validating her experience.

Deconstructive questions invite women to notice how their stories are constructed, to see their story from a different perspective, and to discover other possible narratives. For example, when working with a woman has who has been sexually assaulted, we might at some point, when talking about sexual assault, ask a deconstructive question such as, "How do you think you came to believe that?" This invites the woman to step out of the dominant story and to begin to untangle her web of beliefs. Space is made for not only her current beliefs about women who are sexually assaulted and how she came to hold those beliefs, but also for the possibility of an alternate story in which internalized and oppressive beliefs are re-politicized.

To continue with the example of a woman who has been sexually assaulted, her crisis story might reflect the experience of being defeated. For example, her initial offering of her story might be, "I was walking and he grabbed me and I went limp and then he raped me." This story has defeat as its dominant theme (Morgan, 2000; White & Epston, 1990). The dominant story often holds links to pre-trauma schemas that, if left unchallenged, lead to self-blame and the potential for future trauma. We would respond to this statement by paraphrasing her story and reflecting her feelings. However, we support her in moving beyond the dominant story through deconstructive questioning to illuminate the preferred or alternative story (Morgan; White & Epston). An alternative story might be about how she resisted (by going limp) when she knew she was physically overwhelmed. By asking questions about her resistance, that part of her story comes to the foreground and the crisis experience is changed from a personal defeat to a story of courage in the face of danger.

Making-Meaning Phase

In the second or Making-Meaning phase, we continue the process of externalizing and shift more deliberately into "making meaning" of her crisis experience. Our goal in this phase is to support the woman in reframing her experience within a feminine context. Through the use of metaphor, narrative strategies, reframing skills, deconstructive listening, consciousness raising, and reframing symptoms, we support her to accept her experience without intensifying the powerlessness and without pathologizing her responses into "symptoms." We are shifting from the message that the crisis was her experience alone to one in which it is part of a larger socio-political context. For example, we might hear a woman tell us that she was the target of sexual assault because she was where she "shouldn't have been." We might ask her deconstructive questions such as, "Tell me more about why you think you shouldn't have been there?" or "Talk to me more about why women shouldn't go to the bar alone. Where did you learn that?" or "How is it different for men to go to the bar alone and women can't; what is that all about?"

Affirmation Phase

During the Affirmation Phase, we continue the process of making meaning by providing information about the typical responses women (and people in general) have to crisis events. For example, we might describe the body's reaction to crisis through a discussion of our "dinosaur brains" (i.e., the limbic response to danger). We talk to women about how there are natural reactions to danger, for example to fight, to flee, or to dissociate. The particular action that a person takes in response to danger is based upon previous schemas that have been successful in the past (Damasio, 2005). Damasio suggests that these actions start before the cognitive part of the brain has the time to evaluate the situation and make a logic-based decision. This information is helpful to women who are dealing with guilt or shame around their reactions within the crisis moment. We affirm that "her brain did the best it could to keep her safe" in the crisis moment. We also affirm that "it worked; you are alive."

Affirmation is about providing the woman with feedback that supports the alternative stories of competence, empowerment, and agency that arose from the deconstructive questioning in the previous crisis intervention phases. During this phase, we might use the metaphor of pathways to describe the shift from the old story to the preferred story.

When a new lawn is planted and a path needs to be put in place, there are two ways of doing it. One is to have someone plan a path and make people walk on the designed path. The other is to watch people walk across the lawn and allow the path to be where people have shown they want to go. Even on the planned paths, people encountered barriers such as rocks and potholes, and developed skills for dealing with them. Eventually, people will walk where they need to walk, and over time, planned paths decay as more effective ones emerge. The old paths become overgrown but can still be found many years later, despite not being used regularly. The new ones remain somewhat rough until they get well worn and comfortable. People bring the skills they gained in navigating the old path to the new one and continue to develop skills to negotiate the barriers that might be on the new path.

This story is helpful especially when the recent crisis triggers the woman to recall past trauma, (i.e., a transcrisis point). We can support her in recognizing that she has choices about which path she might be on and acknowledge that the older paths are still available to her if she so chooses. We can also explore some of the consequences she might encounter depending upon the path she chooses. When consciousness-raising occurs, old paths look different and new ones look more possible and inviting. We affirm for women that their coping strategies are transferable, sometimes with modifications, to the new path. Our role in this phase is to help the woman build a richer or "thicker" story of her experience that includes the alternative or preferred story of her competence and resilience. We take on the role of guide in exploring this new territory. We are cautious in this phase to pace our interventions so that the woman remains in control of her experience.

It is difficult to navigate new paths alone. Nielsen (2004) found that women who successfully journeyed on new paths either had strong natural supports or they created them. We encourage women in this phase to identify interpersonal supports (e.g., friends, family, co-workers, etc.) and resources (e.g., financial, physical needs, child care needs, etc.) that might exist and support her in creating them where they do not exist. Where gaps exist, we advocate for her and link her to a web of community supports that can help her to meet her needs. For example, we might refer her to a woman's shelter, a feminist lawyer, or a holistic healer. We might advocate on her behalf with funding agencies and financial institutions. We also recognize our limited role with the woman and link her to feminist support systems that can provide ongoing support.

We recognize that it is not possible to do this work ethically without being part of a larger community of support people. We put the feminist principle "the personal is political" into action by engaging the community in supporting women in crisis. *The Canadian Code of Ethics for Psychologists*, Principle of Responsible Caring holds that psychologists must be knowledgeable about community resources and programs for women, recognize how such community supports and programs can be helpful and empowering, and refer women clients to them as appropriate (The CPA Section on Women and Psychology, 2007).

Action Phase

As we enter into the final phase of the crisis intervention, our focus shifts to planning for the future. Safety planning is needed. Initially, we focus on containing danger. We support women in getting their immediate safety needs met; for example, accessing a woman's shelter, gaining a restraining order, or seeking medical attention. Longer term safety planning might involve referrals to supports that can help her develop financial independence, alternative work options, educational opportunities, and supportive counselling.

Our work with women in the Action Phase is to support a shift of focus from danger to safety. A useful metaphor in this process is to talk about her "personal radar," that part of her that is vigilant for danger and can identify a safe path. We present the story of the radar used on ferries in a harbour. The radar the ferry uses is amazing. If the sensitivity of the scanners is set to "high," fish appear as big as ocean liners. If the sensitivity of the scanners is set "low," ocean liners may seem the size of fish. The extremes are not useful. The captain has to set the scanners to the right level of sensitivity to get through the channel. This means focussing on where trouble (e.g., logs and small boats) might come from and getting enough information to plan the safe route.

We encourage women to explore her beliefs about safety, who she is safe with, and how her beliefs about safety developed. We also ask her about how she learned to "tune" her radar. In doing so, we can explore whether or not she needs to recalibrate her scanners, given her recent experiences. Recalibration is done in a spirit of empowerment where she looks to affirm the power she has as a woman in her world.

CONCLUSION

Gender is a significant factor in the experience of trauma (Gilliland & James, 1997; Newman et al., 1997; Simmons, 2007). Crisis intervention is an important aspect of preventing the development of adverse trauma responses, particularly Post-traumatic Stress Disorder. While there are feminist methods of trauma intervention, there is no literature identifying specific feminist models of crisis intervention. In this chapter, we have explored the issue of crisis intervention from a feminist perspective. We have described a four-stage feminist model for responding to women in crisis.

REFERENCES

Barbera, E. (2003). Gender schema theory. *Canadian Journal of Behavioural Science*, 35(3), 176–184.

Bell, M.F., Goodman, L.A., & Dutton, M.A. (2007). The dynamics of staying and leaving: Implications for battered women's emotional well-being and experiences of violence at the end of a year. *Journal of Family Violence*, 22(6), 413–428.

Bem, S.L. (1981). Gender schema theory: A cognitive account of sex typing. *Psychological Review*, 88(4), 354–364.

Bem, S.L. (1994). *The lenses of gender: Transforming the debate on sexual inequality*. New Haven CT: Yale University Press.

Biever, J.L., DeLasFuentes, C., Cashion, L., & Franklin, C. (1998). Social Construction of Gender: A comparison of feminist and post-modern approaches. *Counseling Psychology Quarterly*, 11(2), 163–179.

Cason, D., Resick, P.A., & Weaver, T.L. (2002). Schematic integration of traumatic events. *Clinical Psychological Review*, 22, 131–153.

Cottone, R.R. (2007). Paradigms of counseling and psychotherapy revisited: Is social constructivism a paradigm? *Journal of Mental Health Counseling*, 29(3), 189–203.

Damasio, A. (1994/2005). *Descartes' error: Emotion, reason and the human brain*. London: Penguin.

Davies, B. (1989). The discursive production of the male/female dualism in school settings. *Oxford Review of Education*, 15(3), 229–241.

Everly, G.S., & Mitchell, J.T. (1999). *Critical incident stress management (CISM): A new era and standard of care in crisis intervention* (2nd Ed.). Ellicott City, MD: Chevron.

Freedman, J., & Coombs, G. (1999). *Narative therapy: The social construction of preferred realities*. New York: Norton Co.

Gilliland, B.E., & James, R.K. (1997). *Crisis intervention strategies*. Pacific Grove, CA: Brooks/Cole Publishing.

Hansen, J. (2006). Counseling theories within a postmodernist epistemology: New roles for theories in counseling practice. *Journal of Counseling & Development*, 84, 291–297.

Kaminer, D. (2006). Healing processes in the trauma narrative: A review. *South African Journal of Psychology, 36*(3), 481–499.

Martin, C.L. & Halverson Jr., C.F.A. (1981). Schematic processing model of sex typing and stereotyping in children. *Child Development, 52,* 1119–1134.

Martin, C.L., Ruble, D.N., & Szkrybalo, J. (2004). Recognizing the centrality of gender identity and stereotype knowledge in gender development and moving toward theoretical integration: Reply to Bandura and Bussey. *Psychological Bulletin, 130*(5), 702–710.

Mercer, D.L., & Evans, J.M. (2006). The impact of multiple losses on the grieving process: An exploratory study. *Journal of Loss and Trauma, 11*(3), 219–227.

Morgan, A. (2000). *What is narrative therapy?* Adelaide, South Australia: Dulwich Centre Publications.

Newman, E., Riggs, D.S., & Roth, S. (1997). Thematic resolution, PTSD, and complex PTSD: The relationship between meaning and trauma-related diagnoses. *Journal of Traumatic Stress. 10*(2), 197–213.

Nielsen, K.M. (2004). *Leaving an abusive relationship and finding hope: Women's experiences in post-secondary education.* Unpublished doctoral dissertation, University of Alberta.

Simmons, C.A., & Granvold, D.K. (2005). A cognitive model to explain gender differences in rate of PTSD diagnosis. *Brief Treatment and Crisis Intervention, 5*(3), 290–299.

Solomon, Z., Gelkopf, M., & Bleich, A. (2005). Is terror gender-blind? Gender differences in reaction to terror events. *Social Psychiatry & Psychiatric Epidemiology, 40,* 947–954.

Street, A.E., Gibson, L.E., & Holohan, D.R. (2005). Impact of childhood traumatic events, trauma-related guilt and avoidant coping strategies on PTSD symptoms in female survivors of domestic violence. *Journal of Traumatic Stress, 18*(3), 245–252.

Strong, T., & Sutherland, O. (2007). Conversational ethics in psychological dialogues: Discursive and collaborative considerations. *Canadian Psychology, 48*(2), 94–105.

The CPA Section on Women and Psychology. (2007). *Guidelines for ethical psychological practice with women.* Ottawa, Canada: Canadian Psychological Association.

Ward, T., Mann, R., & Gannon, T.A. (2007). The good lives model of offender rehabilitation: Clinical implications. *Aggression and Violent Behavior, 12*(1), 87–107.

Welch-Ross, M.K., &. Schmidt, C.R. (1996). Gender-schema development and children's constructive story memory: Evidence for a developmental model. *Child Development, 67*(3), 820–835.

White, M., & Epston, D. (1990). *Narrative means to therapeutic ends.* New York: Norton.

Winslade, J. & Monk, G. (2001). *Narrative mediation: A new approach to conflict resolution.* San Francisco: Jossey-Bass

Worell, J., & Remer, P. (1996). *Feminist perspectives in therapy: An empowerment model.* Toronto: Wiley.

CHAPTER 13

Telling Stories to Make Sense of Job Loss by Arlene M.C. Young

Qualitative research relies on the assumptions, knowledge, and skills of the researcher. The reader infers something about the author from everything written, but in feminist and qualitative research, it is expected that the researcher will provide some biographical information to help readers locate both the research and the researcher.

I am the only child of middle-class Canadian parents, both of whom died many years ago. I am the mother of two grown children, who I raised mostly on my own since they were young. For much of my career and my adult life, I was a student counsellor at a university, and a part-time graduate student. My counselling focussed primarily on career and educational planning, and helping students overcome barriers to their learning. Women comprised the majority of students in the university and thus in my counselling practice. In graduate studies in counselling and educational psychology, I focussed on issues affecting women, particularly women and employment. I have taught graduate and undergraduate students in women's studies and counselling for the past nine years.

INTRODUCTION

In more than 40 years as a counsellor in many settings, I have found that most people explain their needs by telling a story. Telling and listening to stories are things that people seem to do naturally, seldom recognizing how important it is to exploring the meaning of life experiences. I have often heard friends and family discuss another person's painful story, saying how they wish they could do something to help. The point I want to make in this chapter arises from the collaborative approach to storytelling that I used in exploring women's job loss experiences. Actively listening to each woman tell her story and collaborating with each woman to write, revisit, and interpret it helped each woman to discover what that loss meant to her. Making sense of women's experiences came about within the context of our collaboration; that is to say, within the context of our relationships to each other.

Feminist Orientation

I read *The Second Sex* in high school (de Beauvoir, 1949/1974). It was not until I had considerable life experience that I connected deeply with her point that men were considered the norm in human endeavour and inquiry, and women were the "other" and the exception to the norm. In graduate studies, some feminist researchers had a particularly important influence on my research orientation because they listened closely to the women who participated in their research, and thus heard stories and found patterns that differed from the dominant theories of the time (Belenky, Clinchy, Goldberger, & Tarule, 1986; Gilligan, 1982). Gilligan found that women's moral decisions were not directed by others' expectations, as Kohlberg thought, but were informed according to how they demonstrated care for themselves and others. Belenky et al. developed a theory of learning that rested, in part, on the importance of voice to the women they interviewed. They stressed that voice was about speaking up, speaking out, and being heard by others. Other research has expanded the idea of voice to include the power and disabling aspects of silence (Mahoney, 1996).

My master's research was an evaluation of an assertiveness-training work-shop for women. Assertiveness training is an approach to teaching communications skills that I had found effective in counselling individuals and groups. Consistent with Gilligan's (1982) findings, I discovered in my research that women sought to balance their assertiveness with maintaining caring relationships (Young, 1987). Those women worked to find a balance between their needs and those of others as they struggled to find their voice.

Marecek (1995) stated that until the latter part of the twentieth century, men researched and wrote psychological theory and research from a male perspective, for the enlightenment and benefit of men, rather than for the advancement of women. Feminist inquiry, in contrast, seeks to question the assumptions taken for granted by previous knowledge and to generate new understandings by, about, and for the benefit of women. Postmodern feminists acknowledge that the knowledge thus produced, like all knowledge, is partial, situated, and governed by the perspective of the knower (Fougère, 1998; Longino, 1994).

MY INTEREST IN JOB LOSS

My interest in women's experiences of job loss arose from organizational restructuring in which several of my colleagues lost their jobs, and I feared

300

for my own. I did not lose my job, but counselling jobs were being eliminated across the post-secondary educational sector in Alberta. I feared that if I lost my job, I would not be able to find another without relocating. Relocation would mean moving away from my adult children and would force a choice between two loves: my family and my career. As a result of my experiences in organizational restructuring, I changed career direction. I applied to a doctoral program that, in turn, led to an academic appointment. My close brush with job loss, despite its positive outcome, prompted me to wonder what women experienced when they lost their jobs.

The Research Questions

My research focussed on case studies of three women who had experienced job loss. The following questions guided the research process. What were women's experiences of job loss? How did their job losses occur? How did it affect them and their relationships to others and to their work? What meanings can be derived from their job loss experiences? How does gender inform these meanings?

Transitions, Grief, and Mourning

Qualitative studies that consider individuals' job loss experiences have existed at least since the 1930s and have focussed on men's job losses (Kubicek, 1999). A longitudinal qualitative study completed in the 1930s looked at the effects of a factory's closure on the men who lost their jobs as well as its impact on their families (Jahoda, 1982). The factory closure in Marienthal, Austria, resulted in an unemployment rate in excess of 20%. Workers and their families first reacted with shock. Then people adapted to the new situation and recovered to some extent by engaging in organizations and activities that had ceased for a time. Finally, people's adaptation was threatened further as the economic hardship deepened.

Jahoda (1982) reconfirmed a number of psychological as well as financial effects that were found in another of her studies in 1980. In the 1980s in Great Britain, she noted that social programs reduced the financial hardships associated with job loss, but the psychological effects remained. The unemployed found, first, that they had too much time and too little to do. Second, they suffered from reduced social contact outside of their families. Third, they lacked collective activities and goals inherent in employment. Fourth, they lost their work status, which in turn affected their personal identity. Finally, they were without regular activity.

Three qualitative studies have shed further light on the psychological effects of job displacement that Jahoda (1982) found (Gilberto, 1999; Hughes-Bond, 2001; Moore, 2003). Gilberto's study of 18 women from New York found that those who were the most heavily invested in work suffered the most psychologically. Those who fared best had their contributions acknowledged and received explanations for the loss. Those who suffered the worst reactions of shock, hurt, humiliation, and shame had pre-existing mental health issues or had their sense of purpose and status threatened. An increase in the length of unemployment following a job loss also increased anxiety and financial concerns. Hughes-Bond studied 12 Canadian women who lost their jobs in the 1990s. The women were employed in a wide range of occupations and levels in the public and private sectors. Hughes-Bond found that the financial effects were highly variable depending upon the amount of notice, severance pay, eligibility for employment insurance, and family makeup (e.g. whether they had children). They suffered psychological effects like those Jahoda identified, but contrary to Jahoda's speculation, those effects were not alleviated when the women turned their attention to housework and child care. The women missed the structure, goals, and social interaction of their former employment. The losses identified in the previous two studies echo those of other women from the Appalachian region of Virginia. Those women lost jobs in textile factories and lacked the education and skills to make an easy transition to other employment. The study focussed on six of the women who opted for retraining in a local community college. The women spoke of the shock of losing their jobs and the worry about finances, but also recognized that their identities were tied to their previous employment. The women mourned the loss of their long-time work situations and their co-workers. All three studies indicate that women in a number of jurisdictions and occupations have suffered financially from job loss as expected, but they also suffered from psychological effects just as the men that Jahoda studied did.

Bridges (1980) and Pulley (1997) applied theories and research of grief and mourning to job loss. Bridges (1980) focussed on describing the transition process, stressing that every transition begins with an ending. Beginning a new job implies losing or leaving an old one with its attendant routines and interpersonal relationships (Bridges, 1980). Bridges (1980) stressed that all endings, even happy ones, imply loss, grief, and mourning. He also predicted that the labour market would become more volatile and that individuals, employers, and career counsellors must develop new relationships to work and learn to handle job transitions effectively (Bridges, 1994). When a job ends, some people may react with feelings of shock or betrayal; others with relief (Pulley, 1997). Pulley called the period after the job loss the "dark time," filled with negative emotions, and accompanied by serious soul searching. The turmoil would be particularly difficult if friends and family failed to realize that the individual was mourning a loss.

Bridges's (1980) theory about transitions resonated with the theory and research on grief and mourning (Rando, 1984, 1995; Neimeyer, 1999, 2000).

Bridges's (1980) first two stages, endings and the neutral zone, parallel Rando's descriptions of grief and mourning. Rando (1995) described grief as the psychological, social, and somatic responses to the perception of loss; and mourning as active processes of adaptation to changed circumstances. Grief can involve feelings of loss, betrayal, or as Pulley (1997) found, relief. Further, losses can be physical and tangible, or psychosocial and symbolic (Rando, 1995). The death of a loved one would be an example of a tangible loss; job loss would be an example of a psychosocial or symbolic loss. Rando (1995) acknowledged that there was more social support for the loss of a loved one, and that cultural patterns of grief and mourning would be variable. On the other hand, she recognized the lack of acknowledgement of grief and mourning for psychosocial or symbolic losses and that mourners would not receive similar support.

Narrative approaches stress that grief is constructed by the bereaved within a social context and not in prescribed patterns (Neimeyer, 1999, 2000). Given its contextual and individual framework, however, Neimeyer stated that grievers tend to challenge taken-for-granted constructions about life and reconstruct meanings unique to them and their context. Similarly, Rando (1995) stated that psychosocial or symbolic losses have an impact on individuals' assumptions about themselves, and about how things are and work in the world. Neimeyer (2000) explained that narrative strategies focussing on deriving meaning from experiences would be particularly valuable in grief work. Those who suffered less could explain their loss and find some purpose or meaning for it.

RESEARCH PROCESS

The three women who participated in this research made sense of their experiences and found meaning by telling their stories. It is important to note that it is making sense or finding meaning that is most relevant to making sense of the experience and not the content of that meaning. That idea fits with Frankl's (1963/1992) observations that those who survived concentration camps had something to live for—something that could be idealistic, loving, or mundane. What mattered was that survivors found meaning so that they could do what was necessary to survive.

This research can be described best as arising from an emergent design that focussed on three case studies. I did not begin my research with the idea of writing stories. Writing and revising stories collaboratively emerged as the best way to present the information. The three participants told me that talking about what happened, and collaboratively writing their stories helped them to make sense of their experiences.

Participants

Diane, Rebecca, and Susan, the three women who participated in this research, are white, middle-class, university educated, Canadian women who worked in professional jobs, as a social work manager, university counsellor, and engineer. The counsellor is married with one child, and the social work manager and engineer are single and childless.

Interviews

Interviewing participants was my principle way of discovering the three women's experiences of job loss. Each of the women lost her job in the Alberta public sector restructuring and downsizing in the 1990s. All three had many years of successful employment with one employer prior to their job loss.

Franklin (1997) discusses three models of research interviewing. In the first, information extraction, the interviewer structures the interview often with set questions in a specific order. The interviewer is friendly, but avoids biasing the interview by responding substantively to questions or observations. In the second model, shared understanding, the interviewer comes with an open mind and with as few presuppositions as possible. The interviewer clarifies, paraphrases, or interprets while interviewing, and interviews further to corroborate interpretations. In the third or discourse model, both parties to the interview interact and shape what transpires. "Assumptions that the interviewer can (or should) be 'objective' and 'distanced' (as required in the first model), or can bracket presuppositions (as in the second model), are called into question. Interviewers, like interviewees, necessarily see situations from a point of view infused with personal experience" (Franklin, p. 104).

The interviews for this research shared some aspects of Franklin's (1997) understanding and discourse models. The hybrid characteristics were due in part to the requirements of the ethics review committee, which asked for a list of the questions to be asked, and in part to my insecurity at interviewing without a set of prompts. These are the prompts that I used, as required and to keep the interview focussed on the experience, meaning, and interpretation of involuntary job loss.

- What was that experience like for you?

- How has it affected you? Self? Thoughts? Mood? Family? Friends? Work associates? As a woman?

- How did you feel it in your body?

- Is there an incident that stands out?

- What does the experience mean to you?

- Has that meaning changed?

- What keeps you going?

- What will you take from this experience into the rest of your life?

I conducted an initial audiotaped interview with each of the women. I transcribed the interview verbatim, verified the transcript for accuracy, and identified points to clarify. After each interview, I wrote notes, much as I would after a counselling session. I recalled the setting, the major topics covered, and my impressions. Once I had verified the transcript, I erased the tape, and changed the names on the transcript to ensure the woman's anonymity. I read and reread the transcripts, noting parts that I wanted to clarify. Most of those clarifications occurred in a tape recorded and transcribed follow-up interview, but there were also additions and corrections as I wrote and revised the stories in collaboration with each participant.

Analysis

With the transcripts in hand, I was ready to analyze the content of the interviews, identify themes, and sequence events. The process of selecting the significant parts of the transcript is also the beginning of narrative construction and interpretation. Some experiences are selected for inclusion in the narrative and others are not (Bruner, 1991).

My first method for identifying the meaning was simple enough conceptually, but very time consuming. It comprised a thematic analysis of the transcripts from each woman's initial and follow-up interviews. I selected the richest segments of the interviews and put these quotations into a grid. The grid had five columns labelled from left to right: time (before, after, during separation interview), number (the sequence of quote identified for each individual), quotation (verbatim), paraphrase (my restatement of the information and emotional content), and themes. I systematically worked through each interview, addressing each column for each quotation selected. Once I had a complete matrix for one woman's interviews, I made many copies of the grid, and cut it apart at each quotation. I sorted the quotations, by hand, into piles. I compared each quotation to the others and kept only those that expressed new information or a particular theme. Once I had the quotations sorted, I labelled each group according to a second-order theme that seemed to describe it. I reviewed all of the quotations in each group and compared them with the others, reconsidered, and sometimes changed the labels.

The thematic analysis that I have described was, however, only one step in the process of making sense of the data. Having undertaken the detailed quotation-by-quotation analysis, I had to stand back to reflect upon what the women were saying by reading, thinking, walking my dogs, writing, and talking about what I was doing. Some theorists talk about the hermeneutic circle, in which the parts of a text must be understood in relation to the understanding of the whole (Schmidt, 1996). When I speak of finding the meaning of the whole, I look at the following: What happened? How did it feel? and What did it mean? Hermeneutics provided one way to approach the matter, and writing proved to be another (Richardson, 1994). While I did not follow Richardson's method in her way, I found that my understanding developed through the process of writing in my journal, and writing and rewriting the case studies. That process involved cycling back and forth between the transcripts, data analysis matrices, second-order themes, my journal, the participants, and the stories themselves. In rewriting the stories, the participants and I began to understand their experiences in a new way. They stated, and I understood, the role that writing narratives filled in making sense of their experiences.

Narrative Theories

Presenting the participants' experiences of job loss as stories fits naturally with what they said and how they said it. That idea is supported by psychological theories and theories of narrative research (Bruner, 1991; Gergen & Gergen, 1988). The elements Bruner (1991) considered essential for narrative are present in the stories of the participants. The stories were about particular events in time, events that were sharp changes of direction in the progress of their lives. Gergen and Gergen (1988) added to those ideas by stating that the point of the story, its direction, is important in structuring the narrative (for example, how I survived, overcame, learned, etc.) and also in establishing causal links between events. Feminist theorists consider narrative inquiry valuable, but have criticized it for incorporating the dominant male bias of our culture (Gergen, 1997; Sands, 1996; Scholnick, 2000). The usual narrative plots may not fit well with women's lives (Gergen, 1997; Sands, 1996) and may use androcentric metaphors such as argument and building rather than women's metaphors of conversation and friendship (Scholnick, 2000).

Gergen (1997) stated that story forms are gendered such that there are "manstories and womanstories" (p. 205). Gergen examined the narratives inherent in the career paths of several women and concluded that their "career line was important, but it was not an ultimate end point. Whereas men seemed to sacrifice their lives to careers, women seemed to tell the story in reverse" (Gergen, p. 212). She emphasized that women thought their careers and success were important but not the goal of their striving. "The story is about a person who is embedded in a variety of relationships, which all have some priority in the telling of the life. Ambiguity about any outcome complexifies the task of giving value to a particular event" (Gergen, p. 216). The narratives of the participants in this research interwove job, family, friends, colleagues, and community in the ways that are characteristic of women's stories.

I recognize the importance of Gergen's (1997) observations about the complex pattern of what she calls "womanstories." Just as Gilligan (1982) added to the patterns in ethical decision-making, so has Gergen added the socially embedded, long suffering, selfless heroine to narrative possibilities. Gilligan and Attanuci (1988) found that both men and women are aware of and use both principled and care orientations to approach ethical dilemmas. Further, they suggest that women use caring orientations whereas men use principled orientations more frequently. It may be true that women's stories often follow the interconnected pattern Gergen described. It is also possible that single, widowed, or divorced fathers raising children could tell stories that are as complex as those told by the women in her research.

Diane, Rebecca, and Susan all stated that taking part in the research had been important to them because it helped them to understand their job loss in a different and more complex manner. All three stated that they volunteered to take part in the research to assist me in my work, but that they also had benefitted from taking part. The goal of the interviews and subsequent narrative development was to richly describe and interpret the participants' experiences from their perspectives. That meant understanding each other, sharing stories, laughing, and crying together—a relationship sharing some of the qualities of friendship. The big difference is that the interviews were undertaken to meet my research goals. It is both moving and humbling to realize the great responsibility in simply asking questions and listening carefully.

MEANINGS

Research can produce unanticipated knowledge. In this case, the benefit of the research process to participants was not fully appreciated at the outset of the project. Three women's experiences of job loss were told as stories in my doctoral dissertation (Young, 2003). Stories are a culturally familiar, cohesive, and comprehensible way to discuss personal experiences (Bruner, 1991; Gergen & Gergen, 1988). Diane, Rebecca, and Susan told me that they made sense of their job loss experiences through our discussions and through revising the drafts of their stories. Each stated that she had discussed the job loss experience in a different way with me than she had with others. Specifically, each woman had been able to focus on the experiences and to consider what they meant. All three women had been committed to jobs within particular organizations, but as a result of their job losses, they changed their relationships to work, other people, and themselves. The focus here is on the meanings they derived from telling their stories.

Stories told for public knowledge are both subject to and moulded by public evaluation (Gergen & Gergen, 1988). Each of the three women who partici-pated in the research emphasized how their work environment and organiza-tional values had changed to become discordant with their own. Consistent with attribution theory, the women attributed the loss of their jobs to the situation, not to themselves (De Cremer, 2000; Howard & Hollander, 2000). Diane stated that she cared about clients and staff in her social work department, but caring had become less valued in the department. Rebecca and Susan enjoyed teamwork and collaborative decision-making, but organizational downsizing had led to competition between individuals and departments. Each of them told a story of being caught up in organizational restructuring.

The three women's stories of job losses described fragments of the women's lives. When I asked Susan about when the meaning of her job loss would become clear, she said, "I suspect I will always be able to have a different understanding of things I've learned from it, because as you continue to grow, your perspective changes a bit." The stories do not fit a conventional literary form, but are shaped by a theme: "How I survived the loss of my job" (Gergen & Gergen, 1988; Gergen, 1997). I asked them to tell me about their job loss and each responded by telling me a story about what had happened and how it affected them within their context.

Grief and Mourning

Diane, Rebecca, and Susan each went through what Bridges (1980, 1994) called a neutral zone or what Pulley (1997) called a dark time after their job loss. During that time, they had to grasp the personal losses and meanings brought about by their dismissals. Diane was angry at the loss of her social services man-agement job that connected her to the wider community through personally and socially meaningful work. During the two-and-a-half years it took to find another suitable job, she lost relationships with some departmental survivors and friends. She believed that the departmental survivors feared for their own jobs and felt guilty about her job loss, and that her friends did not understand her emotional turmoil. Rebecca mourned the loss of an ideal, collaborative work environment. She was angry at the impulsive decision-making that took away jobs, and she used her anger to demand accountability. Rebecca found another job immediately, but it soon proved unsatisfactory. The two experiences left her feeling sad for what she had lost, and guilty for leaving the second job so soon. Susan was angry about the duplicity of management in fostering a collaborative re-engineering process while the real decisions were made behind the scenes. Similarly, in her subsequent minimum-wage sales job, management stressed teamwork, but actually rewarded competition. Each of the women experienced a dark time filled with negative feelings as they made the transition from job loss to a new situation, employed or unemployed.

Narrative approaches stress that grief is constructed within a social context and that it does not follow prescribed patterns (Neimeyer, 1999, 2000). Nonetheless, like Neimeyer, Rando (1995) stresses that losses have an impact on the individual's taken-for-granted assumptions about the world. Diane, Rebecca, and Susan faced challenges to their assumption that hard work and loyalty would be rewarded with job security. That belief was prevalent, and it was the belief that Bridges (1994) and Pulley (1997) saw as needing revision. They foresaw a transformation in the nature of employment such that individuals could anticipate many losses of employment throughout their careers.

Grief was a reaction to loss, but individuals could choose how to respond to it (Neimeyer, 1999). Diane and Rebecca both focussed on, and were successful in, restoring their careers. Susan tried to focus on her career, but her health worsened, and restoring her health took precedence. Neimeyer also noted that grief is private, but it is linked to the responses of others. Diane was disappointed in the poor support she received from many of her friends and colleagues, and consequently withdrew from some relationships. She continued to have a supportive relationship with her family. Rebecca initiated contact with colleagues who seemed unwilling to initiate them with her, and thus maintained important work relationships. Her relationships with her husband and son remained close. Susan continued to get support from friends, family, and former colleagues.

Financial

Each of the women was affected by the loss of income. Diane's job loss ended her dream of early retirement because she used some of her retirement savings to live while unemployed. Diane was embarrassed that with little income, she could not take part in many social activities, visit her family who lived some distance away, or contribute financially to organizations she formerly supported. Rebecca and her husband needed two incomes to maintain their family and dream home. Over the course of a few years, she had become the primary wage earner, and found that she felt more responsibility for her family's security. Susan suffered greatly financially. Her severance package kept her going at first. As her health deteriorated further and she could not work, she ended up financially broke and on welfare. She felt humiliated by her situation.

Psychological

Diane, Rebecca, and Susan have experienced, in varying degrees, the psychological effects that Jahoda (1982) described. First, each of them needed to take action to structure their time after the loss of their job. Diane engaged immediately in a job search; Rebecca started another job immediately; and Susan started her own business. Second, each of them dealt with the loss of her professional relationships. Diane suffered isolation and kept contact with only a small group of her professional contacts. Her immediate departure from the workplace militated against bringing closure or redefining continuing working relationships. Her isolation was particularly acute because she lived alone. Rebecca and Susan had several months to renegotiate the work relationships that mattered. Susan found later, upon dismissal from temporary, minimum-wage jobs, that relationships with those staff members ended immediately. Susan's isolation, like Diane's, was especially acute because she lived alone. Third, all three women identified strongly with the goals of their former employers and suffered from the loss of a collective purpose. Diane and Rebecca each found another collective purpose after their job loss, but Susan has been unable to do so. Diane initially made job search her focus. It was hard work and resulted in short-term jobs that left her even more disillusioned with employers. She had, however, meaningful volunteer work to fill her need for a collective purpose. Rebecca found a job in another college, had no difficulty investing in its goals, but eventually she left because of the uncomfortable working conditions. Both Diane and Rebecca were able to fulfill the fourth and fifth psychological effects by regaining the status accorded by successful employment in jobs that resonated with their personal identities. Susan's poor health has prevented her from seeking employment. She has, rather, focused on improving her health. Initially, she engaged successfully in consulting and conference organization. Later, she tried to establish her own business, but her deteriorating health militated against success. When she was once again well enough to work, she had short-term minimum wage jobs that further eroded her trust in employers. Unlike Diane and Rebecca, Susan has been unable to sustain employment, volunteer, or contract work, and feels lost without it.

Identity

Each woman changed her status and redefined her identity to some extent. Multiple job losses and frustration with social work administration led Diane to find satisfying work in a related occupation. Moving to a new job and community and finding the new job unsatisfactory helped Rebecca to take a risk. She reconnected with the risk-taking part of her personality that she had foregone in favour of marriage and child rearing. While Diane and Rebecca had to change their daily routines to accommodate new jobs, Susan suffered greatly from the lack of both routine and employment status. She attributed failing to notice her deteriorating health to that lack of routine, and the lack of regular contact with others. She did not notice, and because she lives alone, there was no one else to draw her behavioural changes to her attention. Loss of status and self-esteem affected Diane until she found another job. It continues to be problematic for Susan. Susan has been granted a pension on the basis of a permanent disability. It is a relief to her to have a steady income, but having a disability pension is evidence that her unemployment is permanent. She is still mourning for the loss of her career.

As Women

I asked each of the women to discuss how her experiences of job loss affected her as a woman. The answer to that question most often came, not through direct responses, but through their stories. Rebecca said, "I don't know what is woman and not woman. To me everything is woman. Not being a man, it's difficult for me to see whether these issues are different." That statement begs the question, What, if anything, about the women's stories is particularly womanly?

Diane and Susan talked about the sexism they encountered in their work environments. Diane told me that being a woman affected her because she had worked harder to advance than the men in her department. Susan talked about the quantity and quality of sexism, foul language, and unwanted sexual advances she contended with when working in an engineering department. The women were affected by those experiences because of their gender.

The three women had worked to support themselves financially throughout their working lives. Their self-esteem rested in part on professional accomplishments and their familial and social connections. A good salary meant that they could support the households they wanted, contribute financially to community organizations, socialize with friends, and help family members. Rebecca focussed on her husband and son, and Diane and Susan on their extended families. Their stories are marked by a dual concern for employment, and their social relationships were typical of what Gergen (1997) called womanstories.

Shifts in Meanings

The women's awareness and understandings of their experiences developed as the research progressed. Diane's story demonstrated an adherence to the implicit employment contract that good work leads to continuing employment. She engaged in her job search and new jobs with the same understanding. Rebecca recognized that she gave more to her employer than was good for her or her family. Her new relationship to employment is more tentative, similar to the understanding that she believes is held by employers. Susan came to mistrust employers because of managers' duplicity in both the departmental re-engineering process and part-time minimum-wage jobs. Her declining health and eventual permanent disability deepened her questioning further. She questioned not only the assumption about hard work and loyalty, but also the assumption that employment is the hallmark of a worthwhile person. Each of the women developed new understandings about employment and employers from her experiences and through her work in constructing narratives.

IMPLICATIONS

This research drew on the experiences of three white, middle-class, university educated, Canadian women and may have implications for others who lose their jobs or suffer a loss, and those who support them. The reader is in the best position to choose how to incorporate these implications.

For Those Who Lose Their Jobs

Reach out to those who matter to you. Tell the story of your experience to trusted others who are willing to listen while you make sense of your job loss. Give them a brief outline of your expectations for your discussion. Be sure to state clearly to others whether you want their advice. Other people may be guilty or fearful survivors who do not know what to say or do. You can help them to connect with you by letting them know that you value working together with them or their friendship. You can then discuss with them how your relationship is to continue, at least during the current transition.

For Friends and Family of Those Who Lose Their Jobs

Listen to what those who lose their jobs have to say. Most of all, listen. Diane, Rebecca, and Susan stressed that having the opportunity to focus on what it was like to lose their jobs, and to make sense of and gain meaning from it, was very important to them. Take the lead by asking the questions she wants to address. Do not give advice unless the individual concerned asks for it. You cannot fix the problem or make the individual feel better, but you can be a good listener. Listening alone is helpful.

For Employers

Employees realize that there are changes in the wind (Bridges, 1991, 1994). It is important to inform staff about the plans as thoroughly as possible, to explain the rationale for changes, and to commit the organization to fair treatment of all concerned. As Bridges says, the truth may be difficult, but rumours destroy trust. Give as much notice as possible to ease the transition for those who are leaving. The two women in this research project who had the time to say farewell, and to initiate contact with important others, fared better after they lost or left their jobs. That recommendation seems contrary to the admonition that employers make changes quickly so the organizations can begin to recover (Bridges, 1991). It seems likely that there will be tension between employee and employer needs, and employers must balance the good of the organization with that of individuals. It is important to recognize, however, that employees will suffer less from job loss with time to say farewell. I urge employers to give trusted employees as much notice as possible. Hire outplacement and counselling services to help both job losers and survivors cope with the change. Change and loss of the old structures are difficult for everyone (Bridges, 1994).

For Counsellors

Encourage those who have lost their jobs to tell their stories. Encourage them to use words, or other media if that's more comfortable, and to describe their context in rich detail (i.e., including their race, class, marital status, sexual orientation, ability, whether they were sole wage earners, had children, etc.). The process of telling the story, making sense of it and finding meaning, will help clients through the transition from job loss to the next stage in their lives (Bridges, 1980; Neimeyer, 1999). Counsellors need to be sensitive to age and gender issues (Straussner & Phillips, 1999). Straussner and Phillips found that women lose hope more quickly than men and are more likely to accept any job that is offered. Help those you counsel to identify what gives them hope and to be flexible in their responses to unemployment, and remind them that unemployment is temporary. Group counselling may be particularly effective because some research has shown that the most helpful support is from someone else who has lost a job (Carroll et al., 1995). A narrative process can be used effectively in conjunction with other career planning exercises and inventories to help clients make plans that are uniquely suited to their abilities, preferences, and situations (Cochran, 1997). Integrating narrative into career counselling has the potential to improve the job loss. transition. Cochran's central idea is "emplotment; that is, how a person can be cast as the main character in a career narrative that is meaningful, productive, and fulfilling" (p. x). He states that through their life stories, individuals implicitly or explicitly describe their ideal life course. As they try out options, read about them, and talk with others, they will accept or reject them according to how they fit into their evolving story. The best choices would not only allow people to continue their ideal courses, but would allow them the agency to continue shaping their life stories.

CONCLUSION

These women's stories of job loss are stories of transition and survival. As I worked with the women, I felt privileged to discuss their experiences and feelings. They spent many hours in interviews with me and in reviewing drafts of their stories. Their experiences and the meanings they derived from them make it clear that there is no one way to lose a job, or to react to that loss. Each woman's job loss story has unique characteristics, but each woman gained insight into her experiences by telling her story as part of the research.

Jahoda (1982) pointed out that most of us are speaking of employment when we discuss work. Employment in good jobs with predictable pay and benefits provides employees with the income to provide for themselves and their families. It also gives them the leisure to spend time with their families, to continue their education, or contribute to their community's life in some way. Through employment, people enjoy the psychological benefits that Jahoda identified. Our work structures our time, gives us something meaningful to do, gives us a status, and allows us to engage with people outside of our families and to pursue collective goals. The loss of jobs with good pay and benefits threatens to leave many of us psychologically wanting.

The situation for those who lose their jobs can be difficult, often painful, but there are things that friends, families, employers, and counsellors can do to help. Families and friends can provide support by simply listening to the story of the job loss. Employers prepare employees for the possibility of job losses by keeping them informed of organizational plans and of the planned severance provisions. They can also help those who lose their jobs by ensuring that outplacement services are available. Counsellors can use a narrative approach to help those who lose their jobs to find meanings in their experiences, and to draw on this found meaning to plan the next stage of their lives. The loss of a job may lead to a new beginning and a transformation of work to something more meaningful than what was lost.

REFERENCES

Belenky, M.F., Clinchy, B. M., Goldberger, N. R., & Tarule, J. M. (1986). *Women's ways of knowing*. New York: Basic Books.

Bridges, W. (1980). *Transitions*. Reading, MA: Addison-Wesley.

Bridges, W. (1991). *Managing transitions*. Reading, MA: Addison-Wesley Publishing.

Bridges, W. (1994). *Job shift*. Reading, MA: Addison-Wesley.

Bruner, J. (1991). The narrative construction of reality. *Critical Inquiry, 18*, 1–21.

Carroll, T.L., DiVincenti, M., & Show, E.V. (1995). Nurse executive job loss: Trauma or transition. *Nursing Administration Quarterly, 19*(4), 11–17.

Cochran, L. (1997). *Career counseling: A narrative approach*. Thousand Oaks, CA: Sage.

de Beauvoir, S. (1949/1974). *The second sex*. New York: Vintage.

De Cremer, D. (2000). Effect of group identification on the use of attributions. *The Journal of Social Psychology, 140*, 267–269.

Fougère, M.L. (1998). Women's studies and the politics of relations across differences: The lessons of postmodern epistemology. *Atlantis, 22*, 145–150.

Frankl, V. E. (1963/1992). *Man's search for meaning: An introduction to logotherapy*. Boston: Beacon Press.

Franklin, M. (1997). Making sense: Interviewing and narrative representation. In M.M. Gergen & S.N. Davis (Eds.), *Toward a new psychology of gender* (pp. 99–116). New York: Routledge.

Gergen, M. (1997). Life stories: Pieces of a dream. In M.M. Gergen & S.N. Davis (Eds.), *Toward a new psychology of gender* (pp. 203–221). New York: Routledge.

Gergen, K.J., & Gergen, M.M. (1988). Narrative and the self as relationship. In L. Berkowitz (Ed.), *Advances in experimental social psychology* (pp. 17–56). New York: Academic Press.

Gilberto, L.M. (1997). *Downsized expectations: Older women coping with job loss*. Unpublished doctoral dissertation, City University of New York, New York.

Gilligan, C. (1982). *In a different voice*. Cambridge, MA: Harvard University Press.

Gilligan, C., & Attanucci, J. (1988). Much ado about...Knowing? Noting? Nothing? A reply to Vasudev concerning sex differences and moral development. *Merrill-Palmer Quarterly, 34*(4), 451–456.

Howard, J. A., & Hollander, J. (2000). *Gendered situations, gendered selves*. Walnut Creek, CA: Altamira Press.

Hughes-Bond, L. (2001). *Going home: A study of unemployed female workers' perspectives on unemployment*. Unpublished doctoral dissertation, University of Ottawa, Ottawa, Canada. Retrieved August 15, 2009 from ProQuest Digital Dissertations (ATT NQ67216).

Jahoda, M. (1982). *Employment and unemployment*. Cambridge, UK: Cambridge University Press.

Longino, H.E. (1994). In search of feminist epistemology. *Monist, 77*(4), 472–486.

Mahoney, M.A. (1996). The problem of silence in feminist psychology. *Feminist Studies, 22*(3), 603–625.

Marecek, J. (1995). Psychology and feminism: Can this relationship be saved? In D.C. Stanton & A.J. Stewart (Eds.), *Feminisms in the academy* (pp. 101–132). Ann Arbor, MI: University of Michigan.

Moore, M.N. (2003). *A cross-case study of six women who experienced layoffs in the apparel industry and enrolled in retraining programs at a southwest Virginia community college.* Unpublished doctoral dissertation, University of Virginia, Charlottesville, VA. Retrieved August 14, 2009 from ProQuest Digital Dissertations (ATT 308310).

Neimeyer, R.A. (1999). Narrative strategies in grief therapy. *Journal of Constructivist Psychology, 12,* 65–85.

Neimeyer, R.A. (2000). Searching for the meaning of meaning: Grief therapy and the process of reconstruction. *Death Studies, 24,* 541–558.

Pulley, M.L. (1997). *Losing your job—reclaiming your soul.* San Francisco: Jossey-Bass.

Rando, T.A. (1984). Grief: The reaction to loss. *Grief, dying, and death.* Champaign, IL: Research Press.

Rando, T.A. (1995). Grief and mourning: Accommodating to loss. In H. Wass & R.A. Neimeyer (Eds.), *Dying: Facing the facts* (pp. 211–241). Washington, DC: Taylor and Francis.

Richardson, L. (1994). Writing. In N.K. Denzin & Y.S. Lincoln (Eds.), *Handbook of qualitative research* (pp. 516–529). Thousand Oaks, CA: Sage.

Sands, R.G. (1996). The elusiveness of identity in social work practice with women: A postmodern feminist perspective. *Clinical Social Work Journal, 24*(2), 167–186.

Schmidt, L.K. (1996). Recalling the hermeneutic circle. *Philosophy Today, 40*(2), 263–273.

Scholnick, E.K. (2000). Engendering development: Metaphors of change. In P.H. Miller & E.K. Schonick (Eds.), *Toward a feminist developmental psychology* (pp. 29–42). New York: Routledge.

Straussner, S.L.A., &Phillips, N.K. (1999). The impact of job loss on professional and managerial employees and their families. *Families in Society, 80,* 642–648.

Young, A.M.C. (1987). *The effects of an assertiveness training workshop for women on assertion and self-esteem.* Edmonton, AB, Canada: Unpublished master's thesis, University of Alberta, Edmonton.

Young, A.M.C. (2003). *Making sense of women's job loss experiences.* Edmonton, AB, Canada. Unpublished doctoral dissertation, University of Alberta, Edmonton.

CHAPTER 14

Engaging Women Who Are Mandated to Participate in Counselling by Ann Marie Dewhurst and Karen M. Nielsen

Please see our personal information at the beginning of Chapter 12.

INTRODUCTION

This chapter describes a feminist, community-based approach to counselling women who are mandated to participate in that counselling. It may seem to some that it is not possible to be a feminist and work with women coerced into therapy. It is our view, however, that women mandated into treatment are a unique and vulnerable group of women who are in strong need of feminist therapists. Our review of the counselling and psychological literature confirmed that there is not much written about how to therapeutically support women mandated to participate in counselling. Therefore, we saw the need for this chapter. Our goal is to integrate published literature with our counselling experience gained over many years of working with women mandated to participate in counselling in both community and correctional settings.

Women mandated to participate in counselling are a heterogeneous group with various motivations to participate in or avoid therapy. Some are interested in participating in therapy to gain a particular goal (e.g., the return of a child or a release from custody). Others are motivated by the goal of avoiding negative consequences for their actions (Snyder, Lehman, Kluck, & Monsson, 2006). Therefore, some women are in agreement with the mandating agency. They see the potential advantage of participating, with or without perceiving a personal need for therapy, and therefore engage in the process.

Women may be mandated into counselling by a number of sources. One source might be family and friends. A woman might be told that unless she changes her behaviour (e.g., behaviours related to addiction, violence toward others, or neglect of a child), she may be subjected to sanctions or a report to an authoritative body. A second mandating source might be the authoritative body itself; for example, children's protection services. Women may be told that they must participate in counselling in order to maintain or regain the custody of their children. A third common source of a counselling mandate is the criminal justice system. Women on probation or parole may be expected to comply with release conditions that demand participation in counselling. Finally, the fourth formal source of mandates is the family court system. Women going through divorce and separation are often forced into assessment and counselling situations that review their parenting abilities and inform the courts as to their competence as custodial parents.

This chapter will focus specifically on those women who are mandated to counselling, by any mandating agency, and resist engagement in that counselling process. These women are often described as "resistant or hostile." They are more likely to be in the "pre-contemplation" stage of change (i.e., I don't have a problem, you just think I do) or "contemplation" stage of change (i.e., I know that there is something wrong, but I am not sure what it is yet, or what needs to be done about it) (Prochaska, Norcross, & DiClemente, 1994). Women who are coerced into therapy may not have hope that therapy will be an effective pathway to their personal goals (Snyder et al., 2006). Therefore, engaging this group of women to participate in counselling is a more challenging process than engaging women in the "preparation" stage (i.e., the problem is defined and a solution is being developed) who have more hope that therapy will support their personal goals.

The client who is mandated also differs from self-referring clients in that there is always a third party involved and invested in the outcome of the counselling relationship. The typical referral agent within our practice tends to come from either the criminal justice or children protection systems. Regardless of where the referral comes from, as part of the referral narrative, the referral agent often expresses frustration or irritation with the woman being referred. We often hear statements like, "I have been trying to get her to work with me but she won't," or "She just doesn't get it," or "She just won't get with the program." If the mandated woman is grudgingly willing to come for counselling (but only after being threatened with sanctions), the referral agent may suggest that there is little hope for positive clinical outcomes because the woman is not internally motivated for counselling and not participating for the "right" reasons. In addition, we are often asked to "get her on track" and make sure that she learns what is needed to stay out of "trouble" or to get her children back. There is usually an expectation, either implicit or explicit, that we should make her more compliant in "dealing with her issues."

In many ways, women mandated to participate in counselling feel this shift in focus from her as a person to her "issues." Fels Smyth, Goodman, and

Glenn (2006) describe this tendency to separate women from their contexts as a natural aspect of specialized service delivery models. With specialized services for addiction, parenting, supervision, and so on, the context of the woman's life is lost, and she is reduced to her "problems." She may or may not agree with the interpretation of her life by the system agents working with her. Therefore, women mandated to participate in counselling often use their first appointment with us to express their a) disinterest in the counselling process, b) frustration about being forced to attend counselling, and c) anger at the referral agent or referring agency. Because the referral is typically a result of an adversarial process, the woman may feel powerless to participate in defining her needs in the face of a system she sees as having control over her life. She may also have some doubt about her own ability to change her situation. Finally, the woman may not agree that the specific changes she has been asked to make will actually improve her life. In situations like this, we view her resistance to participating in therapy as logical. Creation of a positive working alliance with the mandated woman then becomes our highest priority. We have a second priority of supporting the referral agent in joining this same process.

Our experience is that referral agents are often trying to do a great deal for their clients with scarce resources and are often making referrals for counselling after other, less intrusive, options have already been eliminated. The negativity or frustration expressed often reflects the agent's anxiety that things will go worse for their client or their client's children. They may also be concerned that the adversarial aspect of their relationship will intensify, thereby restricting the options available to actions that are increasingly restrictive. Rubino, Barker, Roth, and Fearson (2000) suggest that this type of anxiety may result in lower levels of empathy shown to clients, which in turn leads to ruptures in the rapport between agent and client. The agent's attempts to challenge or control the client are often interpreted by the client as hostility and prompts for defensiveness or further resistance (Horvath, 2001).

Clients expect those who counsel them to be responsible for establishing and strengthening the therapeutic relationship (Bedi, Davis, & Williams, 2005). Bedi et al. found that the personal characteristics of the therapist and the therapeutic environment have an immediate impact on the quality of the therapeutic relationship. They found that the client felt connected within the therapeutic alliance when the therapist was warm and engaging, listened without judgment (e.g., used paraphrasing), encouraged the client's perspective, and demonstrated interest in the client's understanding of the situation. Their findings reinforce the value of the feminist orientation in working with women mandated to participate in counselling. The following are the three core feminist counselling principles, all of which are congruent with creating a strong therapeutic alliance (Worrell & Remer, 1996): a) enter into an egalitarian relationship, b) acknowledge that the personal is political, and c) value the female perspective. It is important that we, as counsellors, understand the importance of holding an open and flexible stance at the onset of counselling. It allows the most room for engagement (Horvath, 2001).

Horvath (2001) found three client factors that impact the quality of the counselling alliance: a) the severity of the problem she is dealing with, b) the type of impairments she experiences, and c) the quality of her attachment style. Many of the women who are mandated to counselling are dealing with serious and difficult life problems, have significant impairment in their interpersonal and personal coping skills, and demonstrate fear-based or dismissive attachment styles. Our response acknowledges these realities. We accept that women may have previous life experiences that make their reactions against authorities "logical" responses, and often responses that have worked for them in the past (Wincup, 1999).

We typically ask referral agents to allow us to have a session or sessions with the woman to negotiate whether or not we are a good match with the mandated woman. We take the time to learn from her what her goals are and what she is willing to work on. Often this involves reframing goals in ways that work for both the client and the referral agent. Once we have a level of client agreement that is somewhat compatible with the concerns of the system, we usually accept the referral. If we are unable to engage her in working on a mutually agreeable goal, we have often learned enough about her world view to support the referral agent in developing an alternative strategy with her.

Inherent in the frustration or irritation is the incongruence between the referral agent's expectations for the woman and the woman's behaviour that led to the demand for the mandate. This frustration is confirmed in the literature. Women who behave in non-stereotypical ways, such as those who commit crimes or have abusive parenting styles, are more likely than their male counterparts to be perceived of as "mad or bad" (Wesely, 2006). Men who commit crimes or breach social rules are seen as having agency and rationality in their behaviour, and this is often denied to women (Horn & Evans, 2000). The notion that women are passive, compliant, natural nurturers who put their children's needs above their own does not match the reality of some women's lives. Women who abuse substances or who engage in violent, criminal or other non-stereotypic behaviour do not fit the mould of how we expect women to be (Fels Smyth et al., 2006).

Because referral agents do not have a workable story of how to understand women's misbehaviour, they, like many in society, create a story of how women are actually more deviant or flawed than men who commit similar acts. For example, Grabe, Trager, Lear, and Rauch (2006) found that when women are violent, the media is much more likely to account for that violence with individual-level explanations. Men's violence is more often described on a societal level. Horn and Evans (2000) found that women's criminal activity is often described as related to symptoms of generalized pathology or linked to their mental and emotional state. It appears, then, that men act out violently or abusively because of external factors; women do so because they are "sick" or "unstable." The feminist literature and our experience with women mandated to participate in counselling do not support the popular conceptualization of women's anti-social behaviour.

Having a broader understanding of women's anti-social behaviours is important if we want to be helpful in a meaningful way to the women involved. Statistics collected about child abuse show that women are identified as perpetrators of child abuse and neglect in 54% of substantiated cases (Trocmé et al., 2003). Women are the fastest-growing prisoner population in Canada (Balfour, 2006). However, in order to create a helpful response to women, we need to consider their behaviour in the context of their lives (Fels Smyth et al., 2006). Issues of lone parent families, poverty, victimization, and discrimination are realities in the lives of many women. Trocmé et al. report that their statistics need to be considered with caution given that 42% of substantiated neglect involved lone female-parent families. Belknap (2001) and Bloom, Owen, and Covington (2003) found that women's pathways to crime are more likely to be influenced by experiences of violence, substance abuse, poverty, and the need to care for dependents, and they are more likely to be impacted by racial and ethnic issues, violent partners, and partners involved in crime. Balfour notes that the rise in prison populations appears to follow cuts in health, social service, and education spending imposed by neo-liberal administrations who advocate minimal government interference in the economy and increased use of military, police, and prisons.

Women in Canada are more likely to live in poverty than men (Townsend, 2005). Townsend quoted Statistics Canada's (2004) report that 54% of adults living in poverty in Canada are women. The statistic for Aboriginal women living in poverty is twice that of non-Aboriginal women. Women are more likely to experience longer periods of low income compared to men and are much more likely to be living with greater depths of poverty (Townsend). Therefore, in a political environment where more people are struggling financially, we see a social trend toward dealing more harshly with those who break laws during that struggle. This may account in part for the rise in female offenders and the incarceration of women.

SHOULD WE PROVIDE COUNSELLING TO WOMEN MANDATED TO PARTICIPATE IN COUNSELLING?

There is some debate in the feminist community about providing counselling to women in situations where they have come to be mandated (Pollack, 2007;

Scott, 2004). The reality is that many of the women referred for counselling have been violent, have put someone else's well-being at risk, and have the potential to repeat that behaviour if something does not change in their lives. A trend in Canadian corrections is to ensure that therapy programs for women mandated to participate in counselling directly reduce the risk of recidivism (i.e., repeat of the problem behaviour) by focussing on the specific woman's related needs (Balfour, 2006). While this approach has some face validity, we as counsellors are challenged to learn more about which specific needs are linked to the occurrence of specific problem behaviours. However, while there has been an increase in the number of women mandated to treatment, there has not been sufficient research to identify the relevant risk factors or needs from a women-centred perspective. Most of the research has been adapted from research about men (Hannah-Moffat, 2005).

Pollack (2007) cautions that approaching women mandated to participate in counselling from an individual "risk to re-offend" perspective runs the risk of "de-contextualizing" the woman's life and refocusses on her personal deficits alone. She argues that providing therapy to women in prison, even feminist therapy, pressures the mandated woman to remain in a dependent situation not different from that which led to her offending behaviour in the first place. However, Scott (2004) has more hope that this pressure will not occur when therapy is provided by therapists working "at a distance" from the mandating authority. Therapists working "at a distance" have the potential to reduce concerns about power imbalance, especially when therapy is provided within a community setting.

Clearly, any counselling that is to be helpful to women mandated to participate in counselling must be grounded in the context of the women's lives and mindful of their realities (Fels Smyth et al., 2006). Ward, Mann, and Gannon (2007) suggest that any treatment model must have specific goals and include the person as a whole. While it is important to identify factors associated with the development of the problem behaviour, therapy can not focus on the problem behaviour as an isolated event or as an aspect of the person. Ward et al. suggest that issues of human agency and personal identity are important to integrate into treatment strategies. Further, they suggest that the influence of a person's needs in terms of determining their offensive behaviour must be considered. The overarching goal of intervention is for the client to have a "good life" that does not include harm to others or themselves. We concur that our purpose in working with women mandated to participate in counselling is to support change toward a good life or a better life, not just a life without the problem behaviour.

Our work with women mandated to participate in counselling is informed by feminist, social constructivist (Cottone, 2007), and cognitive-behavioural psychological counselling theories and is expressed through techniques derived from these frameworks. Our discussion will focus on the engagement aspect of the therapeutic process. Therapy with a client who is mandated most commonly breaks down at the engagement phase (DeJong & Berg, 2001). Once engagement has been achieved and a collaborative process has developed, feminist counselling with a client who is mandated does not differ from feminist counselling with a non-mandated client.

FEMINIST COUNSELLING PRINCIPLES

A feminist counsellor acknowledges the imbalance of power inherent in the counselling relationship and processes this deliberately with the client (Worell & Remer, 1996). Each woman's presenting concerns are considered not only in the context of her own life but in the larger societal context as well (Fels Smyth et al., 2006). Valuing the female perspective means supporting the woman in valuing traditionally women-centred ways of being (e.g., relational versus individualistic) and in seeing them as strengths.

Inclusion of feminist counselling ethics supports the therapist in maintaining a focus on issues of oppression and bias (Rave & Larsen, 1995). This means that the feminist therapist must ensure that counselling and assessment tools, techniques, and strategies are applied in a competent manner and are appropriate to use with women (Aglias, 2004; Hannah-Moffat, 2004).

ENGAGING WOMEN IN THERAPY

In this phase of the therapeutic intervention, we seek the woman's co-operation, (i.e., the act of working together to achieve a common aim) rather than compliance (i.e., the state or act of conforming with or agreeing to do something) in the counselling process. The process to gain co-operation begins with the initial contract with the referral agent and continues in the first session with the mandated woman. Informed consent processes with the mandated woman follow a relational autonomy model (Sherwin, 1998). We do not assume that a woman understands why she is attending counselling or has any awareness of what counselling might be like. We take the time to explore her previous experiences of change and her expectations for our time together. It is important for us to talk specifically about our understanding of her situation and the mandating body's expectations of her. We discuss the power imbalances inherent in the therapist/client relationship and the "informer/informed upon" dynamic we are about to engage in. We are clear about the limits of confidentiality and the type (and level of detail) of information we are obliged to report both by law and according to our contract with the referral source. We include the woman in the creation of any written reports and invite her participation in our discussions with the mandated authority. We are careful to ensure that our dialogue is with her, not about her.

This initial part of the engagement process is the most difficult. Sometimes the woman declines services. We then need to discuss the reality of her lack of participation. It is important that we not personalize her resistance to therapy as being a rejection of us as people. As Jan Hindman (2004) states, we need to give women "chances and chances and more chances" (n.p.) to engage.

We value the woman's resistance to participating in the counselling process. We go with that resistance and explore it with her, using it as the beginning of the engagement process. A helpful metaphor to describe this process to the woman is shifting from a "karate" approach to therapy (i.e., where the therapists offers options and the client blocks and counters with a return strike) to a "Tai Chi" approach where we do no violence and work together to increase and strengthen the woman's energy, not only for the woman's health but the health of others.

We raise questions about how it makes sense for the mandated woman to resist participation. We demonstrate empathy for her resistance when we are able to hypothesize a variety of good reasons for her non-participation. Examples we might offer include statements such as, "There may be people in your world that you fear more than children's services," or "You may feel that if you change and other people in your life don't, they might leave you," or "You may not feel safe right now to talk about yourself." Women mandated to participate in counselling often have very different explanations for their behaviour than the referral agent (Fels Smyth et al., 2006). We work with her perspective of her experience. For example, when a woman tells us she doesn't agree that she is a neglectful mother, we ask the woman to talk to us about her understanding about what neglect means as well as what attentive parenting might look like. Then we explore her experience of parenting from her definition, and we look for agreement about where we might be helpful to her.

We sometimes use metaphors to help us enhance the therapeutic relationship and strengthen engagement. This is supported by Stine (2005) and Freedman and Combs (1996). Carey (2002) uses metaphors to support externalizing the problem in her therapeutic conversations with clients. Externalizing the problem is a narrative technique that supports egalitarian practice by separating the person from the problem. It allows both the therapist and client to approach the issue together and avoids pathologizing the client (Tomm, 1989). A strategy to support externalizing the problem is to rename it. We often rename the problem simply as "trouble." It is a generic term that has the added benefit of reducing the demands for shame responses that may get in the way of building a therapeutic collaboration.

Another metaphor we use to engage women who are hesitant to participate in counselling is "the backpack story":

> One day, a group of children took a hike on a mountain trail. The guides for the hike gave each child a backpack containing all they would need for their day. One of the guides secretly added rocks to the backpacks of all the girls. For some girls, the guide added one or two rocks; for others, many were added. As the hike progressed, all the children grew tired, but the girls seemed to feel tired sooner. Some girls asked questions about why they were getting tired, others kept walking, and some just sat down. No one noticed the part of the backpacks that held the rocks. It looked just like it belonged.

We use this story as a metaphor to begin discussion of the issues that bring women to counselling, so we can learn something of the context of their lives, while at the same time setting the stage for goal setting. We ask women to talk about the rocks that might be in their backpack. We ask them to discuss how the rocks got into their backpack. At a later stage, we also ask them about whether or not they are adding rocks to any other person's backpack. This story supports women in shifting from an internalized story of "personal deficit" to an empowered one that includes their context and their reactions to it.

Once a strong collaboration is established, issues central to the referral question can be addressed directly. Therapists often make the error of confronting clients who are mandated with the reality of their behaviour too early in the relationship, before trust has been developed (Hilsenroth & Cromer, 2007). This tends to confirm the woman's belief that she is "lesser than" and that the therapist is not there to help her. Miller and Rollnick (2002) confirm that "attack" or confrontational styles do not increase motivation to change and in fact serve only to immobilize the person and make change less likely. Their research demonstrates that intrinsic motivation for change can only happen in an accepting and empowering atmosphere, where it is safe for the person to explore what are potentially the most shame-based and emotionally painful events of their lives.

As we noted earlier, women mandated into counselling often arrive with the expectation that they will be seen as deviant by their therapist. Their experiences of being labelled "monstrous" are well documented in the literature (Grabe et al., 2006). For example, one client came to therapy following a children's services investigation. The referral agent described the woman as non-co-operative and the "worst child abuser she had ever encountered."[1] The woman's shame seemed to walk into the office with her. Her clothing was ill fitting and not laundered; her hair was tangled and wild. She was emotionally labile during the initial session and struggled to make eye contact. Her description of why she was referred to counselling was laced with sarcasm about how bad a person she was. It was as if she were simultaneously accepting and rejecting the referral agent's view of her as scary and vile. She described herself as the worst mother in the world and said that she had no hope of recovering or of ever getting her child back.

She was invited to tell the story of how she came to be in trouble. She told a long tale of her own childhood experiences of abuse and neglect and the ongoing domestic violence she experienced as an adult. Her abusive behaviour to her child occurred in the context of her being beaten by her partner. The backpack story was introduced to her, and the counsellor reflected back to her that lots of people seemed to have contributed to weighing her down and forced her to figure out how to carry the load. She had developed some load-carrying strategies over the years. Some of these strategies had worked, but some had caused harm. The message that what goes into a backpack can come out and that new strategies can be learned was introduced. She started to cry and asked if that meant that her child could heal the same way. Once she understood that her child could recover, she could work on herself. She shifted from hopeless to hopeful in that moment, her shame moved into the background, and she was engaged in counselling.

Dealing with the woman's shame was one issue. Dealing with the referral agent's perceptions was also important. The first step was to help the referral agent to develop an alternative story of the client. We provided the referral agent with information to raise her awareness of the possibility of change for this woman, and women like her. We also worked hard to help the referral agent separate the woman as a person from her abusive behaviour. We used case conferences as opportunities for the referral agent to hear the woman being responsible and accountable for her growth and change. The new story of developing competence is reinforced.

A second step in situations like this is to talk with the referral agent about the socio-political issues around the woman's situation. The context of the lives of most women mandated to participate in counselling includes the impact of poverty, violence, childhood trauma, poor education, and unemployment. These issues are frequently related to their current situation or to their hope for change. Deepening the agent's understanding of the woman's life allows the agent to re-contextualize the woman's problems. This in turn reduces the agent's sense of helplessness and hopelessness. We continue this process by taking advantage of opportunities to tell stories of other women we have worked with and their stories of "trouble" and change. We do this in a conversational way, being careful not to lecture. When we tell these stories, we are really providing the story of a composite client, one that reflects parts of many women's stories. This supports our maintenance of confidentiality.

Referral agents are often decision-makers or are linked to decision-makers and thus have significant power over the client who is mandated. If they are not able to consider the woman within her context, they may not be able to accept the changes the woman makes. This, then, leaves her vulnerable. One of the realities of working with women involved in crime, substance abuse, family violence, and so on, is that the women have developed strategies that hide their behaviour or avoid the natural consequences that come from engaging in their troubling behaviours. Our clients have often "burned many bridges" before getting to our doors, and referral agents often have protection mandates (e.g., for the safety of a specific child or the community at large). While the referral agent may make a referral for counselling, they may not be willing to accept that whatever change occurs is "real" and to be trusted. We deal with this through case-conferencing and open dialogue, with the woman present. In individual sessions and then again at case conferences, we are clear that we do not have a crystal ball or lie detector. And we do not see being an investigator as part of our role.

We encourage, support, and challenge women to speak for themselves during meetings with referral agents. It is not uncommon for the "support team" to consist of half a dozen or more helpers. We have been at case conferences where the mandated woman is the only "non-professional" in the room. Everyone present, except the client, is paid to be there and comes with an agenda. We prefer to have meetings in places where our clients are comfortable. We encourage her to sit where she feels most confident, often with the easiest access to the door. We start meetings by clarifying the "meeting rules," the most important of which is that anyone can call for a break if they feel one is needed. We understand that part of our role as therapists in these meetings is to support our client in expressing herself. This means that we will sometimes interrupt professionals to check what message our client is receiving. We use the same feminist principles that inform our counselling in these meetings. It is often the case that a woman has been too anxious or intimidated by one or more of her "team" and benefits from having information paraphrased or clarification sought. We regularly use humour to diffuse tensions and to rebalance power in discussions.

We normalize, both in counselling sessions and case conferences, the fact that our clients will only share with us information that they feel is safe to share at the time and will not create more trouble for them or force them to make changes that they are not yet ready to make. For example, a substance-abusing woman may tell us that she has stopped using cocaine because she has regular urinalysis and that can be confirmed. However, she may not tell us about her excessive gambling because she doesn't feel ready to deal with that particular problem behaviour. In accepting this, we are setting our boundaries and expectations. Then if we do learn later about other troubling behaviour, we still have the opportunity to work with her without breeching our therapeutic relationship. One of the things we say to clients is that "we will know things are getting better when you feel safe enough to tell us more of what has been going on."

Another means of facilitating a woman to engage in therapy is to use the solution-focussed strategy of asking a version of "the miracle question" (Pichot & Dolan, 2003). We start from the woman's stated understanding of the "problem" she currently is dealing with, and ask the following question: "While you are sleeping, a miracle happens ... and the problems that brought you here are solved, just like that! How would your life be different?" We need to be prepared to hear a woman tell us that she would not have us (or the mandating agency) in her life! And that is fine, because it can still lead to a discussion of what else in her life would be different. We then have room to develop the discrepancy between her "problem behaviour" and how she would like things to be in her life (Miller & Rollnick, 2002). This motivational interviewing principle holds that motivation to change will increase when the client sees that she is being inconsistent with her own desires. Amplifying this discrepancy through discussion of the miracle question allows the client to see change possibilities for herself (Miller & Rollnick). Another way of framing this for a client is to talk about the degree to which her "inside" (i.e., values, beliefs, goals, desires etc.) matches her "outside" (i.e., their behaviour, living conditions, etc.), given her experience of "trouble."

CONCLUSION

It should be noted that not everyone is comfortable working with clients who are mandated. Therapists have an ethical obligation to engage all clients in non-discriminatory ways (The CPA Section on Women and Psychology, 2007). Therefore, it is important for therapists who choose to work with clients who are mandated to consider, in advance, their own expectations, values, and beliefs about this group of clients.

There is little in the literature on how to therapeutically support mandated women in the counselling process and even less that takes a feminist approach. Women mandated to participate in counselling are used to being seen through the lens of their "issues." They are familiar with their "problem" being examined outside of the context of their lives. The result is that they frequently arrive in the counselling office uninterested in the counselling process, frustrated with being forced into counselling, and angry at the referral agent. A feminist approach that takes into account context and makes space within the process for client choice is empowering to the client and supportive of change. Our approach also emphasizes collaboration with the referral agent, recognizing that this person is also part of the context of our client's life. As a team—therapist, client, and referral agent—we work together to facilitate both the client and referral agent in developing a new more empowering story of the woman's life.

ENDNOTES

1 This example is actually an amalgam of similar stories combined to protect the identity of the women who share their experiences with us.

REFERENCES

Aglias, K. (2004). Women in corrections: A call to social work. *Australian Social Work*, 57(4), 331–342.

Balfour, G. (2006). Re-imaging a feminist criminology. *Canadian Journal of Criminology and Criminal Justice*, 48(5), 735–752.

Bedi, R.P., Davis, M.D., & Williams, M. (2005). Critical incidents in the formation of the therapeutic alliance from the client's perspective. *Psychotherapy, Theory, Research, Practice, Training*, 42(3), 311–323.

Belknap, J. (2001). *The invisible woman: Gender, crime and justice*. Belmont, CA: Wadsworth.

Bloom, B., Owen, B., & Covington, S. (2003). Gender-responsive strategies. *Research, Practice, and Guiding Principles for Women Offenders*. National Institute of Corrections: U.S. Department of Justice.

Carey, M. (2002). What the wild man, the dragon-arguing monster and Camilla the Chameleon taught me about externalizing conversations. *The International Journal of Narrative Therapy and Community Work*, 4, 3–11.

Cottone, R.R. (2007). Paradigms of counseling and psychotherapy revisited: Is social constructivism a paradigm? *Journal of Mental Health Counseling*, 29(3), 189–203.

DeJong, P., & Berg, I.K. (2001). Co-constructing co-operation with mandated clients. *Social Work*, 46(4), 361–374.

Fels Smyth, K., Goodman, L., & Glenn, C. (2006). The full-frame approach: A new response to marginalized women left behind by specialized services. *American Journal of Orthopsychiatry*, 76(4), 489–502.

Freedman, J. & Combs, G. (1996). *Narrative therapy: The social construction of preferred realities*. New York: W.W. Norton & Company Ltd.

Grabe, M.E., Trager, K.D., Lear, M., & Rauch, J. (2006). Gender in crime news: A case study test of the chivalry hypothesis. *Mass Communication & Society*, 9(2), 137–163.

Hannah-Moffat, K. (2004). Gendering risk at what cost: Negotiations of gender and risk in Canadian women's prison. *Feminism & Psychology*, 14(2), 243–249.

Hannah-Moffat, K. (2005). Criminogenic needs and the transformative risk subject. *Punishment & Society*, 7(1), 29–51.

Hilsenroth, M.J., & Cromer, T.D. (2007). Clinician interventions related to alliance during the initial interview and psychological assessment. *Psychotherapy: Theory, Research, Practice, Training*, 44(2), 205–218.

Hindman, J. (2004). *Little Rabbit Foo Foo*. Paper presented at the meeting of The Association for the Treatment of Sexual Abusers, 23rd Annual Research & Treatment Conference, Albuquerque, USA *October 27–30*.

Horn, R. & Evans, M (2000). The effects of gender on pre-sentence reports. *Howard Journal of Criminal Justice*, 39(2), 184–197.

Horvath, A.O. (2001). The alliance. *Psychotherapy, Theory, Research, Practice, Training*, 38(4), 365–372.

Miller, W., & Rollnick, S. (2002). *Motivational interviewing* (2nd Ed.). New York: Guilford Press.

Pichot, T., & Dolan, Y. (2003). *Solution-focused brief therapy*. New York: Howarth Press.

Pollack, S. (2007). I'm just not good in relationships. *Feminist Criminology*, 2(2), 158–174.

Prochaska, J.O., Norcross, J.C., & DiClemente, C.C. (1994). *Changing for good*. New York: Avon Books.

Rave, E., & Larsen, C. (1995). *Feminist therapy code of ethics by ethical decision making in therapy: Feminist perspectives*. New York: Guilford Press.

Rubino, G., Barker, C., Roth, T., & Fearson, P. (2000). Therapist empathy and depth of interpretation in response to potential alliance ruptures: *Psychotherapy, Theory, Research, Practice, Training*, 10(4), 408–420.

Scott, S. (2004). Opening a can of worms? Counseling for survivors in UK women's prisons. *Feminism & Psychology*, 14(2), 256–261.

Sherwin, S (Ed). (1998). *The politics of women's health: Exploring agency and autonomy*. Philadelphia: The Feminist Health Care Ethics Research Network, Temple University Press.

Snyder, C.R., Lehman, K.A., Kluck, B., & Monsson, Y. (2006). Hope for rehabilitation and vice versa. *Rehabilitation Psychology*, 51(2), 89–112.

Stine, J. (2005). The use of metaphors in the service of the therapeutic alliance and therapeutic communication. *Journal of the American Academy of Psychoanalysis and Dynamic Psychiatry*, 33(3), 531–545.

The CPA Section on Women and Psychology. (2007). *Guidelines for ethical psychological practice with women*. Ottawa, Canada: Canadian Psychological Association.

Tomm, K. (1989). Externalizing the problem and internalizing personal agency. *The Journal of Strategic and Systemic Therapies*, 8(1), 54–59.

Townsend, M. (2005). *Poverty issues for Canadian women, gender equity consultation for the Status of Women Canada.* Downloaded August 8, 2007 from http://www.swc-cfc.gc.ca/resources/consultations/ges09-2005/poverty_e.html.

Trocmé, N., Fallon, B., MacLaurin, B., Daciuk, J., Felstiner, C., Black, T., et al. (2003). *Canadian incidence study of reported child abuse and neglect –2003 major findings.* Ottawa, Canada: Public Health Agency of Canada.

Ward, T, Mann, R.E. & Gannon, T.A (2007). The good lives model of offender rehabilitation: Clinical implications. *Aggression & Violent Behavior, 12*(1), 87–107.

Wesley, J. (2006). Considering the context of women's violence: Gender, lived experiences, and cumulative victimization. *Feminist Criminology, 1*(4), 303–328.

Wincup, E. (1999). Women awaiting trial: Common problems and coping strategies. In M. Brogden (Ed.), *British Criminology Conferences: Selected Proceedings: Volume 2.* London: British Society of Criminology. Downloaded August 8, 2007 from http://www.britsoccrim.org/volume2/011.pdf.

Worell, J., & Remer, P. (1996). *Feminist perspectives in therapy: An empowerment model for women.* Chichester, England: John Wiley & Sons.

APPENDIX I

GUIDELINES FOR THE ETHICAL DELIVERY OF PSYCHOLOGICAL SERVICES FOR WOMEN

INTRODUCTION AND RATIONALE

In order to deliver competent and ethical psychological services for women, psychologists need to be aware of, and knowledgeable about, the issues and conditions that have an impact on women's lives in Canada. Psychological services for women should be non-sexist, empowering, and recognize the realities of women's lives. These *Guidelines* provide Canadian psychologists with direction and guidance about how to achieve these ends.

In 1980, the Canadian Psychological Association adopted *Guidelines for Therapy and Counselling with Women.* These guidelines were partly in response to the recommendations of the Task Force on the Status of Women in Canadian Psychology (Wand, 1977) which, in turn, was established in response to the United Nations 1975 International Year of Women. Over the past 25 years, there has been a shift from needing to prove that unjust discrimination toward women exists to a more general acceptance that people aligned with many forms of diversity, including gender, ethnicity, socio-economic status, and sexual orientation are harmed by discriminatory actions.

Since 1980, there have been several positive developments in the practice of psychology. There is clearer recognition that psychologists are not value free; rather, as with members of all disciplines, they are influenced by their beliefs, biases, socialization, life experiences, and degree of privilege and influence. There is greater acknowledgement of the issue of power and how it may be used and abused in relationships. Many psychologists have become increasingly aware of how an individual's sex intersects with the individual's age, race, ethnicity, culture, religious beliefs, sexual orientation, gender identification, ability, and social and economic conditions. There is greater insight into how Canadian women's psychological problems and concerns are often a consequence of social, cultural, and economic conditions (Morrow, 1999; Stoppard & McMullen, 2003).

Within psychology, principles of social justice and social responsibility are slowly being recognized in a profession whose members have often prided themselves in their emphasis on the individual. The *Canadian Code of Ethics for Psychologists* (CPA, 1986, 1991, 2000) expanded the meaning of respect and caring to include the valuing of all individuals, groups, and collectivities with which psychologists may work. The *Feminist Therapy Code of Ethics* (Feminist Therapy Institute, 1987, 1999, 2000) and *Ethical Decision Making in Therapy: Feminist Perspectives* (Rave & Larsen, 1995) led the way in integrating feminist tenets with ethical thinking.

Although progress has been made, sex discrimination still exists, and women and women's roles in society still are often undervalued. Women expend more time in unpaid work than do men, are more likely to have low incomes, to live below the poverty line, and to be victims of criminal harassment and kidnapping (Statistics Canada, 2006). It is well documented that Canadian women and girls are more often victims of physical and sexual violence than are Canadian men and boys (Statistics Canada, 2006), and that abuse and trauma can have an enormous impact on the mental health of women and girls (Fisher, 1998; Rivera, 1999). Although the mental health issues and concerns of Canadian women differ from those of Canadian men (British Columbia Centre of Excellence for Women's Health, 2003; Janzen, 1998; Morrow, 1999) and women are more likely than men to seek treatment (Statistics Canada, 2000), there is a paucity of services that are specific to women's needs (Morrow, 1999; Morrow, 2002).

There is an ongoing need to foster awareness of women's issues in the context of psychological services. In order to provide appropriate and non-sexist psychological services, psychologists must be sensitive to, and knowledgeable about, individual, group, community, and socio-cultural differences. Psychological services also need to be responsive to the complex and varied contexts of Canadian women's lives.

This revision of the original *Guidelines for Therapy and Counselling with Women* (CPA, 1980) is an application of the most recent edition of the *Canadian Code of Ethics for Psychologists* (CPA, 2000) and the *Guidelines for Non-Discriminatory Practice* (CPA, 1996, 2001) to issues specific to the delivery of psychological services for women. The guidelines contained in the current document are grounded in the four ethical principles of the *Canadian Code*; namely, Respect for the Dignity of Persons, Responsible Caring, Integrity in Relationships, and Responsibility to Society. The Guidelines do not duplicate ethical standards in the *Code* and thus should be used in conjunction with the *Code*.

This document consists of:

1. an introduction and rationale (above);

2. a summary of each of the four ethical principles of the *Canadian Code of Ethics for Psychologists* (CPA, 2000), followed by a state-

ment of application of each principle to the delivery of psychological services for women;

3. specific guidelines for the ethical delivery of psychological services for women, referenced to the relevant ethical principles;

4. positive and negative examples of applying the guidelines to the delivery of psychological services for women.

APPLICATION OF THE FOUR PRINCIPLES OF THE *CANADIAN CODE OF ETHICS FOR PSYCHOLOGISTS* TO THE PROVISION OF PSYCHOLOGICAL SERVICES FOR WOMEN

PRINCIPLE I. RESPECT FOR THE DIGNITY OF PERSONS. In supporting the Principle of Respect for the Dignity of Persons, psychologists actively demonstrate the belief that all persons have innate worth as human beings and should be treated primarily as a person or an end in him/herself, not as an object or a means to an end. Psychologists appreciate that the innate worth of a person exists regardless of real or perceived differences in culture, nationality, ethnicity, colour, race, religion, sex, gender identification, marital status, sexual orientation, physical or mental abilities, age, socio-economic status, or any other preference or personal characteristic, condition, or status. Psychologists actively avoid and do not support unjust discrimination based on any of these factors. Psychologists recognize that respect for moral rights (e.g., privacy, self-determination, personal liberty, and natural justice) is included in respect for the dignity of persons, and that the manner in which such rights are promoted, protected, and exercised varies across cultures and communities. They acknowledge and respect such differences, while guarding against clear violations of moral rights. Psychologists also recognize that as individual, family, group and community vulnerabilities increase, or as the power of persons to control their environment or their lives decreases, psychologists have an increasing responsibility to seek ethical advice and to protect the rights of the persons involved.

In applying the principle of Respect for the Dignity of Persons to their delivery of psychological services for women, psychologists ensure that they do not, wittingly or unwittingly, engage in or support any previous or existing sex-based unjust discrimination and/or oppressions (e.g., fewer choices, greater negative consequences, restrictions on personal liberty), whether these factors are based in the individual, the family, the community, or the socio-political context. Psychologists also recognize that, in addition to gender-based unjust discrimination and/or oppressions, a woman client also may be subject, or may have been subjected, to unjust discrimination and oppressions due to other diversities (e.g., race, culture, poverty). Psychologists also understand that such circumstances can increase the power imbalance in the professional relationship, and that special consideration and safeguards for protecting and promoting moral rights are increasingly warranted in such circumstances.

PRINCIPLE II. RESPONSIBLE CARING. In supporting the principle of Responsible Caring, psychologists demonstrate an active concern for the welfare of the persons with whom they work. They try to be of as much benefit as possible. They also avoid doing harm, minimize harm that cannot be avoided, and correct harm when they are able to do so. In order to be of benefit and not harm, psychologists acquire and maintain the competence needed for their work, stay within the limits of their competence, and apply the knowledge and skills that are appropriate for the nature, and the social and cultural context, of a particular client or situation. They also develop adequate self-knowledge regarding how such factors as their own values, experiences, sex, gender identification, race, culture, socio-economic situation, and social context might influence their actions, interpretations, choices and recommendations, and their ability to be of benefit and not do harm.

In applying the principle of Responsible Caring to their delivery of psychological services for women, psychologists understand how women's lives are shaped by their sex in interaction with their culture, nationality, ethnicity, race, religion, gender identification, relationship status, sexual orientation, physical or mental abilities, age, socio-economic status, as well as by other personal characteristics, conditions, or statuses. Psychologists also recognize that their women clients live in multiple contexts and that, while many of these contexts give meaning and satisfaction to their lives, some experiences (e.g., poverty, violence, undue pressure to make specific choices, socialization to a primarily passive and/or submissive role, other abuses of power) are harmful to their well-being. In attempting to be of benefit to women clients, psychologists understand that it is important not to pathologize such harmful effects, but rather to view and treat them as understandable responses and results. In developing and monitoring their self-knowledge with respect to their delivery of psychological services for women, psychologists are particularly sensitive to understanding how the contexts of their own lives might influence or interfere with their attempts to help and not harm women clients.

PRINCIPLE III. INTEGRITY IN RELATIONSHIPS. In supporting the principle of Integrity in Relationships, psychologists are open, honest, and accurate in their communications with others. They view trust as essential to the professional relationship and, to this end, they recognize, monitor, and manage potential biases, multiple relationships, and other conflicts of interest that could result in the real or perceived exploitation of the client and to the diminishment of trust. Psychologists balance completeness and openness of communication with cultural differences and expectations regarding appropriateness. They also recognize and respect cultural differences with regard to boundaries and multiple relationships, while ensuring that the best interests of the client are always the paramount consideration.

In applying the principle of Integrity in Relationships to their delivery of psychological services for women, psychologists are aware of and sensitive to the special trust issues that some women clients might have, including being distrustful or overly trustful of those in authority. Psychologists also recognize how their own biases and early socialization might affect their attitudes and actions towards their women clients, and strive to be as self-aware, objective, and unbiased as possible.

PRINCIPLE IV. RESPONSIBILITY TO SOCIETY. In supporting the principle of Responsibility to Society, psychologists acknowledge that they have responsibilities to the societies in which they live and work, and to the welfare of all human beings in those societies. Psychologists do whatever they can to ensure that psychological knowledge is used for beneficial purposes. When they are used contrary to these purposes, they do what they can to try to correct such misuse. They demonstrate respect for democratically established law and social structures, but also speak out when such laws seriously ignore or oppose the ethical principles of Respect for the Dignity of Persons, Responsible Caring, or Integrity in Relationships.

In applying the principle of Responsibility to Society to the delivery of psychological services for women, psychologists acknowledge that their concern for the welfare of all human beings in society includes concern for the welfare of women in society, and that some psychological theory, research, and practice has distorted, ignored, or pathologized women's experiences. In response, psychologists accept the responsibility to do what they can to change societal laws and structures that unjustly discriminate or lead to oppressions of women. They recognize that there are multiple avenues to improve the lives of women, and choose the most appropriate and beneficial use of their time and talents to help meet this collective responsibility.

GUIDELINES FOR PSYCHOLOGICAL PRACTICE WITH WOMEN

These guidelines provide descriptions of knowledge, attitudes, skills, and behaviours needed for the ethical delivery of psychological services for women. Although the four ethical principles of the *Canadian Code of Ethics for Psychologists* (CPA, 2000) are interrelated, each guideline is referenced to the main ethical principle that the guideline supports.

Appendix I

In psychological practice with women, psychologists:

1. Respect, listen, and learn from women clients, particularly when women clients' life experiences differ substantively from the psychologist's own. (Principle I)

2. Use inclusive and respectful language with women clients; label issues related to women as such (e.g., "women's issues"); use non-specific terms regarding an individual's sex when appropriate (e.g., police "officer"); and avoid language that stereotypes, demeans, or infantalizes (e.g., "girl"). (Principle I)

3. Recognize that women clients might feel in a power-down situation when working with a male psychologist, or with any "expert," be they male or female, and that the power imbalance may make it difficult for some women clients to challenge the psychologist. (Principle I)

4. When needed, take special precautions with women clients (e.g., more time, more reassurance about right to choose) to ensure that any consent for psychological services is informed and voluntary. This includes consent for services and consent for disclosure of confidential information to others who may claim the right or need to know (e.g., partners or physicians).

5. Understand that, with repeated exposure to traumatic events, some women cope through making what may appear to be poor lifestyle "choices" (alcohol abuse, etc), and that it is important to avoid diagnostic labelling that may stigmatize.

6. Are aware of their own cultural, moral, social, and sex-based beliefs and values and how these may influence or interfere with their ability to help and not harm their women clients; for example, how their position of privilege as professionals may lead to de-sensitization regarding the realities of women clients who live in poverty. (Principle II)

7. Keep up to date regarding current research and issues related to working with women clients through continuing education activities such as attending conferences, reading, workshops, and courses. (Principle II)

8. Are aware of how some psychological theory, research, and practice may have distorted, ignored, or pathologized women's experience, critically appraise the applicability of psychological theories and research to women, and only use those aspects that are appropriate. (Principle II)

9. Obtain supervision or consultation, or refer to another practitioner, if their beliefs and values about a woman client's particular situation (e.g., beliefs and values regarding abortion or a woman's role in child rearing) are likely to interfere in any substantive way with their ability to benefit and not harm the woman client. In these situations, collaborate with women clients on the solutions that best services their interests. (Principle II)

10. When needed, consult with others who are more knowledgeable about, and experienced in, working with issues related to psychological services for women. (Principle II)

11. Are knowledgeable about community resources and programs for women, recognize how such community supports and programs can be helpful and empowering, and refer women clients to them as appropriate. (Principle II)

12. Recognize that women clients may live in multiple contexts and have diverse identities, and that gender inequity may be only one of many inequities with which they contend. (Principle II)

13. Assess accurately the source of women clients' difficulties, apportioning causality appropriately among individual, situational, and socio-cultural factors. (Principle II)

14. Help women clients to become aware of the various factors that contribute to their difficulties and, where appropriate, facilitate women client's examination of their experiences of unjust discrimination and oppressions, and support them in making new choices and developing new strategies. (Principle II)

15. Take care with women clients to determine whether they have experienced physical or sexual assault, recognizing that women are more likely than men to have been victims of physical and sexual assault, including in the context of private family discord. In such circumstanc-

es, psychologists hold the view that those who are assaulted are victims of crimes and those who assault are guilty of crimes. (Principle II)

16. Where appropriate, confirm the validity of the reality, variety, and implications of unjust discrimination and/or oppressions experienced by women clients. (Principle II)

17. Are aware that some women's experiences make them more vulnerable to being sexually exploited, and take special care to establish clear and safe boundaries in the current professional relationship. (Principle II)

18. Continually monitor and evaluate their competence, attitudes, and effectiveness in the delivery of psychological services for women clients, adjusting their practices as warranted. (Principle II)

19. Establish an appropriate level of trust through honest, open, and transparent communication that is considered culturally appropriate by the woman client, being careful not to subtly invalidate her questions or opinions (e.g., by not fully listening). (Principle III)

20. Establish an atmosphere of collaboration regarding all relevant decisions, including the goals of the psychological services being delivered, the risks and benefits of possible activities or interventions, any foreseeable problems, and any issues that arise, thus creating a more equal relationship by sharing power and responsibility. (Principle III)

EXAMPLES OF APPLYING THE PRINCIPLES AND GUIDELINES FOR PSYCHOLOGICAL PRACTICE WITH WOMEN

Positive Examples

You are a school psychologist working in a school where teen pregnancy has become a particularly salient issue. The school board has decided to implement an educational program that is aimed exclusively at young women and asks that you deliver the program. You believe that to provide the program to female students exclusively would be sexist and you make an argument that educational programs should target both male and female students.

As Director of a mental health clinic, you have hired a well-qualified psychologist. All goes well until a woman client complains that the psychologist has advised her to ignore her husband's abusive behaviour and to do more to keep him happy. You meet with the psychologist to explore the client's complaint. Based on your meeting, you recommend that the psychologist take a course in diversity, that the assignment of cases to this psychologist be restricted, and that closer supervision be provided. You will review the situation in six months. You also remind yourself that you need to be more sensitive to cultural beliefs of psychologists regarding women's roles, especially when recruiting new staff.

You are seeing a couple for relationship counselling who say they do not want to divorce. Both partners blame the other for having extramarital affairs. After hearing more detail in the second session with them, you suddenly realize that the wife's current lover is a well-known and respected member of the community whose work you have admired, although you have discounted occasional rumours that he takes advantage of young female employees. With this unexpected insight, you decide that you cannot remain objective in counselling the couple, and that you need to find a way to withdraw your services in as sensitive and as caring a manner as possible.

You are a psychologist specializing in the delivery of services related to violence against women. You have heard many stories of the harm done to victims of abuse by previous service providers who have viewed the after-effects of abuse as character defects (e.g., personality disorders). You design educational workshops for the benefit of other professionals.

Negative Examples

After eight years as an employment counsellor, you decide to shift your practice to marital therapy. You have come to the opinion that mothers of dependent children should not work outside the home unless out of dire financial necessity, a hardship that you have experienced personally as a single parent. In your marital therapy sessions, you routinely explore in depth why a mother who is working outside the home is doing so, and emphasize the important role that mothers have in nurturing their children.

You are seeing a woman who was referred for therapy for continuing depressed mood and lack of self-esteem. You learn that her husband, who is always repentant afterward, is physically abusing her. Your client feels guilty for the marital problems, because she believes that wives are primarily responsible for the success or failure of a marriage. Her husband has told her repeatedly that he would not hit her if she were more obedient and submissive. Because she does not wish to leave him, you advise her to be more obedient and submissive, in order to avoid physical harm.

You believe that you are very accepting of women of all races and cultures and describe yourself as a cross-cultural psychologist. One of your goals is to help women immigrants become comfortable in their new country. You believe that some cultural dress codes are repressive and that they will make it difficult for immigrants to integrate into Canadian society. If your women clients wear such traditional clothing, you recommend that they switch to Western clothing.

You are a psychologist who works with women who have suffered from spousal abuse. You are a strong advocate for funding to expand services for the prevention of family violence, and you frequently give presentations at fundraising events for this cause. You always ask one or two of your women clients to be present on the platform to publicly describe their stories as victims or survivors of abuse.

REFERENCES

British Columbia Centre of Excellence for Women's Health. (2003). *Mainstreaming women's mental health: Building a Canadian strategy.* Vancouver, BC: Author.

Canadian Psychological Association. (1980). *Guidelines for therapy and counselling with women.* Ottawa, ON: Author.

Canadian Psychological Association. (2000). *Canadian code of ethics for psychologists.* (3rd ed.). Ottawa, ON: Author. (Previous versions in 1986 and 1991.)

Canadian Psychological Association. (2001).*Guidelines for non-discriminatory practice.* (Rev. ed.). Ottawa, ON: Author.

Feminist Therapy Institute. (2000). *Feminist therapy code of ethics.* San Francisco CA: Author. (Previous versions in 1987 and 1999.)

Fisher, P. (1998). Women and mental health issues: The role of trauma. *Visions: BC's Mental Health Journal, Winter*, 6-7.

Janzen, B. (1998). *Women, gender and health: A review of the recent literature.* Winnipeg, MB: Prairie Women's Health Centre of Excellence.

Morrow, M. (1999). *Hearing women's voices: Mental health care for women.* Vancouver, BC: British Columbia Centre of Excellence for Women's Health,

Morrow, M. (2002). *Violence and trauma in the lives of women with serious mental illness: Current practices in service provision in British Columbia.* Vancouver, BC: British Columbia Centre of Excellence for Women's Health.

Rave, E. & Larsen, C. (eds). (1995). *Ethical decision making in therapy: Feminist perspectives.* New York: Guilford Press.

Rivera, M. (ed). (1999). *Fragment by fragment: Feminist perspectives on memory and child sexual abuse.* Charlottetown: Ragweed Press.

Statistics Canada (2006). *Women in Canada: A Gender-based Statistical Report.* 5th Ed. Ottawa: Author

Statistics Canada (2000). *Women in Canada: A Gender-based Statistical Report.* 4th Ed. Ottawa: Author

Stoppard, J. & McMullen, L. (eds). (2003). *Situating sadness: Women and depression in social context.* New York: New York University Press.

Wand, B. (1977). Report of the task force on the status of women in Canadian Psychology. *Canadian Psychological Review, 18*, 3-18.

OTHER RELEVANT CANADIAN PUBLICATIONS

Boatswain, S., Brown, N., Fiksenbaum, L., Goldstein, L., Greenglass, E., Nadler, E., & Pyke, S. (2001). Canadian feminist psychology: Where are we now? *Canadian Psychology, 42 (4)*, 276-285.

Canadian Psychological Association. (1981). Education of graduate students. *Canadian Psychological Association Policy Statement.*

Canadian Psychological Association. (1981). Female role models. *Canadian Psychological Association Policy Statement.*

Canadian Psychological Association. (1981). Psychology of women. *Canadian Psychological Association Policy Statement.*

Canadian Psychological Association. (1981). Discrimination in employment areas. *Canadian Psychological Association Policy Statement.*

Canadian Psychological Association. (1981). Sexual harassment. *Canadian Psychological Association Policy Statement.*

Canadian Psychological Association. (1982). Discrimination on sexual orientation. *Canadian Psychological Association Policy Statement.*

Canadian Psychological Association. (1984). Prejudicial discrimination. *Canadian Psychological Association Policy Statement.*

Canadian Psychological Association. (1995). CPA response to Canadian panel on violence against women. *Canadian Psychological Association Policy Statement.*

Canadian Psychological Association. (1996). Equality for lesbians, gay men, their relationships, and their families. *Canadian Psychological Association Policy Statement.*

Church, E., Pettifor, J., & Malone, J. (2006). Evolving Canadian guidelines for therapy and counselling with women. *Feminism and Psychology, 16*, 259-271.

Gurevich, M. (2001). W(h)ither psychology of women?: Current trends and future directions for the section on women and psychology. *Canadian Psychology, 42 (4)*, 245-248.

Pettifor, J., Larsen, C., & Cammaert, L. (1984). *Therapy and Counselling with Women: A Handbook of Educational Materials.* Ottawa: Canadian Psychological Association.

Pyke, S. (1996). Sexual harassment and sexual intimacy in learning environments. *Canadian Psychology, 37(2)*, 13-22.

Pyke, S. (2001). Feminist psychology in Canada: Early days. *Canadian Psychology, 42*, 268-275.

Stark, C. (1997). Academic freedom, "political correctness", and ethics. *Canadian Psychology, 38*, 232-237.

Stark-Adamec, C., & Kimball, M. (1984). Science free of sexism: A psychologist's guide to the conduct of nonsexist research. *Canadian Psychology, 25*,

Storm, C., & Gurevich, M. (2001). Looking forward, looking back: Women in psychology. *Canadian Psychology, 42(4)*, 245-248.

AUTHOR BIOS

Kathy Bent is a First Nation Ojibway woman with French and Irish ancestry who is a member of Little Black River First Nation in Manitoba. Kathy has served on many Aboriginal and non-Aboriginal boards and committees in the past and is currently a member of the Canadian Indigenous and Native Studies Association, the Canadian Mental Health Association, the Aboriginal Council of Winnipeg Inc., and Mother of Red Nations Women's Council Inc. Kathy holds a BA in psychology (honours), an interdisciplinary MA, and is currently working on a interdisciplinary PhD in psychology, Native studies and anthropology at the University of Manitoba. Her research interests focus mainly on self-perception, identity, and issues pertaining to holistic self-development, equity, women and minorities, and Aboriginal cultural identity. Kathy is currently an Aboriginal community researcher in Winnipeg. She has authored and co-authored various articles on Canadian Aboriginal issues.

Sandra Collins is an associate professor and Director of the Graduate Centre for Applied Psychology at Athabasca University. Her research and writing is focussed in the area of multicultural counselling, gender and sexual orientation, and social justice. She is the co-author and co-editor of *Culture-Infused Counselling*, the first edition of which won the Canadian Counselling Association's 2006 annual book award. She integrates her focus on cultural diversity in her roles as educator and university administrator.

Bonita Decaire (Dip. SW, BSW, MSW) is a speaker, educator, learner, story teller, actor and social worker. She was born in Edmonton and raised in Calgary Alberta. Currently she lives in a small rural northern community beside the lake in a picturesque setting. She is an active volunteer for many local, national, and international organizations and is a proud feminist. Current research interests include asexuality and work and family life integration.

Ann Marie Dewhurst, PhD, is a forensic and clinical psychologist who has worked with people who have been physically, sexually, and emotionally abusive toward others. She has done this work in correctional and mental health settings. For the past six years, she has worked in private practice. Ann Marie facilitates a variety of courses for the Graduate Centre for Applied Psychology at Athabasca University, with particular focus on applied professional ethics and clinical practice. Ann Marie is a published author in the area of family violence and has presented her research at local, national, and international forums.

343

Deborah Foster, PhD, is a Registered Social Worker who teaches social work and women's/family studies at Portage College in Lac La Biche, Alberta, as well as women's studies and health studies at Athabasca University in Alberta. She has spoken at numerous conferences and published articles on sexuality, women's issues, and topics important to lesbians and their families. Her doctoral dissertation has been published as a book entitled *The Experiences of Planned Two-Mother Families*.

Susan LeBlanc is a faculty member and instructor at Capilano University. She holds a master of arts–integrated studies graduate degree with dual specialization in work, organization, and leadership, and equity studies from Athabasca University, and a bachelor of arts degree in women's studies from York University. Born and raised in Montreal, she and her partner, Michael, currently make their life together in Squamish, raising their children: Katelyn age, 10, Maxwell, 9, and Samantha, 5. Susan has a passion for knitting, reading, and time with family on their island get-away off the Sunshine Coast of British Columbia.

Marie Lovrod is assistant professor of women's and gender studies at the University of Saskatchewan. She completed her PhD in autobiography and feminist theory at the University of Calgary, has directed both Women's Studies Abroad and diversity education programs, and has published several articles and book reviews. She is currently working on autobiographical representations of childhood and youth, and their political functions in a range of contexts.

Judi Malone is a registered psychologist who works as a counsellor and university educator. She is an existential feminist practitioner in a rural private practice, with an active interest in mentoring future Aboriginal psychologists. She is active with many provincial and national psychology organizations, and her research interests include professional ethics, rural psychology, the psychology of women, cross-cultural psychology, counselling and psychotherapy, existential psychology, and disabilities.

Karen Nielsen, PhD, tutors and instructs in undergradauate and graduate courses in women's studies and criminal justice at Athabasca University. She is also a clinical social worker and trauma specialist in private practice in Edmonton, Alberta. She has over 25 years' experience in working with people who have experienced trauma, particularly sexual abuse or family violence. Her PhD research was a qualitative study of the coping experience of women who had left abuisive relationships. Karen is a published author and international presenter in the area of family violence and sexual abuse.

Jean L. Pettifor, past president of the College of Alberta Psychologists, the Psychologists' Association of Alberta, and the Canadian Psychological Association, and adjunct professor at the University of Calgary, has received many awards for her lifetime contributions to the profession, the community, and the promotion of quality in human services. Through her teaching, research, and practice, she has promoted respect and equality for persons and peoples. Today, she is recognized provincially, nationally, and internationally for her work in promoting value-based ethical decision-making in addressing both individual and societal problems in living. Her most recent award is the Honorary Doctor of Laws degree from Athabasca University in 2009.

Cathy Richardson (Kinewesquao) is a Metis woman with Cree, Gwichin, and European ancestry. She is an assistant professor in the Indigenous specializations program in social work at the University of Victoria. She is the co-founder of the Centre for Response-Based Practice, which is involved in research and clinical practice aimed at helping people recover from violence. Cathy is an activist, writer, and co-developer of Islands of Safety, an Indigenous family violence prevention model for Metis Community Services. Her work is based on affirming human dignity and exploring the intersections of social justice, human rights, and counselling. She is married with three children and lives in Cowichan Bay on Vancouver Island.

Janice L. Ristock, PhD, is a professor of women's and gender studies and Associate Vice-President (Research) at the University of Manitoba. Her research interests include same-sex relationship violence, feminist community-based research, and health and mental health issues facing gender and sexual minorities. She received a book award for No More Secrets: *Violence in Lesbian Relationships* from The American Psychological Association, Division 44 (Society for the Psychological Study of Lesbian, Gay, and Bisexual issues) for making a distinguished contribution to LGBT psychology.

Lynda R. Ross, PhD, is an associate professor of women's studies and Chair of the Centre for Work and Community Studies at Athabasca University, where she also coordinates the University Certificate in Counselling Women program. Her research interests centre on the construction of theory, attachment, motherhood, social construction of "disorder," and on women's under-representation in fields of computing and information technology.

Shelly Russell-Mayhew, PhD, is a registered psychologist and assistant professor in the Division of Applied Psychology, Faculty of Education, at the University of Calgary. Her research has focussed on girl's and women's relationships with the body, including eating disorders, body image, and obesity. She is currently interested in the influence of shared risk factors, like body dissatisfaction, media, and dieting, on the concurrent prevention of eating disorders and obesity in a school setting. Shelly's professional experiences with eating-related issues have included clinical work at eating disorder treatment programs and other practice settings as well as various advocacy roles.

Charlene Y. Senn, PhD, is a professor of psychology and women's studies at the University of Windsor and the Faculty of Arts and Social Science Senior Research Leadership Chair (2009–2014). Her research has focussed on many different aspects of violence against women and girls, including pornography, sexual abuse, and sexual assault. She is currently interested in the positive influence of sexuality education on girls and women, and is investigating how educational programs might increase women's ability to emotionally and physically fight off men's attempts to sexually coerce or assault them. With the assistance of funding from the Ontario Women's Health Council, she formed the multidisciplinary Health Research Centre for the Study of Violence against Women at the University. Charlene's interest in issues of male violence against women and health are not merely academic. She previously worked frontline in a women's shelter and is active in her community.

Gina Wong-Wylie, PhD, is an associate professor in the Graduate Centre for Applied Psychology at Athabasca University and an adjunct professor at the University of Calgary and the University of Lethbridge in Alberta. She is a registered psychologist and directs a counselling and consulting practice focussing on adolescent girls and women. Gina is active with the Association for Research on Mothering as a journal and conference advisory board member. She is the Chair of the Status of Women in Psychology Committee for the Canadian Psychological Association and has published widely on issues related to motherhood, specifically in relation to prenatal/postnatal maternal adjustments. She has been recognized and sought as a presenter and advocate on issues pertaining to maternal wellness from feminist and cross-cultural perspectives. Gina also directs the Disordered Eating and Body Image Treatment (DEBIT) Program in collaboration with a registered clinical dietician. Gina resides in Edmonton with her two young daughters.

Arlene Young, PhD, is a registered psychologist who counselled students at Athabasca University for 23 years and has worked as an academic and tutor in women's studies for the past 11. Arlene's graduate studies were in counselling and educational psychology. Her research focusesd on issues affecting women, particularly women in management and the professions. Part of her focus in counselling was on helping students overcome barriers to learning. As part of fulfilling her counselling role with distance students, she edited a book, *Overcoming Exam Anxiety,* and authored and revised an annotated bibliography, *Selected Study Skills Books in the AU Library and Some Websites*, available on the Athabasca University Web site. She currently tutors students in women's studies and in the Counselling Women Certificate Program, and is a course author and instructor in gender issues in the Master of Distance Education Program at Athabasca University.

ACKNOWLEDGEMENTS

I would like to thank all of the authors who contributed to this collection; Susan Silva-Wayne, the press editor and Colleen Wormald, the production manager; as well as each of the anonymous reviewers for their valuable input, work and commitment to this project. —Lynda